Preface

Tom Daly's colleagues at the National Film Board of Canada regard his legacy with either annoyance or affection.

An administrator with filmmaking experience expresses a negative view: 'When I hear the name "Tom Daly," the word "boring" *springs* to my lips. The words "irritatingly Canadian" *spring* to my lips, the words "uniquely Canadian." He has made the NFB introspective, pompous, socially responsible – everything but commercially successful.'

A filmmaker admired for his craftsmanship and versatility summarizes the opposing viewpoint: 'Tom Daly stands for everything the world admires about the Film Board: its commitment to excellence, its experimentation, its ethical principles.'

Which of these conceptions is true? While the latter one predominates among those who have worked with Daly on a film, several who know him well say both assessments have some truth in them. Daly would agree. His way of looking at the world, and at himself, strives to replace judgments of the 'either/or' variety with an understanding that incorporates seemingly contradictory observations.

This striving seems to lie at the heart of Tom Daly's achievements as an editor, producer, teacher, and colleague at the National Film Board. As an editor, he sought, when at his best, a structure that could accommodate more rather than less. As a producer, he worked to turn rebellion into creative collaboration. As a teacher of young filmmakers, he took as his starting-point the director's vision, not his own preferences or preconceptions. As a colleague, he struggled mightily to subordinate his irksome traits to a larger, more helpful, more magnanimous attitude towards others.

When I began this project years ago, I had no idea that this would be the kind of perspective I would reach. The Film Board stood alone among non-profit producers of films intended for the public good. Daly's name was associated with an inordinate share of the Film Board's best films and filmmakers. In most cases, his role was that of editor or producer. Occasionally he both produced and edited. What I expected to delineate was, first, a set of editing rules that would communicate the essence of his skill at structuring film material, and, second, some principles of creative producing. The task seemed straightforward and manageable, and I thought it would be quickly accomplished.

What slowed me down was my attempt to avoid grappling with Daly's philosophical views. Although obviously important to Daly, they struck me as curious but not particularly pertinent. When he talked about them, my mind would tend to wander, and I'd press him to talk about rules of editing. Only when I finally began to sense the close relationship of his philosophical views to how he approached the work of filmmaking did I glimpse their importance. Daly seemed to have a remarkable ability – I haven't seen such elsewhere, in any field, although it must exist – to relate the minutest detail to the broadest whole. He could relate a decision about the precise frame with which to start or end a shot to the intended meaning of a film at its most abstract level, whether he was sympathetic to the film's intentions or not. He could move in either direction, from the particular to the general or from the general to the particular. His philosophical outlook had to have something to do with this ability.

Yet the explanation of Daly's contribution to the Film Board lay no more in a system of ideas than in a list of editing rules. Daly's editing decisions did not derive from his philosophical ideas; the link between them was not one of logic. It was his *attitude* towards them both that forged the connection, giving him a unity of purpose that seemed to underlie his long and productive career. The tie was accomplished through very hard work. It was willed.

Thus the shape of this study itself evolved from reductively analytical to more broadly descriptive and exploratory, from static to developmental. It is a career portrait. It is not a biography in the usual exhaustive sense – although biographical information is adduced where both available and appropriate – and it does not try to 'explain' Daly. It is not a critical study, although critical judgments of films may often be implied and are occasionally explicit. And it is not history in the strictest sense. There are several instances where the actual fact of the matter is in dispute, impossible to determine, or of trivial interest compared to the perception or the memory.

To construct a career portrait of someone whose central creative contribution lay in helping others create poses a special problem. How is his

THE BEST BUTLER IN THE BUSINESS: TOM DALY OF THE NATIONAL FILM BOARD OF CANADA

The Best Butler in the Business is a career portrait of the man who is widely regarded as the most important figure ever to work in the English-language branch of the National Film Board. Heir to John Grierson and Stuart Legg, Tom Daly was also the creative sire of a host of filmmakers, including Roman Kroitor and Wolf Koenig. It was his presence that gave the best documentaries of the 1950s and 1960s their reflective tone – the distinctive mark of the NFB films of that time.

D.B. Jones draws on both the testimonies of colleagues, which reflect Daly's central role in the success of the NFB in its golden years, and Daly's own recollections of key periods and events, including his personal accounts of the production of some of the NFB's classic films and his views on government service. Jones describes in detail the films of which Daly was both editor and producer. Although they represent only a small portion of his total output, they most closely reveal his unique aesthetic vision. Jones also shows how Daly's decisions as a producer often subverted established forms of organizational control and documentary expression.

In tracing the connection between Daly's intriguing philosophical views and his approach to film, Jones presents both a portrait of a great filmmaker and a study of one man's philosophical quest.

D.B. JONES is Professor of Film in the College of Design Arts at Drexel University. He is author of *Movies and Memoranda: An Interpretive History of the National Film Board of Canada.*

D.B. JONES

The Best Butler in the Business: Tom Daly of the National Film Board of Canada

UNIVERSITY OF TORONTO PRESS
Toronto Buffalo London

© University of Toronto Press Incorporated 1996
Toronto Buffalo London
Printed in Canada

ISBN 0-8020-0760-0 (cloth)
ISBN 0-8020-7133-3 (paper)

Printed on acid-free paper

Canadian Cataloguing in Publication Data

Jones, D.B. (David Barker), 1940–
    The best butler in the business

    Includes bibliographical references and index.
    ISBN 0-8020-0760-0 (bound)
    ISBN 0-8020-7133-3 (pbk.)

    1. Daly, Tom.   2. Documentary films – Canada –
    History and criticism.   3. National Film Board of
    Canada – Biography.   4. Motion picture producers
    and directors – Canada – Biography.   5. Motion
    picture editors – Canada – Biography.   I. Title.

    PN1998.3.D35J6 1996   791.4'3'092   C95-932914-5

Chapter 1 is an expanded version of 'Tom Daly's Apprenticeship,' which
appeared in *Film History: An International Journal* 3:3 (1989).

Except where other source is given, photographs are used by courtesy of Tom
Daly.

University of Toronto Press acknowledges the financial assistance to its
publishing program of the Canada Council and the Ontario Arts Council.

Contents

contribution to be described? How does one look at, say, *This Is a Photograph*, and determine how much of it is the work of Albert Kish and how much of it is the work of Tom Daly? It cannot be done. Creative collaboration doesn't unfold in measurable inputs. Daly's contribution was not ten per cent or twenty per cent or fifty per cent; it lay in helping Kish to make as good a film as he could.

One gains a sense of Daly's contribution from Kish himself, and from similar testimonies from other filmmakers. For this reason, statements from filmmakers (with reference, usually, to specific films) constitute the primary form of evidence here for Daly's importance to the Film Board. But since I am also trying to convey a sense of Daly himself and his ideas about filmmaking and government service, Daly's own thoughts and memories constitute an essential aspect of the story. They help illuminate his role in production. They suggest the philosophy behind the art. They also provide the main narrative thread for the portrait as a whole.

This way of approaching such a topic was suggested to me by Herbert Mitgang's vivid portrait of Helen Wolff that appeared in the *New Yorker* some thirteen years ago. Helen Wolff and her husband, Kurt, were book editors responsible for publishing in North America English-language editions of such writers as Franz Kafka, Günter Grass, Italo Calvino, Hermann Broch, and Boris Pasternak. The Wolffs' contribution to the work of their writers seemed much (if not entirely) like Daly's to that of filmmakers. Mitgang relied heavily on interviews with Helen Wolff (Kurt Wolff had died long before Mitgang wrote) and on the testimony of authors they had helped. Their own words were more interesting than any paraphrase or conflation of their words would have been.

I've embellished this basic approach with numerous brief descriptions of films that Daly either edited or produced. Filmmaking is collaborative to an extent that authoring a book and editing it rarely are. One doesn't miss summaries of, say, *The Trial* or *Doctor Zhivago* in Mitgang's portrait of Helen Wolff. Indeed, the inclusion of such summaries would seem odd, even impertinent. The Wolffs helped their writers with fine editing and with publishing, rarely with the writing itself. But editing plays a significantly larger role in documentary film than in prose fiction. And although editing was Daly's purchase on the craft of filmmaking, he was also a producer, and as such he was involved in many projects from their conception and throughout their production. Descriptions of the films are often needed in order for Daly's or a filmmaker's comments to make sense.

For the comparatively few films which Daly both edited *and* produced, the descriptions are much more detailed. These films were more fully collaborative than most of the others, and they come closest to revealing Daly's own aesthetic vision. And most of them, in my view, remain undervalued works of art that reward close examination.

Finally, I have included, where they were available and enlightening, internal Film Board documents, seemingly routine memoranda, letters, and notes, unofficial communications, and transcripts. A wonder of Daly's career – and generally of the Film Board itself – is that such art as he and others made emerged from a government organization that except in its earliest years was subject to the usual bureaucratic expectations. For nearly four decades, Daly was a producer at one level or another. Paperwork came with the job.

I would like to alert the reader to some methodological and conceptual limitations to the study. Interviews are always slanted somehow, by both parties to them. The interviewer has his preconceptions, the interviewee his or her selective memories. Interviews are not of equal value. Some of those I interviewed were more forthcoming than others, or more articulate than others, or more quotable. Some simply knew more about the subject than others. Some may have trusted me more or less than others did. A few did not respond to my attempts to contact them. Several of the people I would have liked to talk to are dead. A few I could not locate.

The interviews took place from the early 1980s into the early 1990s. Where possible, afterwards I sent a draft of whatever portions of an interview I planned to use to the interviewee and allowed him or her to correct misstatements or suggest rewordings. Often there would be follow-up interviews. When correspondence followed an interview, I have treated the correspondence as part of the interview. Often I have combined portions of separate interviews with the same person. I have edited for economy, and made minor changes for clarity, but I have tried to retain the 'voice' of the person talking, even where some additional editing would have saved space or further enhanced clarity.

The films that are described in any detail represent only a small portion of Daly's total output. In most cases, they are among the most interesting films in which Daly was involved, but many really fine films – *Blackwood*; *Stravinsky*; *Emergency Ward*; *Co Hoedeman, Animator*; *Persistent and Finagling*; *In Praise of Hands*; *Kurelek*, for example – are ignored, or mentioned only in passing, simply because the films combined with what Daly or the filmmaker had to say about them would have added nothing new to the account. Dull films are also avoided for the most part.

The documents that are mentioned or quoted represent only a tiny proportion of what must have been generated over the years. A few of those I have included came to my notice by luck or accident. I've avoided using the same kind of documentation more than once or twice. For example, I've used excerpts from two letters sent to Colin Low when he was directing *Circle of the Sun*. Daly wrote several hundred, perhaps more than a thousand, such letters (or telegrams) over the years. Similarly, I've used just one letter to a co-producing agency and one to a film subject, and one memo defending a film, and one memo defending a filmmaker.

Readers familiar with my book on the National Film Board documentary, *Movies and Memoranda: An Interpretive History of the National Film Board of Canada*, might notice that I've reproduced a few documents and quotations that I used there. The note from Wolf Koenig that appears near the end of chapter 2, for example, was quoted in the earlier book (although less completely). Then it was used because it said something essential about Unit B. But it also says something vital about Tom Daly. A published quotation of Donald Brittain is also used again, in this case less for what it says about Unit B and Daly than for what it reveals of Brittain's attitude towards them.

I've tried to avoid other kinds of repetition. I did not want to go over much-trodden ground about Film Board history or to probe in detail John Grierson's idea of documentary film. I try to give just enough for narrative coherence or dramatic interest. For readers who seek more background on the National Film Board, I recommend Gary Evans's two histories, *John Grierson and the National Film Board: The Politics of Wartime Propaganda*, and *In the National Interest: A Chronicle of the National Film Board of Canada from 1949 to 1989*. *Movies and Memoranda* provides thematic summaries of some episodes in Film Board history and an interpretation of Grierson's documentary aesthetic. *Grierson on Documentary* is a good, chronologically organized selection of Grierson's writings and speeches. *John Grierson and the NFB*, prepared by McGill University's John Grierson Project, is an interesting collection of remembrances of Grierson by people who worked with him.

Nor have I attempted to summarize the critical reception of individual films or groups of films except where it seemed relevant to the story as it unfolded. For readers interested in other critical perspectives on some of the films and filmmakers that figure in this study, I recommend three anthologies: *The Canadian Film Reader*, edited by Seth Feldman and Joyce Nelson; *Take Two*, edited by Seth Feldman; and *Self-Portraits: Essays on the Canadian and Quebec Cinemas*, edited by Piers Handling. The first of these includes four articles cited here. I also recommend the relevant sections of Peter Harcourt's *Movies & Mythologies: Towards a National*

Cinema. To my knowledge, Harcourt was the first critic to perceive some shared distinctive traits among Unit B films.

I've declined to entangle this portrait of Tom Daly in the debates that recently have emerged about John Grierson's ideology and the Film Board's value in Canadian society. A fair consideration of the issues involved would distract me from my subject. I do, however, include Daly's own perspective on them to the extent that he has offered one. Anyone interested in exploring them might begin by reading the studies mentioned in the text: Joyce Nelson's *The Colonized Eye: Rethinking the Grierson Legend* and Peter Morris's 'Re-thinking Grierson: The Ideology of John Grierson.'

The legitimacy of even documentary film itself has been questioned in two recent books: Bill Nichols's *Representing Reality: Issues and Concepts in Documentary* (1991) and Brian Winston's *Claiming the Real: The Documentary Film Revisited* (1995). Both books deconstruct documentary's claim on the 'real' world. Nichols begins his book by asking, 'Can we love the cinema and Plato, too?' He concludes that we cannot. That issue, too, I avoid addressing in any direct sense.

I have not attempted to judge or even fully to describe the philosophical system that became an essential part of Daly's life and professional growth. Either task would be beyond me. Instead, I have merely summarized it and then focused on what Daly says about it and how he applied it in practical contexts. The system, in any case, seems to be one which, despite its esoteric tone, encourages individualization and individual verification of any of its precepts. It is more a system of thinking than of knowledge. It appears less bizarre than at first glance when one sees its connection, for Daly, to fundamental themes in Eastern and Western philosophy.

Finally, I have tried to avoid injecting into this account my own explicit opinions or judgments on the ultimate matters. I do not wish to judge Daly, his friends, or his opponents. Rather I try to present issues as fully and fairly as I can within the limits of narrative balance and coherence.

To leave these various matters at that, however, would be disingenuous of me. Although I try to present Daly as objectively as possible, my generally positive view of the Film Board and Daly surely has influenced my choice and arrangement of materials, and of the words with which I frame them. While I don't presume to pass judgment on Daly or his philosophical stance, obviously I admire Daly's accomplishments and acknowledge their relationship to his philosophy. And although I have rejected any impulse to saddle this book, or Tom Daly himself, with the burden of rebutting the Film Board's or documentary film's modern critics – most of whom emerged after Daly's career was over – I think that Daly's legacy itself could stand as a kind of proleptic response to them and the attitudes that underlie them.

I don't want to lay out this last idea in the form of an argument – it is not something I set out to prove; it occurred to me only after the book was finished – but I think some support for such a notion can be found in the portrait that follows. I believe the reader will discover, for example, that if 'multiculturalism' means a respect for other cultures Daly was a multiculturalist – but one more interested in commonalities than in differences – long before multiculturalism became a political shibboleth. He championed an appreciation for Native Canadian cultures throughout his career. More than most English-speaking Canadians can claim, he empathized with the political and cultural aspirations of French-speaking Canadians. At the same time, he contributed to what there is of a specifically Canadian culture. Most of the films in which he was involved sprang from Canadian cultural soil. The Film Board in which he played such a central role was a net exporter of cinematic innovation and style. In his decisions as a producer and as an artist, he repeatedly if quietly subverted established forms of organizational control and documentary expression. He arrived at the basic insights of 'reader-response' theory and intertextuality before the two terms entered the critical vernacular. And as I hope the reader will discover, Daly, in his attitude towards his craft, answered existentially the question raised by Winston and Nichols. He answered it before they asked it. Whatever the adequacy of his answer, it was a lived one, an engaged one, one that mattered.

In the interests of full disclosure, I should mention that I have had professional associations with a few of the filmmakers who are interviewed in the book. I have very minor credits on two of Michael Rubbo's films (*Wet Earth and Warm People* and *Jalan, Jalan: A Journey in Sundanese Java*). I am listed, generously, as a co-producer on Donald Winkler's *The Scholar in Society: Northrop Frye in Conversation*. I have writing credits on two of Nico Crama's non-NFB films. I wrote the screenplay for Martin Defalco's *Cold Journey*. *Cold Journey* is discussed in chapter 5.

For readability, I have dispensed with numbered notes. The interviews constitute the book's primary material. Descriptions of films are secondary material. In those relatively few cases in which I felt a reference was needed, I have attempted to incorporate into the text itself just enough information to allow the reader (a) to know the basic source without having to flip to the rear pages of the book but (b) to find easily, if desired, full reference information (e.g., volume where relevant; page numbers where needed) under 'Works Cited.' I hope that narrative flow compensates the reader for what I believe will be at most an occasional inconvenience.

Acknowledgments

I would like to express my gratitude to people who have helped me complete this project. Piers Handling and the Canadian Film Institute supported the project at its initiation. Donald Bidd, Suzy Bouchard, Isabel Bourbon, Marielle Cartier, Lyle Cruikshank, Terry Ryan, and Bernard Lutz of the NFB, and the NFB officially, helped me enormously, putting up with what at times must have seemed like endless requests for information, access, or screenings. Ron Alexander, Erik Barnouw, Beth Bauer, Al Blatter, Paula Cohen, Julia Epstein, Sheila Fischman, Mark Greenberg, Mary Mulhern, and Paul Swann all helped me answer specific questions or offered valuable suggestions at one time or another. Richard Binder and Deidre Harper of Drexel University's Hagerty Library met innumerable requests for reference material. Peter Bartscherer helped me navigate the word-processing system used in completing the project. Drexel University supported several trips to the Film Board and paid certain other expenses related to the project.

I am grateful to every filmmaker quoted in the pages that follow. To submit to an interview is an act of trust, which I hope none will feel was misplaced.

Ruth Daly showed cheerful forbearance, and Tom Daly, Jr, offered intriguing suggestions. I am especially indebted to Tom Daly himself, for his participation, openness, and patience.

My deepest gratitude is to Dini Wiradilaga, whose insight, judgment, and wisdom delight and teach me still.

Portrait Group: Mrs. R.A. Daly and Her Sons Dick and Tom, 1924-25. Tom Daly
is in the foreground, with the opened book. Courtesy Art Gallery of Ontario,
Toronto.

The blue-suited Daly in the early NFB years.

Daly's two film teachers, Stuart Legg (*left*) and John Grierson, at the early NFB.
Courtesy NFB.

OPPOSITE PAGE and ABOVE: Sequence from *Guilty Men*. 'You think you've seen the hanging through a symbol, then you really see it.' Courtesy NFB.

Hungry Minds. 'Kids aren't so given to self-pity.' Courtesy NFB.

An early NFB party. The birthday *honorée* is Bunty Read, wife of Nicholas Read, director of *Out of the Ruins.*

Daly and Donald Mulholland with Mary Pickford, host of the 3rd Canadian Film Awards, 1951. Courtesy NFB.

Grant McLean in China, 1946. 'Grant had all sorts of qualities I've never had.'
Courtesy Grant McLean.

Colin Low shows an award for *The Romance of Transportation* to *(left to right)* Eldon Rathburn, Tom Daly, Wolf Koenig, and Robert Verrall. Photo by Will Doucette, courtesy NFB.

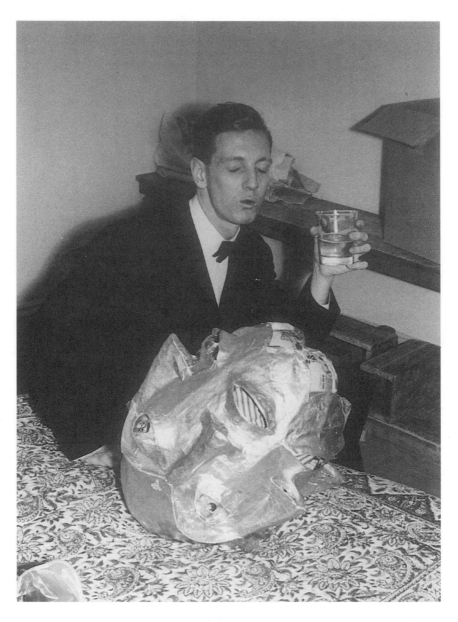

Daly contemplates the Mayan mask made for him by Colin Low. 'You're a product of your past and you wonder about your future.' Photo by Wolf Koenig, courtesy W. Koenig.

Up the Chilkoot Pass, *City of Gold.* Courtesy NFB.

Sequence from *Universe*. The line of attention traces the ray of creation. Courtesy NFB.

Circle of the Sun. Courtesy NFB.

Paul Anka with *Lonely Boy* directors Roman Kroitor *(left)* and Wolf Koenig.
Courtesy NFB.

Stanley Jackson in his NFB office, circa 1960.

Daly enjoying his second 'attention-getting apparatus,' son John, in 1962

Waiting in line for *Labyrinthe*, Expo 67. Courtesy NFB.

The coconut monk prays for peace, *Sad Song of Yellow Skin*. Courtesy NFB.

Albert Kish with Tom Daly, 1979.

Director Derek May, his wife, and Max, *A Film for Max.* Courtesy NFB.

At Concordia University, 1980. Photo by Wolf Koenig.

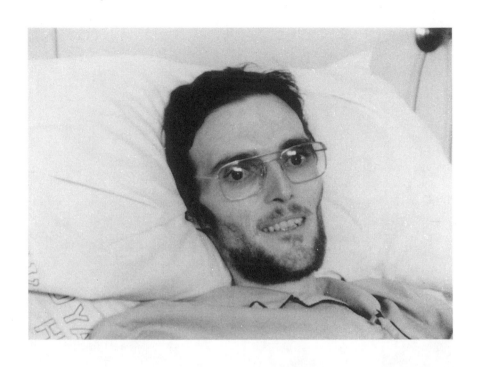

Michael Charette, *The Last Days of Living*. 'When there's nothing left to hide /
And no need to turn away.' Courtesy NFB.

Sequence from *Standing Alone.* Pete imagines the past, then creates it. The fifth shot is from a scene later in the film. Courtesy NFB.

Daly editing, 1983. 'Work can be a kind of prayer.' Photo by Lois Siegel, courtesy L. Siegel.

The poster distributed at Daly's retirement party.

For Daly, this 1989 photo 'looks like I often feel inside.' Photo by Lois Siegel, courtesy L. Siegel.

THE BEST BUTLER IN THE BUSINESS:
TOM DALY OF THE NATIONAL FILM BOARD
OF CANADA

1

A Stretch from Zero

Thomas Cullen Daly, born on 25 April 1918, was twenty-two years old and completing his final year at the University of Toronto when, in the spring of 1940, Hitler launched Germany's fateful blitzkrieg through Belgium and France to the English Channel. Canada officially had entered the Second World War the previous autumn, but Daly, like most Canadians, fully grasped the war's urgency only now. And now, like thousands of other young men and women, he reconsidered his immediate plans. Harvard University had offered him a graduate fellowship to study English literature; he intended to earn a master's degree and then a doctorate. When he asked Harvard if he could postpone the fellowship, he recalls, 'they said no, but that if after the war I wanted to renew it they would be open to that request. I never wanted to.'

Determined to contribute to his country's war effort but lacking martial inclinations and aptitude, Daly sought an opportunity to serve in some capacity he vaguely thought of as 'counter-propagandist.'

'It was the only positive kind of work I was prepared for with my background,' Daly recalls half a century later. 'I had thought of it in terms of written words, because my subject at university was English language and literature. Coming home one day, just before I was to leave for Ottawa to look for such a job, my father said, "I've got another reference letter for you today – from your old principal at Upper Canada College." "Oh, who is it to?" I asked. "I forget the name, but he's the man in charge of the new government film board." I shrugged. I wasn't interested in films. I didn't even go to films. My father said, "Well, if your school principal is kind enough to think of you and give you a letter, the least you can do is go and present it. At least be civil about it."'

The 14 August 1940 handwritten letter from Terence W.L. MacDermot to John Grierson commended Daly as

a first-rate classical scholar at his stage, having a real sense of drama, clever and quick above the average, with a ready pen & refreshing personality. Contra – he is very young – much younger than his years and education, virginal of mind, naive to his fingertips, and as yet unsophisticable. His mind has a tough cortex which throws off worldly ideas – contemporary thought, and so on. But he is full of all sorts of useful high grade quality.

He wants into Min. of Information – in some guise. Remember he can create with his pen, and his flair is dramatic. If you think there is a place for a young possible soldier in that field, I think you would be repaid by his dog-like devotion and talents.

Daly put that letter – the contents of which he learned just before his retirement party in 1984 – at 'the bottom of the pile,' and took the train to Ottawa, where he found that 'everybody else for whom I had references was either away on a speaking engagement or at a Joint Defence Board meeting, or something of the sort. I was finally left with nothing to do but wander over to John Grierson's office at the National Film Board. He too was away – at home, sick. His secretary said they'd get in touch with me. The very next day, she called and said Grierson was still sick, but he'd see me at his home. I couldn't imagine a government civil servant who would invite some unknown job applicant to see him at home. This must have been September 9, 1940. His wife met me at the door and said I'd have to wait. He was seeing someone else. His wife and I sat listening to one of Churchill's speeches on the radio. Lunchtime passed. I kept saying I should leave, but she kept insisting that I stay. Suddenly somebody burst out of Grierson's room and left in a rush. Then Grierson came out in a pair of spotty old grey slacks and a rough, ill-fitting turtleneck sweater, tousled hair, and looking rather pale. He started asking me very sharp, deft questions about Toronto. I couldn't answer most of the questions, which had to do with sociological things or historical facts. And I kept saying to myself, "I'm absolutely no use to this man, I don't know anything about the things he's interested in." After some time he got up, and so I got up, and he said, "Write me notes for a film on Toronto." I was dumbfounded. "I'll give you thirty dollars for it," he said, as he was showing me out the door.'

On 23 September 1940, Grierson wrote back to MacDermot:

Dear MacDermot:

I saw Daly and have given him a small job to do. He seems to me a good boy with a good head. I got a slight impression of conservativeness of mind which always astonishes me in the young. No doubt this is what you refer to when you describe him as 'virginal of mind.'

We shall see what he does with the outline I gave him to do for a film on Toronto.

Yours sincerely,
John Grierson

Daly spent two weeks researching Toronto in local libraries and putting his findings into the form of a script. 'Someone showed me an example of the two-column format – you know, commentary on the right, picture on the left – and I wrote an awful lot on the right and not much on the left. I sent it to Grierson and a couple of days later went to see him. Stuart Legg was there, and so I met him for the first time. I had no idea who *he* was, either, but Grierson apparently had read the script and then given it to Legg for a critique. Grierson walked back and forth making some general comments which didn't sound too hopeful. He then asked Legg to comment. Legg had this habit of looking not at your eyes but at your forehead as he talked to you. He turned over a few pages with those delicate finger movements he had – very exact, refined – reminding himself what was in the script, and then laid it down. He looked into the air, then at my forehead, and said, "Well, you obviously know a lot about Toronto, but it's just not a film."'

Legg's critique survives in a memo he wrote to Grierson on 28 September 1940:

Memorandum to Mr. Grierson
This is Daly's script on Toronto. It has little to do with films, being rather a long literary essay on the city, for which he has secondarily and not too successfully tried to find images. It would be four reels in length and, despite his very considerable knowledge of Toronto, damnably dull.

But there is, through all the writing, a certain grasp of film form and here and there a movie idea.

If you are considering him seriously as a possible apprentice, I suggest that you make him analyse an average two-reeler *quantitatively*, to give him some idea of how much one can get into a film; and *proportionally* as between picture and commentary, so that he gets some idea of the dominating importance of visuals. Then make him re-write, and we might get something.

'I was all set for a polite reject,' Daly recalls, 'when Grierson, to my surprise, said, "Sorry to be so negative about it, but would you mind doing it again in light of the comments we've made?" I was absolutely unprepared for that, but I agreed. In another couple of weeks, I reworked the material into an entirely different form and presented it to Grierson. Well, it wasn't much better, they never used it, but it led to something.'

Long after Grierson had left the Film Board, Janet Scellen, who had been Grierson's secretary in 1940, said to Daly, '"I'm going to tell you something I've kept from you for years. When they had read that script, Grierson said to Legg, 'There's not much there, is there?' 'Well,' Legg answered, 'the research is good, and I need some research. I can use him.' 'Well, if you can use him, fine.'"' Daly was hired in October at twenty-five dollars a week.

Grierson's apparent ambivalence about his new recruit may very well have been rooted in contrary impulses of his own. On the one hand, Grierson valued intellect and formal education. He had been a brilliant student at Glasgow University, winning undergraduate prizes and earning a master's degree in moral philosophy. A Rockefeller grant for postgraduate study brought him to the United States, where his life's mission began to take shape: to harness film for education and national development. He wrote with fire and grace about documentary's latent capacity for poetry and prophecy. His definition of documentary as 'the creative treatment of actuality' reflects his bent for dialectical thinking and remains, in any case, the only definition of documentary that has both cogency and wit. When he made his initial forays into producing government-sponsored documentary film in the 1930s, in Britain, he sought out well-educated, artistically inclined young people, such as Cambridge-educated Basil Wright, who directed *Song of Ceylon* under Grierson's tutelage, and Arthur Elton, who co-directed *Housing Problems* and later built the Shell Film Unit. Later, as commissioner of the National Film Board – an organization of which he was the chief architect – he would personally recruit from across Canada men and women of intelligence and discipline. Stuart Legg, who had worked with Grierson in England and whom Grierson had brought over to the Film Board as his virtual second in command, was a Cambridge-educated historian.

On the other hand, Grierson was even more a man of action than of reflection. He valued knowledge that was practical, useful, applicable in a complex industrial society. He liked people who swam against the current, who didn't quite fit into respectable society, who wanted to change it. Artists appealed to him if they had talent and a tough, angry edge. His chief complaint against Robert Flaherty, whose *Nanook of the North* had helped inspire Grierson's belief in documentary's artistic power, was that Flaherty's attraction to exotic cultures was romantic and escapist.

Daly was not the kind of young person Grierson took to easily. Daly was innocent with regard to societal problems and political issues. He was fastidious and reserved. He dressed conservatively even in informal situations. But in his favour he had a stronger educational background than even the offer of a Harvard fellowship in English literature suggests. His childhood and youth, rich in mental stimulation, seem reminiscent of something one would read of in a Victorian novel. His father, a Toronto financier, studied the New Testament every morning. Although a quiet man, he 'took singing lessons and would, under pressure, sing at parties.' Daly's mother had graduated summa cum laude from the University of Toronto's Victoria College and 'got the "senior stick" from the students as the most popular woman of the year.' She had been a professor of French and German at Wilson College in Pennsylvania before marrying.

When Daly was about nine years old, he happened on a book in the family library that 'was full of black-and-white engravings. It was an early edition of John Bunyan's *The Pilgrim's Progress*. For some reason I found it interesting and read it through. By the time I was eleven, I read it again, with a startling and mind-opening discovery: it was at one and the same time a story on *two levels!* It was a literal story of particular people with particular names and particular events, like any other story, and at the same time a general story of the interplay of different kinds of feelings and values and meanings that affect the life of *anybody* at *any time*. It was clear that this other story was the real story, and the literal story was just one particular example of the big one; and what was important was to realize the general case, since then it could be useful anywhere, and not only in conditions similar to the literal ones in the book.' He soon 'delighted in the discovery of levels of meaning in Aesop's fables, the parables in the New Testament, and, much later, the little teaching stories in Hindu, Buddhist, and Muslim lore, and in certain types of fairy tales.'

There was stimulation in the arts as well. 'The world around home was filled with painters and musicians. Lismer was often a visitor. Varley painted our family portrait when I was six. My parents had an annual party for painters and musicians at home.' Varley's painting is called *Portrait Group: Mrs. R.A. Daly and Her Sons Dick and Tom* and is dated 1924–5. It is now owned by the Art Gallery of Ontario. A colour photograph of it appears in Peter Varley's published collection of his father's work, *Varley*.

Daly took piano lessons from age six to eleven. He sang in school choirs and Gilbert and Sullivan operettas. In his teens, he became adept at competitive chess. He grew interested in Native Canadian cultures and engaged in some amateur archaeology near Toronto. He took a four-month tour of England, mostly by bicycle.

His formal education, as rigorous as Grierson's or Legg's, was essentially classical. He had taken Latin in preparatory school. In upper school, he read Plato in Greek. At the University of Toronto, he started out in the classics course, but switched to English literature when he found that he already had studied much of the material that the classics program at Toronto covered. On the extracurricular side, he served on the Hart House Art Committee and acted in student plays. In his junior year, he produced the 'University College Follies,' whose stars were Lou Weingarten and Frank Shuster, later known as the comedy team of Wayne and Shuster.

In his subsequent career, Daly often would draw on his experiences of classical literature, philosophy, and other arts to help interpret a situation, solve an editing problem, or understand a personal dilemma. Their value to him, however, derived as much from his attitude towards them as from their intrinsic merit. He was open to the classics and to those who taught them. One of his recollections from after his retirement illustrates the personal trait that his school principal had characterized as 'dog-like devotion' and that would have impressed Grierson and Legg if it had come through in their preliminary encounters with Daly. A favourite teacher at the University of Toronto was a professor of Greek, Eric Owen. Daly had studied the *Iliad* with him. 'On graduation day, after convocation, Owen came up to me and congratulated me on my standing. He asked me how I felt, looking back, about my overall choice of courses. I said I regretted only that I hadn't been able to take Greek drama because of my change of program. He said nothing more at the time, but about ten minutes later he came back and asked, "How serious were you about the Greek drama?" I said "Very." He paused for a moment and then said, "What are you doing in June?" "Nothing particular, just waiting to go up to the cottage with my family." Then he said, "Come to my home every morning except Sunday. You can spend the rest of the day preparing for the following morning. We'll take the Oresteian trilogy, and the plays of Sophocles and Euripides on the same subject." And that's what we did.' For Daly, the story exemplifies the outstanding teaching he was fortunate to have had. But it also reveals an eagerness for learning that is as rare as the teaching that encouraged it.

Legg could use someone diligent, studious, and adept at interpretation. The Film Board had been established in May 1939, after several years of planning, as a peacetime organization. Before the outbreak of the war, Legg had come to Canada to make two films on training the unemployed, *The Case of Charlie Gordon* and *Youth Is Tomorrow* (both 1939). But with the outbreak of the war, Grierson had assigned him the daunting task of developing and producing a monthly theatrical series called *Canada Carries On*. The films in this series generally were one- or two-reelers depicting Canada's support of the Allied defence effort. They were narration-driven, using original footage or archival material to support a thesis carefully laid out by Legg and stentoriously delivered by a very young Lorne Greene. At the time Daly was being interviewed, several editions had been produced and released. They bore such titles as *Atlantic Patrol*, *Letter from Aldershott*, *Front of Steel*, and *Wings of Youth* (all 1940).

Legg assigned Daly the task of researching a film – eventually titled *Battle of Brains* (1941) – proclaiming the link between productive scientific research and a successful war effort. It would show examples of Canadian research leading to important military advantages. At this point, however, Daly became an unknowing, minor pawn in a struggle for power that had erupted shortly before his appointment. The National Film Board had been established, initially, as a coordinating, supervising agency without any direct authority over the actual production of films. Film production remained the responsibility of the twenty-year-old Government Motion Picture Bureau, headed by Captain Frank Badgley. Although Grierson and Badgley got along well at first, their relationship deteriorated quickly. Badgley thought Grierson arrogant and imperious; to Grierson, Badgley was a recalcitrant bureaucrat who didn't seem to realize there was a war on. On 27 November 1940, Grierson submitted his resignation to the chairman of the Film Board. In his letter, Grierson complained about the pressures to 'jump through the hoop of Civil Service regulation,' observing that

most governments are finding it necessary to use increasingly such media as radio and film, and everywhere one notices the same tug-of-war. On the one hand, the Civil Servants with their formalities of government regulation; on the other hand, the creative people protesting that Civil Service procedure weakens the vitality and paralyzes the initiative which are necessary for good work. One notices that wherever the weight of influence has lain with the Civil Service, the spark has gone out and the use of the creative media has not been remarkable ...

Films ... are different from other ... government activity in one fundamental ... A routine average will not do. They must either achieve showmanship and distinction or they are not worth doing at all.

Grierson agreed to remain on the job for three months or until a replacement could be found. Because production was under Badgley, Grierson had to send Daly and several other young Canadian recruits to the Motion

Picture Bureau. Meanwhile, Legg, impatient with what he regarded as the Motion Picture Bureau's lethargy, avoided the MPB and worked mainly with Grierson. Daly's immediate boss at the Bureau was Stanley Hawes, another of Grierson's British imports, who was in charge of production and who took over the direction of *Battle of Brains*. During a lull in the film's production, Grierson asked Badgley to return Daly to the Film Board. Badgley refused.

To give Daly something to do while Grierson and Badgley fought over the rights to him, Hawes directed him to clean up, sort out, and catalogue a mass of stock material the Film Board was quickly accumulating. The task seemed formidable. 'There were open cans and closed cans full of nitrate film in all sorts of stages. There were bits of sound negative, sound positive, original negatives mixed up with out-takes, film on reels, on little rollers, in tins, loose film, duplicate film, duplicate tracks, duplicates of duplicates. All of this was just lying around, *very explosive*, and everybody was just going back and forth through this area.'

Daly approached the job methodically and positively. 'In order to do the job, I had to ask everybody, "What's this?" and "What's that?" or find somebody who could tell me. I got to know everybody. I got to know all the films that had been made at the Bureau and all the material we had accumulated. So, in the end, I became the one knowledgeable person, without realizing it, who knew where any old shot was that people might want. I actually became *valuable* for the first time. And when all the captured German material, and Italian material, and, later, Japanese material came in, it was natural to give it to me to catalogue, because I knew how to do that. I knew where all the other stuff was, and I liked doing that. I was good at that.'

While Daly was labouring in probably the least coveted job at the Motion Picture Bureau or the Film Board at the time, Grierson continued his struggle for full control of Canadian government film production. He agreed to a further extension of his Film Board commissionership. Even while engaged in political manoeuvering in high government circles, he pressed for Daly's return. On 7 March 1941, he wrote curtly to Badgley:

I should be obliged to have an early answer about Daly. It is important that I have him back as early as possible.

On 12 March, Grierson's assistant, Ross McLean, followed up with a slightly longer memo. The next day Badgley sent a three-page reply in which he invoked sections of the Film Act, raised questions about the payment of Daly's salary, and referred to the interrupted and therefore not yet completed *Battle of Brains* research. Certain passages reveal Badgley's resentment of Grierson:

We are anxious to keep Mr. Daly because we believe he has definite potentialities insofar as film production work is concerned and we are anxious to build the strength of our creative staff with likely young *Canadians* ...

No one is more aware of the need of building up the creative strength of this Bureau than Mr. Grierson and no one has more strongly advocated just such a course, right along, than he. Yet, when he sends us a young man who appears to have definite possibilities, seems to fit in with our organization and is just beginning to be of some use to us, he suddenly demands that he be released to work for him at a time when we have definite need for the young man ourselves. Surely, amongst Mr. Grierson's galaxy of proteges – literary and otherwise – he can find other talent to meet his immediate needs in the matter of research work.

One thing is sure. I am certainly going to resist, with every means at my command, any effort to turn this Bureau into a temporary haven for persons Mr. Grierson or anyone else may wish to use themselves off and on and have us carry during the 'in-between' periods ... We believe that our need for his services, just now, is greater than Mr. Grierson's ... I regret that I am unable to meet Mr. Grierson's request.

On 11 June, the issue of the Film Board's authority was decided when the Canadian government passed an order in council transferring authority over the Motion Picture Bureau to Grierson and the National Film Board. Grierson's victory set the tone for the Film Board for many years to come. He had won not only control over all government film production but also a mandate to run it free from the usual constraints of the civil service. He could hire and fire – giving his new employees three-month contracts, renewable upon the demonstration of merit – and he won certain budgetary freedoms as well. But it probably never would have worked had Grierson not valued something else as highly as he valued creative control. Steeped in the work ethic, he was fond of calling art 'a by-product of a job of work done.' The Film Board's subsequent pre-eminence resulted not only from the degree of autonomy that the organization and its talented filmmakers enjoyed, but also from the respect for craftsmanship and persistent hard work that Grierson inculcated. This attitude, instilled in the organization's psyche at the very beginning, would help keep the Film Board creative long after civil service protections began creeping back into its employment policies after the war was over.

The lowly 'job of work' at which Daly toiled while Grierson fought his high-level battles marked the beginnings of the Film Board's eventually acclaimed stock-shot library. Almost every Film Board documentary incorporating archival footage has drawn on this library. It is still a resource for filmmakers at the Film Board (and, by permission, for other filmmakers). Daly's work had its most immediate benefit, however, in Legg's development of *Canada Carries On*. 'This is not a documentary war,' Grierson said, 'it's a newsreel war,' and *Canada Carries On* was for Grierson the Film Board's most important ongoing venture.

Legg's memory of Daly, recalled in a letter written more than forty years later (25 July 1983), began at around this time. Legg recalled

talking one day to Grierson about a number of things. 'Oh, and by the way,' [Grierson] interjected, 'I'm giving you one of the new intake. Bright. University. Teacher manqué. Should be our kind. Brutalise him in the usual way.'

An hour or two later a nose appeared round the door of my office. Not receiving a rebuff, more of the nose appeared. Then more. And more. It grew longer and longer. I didn't think I'd ever seen so long a nose. It reminded me of Paradise Lost:

> ... th' unwieldy Elephant
> To make them mirth us'd all his might, and wreath'd
> His Lithe Proboscis ...

It was not, however, th' unwieldy Elephant that finally followed the Proboscis into the room, but a tall, lean young man. He was clean-shaven; and above his Cyranoic nose was a pair of hollow-set eyes which had the uncomfortable habit of turning a haunted stare upon you, through you, and out the other side. The young man was not only clean-shaven: he was clean all over, and – more unusual still for the Film Board of those days – impeccably dressed in a dark blue suit and polished black shoes. Where on earth had Grierson dredged up this pillar of youthful respectability? And the thought darted, as it darted about three times a day, that J.G. had finally gone out of his mind. Until I remembered that J.G. himself invariably wore a dark blue suit and black shoes.

Grierson had learnt his tidy personal habits – oddly pronounced for one who so despised tidy mental habits – in the Navy. Tom had learnt his in the course of a *comme il faut* middle-class upbringing. And I gradually came to realise that his background and mine had much in common. Tom's father wore a bowler hat. So did mine. His mother wore a fur coat. So did mine. His family were of solid professional stock; and, truth to tell, were probably slightly shocked when the apple of their eye embraced anything as low as films. So did, and were, mine. Such staid attributes seemed the antithesis of what Grierson normally looked for in his recruits. Just as I had never understood why he hired me, I was at a loss to account for his eye falling on Tom. I could only recall two of his mottoes: (1) Always cast against type; and (2) Start people at the top of the ladder and let them work their way down. Perhaps he got back at us both by dubbing me 'the solicitor of the documentary movement,' and by calling Tom 'the best butler in the business.' In the latter, anyway, he was certainly right.

Daly saw his job as simply one of helping Legg in any way he could. The burden of writing, editing, and producing *Canada Carries On* left Legg with time for little else. Daly remembers that Legg always had a rumpled look. A caricature drawn by a Film Board animator, Jim McKay, depicted a three-armed Legg at the movieola, his arms in frantic motion.

At first, Daly's ability to help Legg was limited by his own lack of film-making knowledge or skills. 'I couldn't help him with his writing because he really had to do that alone and quietly, but once he had an outline of what he wanted to get, I could do the film research. Legg was making films mainly from stock material. They were international subjects for the most part, and it was impossible for us under wartime conditions either to go and shoot or to get people to shoot stuff especially for us and send it over. Legg's stock-shot type of film meant that you had to have a lot of fresh material on different subjects. He was capable of doing it himself, but he didn't have the time. I would keep asking him questions until I felt sure what the point was of each sequence or exactly what kind of shot he wanted – such and such a meeting of people in that place or that time, or something that would indicate industrial development in some region, et cetera. When I finally knew *why* he wanted it, and in what *context* – should it show a military connection, or an economic connection, or was it a scientific connection? – when I understood how he wanted to use it, then I'd go into the stock-shot library and look at everything I could find. Very little of it was ever what he had asked for. So I'd look at, really, *any* material to see what different meanings it had. Sometimes I got sent to New York to comb through the archives of Pathé and Fox for footage Legg or anybody else at the Board could use.'

Pursuing his characterization of Daly as a 'butler,' Legg remembered

sitting at the movieola, editing; and I decided that I wanted to put back a shot I had discarded. 'Tom,' I said, 'you remember the shot we took out from here? I'd like it back, please.' A few minutes later the tall gaunt form stalked back into the room. In deference to his membership in a profession that demanded physical labour, he had made the concession of discarding his coat, but the rest of his impeccability was still intact: dark blue vest and pants, polished black shoes, clean shirt, elegant cuff-links. Poised on the upturned fingers of his right hand, in the correct position for a silver salver, was the lid of a film can; and in the precise centre of the lid, neatly rolled up and secured with a rubber band, was the shot. He bowed gravely as he presented it to me.

He also had the withering aplomb necessary for a great butler; and one day he turned it full on to Grierson himself. Tom was at the movieola, running a reel of sound he had edited. J.G. happened to wander into the room and stood behind him, listening. After a while Tom became aware of his presence and stopped the movie-ola. J.G. shook his head. 'That won't do at all. Sounds lousy.' Tom slowly raised his eyes, and the haunting stare held J.G. firm. 'Perhaps it has not occurred to you, Mr. Grierson, that I am running the reel backwards.' In his biography of Grierson, Forsyth Hardy attributes this to me, but I'm fairly sure it was Tom who thus reduced the Film Commissioner to size.

As hyperbolic as Legg's metaphor is – Daly can't remember the put-down of Grierson; he doubts that it occurred – and despite its derisive edge, it is rooted in insight. Daly was, in some ways, like a butler in a seemingly manic household. From the 'two or three employees' Grierson had told Parliament (before the war) the Film Board would need, its payroll rose to 55 in late 1941, to 293 a year later, and to 787 in 1945. At one point, the Film Board's co-opted space and improvised facilities were dispersed among fourteen different buildings spread about Ottawa. Grierson's aggressively anti-bureaucratic leadership set the tone for the entire organization. By the standards of the Ottawa of that time, the Film Board's corporate culture was somewhat bohemian, often arrogant, and fiscally free-wheeling. Daly remembers frequent parties, at Grierson's house and in the homes and apartments of others, to which all were invited regardless of rank. But if Film Board employees played hard, they also worked round the clock and on weekends. In the winter, 'the heating in government buildings would be turned off at five o'clock on Friday to save energy. We'd keep working in coats and gloves. We were too excited to stay away.' In Grierson's words, the Film Board's work ethic was to 'bang them out and no misses.' Although a theatrical release date was regarded as a 'sacred commitment,' by 'no misses' Grierson also meant no misses artistically and no misses in terms of purpose. The films should be as well crafted as time and money permitted, but they should never stray from social 'purposiveness,' a value fundamental to Grierson's conception of documentary.

In its war-impelled attempt to forge a quick alliance between rebellious artistic temperament and government-directed social purpose, the Film Board needed a 'butler,' and no one was better situated to perform the role, and probably no one was more suitable temperamentally, than Daly. He was the chief assistant to the producer of the Film Board's most important series. Having created the stock-shot library, Daly was in a position to help all the other filmmakers on their productions as well. Another Grierson recruit, Margaret Ann Bjornson (who married, in succession, filmmakers Alan Adamson, James Beveridge, and Arthur Elton), remembered in 1980 that Daly

lived rather austerely somewhere or another, had no bad habits, was a lovely companion at parties, but he had from the beginning (to the end) an easily held rein over himself, and sometimes the rest of us, and his disciplines were cheerfully unassailable.

Stanley Hawes has recalled that

in the summer of 1941 Jim Beveridge and I were assembling a 40-minute account of the second year of the war called *The Fight for Liberty* (sometimes known as *Empire Cavalcade*). We were working under great pressure – three days and two nights at a stretch were not uncommon – and on the night before it was to be recorded the commentary was still very sketchy. Jim and I were very tired but Tom rallied round that night, as people did in those blessed days – Tom especially – and somehow the three of us had a commentary ready for Lorne Greene at 9 o'clock in the morning.

Daly's first job for Legg after *Battle of Brains* was to find stock-shot material, largely from German footage, for *Churchill's Island* (1941), a film about England's preparations for an expected invasion by the Germans. The film embodied Grierson's ideas about the purposes of film and Legg's notions about structure and pacing. Grierson had been stressing the need for films that were truthful but not defeatist. When NFB films were criticized for acknowledging the strength of the Axis powers, Grierson countered that to deny the strength of the enemy would not only be dishonest but also undermine the credibility of the films. In *Churchill's Island*, the Germans are a ferocious enemy. Sequences depict the bombing of London and the blockade of England. At the same time, the British are shown as quietly brave, undiscouraged, and determined; near the film's end, Lorne Greene, reading Legg's narration, extols England's 'inner strength [and] stubborn calm, which iron and fire and steel cannot pierce.' The film also reflects Grierson's insistence that films show relationships among events; the bombing, the blockade, and England's defence are systemically linked among themselves as well as related to the broader war.

Legg's realization of Grierson's notions of purpose involved two of Legg's favourite principles of documentary editing. One of these was that a film should proceed, emotionally, in 'waves.' A major sequence should build to a crescendo that was followed by a quieter beginning of the next sequence, which should build to a stronger crescendo. *Churchill's Island* starts rather calmly with its sequence of preparations for an invasion. Then comes the bombing sequence, then the blockade, and finally a forceful climax. A second principle of Legg's is embodied in the film's strong opening and closing sequences. 'Catch people at the beginning,' Daly remembers the principle, 'and leave them with something at the end, they'll come and they'll go away with you. If you have any trouble, let it be in the middle.' The middle of *Churchill's Island* is not dull, but it is framed by a suspenseful beginning and a rousing conclusion. The film opens with images of men guarding the coast and the words 'Night and day the watching eyes gaze seaward.' It concludes with Lorne Greene's voice challenging the Germans to 'Come ... if you dare!' *Churchill's Island* also met Grierson's insistence that NFB films should achieve showmanship and distinction: in 1942, it won an Oscar for Best Short Film.

Daly did the stock-shot research for two subsequent films, *Warclouds in the Pacific* (1941) and *Battle for Oil* (1942). *Warclouds in the Pacific*, arguing from geopolitical analysis, predicted a Japanese attack on North America. It was released ten days before Pearl Harbor. 'Everyone thought we were mad,' Daly recalls. (The film was wrong in one detail: it described Pearl Harbor as the 'Gibraltar of the Pacific' and implied the attack would occur elsewhere.) He did the research and the sound editing for *Food, Weapon of Conquest* (1941), *This Is Blitz* (1942), *Geopolitik – Hitler's Plan for Empire* (1942), *The Mask of Nippon* (1942), *Pincers on Axis Europe* (1943), *Freighters under Fire* (1942), and *Battle Is Their Birthright* (1943). These last two were early issues of *World in Action*, a series spun off from *Canada Carries On* for films with primarily international themes.

In researching stock footage for usable material, Daly developed the habit of taking notes on every shot he came across. 'I discovered that the act of writing something down made me actually think about what it was I was looking at. This helped my retention in a way that getting just a general impression couldn't. In some way, connecting the thought with the physical action of actually writing something concrete and specific seemed to

double the memory.' This habit enhanced his ability to see potential meaning in whatever footage he was looking at, and it frequently helped him
solve a specific editing problem for Legg. 'For *Mask of Nippon*, Legg
wanted to do a story about Japanese navy swimmers swimming quietly in
the night among some British ships in the Far East, planting a kind of bomb
that would stick to the hull and be detonated later. He asked me if I could
find anything like that. I didn't think I could find such a thing in a Japanese
newsreel, but in New York, at Fox, I came across a beautifully photographed sequence about a long-distance swim in Japan. It was covered
fully. There were long, lingering shots of the swimmers. It had never been
used, and it was enough to cover Legg's commentary.'

Daly's visual memory soon became renowned among people who had
reason to benefit from it. Years later, in a chatty informational memo about
a variety of topics, Tom Johnston, a public relations official for the Film
Board, recalled an incident from his days in the Film Board's New York
office shortly after the war:

One day I received a call from one of the five newsreel companies then operating in
Manhattan, and the voice at the other end of the telephone said: 'Could you please
get in touch with Tom Daly in Ottawa and ask him if we have in our files a shot of
Sir Winston Churchill made on such-and-such a date at such-and-such a place.'

I must have sounded a bit startled – for I was – but the caller assured me that his
request was on the level and that all I had to do was contact Tom Daly to get the
answer. I made a few rambling remarks such as: 'But Daly's in Ottawa and you are
the one who is at 630 Ninth Avenue and that is where the shot will be if you have it,
so why ...' but he cut me off, with a bit of a laugh, and said: 'Just ask Daly, please.'

So I did ... and that was the first time I learned about Tom Daly's capacity for
remembering motion picture shots. For that New York enquirer he ... told how the
action moved from left to right, the other people in the shot with Churchill, details
of the lighting and camera angle ... and a wealth of other useful data.

Making detailed notes while screening footage was a habit Daly was to
sustain and develop throughout his long Film Board career, even after
becoming a producer and executive producer. Beginning in the late 1950s,
high-ratio, unscripted live-action documentary displaced the largely
scripted and rehearsed documentary as the predominant style at the Film
Board, and directors out in the field were shipping in thousands of feet of
film every day or two. To save time, Daly would screen three sets of rushes
simultaneously, writing notes about each shot on a legal-size sheet of paper
he had divided into three vertical columns. These notes, along with the

memory that they provoked, would be an invaluable resource when structural problems arose during editing.

Daly observed Legg as attentively as he examined stock footage. 'A lot of what I learned from him was just from watching him edit a film. I'd try to guess what shot or kind of shot he was going to put in next. When he did something different, I'd try to figure out why. Occasionally I might not agree with him, but I really wasn't in a position to agree or disagree because it was not something I had positions on already. It was all new to me.'

There was very little formal teaching at the Film Board in the war years. In a talk about editing that he gave at the Film Board right after the war, Legg discussed the creation of new meaning by the juxtapositon of shots and his 'wave' theory of rhythm. By that time, Daly already had absorbed Legg's knowledge of editing through the everyday process of assisting him.

'Although he didn't call it teaching, he used to speak aloud in my presence as his assistant editor. It was his habit or manner or maybe he was doing it for me. I never really knew. For example, he would have all his shots, say, on a bin. He would select all the possible shots for a sequence and hang them out so he could see through them and see which image was which. He would study them, to see which ones went from left to right, which ones went from right to left, which ones were close-shots, which ones had to come in a particular order. Then he would start rearranging them to try to develop a sequence, before actually splicing, because in those days, with hot splicers, you'd lose a frame every time you cut or recut, so it was a good idea to make as many decisions as possible before actually cutting and splicing. This made it very hard to experiment with the rhythm of a sequence. You had to figure it out beforehand, if possible. All the time, he'd be talking out loud, saying things like, "This is a good beginning" or "This sequence kind of peters out" or "Better start over," that kind of thing. It was an absolutely marvellous way of teaching, because none of it was directed at me. He was just thinking out loud, letting me in on his thought process. I got so I could usually guess which shot he wanted next off the bin. If I guessed wrong, I realized I wasn't following his thought, and I would ask him about it, which often led to interesting explanations.'

Daly remembers that Legg was 'very impressed by Russian film editing, which had a lot to do with his ideas about pacing and his amazing ingenuity in relating together different images. At the same time, he was a writer and an essayist. And in the end, in spite of all the great cutting and continuity, I used to feel that he was, basically, illustrating an essay. His shots would be cut to that essay line. But since he was quite a historian, his mind worked in great swatches, and consequently he never got lost in little details. He kept moving on the big line, and found ways to summarize or symbolize a whole paragraph of thought in a very few shots. And I know that unconsciously I learned a lot about that from him. I don't remember him speaking about it. It's just that I was aware of the condensation of material. It was almost the same as a poetic use of language where you talk about "twenty sails" for "twenty ships." The one detail will stand for the whole scene, and the one sequence will stand for the whole war. And he knew how to make a kind of bridge with its piers landing on all the sequences and tying the whole thing together.'

Daly put his own twist on Legg's principle of starting and ending strong. 'I often think as much about working back from the end as I do working forward from the beginning when I'm editing a film, because it's very easy to start well and head off in all directions and then end up somewhere you don't want to be. You can do an awful lot of good work and end up in left field, wondering what to do. If you know where you're heading for, you can get there by the strongest route.'

Daly remembers there being 'a lot of practical principles, a lot of specific details – like if a pan shot was cutting to a static shot, it would be best to let it come to rest for a moment before you cut to it.' But the principles were expressed in the course of solving editing problems, not as part of a theory or system.

One principle stands out from the rest for its influence on Daly. 'The most specific thing I've retained from Legg was his way of showing that the line of the film follows the line of attention in a frame. Movement, for instance, controls our attention. Say you are watching something that moves from left to right or from the left-hand bottom corner to the top right-hand corner, and you cut to something where the center of attention is back again at the bottom left: then there's a big visual jump, your eye has to jump all the way from the top right-hand corner down to the bottom left instantaneously, which it can't quite do. For example, in one of Legg's films – I've forgotten the title – there is a shot in which General DeGaulle is standing up on the right side of the frame, makes a gesture, and sinks back into the bottom left corner. This cuts to a shot of Churchill standing up, moving from the bottom left-hand corner up into the frame. The eye follows this very easily, and the two contrary movements make a kind of visual point and even a political point.'

In October 1981, McGill University hosted a conference on Grierson. In his presentation ('The Growth of a Craft: My Debt to Legg and Grierson'),

Daly connected Legg's 'line of attention' principle to a remembered insight from his teacher Eric Owen. Owen

had said that the emotional line of the *Iliad*, or any other work, was not the line of the emotions in the *Iliad*. Somebody could be laughing in the story, but you could be crying. It was the line of emotions *you* went through following it.

Legg said practically the same thing, that the film is the line of attention you go through, and if you break that line, the connection is gone. I began to really think about that, and watch how it worked.

Thus, Daly elaborates, 'the film that the audience is seeing is whatever they are following in their own line of attention. To some extent you can control it if you want to, and to some extent they are free to look anywhere they wish, but the fact is that other things being equal, a certain movement captures attention much more than something else. For instance, if you are looking at a quiet country scene, and a truck starts to come in from the left, you will look over to see what that is. The audience's attention moves about the frame, and you can be pretty sure it will be on something. The more experience you have, the more you can guess what that something is. If you can put the initial point of attention in the next frame at exactly the same place in the frame as the ending of the last shot, then the audience simply continues their line of attention without a break. You can also break their attention deliberately. My point isn't that you have to keep the attention in the same place; my point is that you use this principle either to make something smooth or to shock, depending on what you need. There are many ways of using it if you really understand how it works.'

Daly learned how to edit sound from Legg in much the same way as he absorbed Legg's knowledge of picture editing. But 'this separate step didn't take very long, because we had no sound effects library at all, and little means of recording useful effects for our sort of film. Legg was drawing upon a very limited supply of sounds, clear of commentary, that were coming in from the British documentaries that were supplied to Grierson. The quality of these sound effects was generally poor. They had of course been recorded on photographic emulsion and quickly deteriorated when copied from one print to another. And we only had means in the recording theatre to handle two effects tracks, one music track, and a live voice recording.

'Just the same, the principles of matching, mixing, synching, and enhancing the sounds were identical whatever the quality, and I took to the challenge with great pleasure. On my own, I began to assemble a library of sound effects, mostly derived from the excellent and advanced sound recordings on captured German material. These sounds were almost always *not* covered by commentary, because the Germans intended that the accompanying text be worked out locally, in the language of each country they had overrun. It was fun to use their sounds right back at them. But we occasionally stole a few more sounds from British and American films as they came by for screening.'

Legg remembered Daly as an assiduous student, 'highly intelligent, with a quick grasp and a good memory,' who seldom had to be told something more than once. But Daly's first attempt to edit a film on his own – *Heroes of the Atlantic* (1941), a fifteen-minute newsreel with a theatrical release date – left Legg doubtful about Daly's future as a filmmaker.

It was, I think, the intangibles of film – the ten percent of feel, intuition, lunacy, which is the filmmaker's *sine qua non* – that he found more difficult to acquire, as many beginners of down-to-earth nature do. When I first gave him a passage of a film to edit himself, [his] nose seemed to twitch with eagerness over the movieola. He went at it full tilt. That was the trouble. When he'd finished, it was a mess – but not an unholy mess. In fact there was not much wrong with it except for one thing: pacing. The first commandment in my unit was 'Thou shalt not be dull'; and in his determination to obey it he had cut every shot to an absolute minimum, regardless of the material's own lilt and rhythm. Consequently, it was just comprehensible, but had no impact. But then, to squeeze the maximum impact from a series of juxtaposed shots is definitely Part II of the learner's syllabus; and Tom was still in the elementary stages. As I recall with shame, I took it away from him and did it myself – which is the worst thing I could have done.

'He took one look at the film,' Daly recalls with serene detachment, 'and I have never seen such a reaction. It was beyond anger. It was beyond comment. He just grabbed the cans, beckoned to me, rushed upstairs to the cutting room, took the picture, and began to tear it apart. I had already felt, during the screening, looking at it for the first time as a whole with him, that it was just like a machine-gun. All the shots were either three or four seconds long. And they never changed. They just kept going, and going, and going, and going. I knew it was a hopeless case, but I didn't quite realize how hopeless he felt it was. He went to the movieola, took the bin, threw everything aside, took the reels, ran them, and as he ran them, broke off shots that he wanted to keep, hung them on the bin, and all the other shots he just threw on the floor. Then he took all the outs, and all the trims, and looked through them, kept this, kept that, and threw away the rest. The

floor was piled high, and he was going so fast, that just to collect the stuff
and get it out of the way I could hardly keep up with him. In a very, very
short time, he had decided, then and there, what he was going to keep, what
he was going to leave aside. He made a cut in four days – a final cut in four
days – which had only three shots left in the same order I had put them in,
and they were cut differently. Everything else was thrown aside. The shots
which I had carefully and judiciously left out because they didn't fit turned
out to be the backbone of his film. They were all the special, difficult, original, unusual shots which were unlike any other shots in the film. And they
were the most interesting ones. I hadn't known how to handle them. I
didn't know how to connect the bloody things. It was just too much for
me. So I had ruthlessly excluded them. But he made the whole film out of
my outs. What a lesson to somebody starting out!'

Legg thought Daly must have found him

a difficult and unpredictable master: for at that time, added to my native impatience
and my neurotic obsession with perfectionist detail, was the unrelenting pressure of
the monthly theatrical release date of the *Canada Carries On* series. The constant
resulting rush, tension and near-hysteria of our cutting-room was far from the
quietly discussive atmosphere usually considered desirable for studenthood. To a
greater extent than most of his contemporaries in other Film Board units, Tom had
literally to pick up his film as he went along. His training, as J.G. had demanded, was
a brutalising process; and that he survived it at all, let alone became distinguished,
speaks of an underlying toughness deceptively masked by his usually placid presence.

A key episode in Daly's progression from apprentice to editor was his
work on *Our Northern Neighbour* (1944). The aim of the film was to promote sympathy for the Soviet Union, suddenly an ally. The film opens with
a drawing of the Northern Hemisphere from a perspective above the North
Pole, which shows Russia's proximity to Canada and visually suggests an
unacknowledged but natural affinity. The main body of the film outlines
twentieth-century Russian history largely from the Soviet point of view.

Drawing first on Daly's stock-shot experience, Legg gave Daly 'a list of
broadly distinct periods of Russian history from the last tsarist era through
the revolution, "new economic policy," and so forth, right up to date. He
also listed the names of all the key people in each period, and the international events, meetings, treatises, and so forth, that were involved. And he
gave me an idea of the cities, industries, resources, land and water regions
whose images could carry much of the necessary commentary. He also
explained *why*, so that if the desired material could not be found, I could

perhaps discover something else that could support a similar meaning. Russian feature films were on the list, because they often treated Russian history – of course from the official point of view of the period – and were shot in Russian style.

'To be able to verify what I was looking at, I found it necessary to learn how to read Russian print in titles, and signs in cities, and on the posters and flags in demonstrations. This was easy, as Stanley Jackson had learned Russian in Winnipeg, and gave two or three of us Russian lessons at lunch hour for about six weeks.' (Jackson, another of Grierson's outstanding Canadian recruits, would spend his career at the Film Board as a talented writer of commentaries as well as an occasional director and valued film troubleshooter.)

In New York, Daly 'found that the newsreels had astounding amounts of material on Russia, all the way back to tsarist times – *most of it never used*, because of the tendency not to publicize life in the Soviet Union, though their news correspondents sent it out anyway. This meant that we would likely have first pick of all this material.

'My visit to the official Communist distributors in New York was not exactly easy, as our government was formerly hostile to the Soviet Union. But as we were now allies, there was a business-like acceptance, after a bit, to allow me to copy pieces of their documentary and feature films, so long as I did the work and didn't bother the distributors. That suited me perfectly, as I didn't have to ask them what the pictures were. I could figure out enough for myself from my new-found knowledge of Russian.'

Because Daly knew the material thoroughly, Legg turned the editing largely over to him. Daly's relationship with Legg on the film became one of 'constant feedback as to what was needed next. From the original screening of the total material available, Legg gave me the order in which he preferred to have the sequences cut. In my turn, I made the longest cut I could of each of these sequences to allow him the greatest latitude for commentary. Then he would tell me what could be omitted and what he wanted rearranged. And so it would go, gradually becoming more and more a series of sections that had an inner shape, a possibility of sound effects or music values, a visual or logical or mood connection between items, and so forth.

'Always the attempt was made to provide not just the *facts* of Russian history and policy, but to convey it with as much as we could of how it would *feel* if we had been in Russia and were Russian, faced always with the official version of events as given out by the Soviet government.'

After *Our Northern Neighbour*, Daly grew increasingly independent of

Legg. Daly trained Margaret Ann Adamson to succeed him as Legg's general assistant. From Legg's outline, Daly edited *Inside France* (1944), a film explaining why France had capitulated to Hitler and urging its reacceptance as an ally. Then he edited *Road to the Reich* (1944) with minimal supervision from Legg. 'I showed it to him now and then for suggestions,' Daly recalls. Using combat photography and captured enemy footage, the film depicts and explains the strategy of the Allied assault on Germany. He edited *Atlantic Crossroads* (1945) and co-produced it with Grant McLean. He edited and produced *Gateway to Asia* (1945). He edited *Ordeal by Ice* (1945), a film depicting cold-weather military training in the Canadian Rockies. Daly enhanced the picture track by laying in synchronized sound effects of howling wind and of boots crunching on glazed snow. These sound effects lent the pictures a kind of presence that had been lacking in the NFB's newsreel films, and are an early manifestation of the attention to detail that would be one characteristic of Daly's later producing and teaching.

Despite Daly's growing autonomy as an editor, these films remained part of the Film Board's war effort. They were individual examples of an approach to filmmaking imposed by Grierson and Legg, and which Daly had absorbed through total immersion. Yet his training under Legg would serve as the foundation for his later role in encouraging radically new styles of documentary film, in helping to salvage troubled films, and in serving as a consultant much sought after by some of the Film Board's most successful directors. Not long before his death in 1988, Guy Glover, who also joined the Film Board during the war years and who spent most of his professional career there, described Daly as 'a first-rate example of someone who has learned *thoroughly a technique* – in his case, the technique of film editing – in a very tough school, that of Stuart Legg. Tom was a fresh-faced, socially rather innocent youth who gave himself up completely to being Legg's assistant. And he was able to take that. He didn't have any false notions of being put upon by Legg's terrible demands. Legg was a kind of English intellectual who was sarcastic, *beastly*. He said terrible things about "poor old Tom, he doesn't know which end is up." But he had also a tremendous respect for Tom, because Tom was doing the work that had to be done to make the films.

'They were compilation films. Without editing, they would have been zilch. Tom learned that kind of editing, and he learned all there was to know about it. It was like a pianist learning from Anton Rubinstein, or a violinist learning from Leopold Auer, the great virtuoso teachers of the nineteenth century. Tom learned virtuoso film editing – of a non-fiction, non-dramatic kind – and he learned it so thoroughly that it lasted him for the rest of his life.

'His knowledge of editing of course expanded out of the kind of narrower type in which he was trained, but the training was reliable enough, and well enough learnt, to allow that kind of expansion. That was a kind of rock-firm thing. He later had to be an executive producer, he had to be an administrator, he had to work with people, and all the other things that producers have to do, but at the centre of it all was this absolutely marvellously learnt technique of film editing. It was through this that he influenced all films with which he came in contact.'

As formative as his training under Legg was for Daly, it constituted only half of the apprenticeship that would change the direction of his life. 'All the filmmaking part and a lot of the history and politics and everything else that was going on was entirely new to me, but the thing that I think excited me most, as a basis to everything, was a kind of one-world view of things at the helm. The world, including all its peoples, was seen more as an organism, in which the role of information – such as our films – was to exchange useful understandings as a kind of circulation of life-blood.

'Grierson and Legg, however much they had to deal with governments and political realities, seemed never to be thinking in terms of nationalism or political divisions that chop up the world map artificially. They spoke of the natural flow of all the world forces – economic, political, and everything else combined – not thinking of them as walls but as organic flow lines like veins and arteries.

'It was from Legg and Grierson, for example, that I first heard of "geopolitics," long before it became generally known elsewhere. Geopolitics was a British invention, conceived by Halford Mackinder, before World War I. He pictured how the control of resources – their sources and supply lines – would give political domination to whoever had that control, regardless of sea power. He brought his ideas to the attention of the British armed forces and government of the day, but they weren't interested. After the war, just before the peace conference in Paris, he published his ideas in a book which was later discovered and studied with great relish by the defeated German generals. They used Mackinder's ideas to build the vast system of land power which Hitler took over later. The irony of all this for the Film Board was that another of Grierson's documentary producer-directors that he brought with him to Canada to teach us was Raymond Spottiswoode, whose wife happened to be distantly related to Mackinder. So it was not surprising that Grierson and Legg knew a lot about geopolitics and were ready to meet it on its own ground, in information and propaganda terms. They already had this kind of world-view themselves. They even made a film about it, *Geopolitik – Hitler's Plan for Empire*.'

Daly found Grierson's one-world view 'far more stimulating than the old nineteenth-century nationalistic kind of thinking, and I found it very exciting that Canadian topics were not only to be dealt with as Canadian topics but also as part of the whole world scene, and that things happening elsewhere in the world, that were important for us to know about, should become a natural part of information in the Canadian war effort. The old view around Ottawa was that you ought to show and promote only Canadian themes, and only nice ones. You mustn't touch anything else. And so it was that the Film Board played a part in the infusion of international thinking into a rather sleepy, old-fashioned Ottawa.

'But it was more a practical understanding than a political one, and it was the first time I'd ever come into contact with a whole philosophy related to practical life. It was a humanistic thing, all around.'

Although Daly's image of Grierson as a humanist who wanted to use film to promote national and international welfare and development has predominated among filmmakers, critics, and public commentators ever since Grierson appeared on the documentary scene, not everyone in Canada has shared it. During the war and right after it, Grierson was widely suspected of having communist leanings. He was also accused of fascist sympathies. His resentful appearance in 1946 before the Royal Commission on Espionage in the Public Service proved nothing but only reinforced the suspicions and embarrassed the Film Board. For the next forty years, however, no one seemed to care. Then, in the 1980s, the benign image of Grierson was again challenged, most notably by Joyce Nelson and Peter Morris. Nelson's *The Colonized Eye* argued that Grierson deliberately subordinated Canada's interests to those of international capitalism and that the associated economic development often was harmful to Canada. Morris's essay, 'Re-thinking Grierson,' probed Grierson's writing and found in the 'organic' thinking that so appealed to Daly an affinity with some philosophical roots of fascism.

When these reassessments were published, many of the men and women who had worked at the Film Board during Grierson's reign were either dead or beyond caring. Those who remembered Grierson seemed mystified by the criticism. Little of it rings true to Daly. 'The greatest impression I got from Nelson's book was that she felt a kind of "intuition" about something that she then set out to document. She may have seriously felt a suspicion, but I know a lot about suspicion, and how it can read anything in a contrary way. I had a suspicion about a lecturer at college talking about how hard the Germans would be to defeat. It seemed like he was preaching defeatism. I had this powerful "intuition" of wrongdoing. I alerted officials to this possibility, but I think it was totally in my imagination. So I've had a personal experience of reading meanings into things that weren't there. I recognized that suspicious tone in her book. She wrote very well when putting the things together to make her case, but if you go back to the sources, you see that she left out lots of key stuff in the dot-dot-dots that would undermine her case. And she was always reading in hindsight with her present-day attitude towards things, as if everyone should have had that attitude back then. For example, in the spirit of the day Grierson expected good results if you developed the northland. Everyone did. Nobody anticipated the bad side-effects.

'Her portrait of Grierson doesn't fit with the Grierson I knew. He was never like what she suggests he was. She *wants* to believe all that. This kind of thing is just in the air. We're in an era of tearing down all icons, all authorities. It's a popular thing to do. But if you, as a society, are consciously against each other, or even unconsciously are "not together," how do you accomplish anything? If you are always suspicious, and ready to blame only others?

'Unless there is inner respect *for* what is admirable in another person, respect which is greater than one's disrespect for what one disagrees with, then I don't think there can be any joint accomplishments of a positive, enduring kind.'

Grierson's critics, both during the war and again in the 1980s, found evidence of anti-democratic tendencies in some of the newsreel films. Daly acknowledges that 'many of those wartime films don't stand up now. They are too time-locked.' But time also has obscured their context. Military alliances and contemporary communication strategies affected the tone and slant of the films.

The Gates of Italy (1943) is one of the wartime films whose context has been forgotten. The film lauds Italy's cultural history and treats the Italian people warmly, praising their honesty and lamenting their suffering. They are seen more as the dupes of fascism than its embracers. Mussolini is presented as a socialist gone wrong, but contemptuous of his German allies, dismissing Goebbels as 'a clown' and the Nazi chiefs in general as 'murderers and pederasts – nothing more.'

Even at the time of its release, the film was criticized for being 'soft on fascism' because of its sympathy for the Italians. But for Daly, who had no official role in the project but did 'help find material for it,' *The Gates of Italy* exemplifies positively the supra-national character of Legg and Grierson's thinking. If the film showed Mussolini ridiculing the Nazis, it in turn denounced Mussolini himself as a power-corrupted fool. Its strategy was less to distinguish Italy from Germany than to distinguish Italians from their leaders, the Italian heritage from its unfortunate present. Daly recalls that 'the war had reached the point where we soon would be going back on the Continent. The minute our boys were on the boot of Italy – about three months later – the perception changed. The film had exactly the right tone. Our boys were working *with* the people of Italy *against* the fascists.' In the 1980s, Daly had occasion to show the film to a group of young people who knew little about the war. 'After the first two or three minutes, they would get fascinated. It holds up as a historical document.'

Our Northern Neighbour is a more troublesome case. The narration lauds Stalin as a noble 'man of steel.' It endorses the official Stalinist line about the Moscow show trials. It extols 'the youthful forward-looking Russia of today' that is 'opening the way to a brighter world, and a broader view of life.'

But Daly stands by *Our Northern Neighbour*. 'Less was known then about Stalin than is known now. And since he was then still in power, there was little to say about the dark side of him that wasn't already part of the general opinion of the Canadian public about him at the time. What was needed was to open *other* feelings towards the Russians, rather than remind our audiences of old suspicions.

'Quotes in the film are actual quotes of Trotsky and others, though naturally incapable of presenting their balanced position. The Moscow trials were not avoided, but were carefully covered by the official statement of the charges by the Soviet government, and not by an outside judgment of the way in which the trials were carried out. All this was consistent at the time with the intent to show *Russia's* foreign policy.'

This aim was the impetus behind the film's innovative artwork. 'For Canadians, the opening polar projection map, showing Russia very close to us in the North, was a new image in those days.' This image suggested Russia's proximity to Canada. To take Canadian audiences inside Russia, 'Legg enlisted Norman McLaren to design for him an animated map which would look west upon Europe from the Kremlin's point of view. It would appear three-dimensional rather than flat. It would show, move by move, Hitler's territorial grabs, moving in organized fashion eastward, towards "us" in Russia, just as in fact Hitler had been doing.

'Norman came up with a clear and simple design, and invented a nameless and shapeless, evolving, menacing black creature, growing out of Nazi Germany and grabbing with unerring clawed, tentacular arms, the lands that led towards Russia. We christened this creature "the Wook,' and it helped in a very short time to convey the fear the Russians had – rightly, as it turned out – that Hitler was aiming to acquire their own heartland.'

Simply getting such a film made and distributed was, in Daly's view, a significant accomplishment and should be weighed against the film's evident flaws. 'It was a remarkable feat of Grierson and Legg to have steered between all the rocks of political danger, such as between two governments, between public attitudes and the need to change some attitudes, between the need for distribution and standard attitudes of commercial distributors, and, finally, to have bridged the border between Canadian audiences, which might be expected to allow something for Canadian-made films, and American audiences, which were much more independent-minded.'

Grierson's critics have found much of their evidence against him in his often provocative writings and speeches. He valued honesty in documentary, but he also said, 'Tell a lie today so that it may become true tomorrow.' He expressed a grudging admiration of Goebbels's claim that the word 'culture' made him want to reach for his gun. He lashed out at the British wartime documentaries for their indirectness and sensitivity. He talked about instilling attitudes and 'patterns of thinking.' Art was a hammer, a weapon. The state should use it to lead, educate, and unite. And before the Royal Commission on Espionage, Grierson refused to make the kind of direct disavowal that might have pleased the commission. Asked if he was a Communist, Grierson described himself as a civil servant in the British tradition of 'the classical Whitehall School,' which meant that he had 'no party affiliations.' Under further questioning, Grierson said, 'I am entirely a person ... concerned with the establishment of good international understanding [and therefore] concerned with the floating of all ideas.' Grierson added, 'I mean, I get as much from Gobineau as I get from Marx.' Grierson's refusal to define his political ideas in the terms demanded of him and his provocative manner of refusal were used in the reassessments of him that emerged forty years later. But while it was Grierson's acknowledgment of his debt to Marx that got all the attention at the time of the hearings, in the 1980s it was his mention of Gobineau.

Grierson said and wrote plenty of things that reveal an authoritarian streak, but Daly thinks that the attribution of communist or fascist sympathies to Grierson ignores his complexity and thereby misunderstands him. What some interpret as totalitarian, Daly sees as holistic. 'I've always resented it when people tagged Grierson as Communist or something like that, because I'm just *convinced* that while he had a lot of the natural sense of the world international "commonness,' which the Communists also tried to use, it was for him just part of a much greater whole. He had no reason not to relate to any side, but he didn't take a side just like that.'

For Daly, Grierson's promotion of national purpose and cohesion was inspiring and liberating – anything but totalitarian. At the McGill University seminar, Daly described how Grierson affected him:

Although I was not so close to Grierson, nobody ever kept you away from him. He was always in the kitchens at all the parties, and of course holding forth against all comers. Because I knew nothing, I was always a listener, and not a partaker ... This was all a great eye-opener to me. But at the same time I think that I was influenced by Grierson as much as anybody in our generation, though not so much through his ideas at that time as by his *being*. It was simply an experience to have someone around us who had a sense of the wholeness of things and how everything related together, whether it concerned practical small things, or the entire world scene in which our little parts fit somewhere. He seemed to be able to show how each one's little part related to everybody else's little part, and that they all had a common purpose and the possibility of a common work with a practical result, worthwhile in the world.

'What's sad,' Daly reflects, 'is that – by the sound of it – Grierson's academic detractors would seem not to have had, in their own education or experience, a teacher with such a breadth of vision and philosophy who could, like Grierson did for me and others, challenge them on their own ground. They just don't seem to be aware of the feel of such encounters.'

The organization of production reflected Grierson's sense of organic structure as Daly remembers it. Although Grierson's leadership was strong, purposeful, and opinionated, he delegated authority to those responsible for making the films. He established twelve production units, each with specific program responsibilities. The *Canada Carries On* team was one such unit. Other units focused on specific areas of Canadian life and economy, such as mining, forestry, fishing, agriculture, manufacturing, labour, the arts, and public information. The compartmentalization that such a structure might seem to imply did not, in Daly's view, come about. Instead, there was a kind of cooperative freedom. 'All the programs needed different types of people. Each could do its own work without interference from others and without having to conform to the beliefs and attitudes of the others. Each unit reported directly to Grierson, who would comment on work, offer advice, and often issue directives. Since Grierson was at home with all these types, we all could live and work in a basic harmony like different organs of the human body, which have different functions and need different kinds of cells to do their work. But their differences don't end up having to clash. In a healthy body, they end up harmonizing.'

Daly was getting a taste of what it was like not to experience life and work as separate things. Recalling a several-day editing marathon to meet a deadline, he remembers that 'the lab was going all night. Everything was going all night, for five days and nights. And gradually everybody was drawn into this. Nobody was *asked* to come. People would just hear about it and ask, "How can I help?" I can remember hunting shots that had been lost – we had a cutting copy print but nobody had kept track of the original sources – and we were hunting all through the night for the footage. Into this, Grierson and Margaret Grierson, his wife, turned up late in the night, unexpectedly, everybody working. Grierson would wander around the place and see everybody and give words of encouragement. Margaret brought in a great sack of sandwiches, and somebody else brought in a bottle of cognac. She would stay to see if there was something she could do. It was just that kind of thing. There was no great separation between life and work.'

This collaborative energy, and Daly's joy in facilitating it, continued through to the war's end. Stanley Hawes recalled that *Salute to a Victory* (1945), celebrating V-E Day,

was made in three days from its first mention by Grierson at 6 p.m. on Wednesday until the screening of the first test print on Sunday morning. A number of us were working on the film and Tom offered to prepare the sound effects track. The cutting copy was in great demand and could not be spared for long. I let Tom have it for a very short time. I believe it was only for about half an hour. Tom in that unruffled way of his took a roll of spacing, placed it alongside the cutting copy, and made a few red pencil marks on it. He then returned the cutting copy, went away with the roll of spacing, and reappeared some hours later with a superb effects track.

Almost always a calm and stabilizing centre amid the turmoil of wartime deadlines, Daly on one occasion relaxed his grip on that 'easily held rein over himself' that Margaret Ann Elton later noted of him. It happened in New York, where, Daly recalls, he 'got famously drunk with Basil Wright. Stuart Legg introduced me to him on a trip to one of the newsreel companies. Wright invited me to dinner in his hotel – a much nicer hotel than the one I was staying in.'

Wright and Daly didn't take to each other immediately, but 'all at once we discovered that we were both classical scholars by education. Everything changed. He opened up. We went up to his room. He had a bottle of Scotch. We were sitting there, talking, and we just kept on sipping. It got to be around three in the morning, and it was time to head back to my hotel. I then discovered that when you try to stand up after drinking so much, it was quite difficult.

'I walked back to my hotel partly to get the air and clear my head. It was safe to do that in those days. I remember being very grateful that New York had such wide sidewalks.

'The elevator man saw me up to my room. When I lay down, my head swam. I didn't know what to do. I tried it again, and my head swam again.

'Finally, I decided to trick it. I sat up, and then slid down just a trifle, and nothing happened. Then I slid down just a little more, and nothing happened. I did this again, and again. I got all the way down this way, finally, and went right to sleep.'

That aberration aside, Daly was content to serve in his sober, quiet way the sometimes raucous unity that characterized the wartime Film Board he remembers. In Daly's view, it was Grierson who set the tone for this spirit of unity – even beyond the walls of the Film Board itself. 'There were little nodal points in Ottawa where several Film Boarders lived together and which had become party spots, so that everybody gravitated there. Grierson used to come, and he'd bring his business and government colleagues. It would always spark something, meeting these kinds of people and talking with Grierson.'

Grierson seems to have been for Daly a real-world exemplar of the academic ideal represented by another favourite university teacher, who 'gave us Plato's *Republic*. The class was large and disparate – Anglican, Roman Catholic, Presbyterian, a couple of "communist"-leaners, two nuns in their black habits, many others – a collection that didn't know each other at all. This professor would read a bit of the text, and then at an arguable point he would break off, and begin to ask individual questions. This produced real arguments, in which he invariably took the "wrong" side, with a very supercilious manner, and always *won* the arguments, in spite of each person's best efforts. Everybody else watched with sympathy and rising annoyance the discomfiture of yet another classmate, until we began to take part in this process *communally*, each one chipping in, trying to corner the professor, and get to the unanswerable question that would make him lose. Gradually, victory would be in sight, but just when we were about two questions from the logical clincher, he would look at his watch and say, "Well, we'd better get on with our study" – to the ohhs and groans of the students.

'One day, during this process, a student came up with the clincher right out of the blue, and everyone leaned forward with expectation, ready for the kill. He wasn't fazed at all. He looked around with the same look on his face and said, "Any more red herrings?" and simply went on with his work, to an even greater chorus of derision.

'But as it turned out – and this had taken most of the fall term – he had effectively moulded us into a single team, a unit, that had learned no longer to take philosophy passively, but was active and precise, and questioning more deeply. And from that moment on, he changed totally and began to offer his own best understanding of Plato and Socrates and the amazingly up-to-date content of the *Republic*, with its three-part soul, and its three-part city-state, and the relation of the parts in their differences and their harmony.'

Grierson seemed to bring to practical matters the spirit of creative debate and positive criticism that Daly's professor had engendered in his classroom. As Daly's career developed, Grierson's example would complement the thorough knowledge of editing that Daly had acquired from Legg. 'I used to be afraid of criticism. But the first time Grierson ever looked at one of my films, I remember him sitting in the second row with his feet up on the front-row seats. I was in the back at the console. As the film was being screened, he'd keep turning around and commenting about it. After only about a minute, he turned around and started telling me what was wrong with the film, missing everything else. I kept wishing he would wait until he saw the whole thing. But when I went away afterwards and thought about what he had said – I can't really recall the details now, but a powerful impression remains – I was astounded. He was right. Everything he said about the first minute of the film applied to all the rest. He was looking at general characteristics rather than details. He was not so much criticizing the film as giving me a critique of what I didn't understand. He had a quality of perception that went straight to the point, and he could transfer that perception to you so that you understood it.

'Grierson could come down with heavy feet on your work, and say in effect, "You're too *good* to be doing such work, you've got too much going for you, you can do better." He'd send you away singing, eager to tear it all apart and start over. He never put *you* down. He put the work down, and gave good reasons.'

Grierson also taught Daly not to fear the genius of others. 'Grierson used to say, "Put any two first-rate people together and the sparks may fly, but the result will be first-rate. Two second-rate people will produce something third- or fourth-rate."' And as much as he promoted teamwork, Grierson valued the individual talent. He had surprised Daly and others by recruiting Norman McLaren and calling him 'the most important filmmaker at the Board.' Grierson's socially and politically conscious filmmaking, his emphasis on documentary, and his embrace of collaborative filmmaking would seem to place a low value on an abstract artist and fanciful animator like McLaren, who was best known for painting or scratching images directly onto film. 'Why,' Daly had wondered, 'had Grierson brought him here? When I saw how McLaren could make something from nothing, I understood. McLaren never looked at what he didn't have. He made something out of what there was. And always first-rate.'

Sometime during the war, Daly encapsulated his view of Grierson in a clerihew, a light verse form consisting of two rhyming couplets about a person whose name must serve as one of the rhymes. Daly had learned the form from reading the *New Yorker*, which often published clerihews written by S.J. Perelman.

Mister Grierson
May seem like a fierce 'un,
But it's a sort of pose
To one who knows.

Daly also wrote one about Legg:

Stuart Legg
Is not the egg
His clothes would suggest
When unpressed.

When the war ended, Grierson and Legg left the Film Board. Many of the Film Board's hundreds of employees left for private industry or other professions. The butler stayed. Daly had lost interest in pursuing a doctorate in English literature. The prospect of an academic career now seemed narrow and constricting compared to what he had glimpsed at the Film Board. 'I was so grateful that the war had broken my career plans and forced me to expand my education into technical fields, emotional fields. Even just socially, it was a marvellous education. Going to the Film Board made it necessary for me to deal with not only intellectuals, but artists, technicians, officials. I had to stretch, from zero in some cases, to learn how to relate to all this.'

When Legg left, Daly was only twenty-six years old. Asked if he had imagined much of a future for his apprentice, Legg wrote:

I think so, though the pressures of the time were too great for either of us to consider what it might be. But in hindsight, put it this way: In documentary films, as no doubt in other creative fields, there tend to be two main kinds of people: those who see films as an end, and those who see them as a means to an end. As an illustration, take the two 'daddies' of documentary, Flaherty and Grierson.

Flaherty was essentially a craftsman. For him, beauty was truth, truth beauty; that was all he knew and all he needed to know. He lived, and put all his genius into, the film of the moment. Where his next film would come from was a hurdle to be taken when he came to it. The world's worries, in their endless complexities, were not ... for him. Thus beyond his films, his outlook was simple. 'John,' he once said to J.G. in my hearing, 'do you realise there are people who are actually *starving*?' 'Bob,' replied J.G. cryptically, 'you amaze me.'

Grierson was a different animal. His was a tortured mind, nagged by the social and political problems of today and tomorrow. He juggled eight, nine, ten balls simultaneously. He thought not in terms of lavishing loving care on a single film, but of the effect of groups and programmes of films. He made only one major film himself, *Drifters*; and for all its excellences, I for one sometimes wondered whether other films on kindred subjects caught more of the lift and plunge of the sea. But he founded schools and units in both hemispheres, and obtained sponsorship for them which must ultimately have amounted to tens or hundreds of millions of dollars. He saw his daily role as that of referee between sponsor and film-maker, balancing the self-adulative tendencies of the former and the aesthetic excesses of the latter, creating an atmosphere in which both could contribute their best. It was a self-denying role, keeping in the background himself, suggesting rather than acting, building up other men and their work.

I do not say that Tom operated on anything like Grierson's scale, but there are similarities of approach between them. In his earlier years at the Film Board, consciously or otherwise, Tom made it his business to smooth our unit's path. It was he who brought you another cup of coffee at midnight, checked that you had the things you needed, saw that our relations with the service departments were as good as they could be (and we were often a brash and demanding lot). And as he matured, he carried this attitude into larger spheres. The butler became a midwife, bringing forth other people's babies, serving others rather than himself, creating a sympathetic, encouraging, contributive climate for his units. In doing this, he denied himself; it is more fun to make films oneself than to father forth those of others. As a result his name is not as well known outside the Film Board as it should be. But his contribution has been greater than that of many whose credits hit the screen more often and stood in larger type.

Legg's summation of the differences between Flaherty and Grierson – who were great friends, if almost always at odds regarding the purposes of documentary film – is the conventional one, undisputed and probably correct in its essentials. Legg's description of Daly's patience and generosity also hits the mark. Daly's most significant accomplishment lay in his contribution to the work of others. What Legg did not understand about Daly, however, and probably could not have understood – few people, even at the Film Board, really did – is that what Legg interpreted as self-denying was for Daly self-fulfilling. It was not that Daly lacked an ego but that, for a film person, he had an unusual way of gratifying it.

Nor did he lack aptitude. He had directed, under Hawes, a live-action sequence for *Battle of Brains*, and the sequence had turned out satisfactorily. And in his only other exercise in live-action direction, his characteristic attention to detail created a scene that even 'impressed Hollywood' – much to the Film Board's momentary consternation.

Legg was editing *Geopolitik – Hitler's Plan for Empire*, and he found himself in need of some material to cover some narration about the Haushofer Geopolitical Institute. When Daly could not find anything in the captured German material that would work, Legg asked him to shoot some footage around the Film Board that could pass for the interior of the Institute.

'What was I to do? It had to feel real, but how could I reconcile it with our aim to show documentary truth? Well, all through the war we would use a gunshot from one battle to cover another battle where we had no actual material. The principle was that if the *essence* of the real truth *behind* the details was honestly suggested, the details could be interchangeable, so long as the film wasn't *stating* that it was the exact footage from that exact place.'

They knew from research that the Institute was a large place, 'very secret, carefully guarded,' that it had offices and a large staff, and that it did research on the land masses of Europe and Asia. From these meagre facts, Daly reasoned out a sequence of shots to suggest the Institute as economically as possible.

'It was *big*. So we'd need a long-shot or two. The most promising place was the upstairs west corridor at John Street, which had length, many doors, and a cross-corridor or two, which could give the impression of a lot of rooms. For "much activity," we had people "coming and going" in the halls – not *too* much, and always under the watchful eyes of a guard in a German helmet, with a gun, perhaps a little out of focus in the foreground ... everything a little shadowy to prevent identification of individuals, and keep a sense of mystery.

'But *what* were they doing? Well, obviously there would be files – oh yes, and maps. That would strike an association at once. So we doctored up one wall map with a not-too-obvious swastika and had office staff members do their usual thing, discussing maps, et cetera. All this in general medium-shots, to get the sense of action, without being too specific, so that *whatever* Legg would say in commentary would be supported.

'Lastly, there'd have to be *some* kind of close-up, to be convincing that they actually did real and meaningful work. So we wanted somebody to be studying details of "luftwaffe aerial photographs." I remembered that one of the ladies then working in the negative room could well pass for a member of the ladies' chorus in *Die Walküre*. So we had her studying photos through a long magnifying glass.

'All of this had to match the usual style of Nazi cameramen, and, as well, the quality of image that reached us in the cans of captured footage. So we put the negative through the duplicating process a couple of times, dirtying it up just a little on the way.'

The film was released. No one around Ottawa seemed to notice the contrivance. But one day the rumour went around that 'the RCMP had informed us that we were harbouring a German spy! In the end, of course, it turned out to be our very own Brünnhilde. One of the Hollywood film executives that used to drop in to see Grierson had not long before been given a guided tour of the John Street building. It seems that his eyes had fallen on the handsome negative cutter as he went by. And when, soon after, he had occasion to look at our film when he got home, he immediately reported to the authorities that a German spy had wormed her way into the Film Board.'

Although he derived 'some real satisfaction' from having fooled a member of 'the reigning centre of fictional film,' Daly loved editing much more than live-action directing. Yet for him editing was anything but passive, or subordinate in creative opportunity. After the war he made two films that apply technique learned from Legg and yet suggest a distinctly personal vision of the world. The first was *Guilty Men* (1945), the second *Hungry Minds* (1948). Both were compilation films, and their styles derived almost directly from the wartime newsreels. (*Guilty Men* was the last edition of *World in Action*.) They were made at a time when North America wanted to forget the war. The wartime style of filmmaking was being phased out; people had become weary of the hectoring tone of wartime propaganda. The two films were late examples of an exhausted style of filmmaking. To the modern eye and ear, the films seem, on one viewing, just like any other wartime film. They have been forgotten and do not appear in histories of documentary film.

Guilty Men reported on war-related trials taking place in Japan and, primarily, at Nuremberg. The film's main purpose was to explain the moral and legal issues to a public for whom the notions of international law and international courts of justice were somewhat new and nebulous. The film's surface tone seems vengeful. Its first shot is a high-contrast drawing of a noose suspended from a post. An image of a hanging body fades in. Then the film's title is superimposed in large, bold letters that start to bleed. Only about ten minutes long, the film races through coverage of trials and other forms of retribution taking place in liberated countries, mentions a widespread feeling that the 'Germans had sidestepped justice after World War One,' summarizes in relative detail the Nuremberg trials, briefly reports on trials of Japanese war leaders, and closes with Lorne Greene's shouted warning that the trials show that 'those who bring tragedy to the peoples of the world must SUFFER THE PEOPLE'S JUSTICE!'

The film's pace and tone almost obscure its structural ingenuity. The early scenes of anarchic retribution form a context for showing the Nuremberg trials as a triumph of due process and international cooperation. Interspersed with short scenes of atrocities, these scenes of lawless retribution weaken potential doubt in the audience about the moral justification for the trials. Daly remembers that 'while we're quite used to seeing dead bodies on film nowadays, in those days a dead body was taboo. You didn't show it even if you had it. It was not acceptable publicly. People objected. I think nowadays people are inclined to a lot of voyeurism about the horrible things that they come across – to kind of go over and over it, caress it, and so on. But that wasn't the point either. We had to prepare the audience for the trials, to show why they were needed, because it really was the first time that political leaders were being tried for what in other wars various generals were the scapegoats for. They were going right to the top, and it was a frightening thing at that time. So the strategy I followed was to catch right at the opening the intensive feeling that everybody really had, show the natural revenge response going on, show what it looked like.'

The four main charges at Nuremberg were war crimes (violations of the 'laws and customs of war'), crimes against peace (overthrowing peaceful governments), crimes against humanity, primarily genocide, and conspiracy to start an aggressive war. Their exposition would constitute the film's main sequence. Because the film was being made during the trials but without any location filming, this sequence would have to be constructed from available archival footage. Daly looked at every piece of material that might conceivably be useful, without any idea of how to structure whatever material he found. His diligence paid off. 'I felt a great moment of excitement when I came across this newsreel of prison guards at Nuremberg bringing food to inmates, looking into the windows of cell doors of these Nazi prisoners, and seeing in close-up that there were names on the doors. It dawned on me that they had happened to photograph names belonging to each of the four charges.' The names and the associated charges were Doenitz (war crimes), Ribbentrop (crimes against peace), Streicher (crimes against humanity), and Goering (conspiracy to start a war). 'I could use these names as "chapter headings." Then I could show from the other material – captured material in our library – what they had done. I could make separate sequences for each charge, show a representative character for each, and why they were being charged. I could be clear about the charges before building a sequence of actual courtroom material.'

Because of the film's timing, Daly faced 'something of a moral problem and a technical problem of guessing the outcome, then writing a narration about it in such a way that it would "read right" before the trials and still "read right" after the trials were over and everybody knew what the verdict was. It was a particularly tricky thing.' Daly's solution was to state the general charge, identify the accused, report what they had done, but not anticipate explicitly the verdict. After stating the charge of 'crimes against humanity,' for example, the narrator says:

Accused on this count were Streicher and Rosenberg, authors and organizers of religious and racial persecution. They brought a new word into the language of human pain: 'genocide,' the murder of races.

An unusual sequence of shots occurs just before the Nuremberg sequence. In an unidentified country, a prisoner for whom we are allowed to feel no sympathy stands under the gallows. The next shot is a still photo of dead bodies in a gas chamber. Then a guard puts a hood over the prisoner and a priest enters the frame. Then there is a shot of soldiers, watching. In the next shot, the noose is slipped over the prisoner's head and around his neck. Even today, it is hard not to cringe: are we actually going to witness the moment of hanging? Suddenly the film cuts to a shot of a seagull soaring across the grey sky, crying plaintively, as if fleeing a scene of imperfect mortal justice, averting our eyes for us. But just as suddenly, the film cuts back to the prisoner, who drops through a hole and out of view, the rope tightening and the body swivelling. It is a jolting, moving, and unusually tough-minded sequence.

The structure for this sequence was a long time in coming. 'This is one of the places where I felt I was doing something a little different from what

Legg used to do, but it is different in part because the material was incomplete. I found this newsreel of the hanging in New York, but everything was shot from the same angle. Any sequence cut from it would all be jumpcuts, and jumpcuts were not something used in those days. I felt that the individual shots were very strong and should be looked at. But how to deal with the empty spaces in between? For a while, I was stumped. I kept coming to this sequence, but, not knowing what to do with it, I would move on to the next. I didn't usually stay stuck when I was editing. If I found I was stuck, I'd just drop that and go to something else where I wasn't stuck. Otherwise, you could use up all your creative energy and get depressed. And I had learned after a while that if you do all the things you can do, then by running them all in a row you often have a suggestion leap into your mind. That's what happened.'

Daly cut a sequence that included a string of three jumpcuts of the hanging. 'After putting all these things together and running them forward at speed, I began to realize that what was happening in *my* mind at the moment of this execution in the film was a reminder of what it was all about, why it was happening, and what it really meant. It occurred to me that it would not be irrelevant to remind people of the reason for the execution. So I cut in the shot of dead bodies. And then I found the shot of soldiers watching, which for me represented "humanity looking on," which includes us. I put that in. But for the third one, I just didn't know what to do, but I had a feeling that it had to do with the ultimate, the future, and what must become of this person about to be hanged, and I couldn't think of anything that would go there until I came across this little shot of a bird. The bird was a little too high in the frame for an ideal shot – in pure cutting terms – but it was better to be high in the frame than low, for the symbolic reasons. And it just managed to have the right length for taking its place in the sequence. So I put it there. People around the place thought I was putting in the shot as a symbol to avoid showing the actual hanging. Then I put in the shot of the hanging. The two then became like a double shot. You drop your guard. You think you've seen the hanging through a symbol, then you really see it.'

The film may be obscure, but the scene of the hanging stuck for a long time in Margaret Ann Elton's mind:

I forget which war criminal [was being] executed, but at the moment this happened, Tom had cut in a wheeling Bird of Omen (perhaps a gull left over from a nature film?). Not that I am anything to go by, but I cried. Out of all the discipline and apprenticeship, even I (who know nothing about Le Film) knew that he was an artist. I passionately wanted (but I think it did not happen) to keep his Treatment and Script and Shot List and Sources and Commentary together, as (well, lamely put, by me) an example or teaching device, or Leonardo notebook.

The scene's artistry, which lies in its editing and the associations implied by the editing, is moral as well as aesthetic, and it becomes even more impressive when judged against the kind of material that was available. In his memo about Daly, Tom Johnston reported that when he asked Daly what footage from the war era remained most vividly in his mind, Daly replied:

There is no possible absolute answer to this. There were many kinds of 'most vivid footage'. But one burning memory remains of some shots that were so shocking they may never be used by anyone: an Italian collaborator by the name of Caruso was about to be executed – tied ignominiously on a chair with his back to the firing squad. Three cameras, with different lenses, covered the event from different angles, and the 3 shots were sent in a row to the newsreels. I saw the long shot first, and the whole top of the man's skull flew off and his brains spattered out as the guns fired off; then suddenly, in closer view he was miraculously alive again, and 'Take 2' of the grisly scene took place, followed by 'Take 3'. It had the nightmare feeling of the director saying: 'Take 1 isn't good enough, let's do it again,' only it was for real.

Guilty Men was a film of retribution, a settling of scores and thus a closing of the books on the war. *Hungry Minds* was a film of reconstruction. Although not precisely a fund-raising vehicle, it sought to engender support for UNESCO's programs for aiding children in the war-ravaged countries of Europe. Its rhetorical strategy employs a threefold appeal. It first encourages patronage, showing children receiving aid from abroad. 'However small the help,' the narrator comments, 'the children are grateful.' Then it shows children in luckier countries, such as England, collecting materials to be sent as 'a miniature aid program' to less fortunate children elsewhere. Thus it evokes guilt. Finally, it tries to arouse fear by suggesting that unless the children are helped, 'from them can spring a new Hitler.'

In two ways, the film departs from the Film Board's wartime newsreel style. Daly integrated into the mostly archival material numerous sketches by the German artist Käthe Kollwitz. And he included shots of people who look at the camera or otherwise show awareness of its presence.

The available footage presented Daly with an unexpected difficulty. 'I think that wherever children are concerned, there is always the wish to develop the most possible future hope for them. It is just an automatic response, I think, that children bring to everybody. From the moment the baby comes, it is like an attention-getting apparatus. Everybody likes to look at it. And every stage in that early period can develop into anything. I think it's that feeling of possibility that accounts largely for our interest in them. But what struck me about the images in the material we had of them was that while the kids had been given a terrible start by the war conditions, they seemed to take it for granted and start from there. It wasn't necessarily crushing them as it did the adults. It was the world they were given, it was home, and they maybe even could do something with *that*, in a freer way than adults could. Kids aren't so given to self-pity, for instance.'

How then to convey the inner terrors these children had experienced? 'In the hunt for material, I came across this "Punch and Judy" sequence, and these marvellous little kids were all engrossed in the show and reacting totally, just a total response coming out of every pore. And I thought that was interesting, it just sort of let things hang out that normally the children didn't seem to want others to know about. You could see it happening. Then I came across the Kollwitz drawings. She was rather "leftist," and these amazing lithographs were used by leftists, but they were all of a piece, with a certain quality of looking deep into the eyes of suffering kids – and adults. It just struck me that they were terribly relevant to the film we had been asked to do.'

Using still drawings in a 'newsreel' film was something new, and Daly's first attempt didn't work. 'I put a sequence of her drawings together, and put it into the film, never imagining any other way of using them. And they were very nice, but the sequence was very slow, and empty – to my enormous surprise, because the pictures themselves worked so well for me, but not coming off the screen. And it was only much later that I began to notice that the newsreel and other archival material we had collected contained images just like the drawings. They had that same quality of look. And it suddenly occurred to me to interweave Kollwitz's images with the other material, going back and forth, finding something in a drawing that led to actuality, and something in the actuality that led back to the drawings. And to do it not only with negative images, but also the positive ones. There was, for example, a powerful drawing of hers showing motherly love. Very warm. I used that to turn the corner from all the dark stuff, to get into something positive.'

Hungry Minds ignores the then-standard admonition to avoid shots of people looking at the camera. This gives the film an immediacy that seems appropriate to its subject, children, who tend to be less self-conscious than adults. One of the several shots in which children notice the camera shows a boy waving at the camera and blowing a kiss towards it. Daly remembers it as 'such an engaging shot, that I thought, What better way to connect with an audience? But it wasn't just from nothing that the thought occurred to me. I remembered from college a painting by El Greco, called *The Burial of Count Orgaz*. In that painting, there are different levels of activity. Count Orgaz is the very white-faced corpse in black shining armour being lowered into a crypt through the floor in a cathedral. A bishop in all his coats is there, and other noblemen are helping lower the body, and so on. But one of them is looking up. And when you follow his line of sight, to the upper part of the cathedral, there is a whole heavenly host looking down, sort of blessing the occasion. The other men are unaware of this scene. Down in the front is a young boy who is quite involved in the burial. He is gesturing towards it with his left hand and towards you with his right hand, looking at you, drawing you into the picture. You were brought into the picture by the painter's use of these two characters, connected both to the world above and the world below. It was an astonishing composition, and I never forgot it. So when this little shot turned up, I remembered the effect the painting had on me, and I had no question about putting in the shot.'

Often in his subsequent career, Daly would return to the editing room, as if to renew or replenish there his knack for finding connections and developing structures. But he would soon serve primarily as a producer and eventually as an on-the-job teacher as well. Legg was right that Daly's main contribution resembled Grierson's in that it was in the service of films other than his own, but Daly's service was responsive rather than initiating, and, as Legg noted, it was as nearly anonymous as Grierson's was public. Daly's contribution was different in another respect: it would span nearly half a century, across shifts in cultural fashion and political climate, whereas Grierson's was essentially spent after about fifteen intense years. Daly's quiet presence in documentary had staying power.

There was one more difference. Grierson was from the outset comfortable in his work. He was never more in his element than when dealing with people, whether above or below him, on practical matters. It came naturally to him. Not so for Daly. He may have found at the Film Board his El Dorado, but he had had to 'stretch from zero' to learn how to relate to it and to be effective in it. He did not yet realize that, save for his mastery of editing, he hadn't moved much beyond zero. 'Legg was such a good teacher, and my job was limited, so my awareness was dim. Until I was responsible for other people, it didn't really become apparent to me ... how lopsided I was.'

2

Meaning Rushes In

As apprentice to Legg and then heir to *World in Action*, Daly had mastered the craft of editing. Had he remained merely an editor, he might have spent the rest of a long career in government filmmaking without facing a serious professional challenge. But he became a producer. This was a natural step for him in a structured setting such as the Film Board. He was meticulous, intelligent, and not at all averse to taking on responsibility. And producing in the Film Board would not require the kind of entrepreneurship, drive, and market daring needed in commercial producing. At the Film Board, where the government supplied the money and filmmakers provided ideas and footage, producing was largely managerial, administrative. But becoming a genuinely creative producer at the Film Board would test Daly severely. Whereas the craft of editing involved arranging pieces of film that others had provided, producing meant working with people and dealing with power, even if the people were civil servants and the power was essentially bureaucratic and political. Daly was far more comfortable serving others than leading them. The mastery now required of him was not just of his craft but of hidden aspects of himself, and achieving it proved to be a more brutal process than his training as an editor under Legg had been.

Daly evolved into producing through his work on compilation films. In 1944, he became the associate producer of *Canada Carries On*, in 1945, of *World in Action*. In 1946, when Legg left, Daly was named producer of *World in Action*. He was producer for *Guilty Men* and *Hungry Minds*. In 1947, he was assigned responsibility for half the NFB's program of production while the NFB underwent a restructuring. The new structure, introduced in 1948, consolidated Grierson's twelve production units into four larger, more comprehensive ones reporting to a director of production. Daly was appointed executive producer of one of the units, Unit B.

At the time, the Film Board was trying to transform itself into a peace-time organization without losing its international focus. *Guilty Men* and *Hungry Minds*, along with two others that Daly produced (*Canada: World Trader* [1946] and *Out of the Ruins* [1946]), were part of the Film Board's effort to redirect its internationalism towards rebuilding a world now at peace.

Although *Out of the Ruins* was Daly's first experience at producing a film made from original footage, its greater importance for his development as a producer lay in 'something that proved of inestimable value in later years – how not to be rigid or self-righteous in the application of important principles while still sticking to them.'

The film was an appeal for support of United Nations relief efforts in postwar Greece. It praises ancient Athens as the source of Western ideas of justice, freedom, and democracy and then laments the near destruction of these values in modern postwar Greece. After surveying the country's economic and political difficulties, the film sketches the United Nations' efforts to distribute food, medical supplies, livestock, and technological assistance.

The director was Nicholas Read, an American who, through Grierson's offices, had served as a cameraman with the Canadian navy in the war. After Read and his crew had returned from Greece and the film was nearly finished, Daly recalls, their Greek location assistant 'showed up unexpectedly. Read welcomed him back onto the project with open arms. The editing was finished and the commentary was being finalized. Some of it was tricky, because of the question of Greek collaboration with the Nazis at high levels during the war, and the continuing strife over that in Greece.

'We thought we were doing a pretty good job of telling the truth fairly to both sides. But even though we had not even released the film publicly, the Department of External Affairs received a diplomatic protest from the Greek ambassador to Canada over "the inaccurate and biased film we were making about Greece."

'The awful truth dawned on us. Our friend the Greek assistant, without protesting to us, had gone to the Greek ambassador and complained about what we were saying in the film. So there was a full-scale diplomatic incident that brought the undersecretary of state down to view the film.

'When the screening was over, he said to us, "Everything you have said in the film is true, and you would be well within your rights to stick by it. But if you don't mind I would like to offer you a piece of advice from my long experience. If you *do* stick by the narration as it is, you and we will never hear the end of it. It will be a thorn in our side, brought up endlessly.

I have a suggestion: make a few verbal changes in the present text, *to say the same thing in different words*, and we will be able to write an official letter to the Greek ambassador saying that we reviewed the film with the NFB, and as a result of our discussions some changes were made in the commentary. And he will be off the hook, being able to report to his government that he made an official protest over something he felt to be against their interests, and as a result of his intervention changes were made. He will be seen to be effectively doing his duty, and we will hear no more about it. Incident closed." And so it was.'

Whatever the now-forgotten details of the compromise, Daly and Read seem to have succeeded in changing the words while retaining some of their bite. At one point in the film, the narrator refers to 'a deep gulf between those Greeks who have and those who have not.' These words are spoken over a shot of a fat man dining on lobster followed by a shot of a hungry peasant.

The internationalist, mildly leftist orientation reflected in films like *Out of the Ruins*, *Guilty Men*, and *Hungry Minds* would soon succumb to the postwar attacks on the Film Board. One complaint against the Board came from private industry. They wanted the Film Board dismantled now that the war was over. Although this may have been the more serious source of opposition, the allegations of communist sympathies received more attention from the media and seem to have had a greater effect on the Film Board's program.

After Grierson's inconclusive appearance before the Royal Commission on Espionage, the Film Board was subjected to three inquiries. The Royal Commission on National Development in the Arts, Letters, and Sciences (the 'Massey Commission') examined the Film Board's mission and its performance of that mission. The second, conducted by a Toronto management consulting firm, J.D. Woods and Gordon, investigated the Film Board's management of its operations. The third, by the Royal Canadian Mounted Police, looked for security risks.

Daly remembers feeling powerless in the face of what was happening. 'I was concerned that a really good thing would be trashed by people who didn't really know what they had. Our only source of information was Jim Beveridge, who had a cousin high in External Affairs, from whom he got hints, which he'd pass on to all of us. But we really didn't know anything. And we couldn't say anything officially outside, because it was still the time when government servants couldn't make statements about policy. We could only keep trying to do well what we were doing: making films.'

In Daly's view, the fortunate timing of the Film Act along with Grierson's sense of the whole proved to be crucial in saving the Film Board. 'Politicians would say, "Now the war's over. We don't have to pay for this." But the Film Board had been created before the war, as a peacetime organization. And after the war broke out, and the NFB took on a major role in propaganda, Grierson resisted pressure to turn the NFB wholly into a war-film machine. He maintained a balanced program, arguing that the men and women at the front needed to know what was going on in Canada, what they'd be coming home to when the war was over.'

While the domestic program won support at home, 'it was also our great good fortune that we were well known abroad. We were respected. Partly because of this, we participated in a postwar UNESCO program though which applicants from occupied or underdeveloped countries could apply for six-month fellowships to study the Film Board – its organization, film production methods, distribution.'

Daly helped select the students and then see that they were looked after in whatever branch or section they were assigned to. 'I still have the Koran of a student from Pakistan, who was killed by a streetcar in Ottawa. Their embassy told me to keep it as a memento of his visit. And I still hear occasionally from a fellow from Burma, who became a successful cameraman and filmmaker there.'

Daly identifies one more factor that helped the Film Board through this period: 'Inside the Board, we were almost totally one family, with almost no divisions.'

The first two reports found the Film Board innocent of all but a few trivial misprisions. The Massey Commission reaffirmed the Film Board's mission, praised its performance, and recommended that its organization become more like that of other civil service departments. The Woods and Gordon team expressed sympathy for the special management problems involved in filmmaking and simply recommended some revised accounting procedures. The RCMP produced a list of thirty-six potential security risks, a list eventually pared to three low-level people, who were dismissed. Brünnhilde was not among them.

The dismissals were accomplished by Arthur Irwin, who was appointed commissioner early in 1950, succeeding Ross McLean, who had been appointed acting commissioner upon Grierson's departure. McLean had asked the RCMP to turn over its records so that he could review the cases of those designated as real or possible security risks. When the RCMP refused, McLean in turn refused to dismiss anyone. The prevailing opinion among those who were around the Film Board at the time is that Irwin was brought in to 'clean up' the Film Board and that he dismissed the three as 'sacrificial lambs' to appease the government without causing any serious damage to the Film Board. But the Film Board emerged from the crisis like someone who has been charged with serious crimes of which finally he is found innocent. He doesn't go to prison, but his reputation has been irreparably tarnished. By the time the results of the investigations were reported and made public, the Film Board had lost a great deal of its confidence as an organization.

The Film Board's retreat from its international focus began well before the investigations were completed. The most significant casualty was a film about China, *The People Between* (1947). The film would be Daly's most significant project as a producer up to that time, althought he wasn't brought into it until the editing stage. It also would involve him with one of the Film Board's strongest personalities, Grant McLean, a nephew of Ross McLean.

In 1946, the United Nations Relief and Rehabilitation Administration asked the NFB to supply a cameraman-director to go to China to film examples of China's effort at reconstruction. UNRRA wanted footage for short newsreel releases and would allow the NFB to keep the negative for its own use. The NFB lent UNRRA Grant McLean. McLean spent an adventuresome year in China. He filmed the expected scenes involving floods, famine, and the arrival of Canadian wheat, but because he found China in the midst of civil war, he wanted to film material involving both the Nationalist forces and the Red Army. In particular, he wanted to film in Mao Tse-tung's stronghold in Yenan. Although he represented the United Nations, McLean recalls that 'it wasn't my diplomatic credentials that got me into Yenan, it was my personal friendships with General George Marshall and Chou En-lai. Marshall loaned me his plane and pilots for the weekend after Chou determined from Mao that I would be favourably received.' According to McLean, in another instance he managed to get to a location for which he lacked permission to visit by pulling a revolver on his driver and ordering him to proceed. McLean shot six thousand feet of film in Yenan.

When McLean returned to Canada with material far richer than that required for UNRRA's purposes, the NFB decided to make a film of its own. Daly was assigned to edit the material, write a commentary, and serve as the film's producer.

Although Daly had edited McLean's wartime film *Atlantic Crossroads*, the China project was 'our first really close contact.' Daly loved editing the material: 'Grant's shooting was so beautiful and atmospheric and alive with the natural flavour of the Chinese, and the footage of Mao Tse-tung's area was such a coup.' McLean was pleased with Daly's contribution, which Daly characterizes as simply helping 'to realize the film that lay in wait inside the material.'

Presented, in a short preamble, as 'the story of China's long struggle for unity and freedom from want and fear,' the film only briefly counterposed Mao's Red Army and Chiang Kai-shek's Nationalists. The film's main focus was the rebuilding of embankments along the Yellow River that had been blown up to stop the Japanese advance in the war. The narration described the project as China's 'biggest ... since the Great Wall.' Thousands of labourers, aided by some donated machinery, were shown lugging enough dirt and rocks to construct a two-mile stretch of embankment a hundred and twenty feet thick. A powerful, visually hypnotic pile-driving sequence near the end of the film, mixing diagonal lines and near-mechanical rhythms, showed the influence of the Russian-derived aspect of Grierson's documentary aesthetic on both McLean and Daly. Some statements in the commentary acknowledged the strength and popular appeal of Mao's forces.

McLean and Daly showed the film to Ross McLean. The commissioner liked it but said it would have to be shown to the Department of External Affairs for approval. Daly remembers that the official who came to review the film 'was no less than Lester B. Pearson, then undersecretary of state for external affairs. He told us that it was a very lovely film, that everything we said in it was true, but that we would have to change some of the narration, because Canada at that time was officially supporting the Chiang Kai-shek side, and we could not embarrass the Chinese government officially. He furthermore told us that it was not up to his department to forbid us to release the film, but if we did release it and public objections arose, his department would not support us, and we would be on our own.'

McLean thinks that while 'Pearson's main point was that Canada could recognize only one government of China, his position was in deference to the U.S. China lobby.' McLean refused to make the requested changes. Daly went along with McLean. The commissioner backed them and left the film alone, hoping that the political climate would change and the film could be released later. A year passed. McLean and Daly finally decided that rather than let such an unusual film 'moulder in a vault,' they would agree to make the requested changes. When External Affairs asked for additional changes, McLean and Daly, as the latter recalls, 'accepted all of them now, believing that the impressions from the picture itself would transmit far more meaning than the verbal commentary, even if softened.' The film was released in January 1949.

Three months later, Chinese Communists fired on British gunboats in the Yangtze River, inflicting heavy casualties. The West reacted angrily, and *The People Between*, with its positive portrayal of the Chinese Communists, was, in Daly's words, 'hissed off the screen.'

The NFB withdrew the film from circulation. The following year, the NFB tried to gain permission to re-release it. Permission was denied. After lying in the vaults for another three years, the film finally was released, but only for private showings to film societies, without publicity.

For Daly, the affair of *The People Between* was a rueful confirmation of the strategy he had adopted for *Out of the Ruins* but, in the atmosphere of political suspicion and resentment that had infected the Board, promptly forgotten. 'Because of our own donkeyness, we misread the realities of the situation to the point that we prevented ourselves from adapting to a really good possibility for too partial a reason. The changes External Affairs wanted after their first visit would not have made the film untrue. It would just be less fully true. But the film would have been released and, having been around for some time before the gunboat incident, probably would not have been so attacked. We were just so angry at the negative response from the Department. That was not somebody else's fault. We understood they couldn't help doing that politically. It was our own fault for not being able to deal with that fully, and still satisfy ourselves.'

A related insight into responding to power involved Daly's reaction to Arthur Irwin once Irwin had restored the NFB to normalcy and assumed his everyday responsibilities as film commissioner. 'Ross and Grant McLean were both so open. Irwin was a non-film man, and he was secretive. He wanted to start a "teach democracy" program for defeated or crushed European nations. This struck us all as strange. Even if one accepted the goals, offering advice like that didn't seem to be a very effective way to achieve them. And it seemed that it was being imposed on us, without any real say from us. I personally found this very hard to take, and I had a lot of anger. I felt I must do something about this, although it was not my nature to be "politically active." I started listing all the ways he was wrong in the way he was dealing with us. The list got about a page and half long. I was called away – a phone call, or something. About two hours later, I went back to look at the list. There were about seventeen or eighteen or nineteen things listed. The question came up in my mind: I wonder how I would rate myself on these same points, with regard to the people under me? I can tell you: my jaw dropped, because one after another – well, I began to think, I'm probably the same. On only a couple of points did I see no applicability to me.

'Three days later, I met Ian McNeill [an NFB filmmaker] outside the commissioner's office. The commissioner was out. No one else was around. We were just chatting outside his office, about Irwin. All of a sudden, Ian looked at me in a funny, guarded way, and said, "You know, you're rather like Irwin." I just burst out laughing. His face changed totally. He said, "I thought you'd get angry." I said, "Well, until three days ago, I guess I would've. But three days ago, I discovered you're right."'

Irwin got the money for the 'teach democracy' program, and as would happen often in the Film Board's subsequent history, the films made under the program bore only a loose relationship to the program's announced aim. Daly remembers in particular a film called *The Man in the Peace Tower* (1951), which was 'basically just a portrait of the carillonneur at work in the belfry of the Canadian Parliament Buildings.'

Daly credits his ability to see himself in his criticism of Irwin in part to a line of study that the more relaxed pace of postwar filmmaking had allowed him to pursue: the ideas of P.D. Ouspensky and G.I. Gurdjieff. His interest in them would grow into a lifelong commitment, and, as it became known around the Film Board, strike many of his colleagues as odd and some as bizarre. Yet it entailed anything but a radical rejection of his classical education or his devotion to civil service; on the contrary, it 'came very naturally, almost as if everything else was simply preparing for it.'

It had begun 'back in the middle 1920s, when life before the financial crash was very comfortable. My mother, with her background, was finding social life very shallow, and was feeling surprisingly cynical about modern values. When she met with an old college chum, the friend heard her story, and thought Mother needed something meaty to occupy her mind fully. She thought she knew just the book that would do it. That was Ouspensky's book *Tertium Organum*, about the fourth dimension and the universe.

'Mother liked to talk about what interested her as much as father liked to be silent. So I heard quite a bit about it, and looked into it a few times when she was out. It later caught a certain interest which stayed with me as a teenager – but very much on the edges of things.'

Then, in the mid-1930s, Daly's mother got a copy of Ouspensky's second book, *The New Model of the Universe*, which 'became much discussed around the house. I was older, and was interested to read parts of it outright ... One part on Christianity struck me so much that, when I looked for it some time later, I was mystified that I could not find it. I remembered it as two pages of tightly written material, very recognizable when I would see the pages. I went through the relevant chapter several times, leafing quickly. Finally, I had to read it in detail. It was there. But it was only a single paragraph on one page, in the middle. It had impressed itself so strongly on my mind, with all its connections, that I had remembered it as having the impact of two whole pages.'

In the paragraph that Daly remembered, Ouspensky discusses the meaning of Christ's parables of the sower and of the tares (Matt. 13:18–30). The paragraph is imbued with Ouspensky's esotericism, but Daly 'was suspicious of that, and didn't let it get in the way.' The insight that excited Daly was that the parables could have multiple levels of meaning. 'On one level, the parable of the sower, for instance, is about the details of the word of truth coming to people. It falls on some people, not on others. But it also could be read on a much bigger scale. An individual person's growth can reach different levels. You can believe something, and if it stays just a belief there's no more growth ... as if a sunflower seed *heard* about growth, and flowers, and so forth, but stayed a seed.

'The same with the meaning of the "grain." It could mean an "idea" planted in man, or it could mean "a man," or it could mean "mankind." I saw that any essentially truthful utterance is not true only on one level. A true utterance of Christ or Rumi or Buddha remains true on many different levels. So too with nature: the same laws seem to apply at all levels of nature. God doesn't change his rules.'

Around this time, 'Mother herself was interested in comparative religion and other studies. She joined a group for some time that studied the *Bhagavad Gita*. She met a teacher of the Baha'i faith, and studied that. This man came several times to our apartment. She read Tagore and Kahlil Gibran.'

In 1949, on a newsreel-hunting trip to New York, Daly came across *In Search of the Miraculous*, Ouspensky's account of the teachings of Gurdjieff. It had just been published. 'I knew at once that *that* was my coming-home gift for my mother.'

Daly bought the book and later 'began to hear from Mother all kinds of things that now struck me as very interesting,' and 'of course began to read it myself with great interest, doubtful about some points that seemed very far out, and which I was unable to accept or verify. But on the whole, everything that was close enough to my own experience to verify proved to be telling me certain things about myself that I needed to know, and far more clearly and precisely than I could put it myself.'

In 1951, a friend who shared his interest in Ouspensky and Gurdjieff 'suggested I meet some people called the de Hartmanns who were in Rawdon, Quebec, waiting for a permanent visa for the United States.' Thomas and Olga de Hartmann had met Gurdjieff at a meeting in St Petersburg in

1917. They became devoted followers of him. Later, in France, Thomas de Hartmann collaborated on a considerable body of musical compositions with Gurdjieff. De Hartmann was in the middle of writing what would become, after his death and with help from his widow, *Our Life with Mr. Gurdjieff*, when Daly met them in Rawdon. 'They took me in for the weekend. Later, with my stories about the de Hartmanns, my parents wanted to meet them, too. And this led to a little group being formed by the de Hartmanns in my parents' apartment in Toronto, from where things grew.'

Gurdjieff maintained that almost every human being remains in an undeveloped, barely conscious, 'mechanical' or sleeping state in which he or she is dominated by one of three aspects of the self: the intellectual, the emotional, or the physical. In this mechanical state, a person has no will. Instead, he or she is controlled by negative emotions, self-centredness, and self-deception. The necessary first step to freedom from mechanical enslavement is the development of an unbiased attitude towards others and, especially, oneself. To take this step, one has to learn to 'observe oneself.' Through self-observation one strives to bring to conscious awareness the three warring aspects of the self and eventually bring them into balance. Acquiring the ability to remain attentive to the workings of one's psyche is itself extremely difficult, and can be achieved only through the guidance of a teacher who has studied ancient teachings, through involvement in group activities and exercises designed to stretch one's powers of concentration, and through daily effort.

Although the Gurdjieff philosophy contains an element of esotericism and projects an aura of mystery, Daly found the teachings practical and thoroughly consistent with his education and on-the-job training. 'What was remarkable was the extension of what I had learned about *attention* from Legg, and from my Greek professor who taught the *Iliad*. Legg had shown me very clearly that a film is the line of attention that the audience goes through, and that if you break that line, you break the connection between the film and the audience. My professor had shown how the reader's line of attention is not the same as that of any particular character. Through this new book, and the teaching that was connected to it, I came to learn that attention is even more than that. It is actually the force or energy that connects our *conscious* life with anything – a thought, a feeling, a sensation, an awareness of self. In fact, one's conscious inner life consists *solely* of what our attention has fallen on since the beginning of our life. There are many blanks in its memory, while the physical body has never ceased to record and respond on its own level to every impulse. But anything our attention has never fallen on is unknown to us altogether. Our entire life consists simply in the thin measly line of what our attention has fallen on. That's all it is. We fritter it away, and everyone else wants to take this attention from us, but it is the priceless thread that connects us to our-selves. So it matters what we put it on, when it comes to our own choice.

'Similarly, the three-part human nature, so simply described by Socrates and Plato, was much further extended in what I was now finding. Many other things, formerly separate in my mind, began to fit together in a much more living way than books in a library. It even took Grierson's and Legg's view of the world as a whole, with its historical, social, cultural, and eco-nomic flow lines, further still.'

While Daly's new researches were extending the world-view he had absorbed from Grierson and Legg, the Film Board's retreat from larger political comment showed itself not only in the fate of *The People Between* and subsequent programming decisions but also in a major administrative appointment. The position was that of director of production, the most powerful position at the Film Board after that of the commissioner.

Donald Mulholland, the commissioner's choice for director of produc-tion, was not the production staff's preferred candidate. They, including Daly, championed James Beveridge. Beveridge had joined the Film Board even earlier than Daly. He was an intellectual, had an activist temperament, and was steeped in what Daly and others understood as the Griersonian tradition. Mulholland had spent several years in advertising in New York. Filmmakers thought he was too commercially minded, that he lacked Beveridge's intellectual scope and social commitment.

To his surprise, Daly quickly took to Mulholland. He found Mulholland direct but not overbearing, efficient but flexible, comfortable with diverse approaches to filmmaking, and interested in promoting quality. Soon after becoming director of production, Mulholland screened a rough-cut of a film from Daly's unit. 'I forget what film it was, but he said that three things would improve it – A, B, and C. Then he told me how he would accomplish A, B, and C. I'm thinking to myself, "I don't want to do those things." At the end he said, "If you feel there's something in what I have said, I expect you to do something about them. But if you don't, then it probably doesn't matter." He was one of those few people who would give you their full feeling about something, but leave it up to you. I tried to meet all three points, but in my own way.'

Mulholland left Unit B's structure intact. This structure was, Daly says, 'basically Griersonian in form. There were separate, self-contained sub-units for different programs or functions. These included, at that time, ani-mation, science films, classroom films, and foreign-language versions. In any emergency, we could always call together the heads of sections, as a kind of inner cabinet, to settle questions affecting more than one section. Help could quickly be brought to the place where it was needed.'

Real emergencies were few. Unit B began to flourish under Mulholland and in the quiet 1950s. The films were quiet, too. They dealt with domestic subjects instead of international issues, they avoided controversy, and they were aesthetically restrained.

Two of the unit's more interesting films were on Arthur Lismer and Frederick Varley, the painters Daly had met in his childhood. *Lismer* (1952), directed by Allan Wargon, is a dramatized portrait of the English-born Group of Seven painter. His belief in the role of artistic training in social and political growth is articulated primarily in somewhat contrived scenes. His development as an artist is traced through his paintings – first an early, naïve response to the power of Canadian landscapes, a middle period of 'storm and struggle,' and, finally, lyricism. In places, the film is charmingly awkward. A scene in which Lismer subtly rebukes a gushing admirer falls flat, but the attempt lingers in the viewer's memory. The narration suffers from occasional academic phraseology, as in 'In the final analysis, it may be decided ...' *Varley* (1953), also directed by Wargon, combines voice-over discourse with scenes of Varley coping with life and with art. A disgust with life and bouts of artistic despair compete with a fundamentally positive, emotional response to 'the beauty and wonder of living.' The film presents Varley's *Liberation*, painted in 1945 when the painter was sixty-six, as the apogee of his career. The film has a direct, succinct quality despite a sometimes ponderous soundtrack.

Shyness (1953), written and directed by Stanley Jackson, was one of a series of films on mental health. While his young pupils play softball at a class picnic, a schoolteacher reflects on his responsibility for helping children develop social confidence. His voice-over narration focuses on Anna, whose shyness is explained by her upbringing but who, with the help of classroom activities aimed at promoting social confidence, makes significant progress towards overcoming her shyness. The film's explanations and prescriptions may be simplistic, but it has a gentle compassion that seems authentic and is engrossing.

The Longhouse People (1951), directed by Allan Wargon, showed for the first time on film certain sacred rituals of the Six Nations Iroquois. Most of the film is set inside the longhouse, once a symbol of Iroquois confederation and now the centre of Iroquois religious life. It is here, the narrator says, that the Iroquois 'express the hopes, fears, and sorrows that are common to all men.' Among the rituals depicted are a rain dance, a harvest thanksgiving, a healing ceremony, a mourning, and a celebration of the choosing of a new leader.

Although the production depended on a remarkable contrivance, *The Longhouse People* set an early standard for the Film Board's dealings with Native peoples. Daly credits this to Wargon's sincerity and patience. 'He won the confidence of the Six Nations group at Brantford, promising that we would not misuse the material if they made a film with us, and that we would not allow others to use any of it without their permission.'

But the cooperation granted by the Iroquois was qualified. 'Some of the social dances and rituals were of great interest, and not so sacred that they could not be filmed in their usual setting and shown to non-Indians. But other rituals took place only in the longhouse itself, which was a very sacred place, and we would not be permitted to photograph there. Allan, as a friend, was permitted to see for himself, but he could not shoot there.'

As months passed, 'it seemed that, with the best will in the world and all their friendliness, the only possibility was to lower our sights and do a more social film, which would have far less of the impressive material that showed the quality, worth, and depth of their religious understanding. We felt the lack of that would make their religion seem much more superficial to non-Indians.'

Finally, Wargon proposed to the Iroquois that he 'build a *replica* of the longhouse on the stage of one of the Ottawa theatres, where we could also control better the sound recording and the quality of colour shooting. If they did not like it when they saw it, they did not have to do their rituals there. But since it was not a *real* longhouse, if they let us film them there they would not have to go against their rule. It would be like putting on a play.

'They accepted in principle. Allan took all the measurements and made detailed sketches of the longhouse. He built a complete set to exact scale, with removable walls so that the camera could always have room to manoeuvre. We booked the theatre for the number of days needed for the shooting, but we still didn't know if they would agree.

'The day they all came we were on tenterhooks. We sat in the theatre seats while they looked the set over. In the end, they were enormously impressed. They said they felt just the same as if they were in their own longhouse at home. They would agree to going ahead. But before we could begin shooting, they had a ceremony of their own, which we could watch but not shoot, to consecrate the set itself as a place where the agreed-to rituals could take place. It was very moving. After that, the shooting took place without a hitch.

'When the finished film was shown to them for their impressions, there was nothing they wanted us to change. Allan was made an honorary member of their band.

'In later days, some outside filmmakers, who were interested in comparing the Iroquois dancing with other kinds of dance in a more secular way, asked the NFB for stock shots from the film. But none were ever given without their permission. In this way, we became more and more trusted by Native peoples to not distort their views and values.'

The film that most nearly epitomizes the Film Board's retrenched postwar orientation was *Royal Journey* (1951), an hour-long account of a visit to North America by Princess, later Queen, Elizabeth and the Duke of Edinburgh. The film opens with a rolling title sequence that 'presents' the couple 'in' *Royal Journey* as if they were stars in a Hollywood spectacular. The visit is covered with geographic thoroughness, including not only scenes in almost every major Canadian region and in Washington, D.C., but also brief and refreshing transitional sequences on the varied means of transportation used during the trip. The narration occasionally exceeds restraint: 'The pent-up enthusiasm of waiting thousands finds release. The autumn air is filled with cheers. And the massed crowds break, running through the streets.' Each major sequence includes a scripted voice-over comment ostensibly reflecting the thoughts of observing common folk. When the Princess speaks briefly in Washington, a jaded 'newsreel cameraman' is impressed that 'she says the right thing, and she keeps it short – which is something you can't always say about every important person, especially when the V.I.P. is a lady.'

Despite its often hokey style and various now-unpopular sentiments, the film is surprisingly watchable. The transportation sequences lend a sense of grandeur to the visit. Some of the sequences, especially one of an extremely windy departure day in St John's, seem grippingly real.

And the film probably contributed more than any other film of the early 1950s to the Film Board's political rehabilitation. It seems to have pleased everybody. Yet this triumph was not achieved without risks.

For one thing, the film was made for theatrical distribution before the era of television, when, Daly notes, 'commercial theatres were still *the* place to see the latest news. The NFB took an enormous chance and qualified gamble by being the first organization anywhere in the world to shoot a public film for the commercial theatres in the new Eastman colour negative. The advance tests with this new stock had been very promising, but if we made a mess of the film we would never hear the end of it politically.'

Another risk had to do with regional representation. 'Every community in every part of the country where the royal couple was to appear wanted *everything* in their area to appear in the film.' To achieve a reasonable balance among the various locations without sinking the film aesthetically, Daly decided, first, 'that from the huge collection of events the royal couple would be subjected to, we would choose those which showed best the country itself, the variety of its peoples, the moods of nature, and the ways we get about. In other words, the film would be essentially about *our country*, through the medium of a royal visit.

'The second decision was that, except for minor details of continuity that might be unavoidable, we would deal with each theme or group that would be presented to the visitors *only once*. Since the royal couple tended to go through the same series of parades, speeches, and shows at *every* place, it would be boring to see the whole visit as it actually happened. So we decided that we would have only one sequence, somewhere in the film, on each group like the army, the navy, the air force, the RCMP, and so forth, and only one natural wonder, one cultural event, one laying of a wreath, and so on. And as far as possible this variety of scenes would be telescoped together, so that the Winnipeg Ballet evening became at once a prairie event, a cultural event, and the only event with the Princess in formal evening dress and diamond tiara.'

The whole scheme almost collapsed near the end of the shooting. 'It so happened that the final leg of the visit was in the Atlantic provinces. Bad weather prevented many planned events from happening outside. The rushes that came back showed only the usual, perfunctory activities that had happened everywhere before. Except for a visit to a roaring steel mill, *everything* seemed anticlimactic after the earlier events.'

Daly was further discouraged 'when we heard that the final departure from St John's by ship took place in such dark and dismal stormy weather that the cameramen weren't sure the material would be visible in colour printing. But to our immense relief, the new Eastman stock came through with flying colours, figuratively and literally. The obvious drama of the royal couple and the Newfoundland people braving a tempest of wind and rain, with the ships tossing, and the gale roaring, and the flags rippling out flat, turned out to be one of the very best sequences in the film.'

Mulholland, who had supported Daly's gamble with *Royal Journey*, was generally sympathetic to Unit B's artistic ambitions. Unit B's projects tended to take longer and cost more to complete than originally estimated, but Mulholland, as Daly recounts, 'thought that better films might very well merit more money, and if more money would likely make it better, he was willing to consider it, within reason. I *know* my own unit's original budgets were often exceeded, but in general the difference made a much more usable film. A wonderful moment: I was in Mulholland's office for something, and the phone rang. It was Irwin, asking about a cost overrun on *Varley*. Mulholland winked at me and defended the *Varley* overage very effectively, in a way I wouldn't have been able to do.

'Once Mulholland stopped me in the hall and complained about a producer who *always* came in under budget but made plodding films. Mulholland said that if the fellow would make better films with more money, he would gladly give it to him. But he didn't think it would make any difference.'

Even the best of the unit's films, however, although skilfully crafted and interesting in content, had a pedantic cast to them. They were safe and artistically conservative, even stodgy. This would change when four of the Film Board's most promising postwar recruits combined with Daly and two veterans to create an informal but cohesive team of filmmakers who were extremely talented in different but complementary aspects of film-making. Three of the new recruits were Colin Low and Robert Verrall, who were animators by training, and Wolf Koenig, who had started as a splicer, learned animation, and bought a Bolex to teach himself camera-work. One of the veterans was Stanley Jackson, who had become a skilled narration writer and an insightful critic and collaborator. Although not a member of Unit B, the composer Eldon Rathburn frequently would play an essential role in postproduction, creating original scores for some of the unit's best films.

In addition to his administrative role, Daly would provide immense editorial skill and, for some, an access to new philosophical ideas. Verrall, for one, found Daly's 'enthusiasm about the world of Greek wisdom and mythology nourishing. I had never read the *Symposium*, and it was wonderful that he introduced me to that.' Colin Low remembers Daly talking to them about the *Iliad* and the *Odyssey*. 'He knew them in detail. He'd tell you who the hell Agamemnon was, and what they were all doing ... and he'd tell it in an interesting way.' Low also met the de Hartmanns through Daly and was introduced to the study of Ouspensky and Gurdjieff.

Daly credits to Mulholland's trust and flexibility one key additional member of the team: Roman Kroitor. Kroitor originally had come to the Film Board as a summer intern. Now he was a full-time employee, but still a trainee unassigned to a specific unit. He had done work for Unit B, and Daly thought him immensely talented. But Kroitor had annoyed the administration when he took an extra week of Christmas holidays without permission, and other filmmakers and producers disliked him. 'Roman,'

Daly recalls, 'had incensed almost everyone with his direct comments and criticisms – the more so because they were often so close to the bone. Mulholland knew I had been using Roman on some projects, and he came to me one day and said he was afraid he'd have to let Roman go. None of the other producers wanted to work with him. I thought quickly, and said that I didn't find him a problem to work with, and that his contribution to *our* unit was fine. And then I asked him, "If I can keep him fully and usefully occupied for the whole [fiscal] year, do you have any objection to keeping him in my unit?" Mulholland accepted that.'

Low, Verrall, Koenig, Kroitor, and Rathburn collaborated on the first Unit B film to make a significant inroad against postwar Film Board pedantry: *The Romance of Transportation in Canada* (1953), an educational film intended for the classroom. In cartoon animation, the eleven-minute, tightly structured film races through the history of Canadian transportation, relating technical breakthroughs, such as the internal combustion engine, to new modes of transportation. The film incorporates several variations on Hollywood cartoon clichés; a representative scene depicts a sled sailing off a cliff, pausing in mid-air, and falling out of frame. Guy Glover, at Koenig's urging, was recruited to write and speak the commentary. The film's lighthearted, anti-chauvinistic tone disarmed audiences.

In its use of cel animation, the film departed from the experimental approach to animation pioneered by the Film Board's Norman McLaren. His *Fiddle-de-dee* (1947) had translated the sound of a fiddler's rendition of 'Listen to the Mocking Bird' into images hand-painted directly onto the film. In his internationally acclaimed *Neighbours* (1952), he had applied single-frame photography to live action. McLaren had trained Low, Verrall, and Koenig – and Koenig had photographed *Neighbours* – but they were eager to try cel animation, and some government departments had asked for more conventional animation than McLaren was interested in doing.

What was distinctive about *The Romance of Transportation* was its refusal to take itself or its governmental provenance too seriously. Daly remembers that 'the educational functionaries of that day regretted that the serious purpose of the film had degenerated into a comic cartoon, hardly fit to carry the noble and heroic tale originally hoped for, but children enjoyed it and teachers loved it.' It was nominated for an Oscar and won several international awards.

Daly had never been happier. His philosophical work was leading to new insights about the world and into himself. He felt secure in his value to the Film Board. He was confident of his ability to serve those above him and to administer those under him. His immediate boss supported him. Under his wing was an impressive team of brilliant young filmmakers. He thought of himself as a knowledgeable, wise, democratically inclined administrator of a healthy, 'organic' unit. But unbeknown to him a problem was festering within the unit which had the potential to destroy it. The problem was Daly himself.

Kroitor remembers Daly giving him and Koenig a lecture on editing that was based on what Daly had learned from Stuart Legg. 'It was fantastic, tremendously well organized. I could practically deliver the lecture now, it was so clear. But Tom had two sides. Wolf and I went off to the cutting room to cut some footage on the basis of the principles Tom had just taught us. It worked very well, but when Tom saw it, it really upset him. Somehow one got the feeling that Tom had spent three or four years getting this from Legg, and now it was easy for someone else to do it. So instead of recognizing the role of his teaching, he became negative. There was a shot at the end of the sequence that was grainy. This was just an exercise for us, but Tom got very upset about the grainy shot.'

Colin Low's first assignment under Daly 'was a "scrape-off" job, making a route-line on a map. You'd paint the pattern on glass, then scrape off the edges with a razor blade. After a while, you learned to dull the blade so you didn't scratch the glass. If you scratched it, you'd have to repaint it. This was a rush job, though, and so I must have scratched the glass several times. The more I rushed, the more scratches I made. I thought most people wouldn't notice. I made the mistake of showing it to Tom. He made me do the whole thing over. The notion of him being that particular just drove me nuts. I almost quit.'

Verrall remembers that 'there was a kind of stuffiness about him, a kind of unctuousness, that got in the way of things we wanted to do. He'd nit-pick. He'd drive us nutty, nattering away about details we didn't care much about.' At the same time, Daly's impulse to encourage contributions from all members of the unit could infuriate this talented group. During the making of *The Romance of Transportation*, remembers Verrall, 'Tom wanted to be very democratic about everyone's contribution to the film. Some sound effects had been put in that we thought were corny. Tom said, "Well, the sound editor has to make a contribution." Finally, Wolf and I cut these effects out of the master and recut the negative without asking him. There was quite a flap over that.'

'It is very hard,' Koenig reflects, 'to be specific about it. Largely it was a matter of style. Tom was prim, kind of boring. Long-winded. He'd have one of us over for the evening, and he'd talk for hours about philosophical ideas. Gurdjieff. Plato. Once he had me over, and he kept talking into the night, and I sort of fell asleep with my eyes open. I was dreaming with my eyes open. One dream was that it was no longer Tom across from me, but my brother. The next day Tom said to me, "I had a feeling that I disappeared during our talk."'

Verrall, Low, Kroitor, and Koenig went to Mulholland and told him they wanted out of Daly's unit. Daly, they said, spent too much of his time getting angry and upset. But, as Verrall remembers the meeting, 'Mulholland proved wiser than we had expected. He said, "Tom is too important to this organization, and he's too important to you guys. You find a way to work with him. If I pull you out, it will destroy him."'

The group decided to confront Daly with their complaints. 'One day,' Daly remembers, 'they arranged to come to see me on the weekend. I suspected something was up, but I had no idea what it would be. They first made it very clear that they were supportive. They told me that they didn't want to work with any other producer at the Board, but if I stayed "*like that*," they couldn't continue with me. I didn't know what "*like that*" meant. One example they gave was that I was always negative in relation to them and their work. I couldn't understand that at all. It wasn't what I felt. I was always enviously *admiring* of their work. So I couldn't see how they got that other impression. I asked them how it showed. They said, "Well, you're always rushing from one thing to another. You come in, look at the film we're working on, give us five minutes, mention four things wrong with it, and rush on to the next thing." I said, "That's not the way it looks to me. True, I rush about, but it seems like I come in and see something that's ninety-six per cent perfect, and see three or four other things that could improve it, so I tell you that, and go on." "But that's all you ever say. One hundred per cent of what you say is 'that's wrong.'"'

'This was,' Verrall recalls, 'very hard on Tom, a very tough moment for him.'

Daly easily could have walked away from the confrontation. He was firmly established in the Film Board. These young filmmakers were talented but unproved, and they were widely perceived as arrogant. But just as they had had the character to present Daly with their complaints, Daly chose to listen to what they were telling him.

'I began to watch how things went, with their criticism in mind. They were right. I was only saying what could be better about a film, but not saying all the things I liked about it – how much I liked it, what way I liked it. Without actually thinking about this, I had assumed they understood how much I liked and admired what they were doing. Once they had brought this out in the open for me, it was quite practical to think about that, and to learn to respond differently. But it hadn't occurred to me.'

There was more to it than that. As Daly explains in terms of his then newly adopted conception of the self, 'They were aware, as I was not, that my logic and thinking were pretty good, and my eye for physical material, for putting it in order, was very good, but I was not attuned emotionally – to life, therefore to the material, and to them. They found a way to make it clear to me that I needed a whole lot of development in that area to be able to work effectively with them.'

'We had confronted him about it,' Kroitor recalls, 'and he's the only person I've ever known who really took something like that to heart. He consciously, deliberately changed his style. It was as if he decided, "I want to change," and *did it!* I have tremendous respect for that.' Koenig adds simply, 'Tom didn't want to be that prim schoolmaster, and he remade himself.'

More than the others, Low knew it wouldn't be easy: 'Tom's awkwardness – socially and between the sexes, and his humour, which frequently didn't work – he wanted to change this. But I didn't really understand Tom until I saw him with his parents. His mother was a talker you wouldn't believe. A marathon talker. A snob, in a way. His father was simple, quiet, and often seemed irritated by her. There was a lot of tension between them. Tom was aware of this. I liked them both, by the way. But you could see Tom in both.'

Low attributes Daly's turnaround largely to his involvement with the Gurdjieff group. It offered him a way to comprehend his problem and act on it. Daly agrees that his study of Gurdjieff helped prepare him to transform the pain of self-knowledge into a positive force. Gurdjieff's insistence that 'an unbiased attitude is the first step to freedom' resonated with Daly. 'It has to do,' Daly explains, 'with self-observation. If you begin to observe yourself, you realize that you have judgments. You think *this* is good in you, and *that* is bad. And the same with other people. You think perhaps *this* is good in them, and *that* is bad. All the time you're making judgments. After a bit, you discover that the judging is going on on the level of reaction, but whatever it is in you that can observe that, when it is not caught in it, is seeing that but doesn't judge it. It is aware of it, and realizes what it does to your life, but it doesn't make the judgment. So when your attention actually gets cleanly into that, whether it's seeing yourself or a situation, you have the possibility of unbiased perception, which treats yourself just the same way you treat anybody else.

'So instead of being afraid of discoveries about myself, I had already begun to realize that the power of turning one's own observation on one-self, and also on that eager element in other people – that it was largely from that level that one does understand things. When you have a dawning, a realization of something, suddenly there's a meaning to things that you didn't have a meaning for before – that light wonderful feeling when the meaning rushes in and you realize something that you didn't realize before. It's at that same level that you can look at yourself. Somehow or other, that's the level where the real relationship between people exists.'

Although Daly had embarked on a program to transform himself and his manner of relating to others, he did not try to deny the fact of his less attractive side. Acknowledging its existence was entailed in maintaining an 'unbiased attitude.' At a Hallowe'en party at Verrall's house in 1954, Daly appeared in a mask he had asked Low to make for him. It was modelled from a photograph of a terra cotta figurine that Daly had seen in a book on Mayan artefacts (*Mexique précolombien*, by Gisèle Freund). The figurine depicted a woman with two faces, each with a separate mouth and nose but sharing a third eye. The point of the mask, Low remembers, was to express 'how, without knowing it, we shift from one personality to another.' The third eye, Daly adds, suggests the true or growing self that includes the others. He saw in that mask something that for him is also expressed in the image of the Roman god Janus: 'Those two faces aren't separate things, but are linked to the being in between. The real being is inside looking at the past and at the future. The present moment is in the middle, where you are. You're a product of your past and you wonder about your future.'

Along with helping Daly understand himself, the practice of self-observation and the notion of the three-part psyche suggested to him a model for analysing films both structurally and according to how they are received by an audience. In 1954, in a talk ('The Audience Is Part of the Film') to the Toronto Film Society Study Group, Daly outlined this model as it might apply to interpreting Sergei Eisenstein's *The General Line*. As recorded in his notes for the talk, he began:

In discussing films and criticizing them, we always tend to talk about the picture and the maker of the picture, and forget what is involved in the reactions of the people in the audience – that is, ourselves. We take it for granted that there is only one film in question – up there on the screen – and that we are all equally absorbing it. We forget that the film is only a 'thing,' a piece of celluloid, a matter of physics and chemistry, until it is completed by making contact with the members of the audience.

When anyone afterwards speaks of 'the film,' he really speaks only of the flow of impressions and reactions *he* experienced. Probably no one is capable of experiencing 'the whole film.' Each is particularly interested or absorbed by certain parts or aspects. Other parts or aspects may go unnoticed altogether. And so it is possible that ... two critics can argue about, say, *The General Line*, from opposite points of view and yet both be right, because they are not really discussing one film, but *two* films – the two subjective streams they separately experienced.

How, then, are we ever to hope to understand one another? Is there any more objective basis of criticism? Can we establish some sort of criterion which will take into account the limitations of our own perceptions as well as those of others? Yes, I think so, if we learn something of how we make judgments from moment to moment in everyday experience.

Daly then described the physical, emotional, and intellectual aspects of the psyche. Then:

All of us, of course, have all three of these apparatuses. And each of them properly should provide us independently with a different aspect of the whole truth about any experience. The trouble is that practically none of us – neither artist nor onlooker – has a natural balance of the three functions. In each of us, one of them tends to predominate to the extent of weakening the other two, or preventing their development. The predominant function is also the most comfortable one, and we rely on it more and more, until finally it tends to govern the whole of our life, instead of only a third of it.

A person dominated by his intellect attempts to like (and make other people like) 'what his mind has decided is right, whether he really enjoys it or not.' He tends to be dogmatic and to expect art to illustrate 'meaning.' The emotional person assumes that if he likes something it must be right. In art, he will tend to emphasize mood, atmosphere, and character at the expense of structure or theme. The physical person is impulsive, quick, and practical. For him, thought inhibits action, and emotion tarnishes it. He tends to be a physical virtuoso: a tightrope walker, an auto racer, or ordinary lover of sport. In art, he prefers realism.

Although one apparatus tends to dominate, the other two are nevertheless present, and

each makes its own separate judgment on what is placed before it. We can be intellectually convinced, without being emotionally convinced – and so on for all the possible combinations. Unless all three parts of us are simultaneously convinced, it is not a complete conviction.

Daly then gave several illustrations from *The General Line*. One involved

an interesting visual comparison of mower blades with the serrated legs of a grass-hopper. Physically, this is an apt simile; they look alike to the eye, and they are both associated by the ear with an oscillating sound. Mentally, they are both connected with harvest fields, and with the cutting of crops. Emotionally, they form a clear contrast – one works for the good [of] man, the other to his detriment. And so all three parts of us accept to some extent the validity of the simile. We get a 'kick' out of it.

A less successful instance occurred

in the cream-separator sequence ... where the agricultural representative removes the cover from the separator. In order to heighten the dramatic effect, Eisenstein has tried to hold on to it, to lengthen it. How? By repeating the action from three different angles. There is nothing displeasing to the mind in the attempt to prolong the moment. And our emotions would be all the more delighted if the attempt was successful. But the physical sense ... objects at once, 'He didn't take off the cover once, he took it off three times.' And this spoils the acceptance of the moment for some people. It is intellectually calculated; it is physically phony.

Daly concluded his talk by summarizing the implications of this analysis for the artist and for the critic:

What applies in detail also applies to the whole. In the creative work of the artist, all three functions play their separate parts. If they go deep and work together harmoniously, we have 'inspired' art, in which the meaning and the intensity of emotion are one with the physical embodiment or rendering. On the other hand, if any of the artist's functions are underdeveloped, warped, or out of balance, the work of art suffers the corresponding imperfections.

But the *experience* of the work of art is incomplete until we add to all this the perception of the viewer or critic. Objective criticism requires that the critic understand his own pyschological make-up, as well as the artist's ... If a work of art does not arouse or please him, it may be due to the imperfections of the artist ... but it may also be due to his own lacks, limitations and imbalances. This, too, is part of the material to be criticized. And the hopeful thing is that it is possible for us to extend our own capacity to perceive and to criticize effectively, by discovering which of our functions are least developed and learning how to balance them up and make them work together. Too often our role in the audience is an automatic, passive one. It ought to be, and *can* be, an active, creative one.

Although Daly's presentation distinguished between filmmakers and audiences, his advice to both applied equally to himself, and it was directed to himself as well as to others. He already had come to see the task of editing as largely the achievement of a balance among the three psychological functions in a film; as a producer he was discovering a need to respond more fully and more generously to the ideas and aspirations of the filmmakers under him. It was an idea that, for him, embraced both the aesthetic challenge of editing and the social challenge of relating effectively to others.

But the philosophical ideas behind Daly's new attitude, as helpful as they were to him and as much as he tried to share them, made sense to few others. Except for Colin Low and one other filmmaker at the periphery of the unit, Daly's filmmaking colleagues remained cool to the ideas of Gurdjieff and Ouspensky. Daly's enthusiasm about them could strike others, as it did Verrall, as 'just a little bit spooky.' But, Verrall adds, Daly's 'basic respect for the convictions of others prevented him from being an obnoxious proselytizer. If he sensed you weren't going to open up to Gurdjieff, that was fine. Finally, it wasn't as important in what mattered as even Tom thought.'

What undeniably did matter for the history of the Film Board and of documentary was that the unit stayed together with Daly as its head. Had the key members of the unit scattered or had Daly been removed, the place of *The Romance of Transportation* in Film Board history might well have remained merely that of an interesting little film, a minor oddity. Instead, it marked the beginning of a glorious decade of filmmaking for Unit B and an enrichment of possibility for filmmaking – especially documentary – in the government service.

In the early 1950s, documentary film had become a rather dull thing, within the Film Board and without. The compilation film, perfected in wartime, seemed ill suited to a world that no longer generated shiploads of combat footage or presented starkly partisan choices. And live-action documentary, encumbered by a 35mm technology that made synchronized sound awkward to achieve, required so much scripting and rehearsal that spontaneity usually was lost. The organizing strategy for both approaches was almost always one of relying on extensive, voice-of-God narration to achieve coherence.

The constraints on documentary style were matched by restrictions on content. Although the Film Board already interpreted government service more broadly than government film operations in other countries did, it generally limited its range of topics to domestic issues directly related to government programs or priorities. Unit B's program of productions for 1953, the year of *The Romance of Transportation*, itself a film intended for schools, included such titles as *Canadian Notebook*, *The Newcomers*, *Poison Ivy Picnic*, and *Fighting Forest Fires with Power Pumps*.

The one NFB filmmaker who had managed to break through the largely unquestioned constraints on style and content at the NFB was Norman McLaren. But McLaren had enjoyed a special status at the Film Board from the day Grierson hired him. He was, in effect, the 'house artist.' And he worked in an inexpensive, abstract experimental genre that attracted little bureaucratic interest.

Now Grierson's gnomic wartime remark that McLaren was the most important filmmaker at the Board revealed a new prescience. Then, it had seemed to mean that McLaren exemplified for others at the Film Board the willing subordination of artistic talent to didactic purpose. His contribution to *Our Northern Neighbour* was one example. But McLaren had come to represent a standard of aesthetic excellence that perhaps documentarians could aspire to. Low and Koenig, from working with McLaren, and Kroitor, through them, had absorbed McLaren's urge to innovate and wanted to apply it to the more contentious field of documentary.

If they possessed the requisite drive and imagination for such an adventure, Unit B provided them with an appropriately nourishing environment. It insulated its members somewhat from the bureaucratic imperatives and tendencies that could suppress creative daring in even the freest of government filmmaking organizations. And, in Eldon Rathburn, Stanley Jackson, and, especially, Daly, the unit provided an essential structuring discipline to balance and bring into harmony the wilder impulses of its younger members.

This balance between innovation and structure is a common feature among the six films that probably remain Unit B's best-loved works and best display the range of Unit B's documentary achievement. The films are *Corral* (1954), *Paul Tomkowicz: Street-railway Switchman* (1954), *City of Gold* (1957), *Universe* (1960), *Circle of the Sun* (1961), and *Lonely Boy* (1961), and they were primarily the work of the group who had met at Daly's apartment to discuss his style of leadership. Low directed *Corral*; Koenig shot it. Kroitor directed *Paul Tomkowicz*. Low and Koenig co-directed *City of Gold*. Kroitor provided a story-line and technical innovation, and he contributed to the editing. Low directed *Circle of the Sun*. Kroitor and Low co-directed *Universe*. Koenig and Kroitor jointly made *Lonely Boy*. As head of Unit B, Daly was of course executive producer for all six, but he also edited all but *Paul Tomkowicz* and *Lonely Boy*. Others made essential contributions; among those who contributed significantly to more than one of the films were Jackson, a writer for four and adviser on all, and Rathburn, who created original music for all but *Paul Tomkowicz* and *Lonely Boy*.

Corral was the watershed Unit B documentary. It was made as part of a series of short films (*Faces of Canada*) that sent several young filmmakers back to their home provinces to make a low-budget, short documentary portrait of someone of interest to the filmmaker. Low had grown up on a ranch in Alberta. With Koenig as his cameraman, he returned to make a film about a man saddling a half-broken horse.

A short, deceptively simple film, *Corral* exemplifies the creative tension in Unit B between innovation and structure. The film broke two Film Board stylistic conventions, and it succeeded in this largely because of the structural resources and support that were available to it.

Koenig was not officially a cameraman, and the Camera Department refused to give him a camera for the project. Daly authorized the rental of a camera from a commercial company. Out on location, Koenig often removed the bulky, 35mm machine from its tripod, put it on his shoulder, and manoeuvered into the corral with the cowboy and the horse. This probably was the first instance at the Film Board in which a camera was hand-held deliberately, with exciting imagery in mind. And it was an early example of Unit B's willingness to skirt standard organizational procedures in pursuit of artistic goals.

Corral also seems to have been the Film Board's first significant documentary not to have a commentary. When the film was nearing completion, Low, Daly, and Jackson, who had started working on a commentary for the film, came to realize that perhaps the film did not need a commentary – that music alone could carry it, and perhaps carry it better, with more emotion, than a soundtrack laden with words.

But *Corral* is also a virtuoso demonstration of classical continuity editing. As executive producer, Daly would spend considerable time looking at rushes and rough-cuts of all Unit B projects, but mainly as a critic and consultant. For *Corral*, he took on the primary editing job himself. Daly was happy to be in the editing room: the material was both exciting and challenging. Koenig's unscripted, often stunning hand-held shots did not easily fit together, but some of the film's most exciting, seemingly fluid moments are built largely from Koenig's hand-held material. A sequence in which the cowboy tries to control the roped but as yet unsaddled horse is composed almost entirely of close-ups of the horse, boots, hands, and rope. The apparently simple setting, too, posed a problem for Daly. Because the corral was circular, 'material from every angle looked more or less the same. Only by keeping a very close watch over the direction of sunlight in the sequence could clarity of action be achieved without the viewer having to think about it. For this, transition shots became all-important, shots in which the direction of sunlight changes within the shot itself.'

The film that was taking shape was visually so lucid and rhythmical that the planned-for commentary began to seem, in Jackson's words, 'like a fifth wheel.' Daly explains the decision to forego commentary in terms of his new way of thinking about film structure. 'All the images were very, very strong physically, and all the little events between the man and the horse produced a natural and strong emotional response. But when it came to the intellectual element, nobody could think of anything to say. We finally realized that there was no need to talk about it, because you could see and feel almost everything that was necessary.'

Jackson played a key if somewhat renegade role in the commentary for Kroitor's *Paul Tomkowicz* (another *Faces of Canada* film). The film is a portrait of a sixty-four-year-old Polish-born Canadian whose job is to clear mud and snow from streetcar rail switches in Winnipeg. Tomkowicz works the night shift. In crisp black-and-white photography, the film mixes images of cold and darkness (even the snow looks dark) with images of heat and light – steaming coffee, vapour from a vent, smoke from a smokestack, electric sparks. Its voice-over commentary seems unpretentious and natural.

Kroitor had recorded a long interview with Tomkowicz and planned to cut the voice-over commentary from it. But Tomkowicz's accent was so thick that he was hard to understand. And the technical quality of the recording was poor. Jackson and Kroitor went to New York to get a Polish actor to read Tomkowicz's words. This recording didn't work out, either. Finally, Kroitor remembers, Jackson 'suggested that a friend of his in Toronto – Tommy Tweed, then a famous Canadian radio actor – might be able to do the narration, and we drove down secretly to Toronto to do the recording. I didn't dare ask Tom for permission because the film was already over budget.' The recording was 'sneaked in on another production's time, with their connivance.'

City of Gold tells a story of Dawson City during the Klondike gold rush of 1898. Pierre Berton, who was then well known as a journalist and who had been born and raised in Dawson City, narrates the story, and Eldon Rathburn's unbroken musical score based on music from the era underlies the entire film. Brief sequences of live-action footage of Dawson City in the mid-1950s frame the film's main section, which is composed entirely from still photographs taken in or around 1898. These photos are arranged in an essentially chronological account of Dawson City's summer of greed and glory. We first catch a glimpse of the ordeal undergone by the men who climbed the Chilkoot Pass in order to reach the gold fields; then we experience their disappointment as they discover that they have arrived too late, that the best sites have been claimed. The emphasis shifts to Dawson City itself. Pieces of factual information are interwoven into an account that is funny, informative, and moving. Berton tells us about characters such as the Evaporated Kid and Montreal Marie, about gold miners and gold dealers, about the tolerance the North-West Mounted Police displayed for sins of the flesh, and about the astounding civil order – not a single murder occurred during that summer – that was maintained in a boom town populated mostly by adventurous foreigners. During the film's account of a combined Fourth of July and Dominion Day celebration, Berton asks what these people were celebrating. Most hadn't found any gold. He suggests that they were celebrating the venture itself – in other words, life and the bold living of it. The film ends with toothless old men chatting and joking on a boardwalk, reminiscing about a past whose deepest meaning belongs only to those who experienced it. The film leaves a receptive audience in a mood of uneasy elation – a feeling that the time for adventure in a person's life is brief, singular, and ultimately private and yet, as celebrated here, available to us all.

The idea for *City of Gold* arose by chance. As Low remembers it, 'The Film Board was still in Ottawa. I had a habit of going to the National Archives to look at stuff. They'd been a great help to me when I did *Age of the Beaver* [a 1952 film about the fur trade using paintings, drawings, and animation]. A very nice lady said to me one day, "Oh, have I got something for you to see."

'She showed me these marvellous photos made from a lot of glass-plate negatives that had been found in a sod-roof cabin in Dawson City in the late forties. A local jeweller named George Murdoch had printed some up and sold them to tourists. He did it in collaboration with a local radiologist, who had the equipment for it. He sent some prints to Whitehorse. Someone from the Archives saw them – he must have been up there, in Whitehorse. He ordered a complete set of the prints from Murdoch.

'I called up Wolf and Verrall. They came right over. We agreed right there that the photos would make a good film.' Koenig adds that they 'had just seen an American film, at a film society screening, called *The Port of St. Francis*, done entirely with still photos, so we knew it could be done. Once we got approval for the idea, Colin began to scour the country for other stills.'

Low wrote to the Library of Congress in Washington, D.C. 'They told me to try Webster and Stevens, an old photographic company in Seattle. I wrote them and asked if they had any photos of the Gold Rush. They wrote back and said yes, they had about four hundred. They were also from glass-plate negatives.

'A lot of both collections were by A.E. Hegg, a top photojournalist of the time. He had gone over the Chilkoot Pass with the prospectors. He processed the plates in a tent on the Pass. He carried them on his back. He spent about two years up in Dawson City.' One of Hegg's photos of the climb to the Chilkoot Pass, used in *City of Gold*, had inspired the famous Chilkoot Pass scene in Charlie Chaplin's *The Gold Rush*. There were also, Daly adds, a number of photos from a photojournalistic team known as Larss and Duclos. Later, when Koenig and Low were in Dawson City shooting the live-action material, they found even more photographs.

The main triumph of *City of Gold* is its conversion of these photographs into cinema. Still photos have become commonplace in documentaries, but their use is rarely inspired with cinematic values. When a still-photo sequence comes on, suddenly any art that might have been employed in the documentary is put on hold. To create some motion, the filmmaker typically zooms in and out, pans right or left, tilts up or down, his camera remaining on a tripod. The result is usually lifeless and clichéd. Dissatisfied with such techniques, Kroitor invented a camera-tracking device that combined some of the fluidity of a hand-held camera with the precision and control provided by mechanization. His device allowed the camera to combine panning, tilting, and zooming into a single and highly controlled movement. The camera movements employed in filming the photographs in *City of Gold* thus mimic the camera movements normally associated with live-action filming. A border of a photograph is never shown in *City of Gold*, and the camera moves around within the frame with such freedom, selectivity, and purposiveness that audiences forget, at least at some level of attention, that they are looking at still photos. The sequence begins to look like location filming.

Matching the film's technical and stylistic inventiveness is its richly layered structure. Long before filming, Koenig, Low, Kroitor, and Daly sifted through the photos, eliminating all but the best. They pre-edited these into a story-line that, although based on historical research, would involve its audience cinematically. For example, the sequence in which the audience comes to identify with the men who climbed the Chilkoot Pass in order to reach the gold fields is followed immediately by shots of hard-bitten miners staring at the camera. By implication, they are staring down the hapless latecomers; by identification, they are staring at us.

Even more remarkable than the shot-by-shot organization of the film's still-photo body are the two transitions between live action and stills. The opening sequence consists of twenty-eight live-action shots of unscripted material, yet their organization works gradually towards the moment at which live-action will become still photography. The first thirteen shots are of people – a young boys' baseball game first, and then old men hanging around in front of a store. The last fifteen shots in the opening sequence are devoid of people: faded signs on sagging, abandoned buildings ('Yukon Saw Mill Co.,' 'Red Feather Saloon,' '3rd Ave. Blacksmith Shop'), an old steam locomotive almost overgrown with tall weeds and young trees, a beached river boat, wooden grave markers. In the final shots of the sequence, the only visible motion is that of drifting fireweed seeds or the shadow of a weed gently nodding in the breeze. The next shot is a panoramic view of snow-covered mountain peaks; the shot is so wide but its content so motionless that it could be either a location shot or a still. Two shots later (in the photo that had inspired Chaplin), the camera pans down to the long line of men making their way up to the Chilkoot Pass, and only then is it certain that the shot is of a still photograph. On first viewing, however, most audiences aren't conscious of the transition to stills, for the filmmakers' intent, which the film realizes, is to achieve the transition imperceptibly. Only on repeated viewing does their sleight of hand reveal itself in the gradual progression from activity to stillness, youth to age, faded signs on existing buildings to still photographic images. And not only are the camera movements in the location material repeated in the filming of the photographs, but even the low evening light of the northern summer is common to the live-action footage and the still photos that immediately follow.

The same artistry is employed, in reverse, in the transition from the still-photo main body back to live action for the concluding sequence. A shot of a pile of picks and axes is followed by a shot that looks up on a stack of long-handled shovels leaning against a wall. The third shot is of an oil lamp in a window; rippling waters are barely in focus beyond the window. Next is a shot of a large book opened up; tall grass sways softly outside. The next shot is of a high-heeled shoe on a window-sill; it is draped in cobwebs, and its price tag flutters slightly from a draft. Then there are several more shots from inside abandoned buildings, followed by a few shots of the ball players, then several of the old men. A shot of an oil truck kicking up dust is inserted into the unheard conversation of the old men. They seem to turn to look at it before resuming their conversation. The film ends on a wide-shot of the men, who by implication experienced Dawson City's wild summer of 1898.

The seamlessness of the film's cuts and transitions contributes to a larger connectedness among three layers of time. The main story in *City of Gold* takes place in 1898. The live-action sequences that frame the main story show Dawson City in the mid-1950s. Berton's remembered childhood is from the 1920s. Yet the vitality of each time period within the film varies inversely with its nearness to us in time and with the apparent liveliness of the image. The film is pleasant but least engrossing in the earliest and latest live-action shots of activity in Dawson City. The film becomes involving when Berton reminisces over shots of rotting ship hulls and decrepit buildings. The still-photo sequence is the most immediate.

The narration meshes fluidly with the visual track. Again, Jackson played an important role in the narration. Koenig had suggested Berton as the narrator. As Kroitor remembers it, however, 'Berton's first narration was hopeless, and Stanley rewrote it to work for a film. Berton then rewrote that, to put it into his personal words.'

In an interview conducted twenty years later and published in a Film Board newsletter under the title 'It's the Mind That Moves ... ,' Daly offered an explanation for the film's successful reversal of expectations about time and movement:

Now, there's an old story of Buddhist monks arguing about a flag flying. One monk argued that it was the flag that moved. The other said it was the wind that moved. As they couldn't decide which one was moving, they went to an older, wiser monk for the answer. He laughed at them, and replied, 'Neither! It is the *mind* that moves.' [The] reason I think *City of Gold* works is that your mind is following the story just as actively and fully as it would if every shot were a motion picture shot. In other words, there is no feeling of limitation created by the lack of movement, no limitation to the effect on you of the story and events. They feel just as if they were real life ...

[For instance, at] the beginning of the film, after we had shown the live present day activity we gradually shifted the attention to the houses behind them which were full of broken windows and empty doorways and boarded up areas. Then we moved away to old locomotives in the forest and decaying ferries aground and then to a ship's rope that was thrown down carelessly and left rotting on the gangway. Without seeing him, you feel the presence of the person who once threw it there. Then we take you to the crosses in the cemetery, with the grass grown up around the graves. Again you feel the individuals of those days in their numbers though, of course, you do not expect them to move ever again. You know they are dead. So even the unconscious expectation of their moving is already ruled out by the order of the images up to this point in the picture. The next time you see these people they are appropriately still, forming a line wending its way into the Yukon.

You can see that the effect was achieved not only by picture. It was also done by calculating the kind of progression of thought and feeling that would be generated in the audience from the order and progression of the images, gradually draining away the expectation of movement until there was no need for it any more, other than camera movement over the stills. At the end of the film we came back from past to present through a similar process in reverse, like coming out of a dream ...

I think the team working on *City of Gold* actually did more searching work on the philosophy of it, the techniques and methods of it, the inventiveness of it, and the variations on its handling, than has probably ever been devoted to any other stills film before or since ... A lot of the elements in it have perhaps individually been done as well, or better, since, but part of why I love that film and can still look at it with pleasure, is because it seems an organic whole. All the parts hold together as if there were just the right amount of whatever it required. And that's pretty rare.

What *City of Gold* does for historical time, *Universe* accomplishes for space. It conveys a sense of the scale of the universe while managing to suggest, through visual structure, a traceable physical connection between earthly existence and the remotest phenomena. The film is anchored in an astronomer's lonely night's work at an observatory near Toronto. After an introductory consideration of the sun's relationship to the earth, the film moves to the observatory. There follows an extraordinary probe into the solar system, in which the filmic material consists largely of three-dimensional models of the moon and most of the planets. The film returns to earth and into the observatory. A second probe takes us beyond the solar system into our galaxy, whose 'billions of suns scattered through stellar space' include twin suns, multiple suns, giant and dwarf suns, and supernovas. After another sequence in the observatory, a third and final probe asks the audience to imagine being able to 'move with the freedom of a god ... so that a million years pass in a second.' We would come to 'an endless sea of night' dotted with islands of stars – galaxies – so immense 'that they have been observed slipping through one another like phantoms.' These are the birthplace of stars and planets, 'sometimes planets that must be suitable for life.' The narrator notes that the light from these galaxies started 'long before the dawn of life on earth,' and he wonders 'what civilizations have risen, looked into the night, seen what we see, asked the questions that we ask ...?' Back at the observatory, the sun rises and the astronomer rubs his eyes. In a very long take, he goes outside, embraces the early morning, walks to his car, and drives off.

Like *City of Gold*, *Universe* owes much of its power to its stunning imagery. The nature of its imagery, however, differs profoundly from that of *City of Gold*. Most of its location material is scripted, and its studio-shot material is imagined and manufactured, not discovered and largely spontaneous at its origin. The sequences with the astronomer in the observatory are carefully planned and lit, and they are shot in classic matched-action style. The illusion of motion in the space-probe sequences is created by camera movements within three-dimensional sets carefully calibrated to suggest the dimensions of real space and time. A particularly impressive instance begins with the moon's dark side filling the frame with blackness. As the camera moves left, the earth emerges from behind the moon's dark horizon. The camera continues to move left to reveal the sun behind the earth. This creates an illusion of the moon and the earth moving in their respective orbits.

While the imagery of *Universe* can look primitive after years of computer-generated advances in animation, the film's meticulously elaborated underlying structure has never been equalled and continues to give meaning to the film. This structure was more complex than even that of *City of Gold*. *City of Gold* had needed only two transitions to join its three sequences. *Universe* required seven to tie together its introduction, its three space sequences, and its four earth sequences. And whereas *City of Gold* rendered the exact moment of each transition imperceptible, *Universe* accomplishes each of its transitions by inventive but extraordinarily lucid applications of ordinary filmic and verbal logic. The first shot of the film is of a starlit sky. The second is a full shot of the sun. The third is of a sky-scraper, seven windows of which reflect bright images of the sun. The film cuts to a high-angle shot from the top of the building to the busy street far below; shadows of surrounding buildings are large and long, suggesting late afternoon. Next is a closer overhead shot of a busy street corner on which pedestrians cast long shadows. The narrator comments that 'the ground beneath our feet is the surface of a planet, whirling at thousands of miles an hour, around a distant sun.' As he nears the end of this line, the camera is at knee-level on the street. The effect is oddly disconcerting in the way that a Charles Addams cartoon, with its ostensible centre of action menaced by an unnoticed off-frame presence, is chilling. Yet the entire sequence has been constructed from well-chosen but ordinary, everyday images.

After two more shots of the street, the film cuts to a long-shot of the observatory, backlit by the setting sun. Inside, the astronomer is preparing for a night's work of observations. The sequence ends with a shot looking out from the observatory as it opens to the night sky.

The probe of our solar system begins with the moon. From the moon, we go past the earth to the other planets. At the end of the planetary tour,

Halley's Comet brings us back to the sun, which is 'flooding its planets with radiant energy [that] sustains human life.' The next few shots are of city night-life, and then the film returns to inside the observatory. Several shots of clockwork mechanisms remind us of the structure of the solar system. This observatory sequence ends with the telescope pointed towards the night sky. A moth flits about the telescope. The second probe – beyond the solar system – ends when the narrator comments that until recently this vast realm of stars, gas, and dust seemed chaotic. We then return to the astronomer recording his painstaking observations. The final probe simply asks us to use our imaginations; at the end of the sequence, after its anthropocentric musings, the film cuts to the weary but contented astronomer. Thus not only have these ventures into space been organically connected to the working astronomer, they – and he – have been integrated into the passing of a single night – a structural metaphor for the motion of the planets.

There is another and rather astonishing level of meaning in the film – or that can be read into it. Although *Universe* was based on current scientific knowledge and was acclaimed for its scientific accuracy, its filmic structure resembles the account Ouspensky gives in *In Search of the Miraculous* of Gurdjieff's notion of 'the ray of creation.' The ray of creation, viewed from man's position, sees the moon as furthest from the source of all energy, which is the Absolute. Next is the earth, then our sun's planets, then the sun, then all suns, then all worlds, and finally the Absolute, which no man has seen. Ouspensky diagrams the ray of creation thus:

O   Absolute
U   All Worlds
O   All Suns
O   Our Sun
O   All Planets
O   Earth
O   Moon

In Gurdjieff's scheme, the emphasis is on the life-giving energy that emanates from the Absolute through each lower level. Contrary to the accepted scientific view, the moon for Gurdjieff was not a dead planet but a future one. Eventually it will become like the earth. The earth will become a sun.

Universe makes no such claims, but its exploration of space is ordered along the lines of the diagram. The journey begins with the moon, then tours the earth and the planets. It is at this point that the sun, although seen earlier and again later, is described. Then the film takes us to 'all suns,' or the billions of suns in the Milky Way. Then it takes us to the realm of 'all worlds,' the galaxies, and speculates on what might lie beyond. And whenever the film brings us back to earth, the earth seems drenched in radiant energy.

Daly says there was no conscious attempt in *Universe* to reflect Gurdjieff's scheme. Kroitor, who was the film's chief structurer at the conceptual level, insists that there was 'absolutely no attempt whatsoever to convey the ideas of that ... philosopher ... that Russian. The film *did* have a lot to do with the idea of there being layers of understanding available to us with regard to the universe.'

Daly attributes the artistry of *Universe* in part to administrative flexibility: 'The film started getting longer than we had planned or budgeted for, and the reason was intrinsic to an unforeseen factor very much at the essence of the subject. It had to do with scales of time. Animation familiarly can telescope a long time into a short movement, as in *The Romance of Transportation*. That is part of the charm of animation. But in handling such a scene as the movement of a moon around Mars – the planet being represented by a good-sized globe, painted suitably, and the moon by a ping-pong ball – at a certain pace that would bring out the length of a shot at the estimated – and budgeted – length that we needed, the shot looked exactly like a ping-pong ball zipping around a globe. But, by experiment, when the ping-pong ball was made to move three times as slowly, the scene took on the look of a moon actually floating around a planet. And so it was that the film kept getting longer.

'There was some trepidation on the part of management at the rising costs, although everyone loved the quality of the images. At one time, Mulholland suggested we might break it down into a series of three separate classroom films: one on the solar system, one on our galaxy, and one on the multiple worlds beyond. But we argued that the main point was to retain this sense of the organic wholeness of the universe and the remarkable fact that any human being, bound to this planet for a lifetime, could nevertheless extend his or her perception in an unbroken thread of awareness all the way out from our solar system to the limits of visibility. That unity and impression of the continuous ladder of scales would be shattered by breaking the film in three and running the parts separately. Mulholland accepted that point of view, defended the project to his superiors, and found other ways of providing the funds over several fiscal years.'

Daly apparently was unaware of one reason for Mulholland's acceptance. Kroitor had gone to see Mulholland on his own: 'I made a pitch to him, and he said, "I can't decide this. If you persuade the commissioner, I'll go along with it." A meeting was arranged between me and the commissioner, then

Albert Trueman. He had been a university president, and it was possible to talk to him honestly about the overall concept and how it was more than a classroom film and would be gutted if it were not a unity. He was completely understanding. He talked with Mulholland, who worked out the basic budget methodology.'

The film's ultimate length was twenty-six minutes. Daly remembers that at first there was not a lot of interest in it. 'Educators found it too long for their purposes, especially since astronomy was not studied very widely at the time. But, as fate or accident would have it, just before we completed our film, Sputnik went up into space, and the space era had begun. Far from being a dull and remote academic subject, astronomy became a subject of general public interest everywhere. Our film was the only one available in this field for a very long time – very relatively speaking!'

Circle of the Sun, although lacking the innovative flair of *City of Gold* and *Universe*, is as visually rich and shares their vision of the connectedness of things. Its key interpretations were based on what the Blood Indians of Alberta told the filmmakers and on two books by the Sioux Black Elk, *The Sacred Pipe* and *Black Elk Speaks*. The film meditates on the meaning of the sun dance for the Blood tribe of southwestern Alberta and ponders the likelihood that the sun dance will survive. It depicts the sun dance through the eyes and voice-over thoughts of a young Blood male, Pete Standing Alone. He has spent years in the United States working on oil rigs and expects to work on them again. He attends his tribe's annual gathering but does not participate in the ceremony. He remains an observer. This was the first time the sun dance had been filmed, and the implication recurs throughout the film that future generations of Bloods might know the ritual only through such recordings. Although Standing Alone's voice-over provides most of the narration, there is also some impersonal narration. This narrator, Stanley Jackson, describes the dance as 'a dying echo of their people's history.' In voice-over, Standing Alone muses that 'the old Indians say in a few more years there won't be any more sun dance ... In time, the old way of life will all be forgotten.'

But structurally the film suggests hope for a cultural revival or, failing that, perhaps some larger continuity. Near the film's climax, several successive shots reveal circular forms: rocks arranged around a fire; a round pendant on a necklace; the opening at the top of a tepee; Indians sitting in a circle. Then, as a slowly circling aerial shot reveals the circular organization of the entire gathering, Jackson says, 'Some observers say a key to the old religion is to be found in the circle. The power of the world works in circles. The sky is round. The stars and the earth are round. The seasons form a great circle. The life of a man is a circle from childhood to childhood. And so it is in everything where power moves.'

Editing, light, and voice-over underscore this theme. As Pete Standing Alone reels off the names of several dances, the film cuts to shots of the animals for which they are named. Although the animals were filmed separately, the overlapping of sounds from the ceremony suggests that they are just outside the camp's perimeter. Most of the dance shots near the end of the film are washed in low-angle light from the setting sun. At the end of the film, after he says that he plans to go south again to make some money, Standing Alone concludes, 'I'll be back here. I always have come back.'

Circle of the Sun is all location footage, and much of it is very beautiful. As is often the case in memorable documentary material, contrivance and chance enhanced a filmmaker's considerable talent. Daly says that when Low found 'that the natural light balance in a canvas tepee would never give adequate detail on the faces of those inside, he had the Indians make a decorated lining to cut down the contrasts – with very nice results for Kodachrome at that time.' But some of the strongest imagery, the faces of onlookers seen intermittently behind foreground splashes of colour from out-of-focus dancers, almost got rejected as unusable. 'John Spotton, the cameraman, nearly stopped shooting as the passing dancers first interrupted his vision, but then he saw the beauty of it, and he kept on shooting.'

Some surviving documentation from the project provides a glimpse into how extensive Daly's involvement with Unit B films could be. He had developed the practice of screening material sent in from the field and then sending out his reactions by wire or letter. His notes could be very detailed. On 23 July 1957, for example, he sent Low a seven-page handwritten letter 're: Rolls 1–16.' After warning Low that the notes 'are irregular as they [i.e., the rushes] were screened in higgledepiggledy order, and not slated,' Daly organized his comments under nine headings, each referring to groups of related material. Of some footage shot at a rodeo:

Details connected with riding – All sorts of shots of bucking itself – plenty – throwing steer stuff not so good or so well covered – good shots of rider and steer leaving chutes. Less good of action itself, or completion of action. Not sure any of them were successful – By contrast the horse stuff is pretty full – shows good riding in spite of some very difficult starts – some excellent shots of starts – terrific shots of horse running out with hoof caught in fence, & activity to free it. (As a purist, I'm sorry you didn't get the actual moment when the hoof was freed, if it ever was! Did they shoot the horse?) – nice shot of a foal that got loose in the ring, though

cut a little short – good shots of 3 horses with 3 competing teams of 3 men to saddle
& ride them – Good shot man *pulls lever* to open chute (would like to see this detail
closer) – when fellow in red jacket got on horse, & got away, there are 2 beautiful
shots of his riding, the horse kicking up dust which is caught by the light of the low
sun, & later there's a pan shot of him going past the sun, & there's a brilliant flare
in the middle of the pan shot which makes it quite spectacular, while the rest of it
has that backlit-dust quality which goes with the previous one (*very* good) – good
shot rider falls off, makes gesture of 'shucks', picks up hat & away – good man
limping back to chutes – *very* good bit of shooting in connection with the serous
injury; it was a brilliant idea to get the approach shot of his *feet* limping as he is
supported (with his wonderful boots); that's better than the more usual kind of
shot which follows, where they carry him away. It seems to suggest stamina, &
'will not give up'.

Two days later, a six-page letter responded to rolls 18–24. A half-page
sample:

Motorbikes and truck sequence – All shots are good. I think you will find one part
of one roll has some vertical streaks in it, & I think they are in the orginal – but they
are either so minor that in a cut action-sequence they wouldn't matter, or there
were so many takes you could easily cut round them. (I didn't bother examining
more closely, because this was the way I felt.) The *near accident* shot is very effective. I felt my stomach tighten when it happened. If it is psychologically all right to
include it in the film (say just before they *do* decide to pass) it would work fine. But
maybe when we feel the whole shape of that sequence it might be a wrong shock
OK either way anyhow.

Low recalls that some filmmakers thought that this kind of response to
rushes was picky. 'But I found it very useful. When you couldn't see your
own rushes, it was a great comfort to know that they had come out all right
technically or that they were doing what you wanted. The encouragement
was important, too.'
From the beginning of the project, Low wanted some personal commentary by Standing Alone. But the way he initially went about it almost
sabotaged the project and served, Low confesses, 'as a lesson in ethics for
me.' As recounted by Fraser Taylor in *Standing Alone: A Contemporary
Blackfoot Indian*, Standing Alone agreed to spend a day with Low talking
about himself and his life. This, he thought, was simply exploratory. They
met in a motel room. A case of beer was on the table. Standing Alone drank
one after another, while Low, a non-drinker, nursed a single bottle. As the

day wore on, Standing Alone got drunk. His tongue loosened. Later they went out to eat. When they returned, Standing Alone went to the bathroom, where he discovered a tape recorder, which was connected to a microphone under the table where they had been sitting and talking.

Standing Alone accepted Low's apology. Low hadn't planned to use the material. His aim was to let people at the Film Board hear what Standing Alone sounded like.

As the editing of the film neared completion, the Film Board agreed to try Standing Alone as the narrator. But, Daly recalls, 'we realized we couldn't really do what Colin wanted without having Pete involved in the writing. We got Pete here. It was understood that Stanley would write something not for Pete to speak, but to give Pete an idea of what was needed.

'Stanley was reading to Pete at the movieola. After each paragraph, he'd ask Pete, "How was that?" Pete would say, "All right." Finally, there was a paragraph which Stanley was *sure* Pete wouldn't like. "What about that?" "All right." Stanley said, "No, it's *not* all right. I *know* it's not all right. What's wrong with it?" Pete paused and said, "Well, there's only one thing wrong with it. It isn't true."' After that, Standing Alone was involved in shaping the thought of each passage.

The film's most memorable image is its final one. It is a shot of a huge, fiery red sun setting behind an oil derrick. The shot exists thanks to the persistence of Low and Spotton, but it is a setting sun only because of the simple magic of editing.

For days, Low and Spotton rose well before daybreak and positioned themselves for the shot. But each morning, clouds hid the sun as it rose. After about a week of this, they finally got the shot they wanted. Low loved the shot and had intended to use it at the beginning of the film. But during the editing it gradually made its way back towards the end of the film.

Daly explains how this came about. 'All of Colin's early morning sequences had been shot in soft pearly grey light or were in full daylight, looking *away* from the sun. So this magnificent shot of a blood-red sun and black derrick never fitted into the colour atmosphere or mood of the action sequences.

'For the end of the film he had this marvellous sequence of the gathered clans taking part in the communal social dances in the afternoon ranging into the setting sun. Either for that purpose, or for other reasons, he had got wonderful shots of wild animals and tame animals, etched in burning reddish light from the setting sun, their dark figures set off against a nearly night sky. We used them there, as if they were naturally listening, or drawn out by curiosity to see, their human brothers and sisters honouring the powers that be.

'I guess Colin had been so tied to the experience of getting a shot of the rising sun that he had not thought of using it as the setting sun. But I had no such ties, not having been there, and being used to looking at shots for all their various possible relationships. So it found its perfect place there at the end, in the same brilliant fiery light, at a point where the title itself was packed with most meaning by all the events and information accumulated in the course of the film.

'I'm sure nobody stopped to "think" about all that, but I'm also sure that the shot had a much more profound impact in that place that it found for itself.'

The excitement of getting and placing such visually rich imagery made filmmakers dissatisfied with the limitations they faced in getting comparable sound imagery. Commentary or music, usually both, did almost all the work of the soundtrack in the films. Synchronized location sounds were sparse or absent. There was no lip-sync of any importance in these films.

The limitations were mainly technical. The equipment for sync-sound location filming was too awkward to do justice to both picture and sound. To get good pictures, the camera had to be mobile; to get good sound, it had to be quiet, preferably still. One available sync-sound shooting device was an Auricon camera that recorded sound directly onto the film – but twenty-six frames ahead of the picture. At any cut, the sound extended twenty-six frames into the next shot, at which point the sound for the second shot would commence. This severely limited editing options, making fine-cutting almost impossible.

While Unit B itself generally avoided single-system technology, the NFB was using it for news magazine programs for television – then a new outlet for NFB films. Daly remembers being challenged to solve a problem that another unit using the Auricon system had encountered. 'It was an item on a Canadian aircraft carrier, showing the process of planes taking off and returning, intercut with the host of the series talking to us while these other activities were going on. The problem was that *all the time* in the background of just about *all the material*, plane sounds were heard rising up, coming down, increasing in volume or decreasing, and curving around in patterns – all much more audible than the narrator. The sounds were too frequently more annoying than the pictures were interesting.

'The solution I found was to make a chart of all the patterns of sound movement, and then see how many "down" movements at the end of a shot could be cut to another "down" movement at the beginning of another shot, where the sound would change direction to accommodate a third shot, and so on.

'This method required shifting around the order of the shots, but there were enough choices so that much of it could seem to have been meant to go together. Afterwards, people didn't notice the problem, having been a little bit habituated to hearing the late sound cut. But I never wanted to have to cut another item like that!'

But new developments in sync-sound filming were occurring rapidly in the late 1950s – at the Film Board and elsewhere – and Unit B filmmakers, led by Koenig and Kroitor, wanted to take advantage of these developments aesthetically. In 1957, when *City of Gold* was being completed, *Circle of the Sun* was being shot, and *Universe* was being extended, Kroitor and Koenig proposed a series of documentaries that would attempt the unscripted, mobile camera, high-ratio approach that would come to dominate documentary filmmaking by the 1960s and is commonplace today. Sometimes it is called *cinéma vérité*, especially when interaction between the filmmakers and the subjects is featured; sometimes it is called 'direct cinema,' particularly when unobtrusive observation (or the illusion of it) predominates. The Film Board called its initial version of it *Candid Eye*, but the term has not entered common parlance. Although the distinctions between the two more common terms are sometimes blurry, 'direct cinema' seems more descriptive of *Candid Eye*'s intentions than *cinéma vérité*.

In a 1967 publication of La Cinémathèque canadienne edited by André Pâquet, *How to Make or Not to Make a Canadian Film*, Koenig recalled the beginnings of *Candid Eye*:

This is roughly what we proposed: Record life as it happens, unscripted and unrehearsed; capture it in sync sound, indoors or out, without asking it to pose or repeat its lines; edit it into moving films that would make the audience laugh and cry (preferably both at the same time); show it on TV to millions and change the world by making people realize that life is real, beautiful and meaningful, etc. Management was understandably puzzled by this proposal.

Koenig and his colleagues had found inspiration and guidance for what they had in mind in a book of photographs by Henri Cartier-Bresson, *The Decisive Moment*, which Koenig had been given as a present. Koenig was as impressed by the author's preface as he he was by the photographs:

It spelled out, word for word, what we must do to make the kind of films we talked so much about. I think all of us studied the book: Roman Kroitor, Tom Daly, Terry Filgate, Colin Low. And I ... think it played a large part in [Mulholland's] decision to let us go ahead and try a pilot film.'

Koenig quoted Cartier-Bresson's preface at length. For Cartier-Bresson, meaningful photography – photography that captured the essence of life – involved 'a joint operation of the brain, the eye, and the heart,' the aims of which were 'to depict the content of some event which is in the process of unfolding, and to communicate impressions.' Photography was the only medium that 'fixes forever the precise and transitory instant.' The task of photography was to perceive reality and almost simultaneously record it. While photography should be unobtrusive and non-manipulative, form was as important as spontaneity. Form was not to be imposed but was to develop organically: 'Composition must have its own inevitability about it.' Because photography depended so deeply on other people, 'a false relationship, a wrong word or attitude, can ruin everything.' Furthermore, the photographer was himself part of the subject, and this demanded that photographers 'be lucid toward what is going on in the world, and honest about what we feel.' Finally, Cartier-Bresson posited a unity between life and the act of photography, proclaiming that 'the discovery of oneself is made concurrently with the discovery of the world around us which can mold us, but which also can be affected by us.'

The desired unity between life and photography implied a redefinition of the role of the cameraman in the Film Board documentary. At the time, cameramen were not part of units. They were technical staff and were considered, by management, as largely interchangeable. In a memorandum dated 21 April 1958, Koenig argued that cameramen should be incorporated into the *Candid Eye* staff. The type of filming required special talent and inclination; productions would benefit artistically from cameramen's involvement in the planning and editing stages; cameramen would 'be much more creative if they feel that they are participating in a whole production'; constant changes in personnel entailed constant re-education; only cameramen who felt committed to the new style of documentary could be asked to contribute the necessary overtime hours.

Other role definitions were relaxed for the series' pilot film, *The Days Before Christmas* (1958). All filmmakers who were interested in the idea were invited to join the production team. Kroitor and Koenig acted as producers, the film had three credited directors, and its two main cameramen were French-Canadians.

By any reasonable standard, *The Days Before Christmas* was a successful film. It has a consistently detached, observational style and holds together as a mosaic of holiday impressions and moods. Images of familiar activities – choirs rehearsing, parents shopping – are intercut with some darker ones, such as a pair of guards whose guns are drawn while bags of money are loaded into a truck. Many of the images are fleeting ones of anonymous people doing nothing extraordinary: a woman wiping melted snow off her glasses; a driver waiting; a guard yawning; grimly determined shoppers trudging through the snow. A startling transition occurs near the end of the film and sums it up. Schoolchildren, dressed as cherubs, are performing a school play. We see a man who appears to be in the back of the auditorium. He looks wistful, as if remembering his own childhood or regretting something. We assume that it is the play that provokes his mood, because the voices of the children have continued over the image. Then we discover that the man is sitting in the bar of a nearly deserted bus depot, late at night (presumably Christmas Eve), as a janitor mops the floor.

But the film also raised some problems that have vexed direct cinema since its discovery. Can the camera be unobtrusive without being voyeuristic? If it openly intrudes, does it also invade? Does its presence alter the supposed authenticity of the material? And how can a meaningful unity – something deeper than just an impressionistic, 'slice of life' structure – be forged from material shot without a script and in response to unfolding events?

In several respects, another well-known *Candid Eye* film, *The Backbreaking Leaf* (1959), seems to have been a reaction against the detachment of *The Days Before Christmas*. The film depicts the tobacco harvest in southern Ontario. The crop has to be picked by hand, one leaf at a time, then quickly tied and put into a drying kiln. Recurrent sequences of picking and drying emphasize the gruelling nature of the work. The resulting rough-edged rhythmic structure is much more forceful than is the serene mosaic of *The Days Before Christmas*. And the photography is more participatory. There are more close-ups of people, the camera's presence is acknowledged, subjects speak to the audience, and the director's off-camera questions are sometimes heard. And in contrast to *The Days Before Christmas*, the film had only one director, Terence Macartney-Filgate (one of the credited directors on the pilot film), who also did the camerawork and recorded the sound.

But the nitty-gritty, closely observed material presented an editing challenge. As Daly remembers it, Macartney-Filgate's photography, remarkable for its toughness and intimacy, 'was mostly shots of tobacco picking and tying and *more* picking and tying. How to make some kind of dramatic development out of all the same kind of material? We solved the problem in the editing room by selecting a different aspect of the activity for each sequence, and withholding that aspect from the other sequences, so each one was "fresh." The first sequence – on the morning of the first day – was a descriptive one, using straightforward shots to show clearly the various activities, how they were carried out, and how they related in sequence. After a break for lunch, the second sequence used all the tough, more intensive and repetitive material to show the physical demands, fatigue, and pain the work engendered. A third tobacco-picking sequence was made of a beautiful early-morning mood combined with the physical chill of having to work in the icy dew. And a fourth took advantage of a thunderstorm interrupting the work.'

The intimacy in *The Back-breaking Leaf* was essentially physical. When direct cinema achieved a strongly emotional intimacy, as it did in *Blood and Fire* (1958), it entered now-familiar ethically ambiguous territory. The film follows a Salvation Army band around on its marches, interviews its leaders, and observes its religious services. The film's climactic and controversial scene occurs at a service when two men decide to step forward and 'come to Christ.' A Salvation Army officer kneels with each man, puts an arm around him, and talks very softly with him. One man is in tears. The camera moves in close. Although the words cannot be heard, the man's anguish is uncomfortably apparent. He looks at the camera, and he seems to resent its presence.

Daly remembers that those opposed to the use of the close-up objected 'on the grounds that it was painful to the person concerned and invaded his privacy. Those of us chiefly responsible for the film were of the opinion that it was the one piece of evidence that showed that the Salvation Army actually *affected* people. All the other material simply showed their activities, descriptively. And it so happened that each of us had experienced some such moral crisis of our own, and that the sense of relief and self-worth from coming through it, with help, showed that such moments were not "evil" or to be avoided, but needed to be understood as moments of inner growth. So we stood by the shot, merely being very careful about its length.

'One secretary was most insistent that it was "wrong" to use it, wrong to invade anyone's privacy like that. I happened to ask her if it would have been okay if she had known it was acted rather than actual. She said yes. I asked if, in fact, the actors looked like these two men, and everything looked exactly as it did, only she knew that it was acted, would she still feel it was okay? She said yes. So I said, "Then the only thing you object to is the reality of it, that it is not imaginary, which is exactly what we found convincing about it, and what we have been trying to reach: the look and sound of reality – of real people and real feelings."'

Even the reality of such feelings soon came into question. If the spontaneity, the authenticity, extolled and perhaps captured by still-photographer Cartier-Bresson could be achieved in direct cinema, it had to be in spite of the inevitably altering presence of a film crew. Was the man's anguish in *Blood and Fire* intensified by a sense of humiliation at being filmed? A viewer of the film has no way to tell, and the filmmakers couldn't have known for sure even if they had tried to find out.

Thus very early *Candid Eye* had encountered – in other films as well as these – what persist as the probably three most difficult challenges in direct cinema: structuring unscripted material; achieving intimacy unexploitatively; and acknowledging filmmaking's inevitably manipulative aspect. Each problem presents difficulties of its own; films dealing satisfactorily with all three are rare. To a degree, the Unit B filmmakers who continued working with direct cinema skirted or minimized these problems by choosing subjects somewhat removed from the grittier realities and less vulnerable than tobacco pickers or down-and-outers. Several films were portraits of successful artists such as Glenn Gould and Igor Stravinsky. Meanwhile, the direct-cinema approach gained wider acceptance in the Film Board and increasingly was incorporated into documentaries as just another technique.

Nevertheless, the main instigators of direct cinema at the Film Board eventually collaborated on a film that achieved a harmony of spontaneity and structure that approaches what Koenig, Kroitor, and Daly saw in Cartier-Bresson's photographs. They did it with a documentary portrait that is incisive without being unduly invasive, and one which also acknowledges its inevitable manipulations.

Lonely Boy is a portrait of Paul Anka, then a nineteen-year-old entertainer from Ottawa who had achieved phenomenal success in the United States. The film begins with a shot from inside a speeding car as it passes a billboard advertising Paul Anka's appearance at the Steel Pier in Atlantic City. On the soundtrack, Anka sings the title song, the first two lines of which are 'I'm just a lonely boy, lonely and blue, / I'm all alone, I've got nothing to do.' After some shots establishing Atlantic City's boardwalk and nightclub areas, Anka, inside, walks on-stage to be greeted by shrieking teenage girls as the song concludes. Following the film's title is an outside scene of young girls shouting for Anka and, when he emerges, thrusting photos at him for him to autograph. Interspersed with such shots are interviews with several girls: 'He's so nice, oh I love him, he's a god'; 'He's so sweet, so cute, I like him'; 'I've got five hundred and fifty pictures of Paul Anka all over my room.' Then the film's only substantial passage of narration introduces the film as an examination of 'the astonishing transformation of an entertainer into an idol, worshipped by millions of fans around the world. This is a candid look at Paul Anka, from both sides of the footlights.'

The rest of the film counterposes frontstage and backstage scenes of Anka on his Atlantic City tour. The frontstage sequences show a confident Paul Anka reducing young girls to paroxysms of ecstasy and yearning. The backstage material samples the things involved in the making of a star: Anka racing into his room and quickly dressing for a performance; Anka describing his transformation from an awkward, overweight, unappealing youth to an attractive young man with sex appeal; Anka's manager saying that it's 'no secret' that Anka has had a nose job; Anka in an empty theatre tentatively rehearsing a new song; and a hilarious bit of schmoozing with the owner of the Copacabana nightclub in New York City. The film's last frontstage image shows Anka putting his arm around a fan's shoulder as he sings to her and the crowd; the camera starts tight on his hand, which is extended in the manner of the hand of God in Michelangelo's painting in the Sistine Chapel, then tracks up to Anka's face.

The film then cuts back to the opening highway scene, only now the camera is inside the car with Anka and his small entourage. As his manager prattles on about logistic details involved in the next engagement, someone in the back seat leans forward to massage Anka's shoulders. Anka looks weary and depressed. The man in the back seat asks out loud, 'Where's my wife and daughter? What am I doing here?' Annoyed, Anka responds testily, 'You know what you're doing here,' laying heavy stress on 'know' and inflecting 'here' to turn his response into a reprimand that contains a hint of a threat. 'I know, I know,' the man quickly agrees. An entirely new dimension of meaning has been added to the title song, which comes back on the track before the film ends with a long take of the roadside from inside the car.

The film exhibits the visual characteristics that became standard direct-cinema signals of authenticity (and, often, excuses for loose construction): interviews with off-camera directors; off-camera comments by the filmmakers; jumpcuts within interviews; an occasionally shaky camera; subjects reacting to the camera; the camera sometimes apparently wandering in search of a scene's centre of interest; microphones in the shot. And yet the film coheres in its details as well as thematically. The frontstage-backstage transitions often are accomplished in a visually logical manner; after Anka rushes out of his dressing-room, for example, tying his tie, he next appears walking confidently on-stage to his waiting fans (although the shade of his suit changes from dark to light). Frequently, though, the filmmakers manage to relate the words or theme of a song that Anka is performing or practising to the sequence that follows it. The line he is working on in his new song is about 'the wee small hours of the morning, when all the world is still'; the next sequence is an interview with his manager, who says that he and Paul often talk 'into the wee hours of the morning about his gift.' Onstage he sings 'Thanks for helping my career get underway' to his fans; this is followed by an interview in which Anka talks about the sexual basis of his appeal. During the important Copacabana engagement, after a performance in which he sings 'What a feeling, what a glow, / What a thrill for me to say hello,' we meet the club's heavily jowled, crusty, cigar-smoking owner. Soon Anka joins him, flatters him, gives him first a gift of jewellery and then a large portrait of Anka himself. 'Beautiful,' the owner says several times, as if he hopes repetition might conceal his lack of enthusiasm.

What finally makes the film so entertaining, however, is the way in which the filmmakers integrate moments of reflexivity into the film. Early on, as he rushes into the dressing-room, Anka seems momentarily taken aback when he notices the presence of the crew. At the Copacabana, one of documentary's funniest instances of demystification occurs when the crew interviews the owner. He is sitting in an open booth, his back to the dining area. At the scene's beginning, he looks puzzled, as if he doesn't quite understand the purpose of what the crew has just asked of him. 'You want the waiters to move around a little bit? All right,' he says, compliantly if not with full comprehension. He turns to look off-camera. 'Bruno!' 'Yessir,' Bruno responds smartly from off-camera. The owner then instructs Bruno, 'Tell the waiters to, like, move around, like they got action.' The interview proceeds, and soon waiters, somewhat uncertainly, are passing back and forth behind the booth. Later, when Anka kisses the owner, something shakes the camera. From off-camera, Kroitor asks them to kiss again, causing the two men to become self-conscious, a condition they mask with feigned hilarity. These instances of reflexivity are self-deprecating and funny, they appeared years before reflexivity became a prescription for demystifying film's relation to 'reality,' and they lack the awkward sanctimony so frequent in attempts by later filmmakers to incorporate reflexive gestures.

The unity of material and structure in *Lonely Boy* lacks the lyrical grace of *Corral*, the lapidary clarity of *Universe*, the deceptive fluidity of *City of Gold*, the explicitness of *Circle of the Sun*. Unscripted, ultraobservational material renders those qualities all but unreachable. As *Candid Eye* developed (and continued under other names), 'we found,' Daly recalls, 'that in structuring a candid, unscripted film, continuity depended far more on emotional factors than on logical connections or physical or time sequence. Logic could make it meaningful, but too often dry and boring. Physical and time sequence make the continuity clear but obvious, and the mind often races ahead unsatisfied. In *Lonely Boy*, a very good balance of all these elements seems to have been reached, without any sense of being limited by the fixed half-hour format. I was finally convinced we had made a candid film "in the round" when we got such different reactions to it – from "how could you put out such a blatant commercial for them" to "how did you ever get away with that." It is one of the few films I have ever been involved in making that I can still look at without impatience.'

These now-classic Unit B films epitomize a faith in documentary art that perhaps (in retrospect) could flourish only briefly, at a high point of aesthetic and technical innovation but before old cultural assumptions about the relationship between images and reality gave way to widespread scepticism about knowledge, meaning, and value. Each film – even *Lonely Boy* – was a conscious construction that its makers nevertheless believed to represent truth. Each was an imaginative arrangement that assumed a relationship of correspondence between its images and their referents. Each, to varying degrees, affirmed and embraced 'reality' as it is encountered or imagined. The filmmakers sought a unity of spontaneity and structure. In this way, they tried to maximize simultaneously the two main terms of Grierson's early definition of documentary as 'the creative treatment of actuality.' They explored the world as openly as filmmakers had ever done and yet sought and found imaginative forms for their researches.

None of the members of the team thought of it quite that way. Jackson, a pragmatist at heart, liked to identify Unit B's distinguishing characteristic as 'an attitude towards the craft' loath to accept a second-rate or second-hand solution to a filmmaking problem. Kroitor was an adventurer whose uncharted territory was aesthetic structure but who also had a flair for technical innovation. Low was blessed with an intuitive lyricism but was disinclined to intellectualize about it. For Koenig, the aim of filmmaking was to show that 'life is true, fine, and full of meaning.'

It might seem that, for Daly, the films represented the kind of structural thinking he had discovered in Ouspensky and Gurdjieff. In the introduction to *A New Model of the Universe*, Ouspensky wrote that the 'esoteric method ... connects every given thing, however small it may be, with the whole.' *Universe* embodies this principle thoroughly. *City of Gold*, with its three waves of time and the almost imperceptible seams that join them, has an element of this impulse. Concentric circles constitute the chief metaphor in *Circle of the Sun*. The sun and its shadows provide the only spatial orientation in *Corral*. Even *Lonely Boy* has an element of this drive for connectedness, its title echoed in the film's title song, in some of its images, in Paul Anka's character, and in the film's framing device.

In his own summation of 'what our films were *for me*,' Daly says, 'I think the nearest I can get to it is that I tried, in so far as it was in my capacity to do it, to see each film as an organic unity, touching all sides of people, and hopefully containing at least one "moment of truth" when the viewer might wake up to a greater awarenesss of "the wonder of it all." Oddly enough, we often do not take the time to do that in the midst of "real life."'

Perhaps one reason the films seem so rich and vital despite their rigorous structure is that the 'given thing' is rarely diminished in importance in order to fit some preconceived whole. 'I was never trying to make the material fit any other form than the one I could see in it. For that I had to empty my mind of all other thoughts, words, "philosophies," expectations – even the original script or outline in cases where the material did not match it. The Gurdjieff teaching, in its *practice*, had the effect of sensitizing me more and more to all the variety of connections and uses that the individual shots had in them.'

Daly believes that any resemblance between the world as depicted in Unit B films and the world as described by Gurdjieff and Ouspensky derives from a common pursuit of truth over which neither the philosophers nor the films have any privileged claim: 'In my view, it is possible that if you looked as closely into various branches of Buddhism or Hinduism or Islam, you might just as easily notice parallels among those. The same with Socrates and Plato. The same with the medieval cathedral builders.

'The fact is that each and all of these systems are expressing their vision of the same real universe, and in so far as they express the truth, it is the *same truth* they are talking about, in different forms and terminologies.

'Gurdjieff has no "monopoly" on the truth, nor has any other. It so happens that his system was derived to help include Eastern thought and practice in terms more understandable and accessible to the West. For me personally, his teaching has allowed me to understand much more in these other systems, and see more precisely how things are related, in many cases with a kind of "bifocal vision" when comparing two together, and sometimes even "multi-focal vision." But the truth is not on the pages, it is more realizable in moments of intense awareness.'

And of course each film was the product of a team. Besides the Unit B regulars, each project drew in additional members on an ad hoc basis. Daly's summation of the main contributions to *Universe* epitomizes how these teams operated. 'The data, facts, arrangement of things were given by the astronomers. Colin had to try to match the space effects as closely as he could to their descriptions. The observatory people cooperated marvellously, but the lighting difficulties were wonderfully overcome by Denis Gillson. Wally Gentleman provided technical wizardry. Roman, among other things, found the plodding, logical unfolding of the order of the original script too dull and predictable. He rearranged the order so that you never lose contact between man on earth and wherever the film has reached in outer space. Wolf shot the "planet earth" exteriors always so that the solar radiation was in evidence. Stanley put the facts and feeling of all of us into words for the soundtrack. Eldon wrote music responding to the sense of wonder intended by the images. No one tried to make the film fit anything else but the givens.

'Even the narrator seemed to fall into step. As I remember it, Douglas Rain was so good professionally that, when he had done the whole text once through to his own satisfaction, he said, "Is that it?" and was ready to get up and leave. But when Roman made it clear that *he* was not satisfied yet, it seemed to touch Rain's professional pride in the right way, and his changed state of emotion brought forth the tones of voice that still can bring shivers down my spine when I hear them today.'

Daly identifies the central motivation of the team at its best as 'a desire not to be separate,' an urge to combine the specific talents of several people so as to create something greater than any of the filmmakers alone could do, to orchestrate the elements of film into larger harmonies. 'None of us,' says Koenig, 'was a raving genius. All of us were in some way incomplete. Tom knew that and encouraged us to work together. It was the "lame man, blind man" thing. We all compensated each other for our shortcomings. Nobody ever said it was "my film." It was always "our film."'

Yet it was not an easy harmony, even after the confrontation in Daly's apartment. In 1976, more than a decade after the end of the unit system at the Film Board, Koenig and Daly were reminiscing about Unit B. Koenig suggested that the key to Unit B's success had something to do with the creative management of tension – much of it caused by Kroitor. Kroitor was as important a mentor for Koenig as Daly was. Kroitor had a master's in philosophy. His intelligence equalled Daly's. But while Daly's mind was expansive and accommodating, Kroitor's was aggressively critical. 'Roman,' Koenig says, 'would thrash me with his logic. Once I was on the verge of tears. I took it from him, though – thank God.'

A few days after talking with Daly, Koenig elaborated his idea in a two-page typewritten memo to Daly. Over the top of it, Koenig scrawled, 'Tom, this is a very glib summary of that thought I talked to you about. It really needs more thought to do history the justice it deserves. Anyway here is something. Please destroy it if you think you should.' The memo:

For all the rosy light cast on old Unit 'B' by the haze of memory and nostalgia it should be remembered that it had a very tough strand running through it. It's this strand, in my opinion, which made it functional (like the wires inside Michelins). And what it consisted of was opposition and conflict! What made the unit function under such apparently self-destructive impulses was that Tom Daly, our Producer, accepted this conflict and, intuitively, used it as a source of energy for the group.

The polarities within Unit 'B' were best expressed by the two major personalities within it: Tom Daly and Roman Kroitor. The personalities of these two men were almost diametrically opposed to each other. Tom, the conservative, pragmatic, technically and artistically accomplished, apparently unemotional administrator; raised in the traditions of Upper Canada College; apprenticed to film aristocrats like Grierson and Legg; always conscious of his obligations to pass on tradition and to serve the public's needs. In other words, truly Anglo and the nearest thing we have in Canada to an aristocrat.

Roman, on the other hand, was a rebel (in his way); an accurate but devastating critic; a Saskatchewan Ukrainian – therefore highly emotional; a brilliant student at University (a gold medal winner); a highly creative filmmaker without (at that time) a full technical knowledge, but learning fast; very nervy and, at times, disrespectful of the opinions of 'older and wiser' heads; with long hair when it was unfashionable and a life style which bordered on the 'Bohemian'. He was the object of envious ridicule by some but, like Tom Daly, he was dedicated to the public good (although he saw it from another angle).

Well, these two personalities clashed, mostly in discreet ways, sometimes not so discreetly. Tom certainly could have gotten rid of this Kroitor guy in about five minutes and he would have been applauded for doing so. But he didn't. Instead he helped to train him and supported him in films which were, to many, very far out. At times he fought for Roman against management even though this went entirely against his own traditional upbringing (and, sometimes, against his better judgement). So, to make a long point short, it was between the polarities of these two men that the strand I mentioned earlier was stretched, and to such a fine tautness that all the rest of us could balance on it. (Often we fell off, but that was our own fault.)

Tom Daly understood this principle of opposites (perhaps based on the old 'her Majesty's loyal opposition' principle) and used it wisely and well to turn conflict into useable energy. I think that Tom's understanding and application of this principle taught us as much, if not more, about filmmaking than his knowledge of editing. It taught us that life is made up of tensions and opposites and connections which, if understood, can create a lot of strength in individuals and in their community (and Unit 'B' *was* a community). Finally it came to us (very slowly) that film, like life, works the same way – that between the beginning and the end stretches that tight rope on which all the characters dance.

Anyway, that's what I think was behind (or through) the old Unit 'B', the animating principle, the thing that made the balancing act possible: a wire stretched between two strong points.

For Daly, the balancing of tensions within the group resembled the ordering of shots and sounds into an effective film. Both, in turn, depended on a degree of harmony among the warring aspects of the psyche. Moments of pure harmony were rare. But they occurred now and then, and the one that Daly remembers the most vividly involved his temperamental opposite, Kroitor. 'We were making a film called *Farm Calendar* [1955]. It was a sponsored film for the Department of Agriculture in Ottawa. The next morning, the sponsors were coming to see the cutting copy, and we had enormous work to do. We had worked all day, and without consulting each other we just somehow *knew* that we would go on working through the evening as long as seemed sensible. And a kind of working rapport began to operate after we had been out for supper. I was sitting at the machine, doing the physical cutting, but we were making decisions together. Somehow at the end of each sequence, a clue to what to do with the next one arose, and gave us a kind of momentum to work on, and we went to the next sequence. And again, somehow at each join with the next sequence, a clear clue arose and – it's very strange for this kind of thing to happen – but it *kept going* like that, and we never *looked* at the time or *thought* about the time. We just went on working. And I know that eleven o'clock went by, twelve o'clock went by, one, two, four, five, six. We were full of energy the whole night. It kept revitalizing at the beginning of each new sequence with this exciting clue of what to do with the next thing. And around seven o'clock we reached the last sequence. And somehow at the very last sequence, at around eight o'clock, we didn't know what to do and we suddenly felt tired and the work was at an end.

'There is a characteristic of being on beam with this finer energy in oneself and being in relationship with somebody. If you have to stop and talk about it, you've lost it, but while it's there, somehow both people are tuned in on it at the same time. And as long as it stays like that, somehow you are working more totally, and not only separately, but really together. This is simply a case where it lasted for hours. It's not a great and important *film*, but to me it was a great and important *evening*, both for work and for development of relationships.'

Kroitor, who confesses, 'It was probably my fault that the editing wasn't finished,' remembers 'both the night and the intensity. It was enjoyable. But for me it wasn't any more than that.'

Kroitor's lifelong reserve with regard to Daly is rooted in the very perception about Daly that inspires Kroitor's deep and abiding respect. 'I'm generally sceptical,' Kroitor says, 'about people who philosophize about "the meaning of life" and how one should live. Most people who philosophize about life don't in fact live the philosophy. They deceive themselves. But Tom is rare. He would actually listen to what people told him, and he worked very, very hard to change himself. So his philosophy did in fact change his life.

'He has struggled his whole life long with a predisposition to be analytical, rational. And he has overcome that. He's more rounded. My problem is ... I always feel there's a kind of ... *limping* behind it. The effort is so apparent.'

3

What Gets in the Way

From 1954 through 1964, Unit B produced more than a hundred films across a range of genres. While *Paul Tomkowicz: Street-railway Switchman, Corral, City of Gold, Universe, Circle of the Sun*, and *Lonely Boy* seem to embody most fully a consistent and original Unit B aesthetic, many other Unit B films were distinctive in various ways. Guy L. Coté's *Roughnecks: The Story of Oil Drillers* (1960) combined Eugene Boyko's sensual and stark photography with the subject's ostensible voice-over in portraying the life of roustabouts drilling for oil in the Canadian wilderness. *Emergency Ward* (1959), a *Candid Eye* film by William Greaves, conveys moments of human misery primarily through off-camera action. The amiably anti-American *Days of Whiskey Gap* (1961), directed by Colin Low, uses for commentary the recollections of several old-timers. Low's *The Hutterites* (1964) was the first film allowed by the Hutterite community in northeastern Alberta. While the film shows the sect's authoritarianism, uniformity of thought, and austerity, it also conveys some softer impressions: children engaged in rough horseplay; a woman telling a story to a child whose hair she is affectionately braiding; and a young woman's hope chest, which contains a valentine, a Christmas card, and lace.

I Was a Ninety-pound Weakling (1960), by Wolf Koenig and Georges Dufaux, is a funny and prescient look at obsession with physical fitness. In one scene, an exercise equipment promoter, while working out on a motorized cycling machine, praises the machine's ability to provide non-exerting exercise. Another interviewee predicts an eventual proliferation of home exercising equipment. *The Living Machine* (1962), by Koenig and Roman Kroitor, explores the emerging field of cybernetics, and, from that, ponders the nature of man.

Two films directed by John Feeney lovingly depict the close relationship between art and life in Inuit culture. In *The Living Stone* (1958), a story narrated by an Inuk helps establish a unity among Inuit art (in this case, stone carving), mythology, and approach to life. Feeney's *Eskimo Artist: Kenojuak* (1964) pursues the subject further with contrasting metaphors of light and shadow pervading the film.

The interior scenes in these films required a degree of artifice reminiscent of *The Longhouse People*. The colour film stock available to Feeney, Daly explains, 'required very much light. The lights we had were very hot. The natural warmth in an Eskimo snow igloo, with perhaps an ice window for light from outside, or a seal-oil lamp in the centre, is a little above freezing in the centre of the space, and below freezing at the walls – otherwise the whole structure would melt. The light needed in order to get good shots inside such an igloo would melt it quickly.

'Feeney's solution to this problem was to make an artificial igloo out of chunks of plastic foam cut and shaped by the Eskimos and built by them into a true igloo construction that was built right near sources of electric power in Cape Dorset. The Eskimos loved it.' The contrivance had an unexpected bonus. Filmed from the outside, 'it gave the same kind of effect of filtered luminosity as a real igloo on a dark night, before the seal-oil lamp was extinguished.'

The Jolifou Inn (1955), directed by Colin Low and edited by Daly, portrays the Dutch-born artist Cornelius Krieghoff strictly through his many paintings of Canadian life. The camera enters each painting and then films it as if it were present in the scene depicted. If the camera is tight on the image of a man pointing, it pans to what he is pointing at; it tilts down with falling snow; it follows a line of people entering a house. Daly's editing complements this technique in spite of the fact that 'Krieghoff made very few large-scale canvases which could be used as "long-shots" to give distance and breadth to his images. His favourite and most popular subjects were often detailed moments of habitant life, which produced the effect of a great many "medium-shots" without a corresponding amount of long-shots and close-ups. As a result, the structure had to be made less by developing the action within the paintings themselves – as in the manner of *City of Gold*, two years later – and more in grouping them around a progression of narration themes, which added breadth to what was not explicit in the paintings themselves.'

A Is for Architecture (1960), co-directed by Gerald Budner and Robert Verrall, uses colour drawings to survey the history of architecture. The film interprets each era of great architecture as the reflection of the central ideas of the culture that produced it. The narrator says that the Greeks, being 'more interested in living this life than the next,' placed figures of their gods close to man, and they carved pillars to please the eye. The Romans, a 'race of conquerors,' invented the triumphal arch. Medieval Christians built churches whose 'pointed arches soar up,' whose 'slender, vertical lines ... lead men's eyes upward, to heaven.'

Daly attributes the liveliness of the film's static drawings to 'Verrall's inventiveness in adapting the limits of the animation camera and apparatus of the time to the more sophisticated needs of the human eye's curiosity. For the richly rendered section on medieval cathedrals, he was limited by our panning mechanism, which could only move in a straight line in the same field. But by carefully distorting a flat drawing he was able to give us the impression of standing at the centre of the cathedral floor, looking towards the west wall, then sweeping the eye upward and overhead and beyond, and then down again to rest on the eastern half of the interior, with the choir and east windows ablaze with colour.'

Following upon *The Romance of Transportation*, Unit B continued to make mildly subversive animation films. *My Financial Career* (1962), directed by Grant Munro and Gerald Potterton, was an adaptation of a popular short story by Stephen Leacock. In it, a shy man recounts his first and last attempt to deposit money in a bank and open a checking account. Underlying the film's comic tone is a suggestion of the power of institutions to strip individuals of their dignity. Daly remembers that the humour was almost lost when 'a "name" narrator was engaged to record the text. Unfortunately, the result wasn't very funny. In desperation, we called Stanley Jackson in to record a guide track that might help the narrator to take fire. That effort was not successful, but Jackson's own recording was. The whole roomful listening to it laughed themselves sick. So Stanley's guide track – cleaned up a bit – was used as the final narration. Even the slightly amateurish elements in it made the Leacock character sound a hundred times more like a real person. Nobody could tell a story with more empathy than Stanley Jackson. I remember having the purest delight in slightly trimming the sound and picture for the final, final editing to make the timing flow just right.'

The unit's most memorable animated film was made for the federal Department of Labour to promote winter employment. The film, *It's a Crime* (1957), was directed by Koenig from a story-line by Kroitor. In the film, a safe-cracker narrates a tale of woe. When economic activity slows down in the Canadian winter, the safes are empty. He turns to robbing private homes. In one, he discovers some old photographs suggesting that in a less industrial era Canadians became used to working hard in the summer and waiting out the winter. He concludes that the solution to Canada's problem – and his – lies in breaking this old habit. He takes the initiative himself by using modern technology to print counterfeit money. The film is fast-paced and irreverent. In part a parody of Carol Reed's *The Third Man*, the film also pokes fun at the Film Board itself: eluding the police, the thief slips into a theatre, where he chances upon 'a most absorbing movie,' which turns out to be a spoof of the conventional Film Board sponsored film, its narrator extolling in thunderous alliteration the development of the Canadian North:

TODAY, SCIENCE has given us TECHNOLOGY ... the power to WHIP NATURE into SUBJUGATION! We are TAMING the TREACHEROUS TREASURE-LADEN NORTH!! DEFYING the FURY of our SOLEMN CLIMATE!!! CONQUERING our SPACE ITSELF and its OUTRAAAA-GEOUS GEOGRAPHY!!!! VICTORY – at LAST – is OURS!!!!!

For Daly, *It's a Crime* was 'a special milestone. The style of dealing with sponsors' messages at that time was to list all the points the sponsor wanted mentioned in the most sensible order the filmmaker could find, which took the form of a little propaganda essay. The more points included, the happier the sponsor.' The story approach limited the number of points that could be covered, but 'called up greater attention and interest on the part of the viewer, and hence greater receptivity to the message. The sponsor had a hard time accepting the "novelty" at first, but finally came through handsomely.'

It was such a heady time for Daly that even shelved projects could produce a feeling of rightness with the world. In 1957, the United Nations commissioned the NFB to chronicle the UN's efforts to restore peace in the Mideast after the Suez crisis of 1956. The film was called *Blue Vanguard* and was directed by Ian MacNeill. Daly regards it as one of MacNeill's best films, but the political situation was 'very touchy, and the UN demanded some changes after the film was completed. Ian and I took the revised film to New York. [Secretary General] Dag Hammarskjöld himself came to the screening.'

After the screening, 'everyone looked to Hammarskjöld to hear his reaction. He paused a little, and then said something to the effect that the film was everything they had hoped for, but he was still not absolutely sure in his own mind that the release of the film would not "reopen the old wounds" and cause a backlash. He would think about it further with his aides and let us know the answer.'

In the end, the UN decided not to release the film. But Daly was disappointed more for MacNeill than for himself or the Film Board. 'In spite of all the work we had done on it, I was overwhelmed by the fact that we had a real secretary general of the UN who could, because of listening to his own *conscience*, still make a decision in the interests of true peace in the world, although there was not a single untruth in the film, and its tone was itself conciliatory. There was something about the stature of the man that showed it was not at all a political decision, but one made entirely from his heart as an honourable human being.'

Although Unit B films typically celebrated life as 'true, fine, and full of meaning,' Unit B also produced a filmmaker whose nihilist vision in his first film probably had a wider influence on North American film culture of the time than the celebratory films did. Arthur Lipsett's *Very Nice, Very Nice* (1961) is a dour jeremiad constructed almost entirely of scraps of film and tape salvaged from material discarded by other filmmakers. Lipsett's visuals, most of them held on-screen for less than a second or two, mock the snippets of dialogue and narration – some of it by Stanley Jackson, who by now had achieved near-legendary status around the Film Board for his skill at commentary – heard on the soundtrack. The film, made a year before the Cuban missile crisis, is preoccupied with the prospect of nuclear war. Shots of nuclear reactors and a cloverleaf intersection are intercut with pictures of palaces and pyramids; Einstein is intercut with a skull. There are shots of rocket launchings, jet fighters, and hydrogen bomb blasts. John F. Kennedy is heard briefly on the soundtrack; photos of Khrushchev and Eisenhower are made to oscillate frantically.

Very Nice, Very Nice was begun as just a soundtrack put together without a budget. Daly's 'first inkling of it was when Wolf, and I think Bob Verrall, came down from the Animation Department and said, "We've got something unusual," and we went up and we listened to the track on the movieola. Arthur had put it together from pieces of sound he found in NFB trash bins, the mistakes and muddle-headed utterances of people, including our own staff, when they were off guard or caught in mid-boo-boo. We weren't sure what to make of it. But it was original and fascinating. It was already rather completely made, so then the question became how to make a picture for that track without it feeling like an illustrated thing. Obviously the mind that had put together the track would best be able to come up with what kind of pictures to go with it. So we let him go and collect pictures from various sources in the same way he had collected the sound. And gradually he put together the film that way.'

One of the Film Board's first feature-length dramas, Don Owen's

Nobody Waved Good-bye (1964), came out of Unit B. The film's originality lies in its application of improvisational acting and direct-cinema shooting technique to fiction. And this combination also had a lot to do with the film's becoming a feature. Originally it had been budgeted as a short drama. But, as Roman Kroitor remembers it, 'Tom was away and I was in charge of the unit, and Owen called me and said, "I think this can be a feature film. Can I shoot enough stuff?" And I said, "Go ahead."' Daly, who doesn't recall knowing about Kroitor's action, remembers viewing the first rushes. He thought that while the improvised scenes 'did, indeed, feel like live people in a live situation, the drawback was that the scenes tended to be too long. There was none of that artificial tight editing of script, or careful "signposts" planted here and there to "telegraph" the story.' After talking with Owen about this problem but impressed by the engaging quality of the rushes, Daly 'decided there was no better way to proceed than to go on as planned, trying where possible to simplify or shorten the scene development.' Only so much compression proved possible, and – after some intense administrative controversy – the film became an eighty-minute feature. (In an article by Natalie Edwards in *Cinema Canada*, Owen took sole responsibility for the decision to keep shooting and turn the project into a feature.)

All this experimentation and creativity was gathering notice in the international film community. By the early 1960s, Unit B films had garnered scores of prizes and awards. *City of Gold* had won first prizes, gold medals, or blue ribbons at nine international festivals; it was nominated for an Oscar; it won Best Film of the Year at the Canadian Film Awards. Its innovative use of still photographs, reports Erik Barnouw in his documentary history, inspired the American television series *The Real West* and *End of the Trail*.

Universe got twenty-three awards, as a science film, animated film, and documentary. It inspired Stanley Kubrick to hire its narrator to be the voice of Hal in *2001: A Space Odyssey*. Kubrick also visited the Film Board and pumped Colin Low for ideas. He recruited Wally Gentleman for special effects. Kubrick's opening shot seems to have been inspired by a very similar shot in *Universe*. (But Kubrick's film did not acknowledge any debt to the Film Board.) The United States National Aeronautics and Space Administration bought hundreds of prints of *Universe* and, in 1964, produced its own version, *The Universe*. NASA's remake imitated the muted, awed tone of the original narration and adopted the dramatic use of cymbals and drums in the original score (but did not include the NFB among its sixteen acknowledgments).

Lonely Boy got ten prizes. The series which engendered it, *Candid Eye*, influenced *cinéma vérité* in France and direct cinema in the United States. (*Lonely Boy*, too, eventually got copied without acknowledgment, in certain scenes in the 1984 Hollywood film *Top Secret*; some NFB people thought that Peter Watkins's 1967 fiction film *Privilege* borrowed much from *Lonely Boy*.)

Other Unit B films shared in this glory. *Circle of the Sun* received eight awards and substantial praise from Canadian Indian spokesmen. *The Living Stone* got eleven awards, *The Romance of Transportation* got nine, *The Hutterites* eight, *A Is for Architecture* six, *Roughnecks* six, *The Jolifou Inn* five, *Corral* five, *It's a Crime* three, *The Back-breaking Leaf* three, *The Days of Whiskey Gap* three, *My Financial Career* three. *Noboby Waved Good-bye* (four awards) was hailed as a breakthrough for low-budget, socially conscious feature filmmaking. New York critics praised it; Judith Crist put in on her Ten-Best list for 1965. Canadians saw in it a model for a Canadian kind of drama. *Very Nice, Very Nice* (three awards) became a much-copied prototype for 'experimental' cinema. Eight Unit B films received Academy Award nominations.

In addition to praise for individual films, Unit B was getting outside attention as a distinct entity, most impressively by Peter Harcourt in his article 'The Innocent Eye,' published in *Sight and Sound*. Although it seems to have originated as a report on recent work of the Film Board in general, the article focused almost exclusively on Unit B, describing its collaborative approach to production and detecting in its best films a sense of detached wonder. Harcourt found

something very Canadian in all this, something which my own Canadianness prompts me to attempt to define. There is in all these films a quality of suspended judgment, of something left open at the end, of something undecided. And if one thinks of the films of Franju, Marker, or Robert Vas, of their insistently personal quality, there is also something academic about the way the Canadian films have been conceived. There is something rather detached from the immediate pressures of existence, something rather apart.

Harcourt added that it may be just this freedom from pressing needs that had enabled the Unit B filmmakers to explore those questions that lie at the heart of their best work. But the specifics of Harcourt's analysis may have been less significant within NFB circles than the impression that Unit B's importance had superseded that of the Film Board as a whole.

Unit B exerted a strong influence within the Film Board. The unit's repeated triumphs and aura of success attracted other filmmakers into the team's ambit or to its fringes. So did Daly's growing stature. William Greaves, Unit B's chief editor from 1956 to 1960, directed one of the best *Candid Eye* films, *Emergency Ward*. He left the Film Board in 1960 to become an independent filmmaker (*Ali the Fighter* [1971], *The Marijuana Affair* [1974]) and television producer (*Black Journal* [1968–70]) in New York. He was the executive producer of Universal Pictures' *Bustin' Loose* (1982). Greaves remembers Daly as 'something of a mystic.' But 'looking at him, you'd never know that there was this flaming, artistic person there, because he didn't conform to the conventional notion of what the artist should look like – you know, long hair, jeans, dishevelledness – but was always very proper, with a white shirt and tie.' In the editing room, 'Daly would constantly maintain a dialogue with you over the relative merits of this or that particular editing solution. There was constant reviewing – not arguing, but debating and discussing – and there was always room for improvement in everything. He simply prodded your mind with stimulating questions that you were forced to answer, provoking new ideas, new feats of imagination that you didn't realize you had.'

John Spotton had been a cameraman before accepting a pay cut in order to leave the Camera Department and join Unit B to learn editing. He didn't want to give up camerawork, but he wanted more order in his life and a larger creative role in the projects he worked on. His first assignment was to watch Daly edit *Circle of the Sun*, which Spotton had shot. 'I sat every Tuesday and Thursday evening with Tom and Colin in the cutting room, all winter long, until ten o'clock or so at night. It was an *incredible* introduction for me! What a lucky break! Not only did I get lots of comments from Tom about my shooting, I began to see how the shots could be used. He'd look at the shots and "read" them, tell me things about them that I didn't have a clue were there.'

Editing came hard for Spotton. 'I worked on *Lonely Boy* up through about ten different structures. I was at the end of my tether. Koenig wanted to replace me. I'd work and work at the material, then screen it for the gang, and then we'd retire to Tom's office, and these guys would sit around and talk for two hours. Most of the time, they were talking so far above my fucking head I didn't know what they were talking about.' The sessions would end with Spotton mystified and the group asking him when they could see the next version. 'I used to go home and cry. I just wanted to quit after every one of those sessions. And I know Tom recognized that. When I was down, he'd mysteriously arrive in the cutting room, and spend a lot of time with me, just talking, not about the film but about life. He's the only guy in my whole life who did that.'

Filmmakers outside Unit B had ambivalent feelings about it. In the late 1950s, Martin Defalco, later a director, was a technician in the mixing studio. 'The Unit B people moved like a swarm, always together. When we saw them come in, we knew we'd be working late, maybe all night, with no overtime. We hated to see them come in. We liked the hacks. In and out. But Tom was developing in Unit B a commitment to excellence, and other filmmakers outside of Unit B began to absorb it.' Hans Möller joined the Film Board in 1955 and worked under Daly before being put in charge of a unit responsible for producing film-strips. Möller says Daly 'was a better producer for some than for others, and I was one of the others. But I think I learned something from his ceaseless search for excellence, which I tried to implement in the film-strip unit.' Guy Glover would cringe when reminded of Unit B's mystical strains: 'Tom and Wolf and Colin and Roman all had a peculiar religious side. It was not that they presented an absolutely unified religious front, but the vibes they gave off to people who were not of similar views were really quite maddening, and to many people quite incomprehensible. But let's face it, they had more successes than they had failures, with people and with films, and that's the test, finally.'

One member of the original *Candid Eye* team who found Unit B's character alienating was Terence Macartney-Filgate. When the Film Board moved from Ottawa to Montreal in 1956, most of the English-Canadians chose to live in the suburbs or the country. Filgate moved downtown. Filgate says he was 'brought in to work on *The Days Before Christmas* because I knew downtown like the back of my hand and was used to going into nightclubs and taverns and such places of ill repute!' Filgate directed some of the most memorable films in the series, including *The Back-breaking Leaf* and *Blood and Fire*, but he did not fit in with the group. He had spent part of The Second World War with a bomber crew in the RAF, and 'so I probably exhibited a certain surface callowness that did not sit well with more sensitive souls. I'm a sarcastic, irascible guy. They'd be talking about some cosmic aspect of a film, and I'd say something like, "I didn't know God went to the movies." When Wolf made *I Was a Ninety-pound Weakling*, I told him his film was like looking through the keyhole of a john, that he shouldn't snigger at people.' Worse was a 'squishy rural romanticism' that Filgate regards as 'the curse of the Board. In the first *Candid Eye* season, there was a "romantic rural" film [*Country Threshing* (1958)], complete with a very Anglican choir warbling about bees and honey. I shot a lot of this film and was rather vocal about its treatment of the subject. It is probably lost in the archives now, but Tom and Roman and Wolf and Stanley just loved it. I should have kept my mouth shut.'

In 1960, Filgate took a leave of absence 'to see if there was a world outside the Board. I went straight to work with Leacock, Pennebaker, Maysles, and Drew on *Primary* and then some other Time Broadcasting films, but when I asked for an extension of my leave I was refused.' He wrote two technical scripts for the Film Board as a freelance. In 1969, the American filmmaker George Stoney, who had been hired by the NFB to run its new 'Challenge for Change' program, engaged Filgate to direct *Up Against the System* (1969). But he was not brought back on staff.

Filgate has always suspected that the Unit B team had something to do with his not being rehired, but his irreverent memory of the unit and of Daly is leavened by charity: 'Those films – *City of Gold, Universe, Lonely Boy* – they're landmarks in documentary, of that there is no doubt. Wolf was a wonderful cameraman with an exquisitely sensitive eye. Roman had a great sense of structure. And Tom, he somehow got the money for the films, he protected those guys, he'd insist on the extra months if needed. He wanted every film to be the very best it could be. Without him, Unit B wouldn't have worked.'

Albert Kish emigrated from Hungary after the failed revolution of 1956, came to Canada, and joined the Film Board after Unit B's era had passed. But one reason he chose Canada was the good-natured irreverence of *The Romance of Transportation*, which he had seen in Hungary. He thought that any country that could make light of itself through a government information agency would be 'a nice place to live.' Years later, in 1979, Kish was assigned the job of making an NFB film on the Film Board's first forty years (*The Image Makers*). 'I looked at over six hundred NFB films,' Kish recalls, 'and, oh yes, there are many talented filmmakers here, but the films coming out of Unit B, with Daly's name on them as producer, had a very *different* quality. They were very polished, with lots of artistry. They had a lyrical quality. They were strong technically and also told good stories. You never had a feeling of being cheated, that something was missing, and every film was just the right length.'

Although he could seem the epitome of Anglo-Canadian reserve, Daly played a helpful role in the development of French-language filmmaking. In the 1950s, he became a beacon for French-Canadian filmmakers, who at that time were a hardly noticed presence in the Film Board. Bernard Gosselin, who entered the Film Board in 1956, recalls that he and other French-Canadians often would seek Daly out to talk about films and making films. 'One day he said to us, "Why don't you stop talking and do something?"

'"What do you mean?"

'"Make a film."'

In 1962, Daly helped Gosselin and Jean Dansereau get money for *Le Jeu de l'hiver*, a short film that is regarded as one of the inaugurating films of serious French-language filmmaking at the Board. Neither filmmaker has forgotten Daly's support. Gosselin says that Daly 'never took us as people who knew nothing. He always took us as guys with lots of possibilities. He gave us confidence, and a goal of quality that I can still value, that lets me say to myself that I can still improve.' Dansereau, who says he had got on the bad side of senior French-language management, 'found in Tom not only someone who helped me regain my self-confidence, but a man who could give me a sense of what cinematography was all about. And of film editing, not just in the technical sense but in the sense of using picture and sound to transmit feelings and ideas – using the elements of *film*, not literature.'

Georges Dufaux joined the Film Board in 1956 as an assistant camera-man. He soon became a cameraman. He worked with Colin Low on *City Out of Time* (1959), a film on Venice. 'Then the *Candid Eye* team asked me if I'd like to work with them. I worked with them for about two or three years, on *Blood and Fire*, *The Days Before Christmas*, and *I Was a Ninety-pound Weakling*. People were really involved in the total aspect of film. Before, a cameraman was just a cameraman. It was a liberation for me.' Dufaux also believes that the kind of filmmaking he learned from *Candid Eye* offered 'a way for Quebec to discover our own reality, which before we had seen through all the filters of conventional filmmaking.'

Michel Brault joined the Film Board in 1957 and quickly became involved with Unit B through the *Candid Eye* series. Although he is cred ited as the main cameraman on *The Days Before Christmas*, Brault regards a shot by Wolf Koenig as 'the turning point in the liberation of the camera in cinema. Wolf took the camera off the tripod and held it close to the Brink's guard's gun, and just followed it as the guard walked through the store and outside to the truck. He was holding the camera in his hand with-out even looking through the eyepiece.' Brault went on to become one of Quebec's leading political filmmakers. In 1963, with Dansereau, Gosselin, Pierre Perrault, and others, Brault made *Pour la suite du monde*, a stunning feature-length documentary using an improvised approach. In 1971, he co-directed, with Perrault, *L'Acadie l'Acadie?!?*, a documentary on a protest at the Université de Moncton, where students demonstrated for greater rec-ognition of the French-Canadian presence in New Brunswick. Later, in private industry, Brault directed *Les Ordres*, a dramatic feature about the October Crisis of 1970.

Werner Nold, a native of Switzerland, came to the Film Board in 1955, at age twenty-two. He says, 'Daly was for me, and still is, the best documentary editor around – French, English, Canadian, or American. If you think of Grierson as the father of documentary, his best son was Tom Daly. His best student. Tom Daly had the same approach, the same spirit, as Grierson. I did one job with him, editing the English version of *La Lutte* (1961). Tom gave me some advice. He was so sensible, so precise, so patient with me. It changed my life. I learned that day that to be a good editor, you have to be patient, and try many, many things, and don't stop before you're completely satisfied. We tried again and again to make the film better. Ever since, I've always asked him in if I run into a problem in editing.' When Nold was the chief editor on *Vingt et un olympiad* (1977), he 'invited Daly to every important screening of the film, especially the four-and-a-half-hour version. We would talk, he'd give me advice and prod me to go further. When the film was finished, he grabbed me and paid lots of compliments. I think that was the greatest reward I got from the film. He's the only producer I've ever known who worked so closely with the filmmakers, trying to make the film work better, for every filmmaker. He was fantastic for filmmakers.'

Jacques Bobet, himself an experienced producer at the time of Unit B's prominence, defined Daly's significance for the younger French-language filmmakers thus: 'What Tom did, actually, was to *trust*. He had a knack of never turning his back on what he saw.'

And yet, Unit B's amazing run of innovation, triumph, and influence rode atop an undercurrent of increasing tension with the organization of which it was a part. As before, Daly was at the centre of this tension, but this time the problem was not merely internal to the unit. It involved management. At some point in 1957 or, more likely, 1958 – no one involved remembers precisely when – Unit B's leading filmmakers confronted Daly with a new complaint about his leadership.

'You think you see it all, but then something happens that shows you much more. They came to see me again. They felt I was blocking them from doing things they felt they wanted to do, because of a characteristic of mine, which they described as my ... *fear* ... for instance, of Grant McLean.'

In 1957, long before *Universe* would be completed, Donald Mulholland had taken ill and could not continue as director of production. Grant McLean was appointed to succeed him. The choice of McLean was popular around the Film Board. His background included extensive location filming as a cameraman and director. After *The People Between*, he had made several social documentaries, including *Farewell Oak Street* (1953), an imaginatively photographed, award-winning dramatized documentary on slum housing. He produced other films acclaimed at the time, such as *Dresden Story* (1954), a report on racial strife in an Ontario town, and *Monkey on the Back* (1956), a tough-minded look at drug addiction for an early NFB television series (*Perspective*, which he developed). He also had been head of the Camera Department, and he subscribed openly and passionately to Grierson's conception of film in the public service. Filmmakers were confident that McLean would understand their needs and problems and that he would support the Board's mission. Daly also felt pleased about the selection.

But two people could hardly be more different in personality than Daly and McLean. Daly was polite, cautious, meticulous, scholarly, and nonconfrontational. He didn't smoke. He drank only socially, and minimally. 'You couldn't swear in front of Tom,' Verrall remembers, 'you couldn't talk dirty.' McLean, by contrast, had the personality of a swashbuckler. 'He was a raw, brutal character, a hard drinker, a poker player, a jock,' Koenig recalls. 'He'd challenge people in the Camera Department to arm wrestling. He liked to race his car, full of people, to a level crossing ahead of an oncoming train. On Friday he'd go to a map on the wall, close his eyes, pick a spot, and – wherever it was – go there and be back for work on Monday morning.'

McLean brought this same sportive approach to administration. Longtime NFB filmmaker Roger Hart remembers hearing of McLean that he 'would "cut" you for a raise, cut the cards. If you won, you'd get the raise. Or let's say you came in and said you wanted to be paid what you thought someone else was getting. He'd pull out a salary sheet, glance at it, and then call you on your raise request. "Do you *really* want to be paid what he's making?" If you said yes, he'd agree to it, and if the guy was making more than you, you'd get a raise. But maybe he was making less. If so, you'd get a pay cut.'

Such perceptions of McLean eventually became part of public legend. Long after McLean had left the Film Board to become a commercial producer, a capsule portrait by John Reeve in *Quest* magazine lauded his exploits as a filmmaker, citing several of McLean's NFB films, his success in the private sector, and his work as a United Nations cameraman during the Korean war, where he

covered the Inchon invasion, and achieved something General MacArthur never did: armed only with some 'Please don't shoot me' arm bands and a bottle of Three Feathers rye, he penetrated the North Korean lines for a personal inspection of the Yalu River.

After praising McLean's Griersonian commitment to film as a tool for social change, Reeve expressed comparable fascination with McLean's off-duty persona:

Beyond McLean, the filmic force, lies another McLean – the sportsman – sybarite. As an automobile rally enthusiast, he was four times Quebec driving champion and top national driver once; he took a First in the Shell 4000, and was the first Canadian to complete the Monte Carlo Rally. He is also a formidable high-stakes bridge, gin, and golf player; moreover, if money is involved, he can hold his own at billiards, and – oh yes – he can also fly. McLean bears a marked physical resemblance to television's Frank Cannon, and he shares that worthy's gourmet palate and gourmand appetite. To confront his leviathan capacity for Scotch is to know how Hillary felt on first beholding Everest.

Daly too held McLean in a kind of awe. Working with him on *The People Between* had been 'a wonderful and exciting experience. Grant had all kinds of qualities I've never had – first of all, the drive and clever manoeuvring to get permissions and authority and equipment and supplies, and the necessary gall and sheer bravado to get past frontier guardsmen by hook or crook, and the daring to take chances of getting into Mao's territory without knowing how he was going to get out. All his gambling instinct and aggressive way of getting through difficulties was quite foreign to my nature and training and capabilities.'

McLean once offered Daly a ride from Ottawa to Toronto. 'For a while, I was scared stiff by the chances he took, like passing a car just before an oncoming car in the other lane could hit us. But realizing I would have several hours of this, I began to study his timing in such situations. It wasn't long before I realized that his timing was not erratic, but exact, and that if I had been able to act at that speed, I would myself have figured out that the overtaking was a safe bet. Then I actually relaxed and enjoyed the rest of the trip. But I could never have done it myself.'

Although McLean appreciated Daly's editing contribution to *The People Between*, he had come to regard Daly as 'smug, or worse,' and didn't think much of him in his new capacity: 'He didn't discipline himself, he was too weak as a producer.' McLean meant that Daly couldn't keep to a budget or a schedule, and couldn't control his charges. Perhaps with *Universe* in mind, McLean recalls that 'Unit B was notorious for missing deadlines – not by weeks but by years.'

While McLean felt that Daly was too indulgent towards his filmmakers, they were telling Daly that he didn't support them nearly enough. Although he had learned to respond helpfully to their works in progress and had found money to rent a camera for *Corral*, he was still, in their view, too much a stickler for rules. Kroitor and Jackson had not trusted him to approve their attempts to get the commentary right for *Paul Tomkowicz*. And he could be very discouraging, and in an unsettling way, when he felt his filmmakers were pushing him to take risks himself. Kroitor remembers a time when he and others were interested in working in dramatic features. 'We went to him, we told him we wanted to work on a feature film. He exploded. He told us we didn't even know how to make short films yet. How could we make a feature? This took the wind out of our sails. He was right. But what if he had been encouraging in that area? Maybe we *would* have developed some skills in features.'

Nobody Waved Good-bye, made well after this confrontation, seems to have become a feature partly through default, partly from Kroitor's casual go-ahead as Daly's stand-in, and partly because Daly's editing skills gave him confidence the film could work as a feature. 'If somebody on location did something wrong that I could correct myself, I had no problem. If, however, it was something I didn't know how to go about dealing with, I would get angry in myself if not at them.

'My anger came from being afraid – of ignorance, of falling by the way-side, of not being able to function as needed – whatever. This made me for a long time incapable of launching out on projects for which I couldn't see a better-than-average chance of success beforehand.'

A meeting between McLean and Daly was, typically, an ordeal for both. McLean, Koenig says, 'couldn't stand Tom's on-the-one-hand on the other-hand approach.' In turn, McLean – daring, open, direct – personified for Daly all that he felt to be lacking in himself. 'Tom didn't know how to handle a meeting with McLean,' Verrall recalls. 'He'd kind of wring his hands.' Often Daly would find a stereotypically bureaucratic way to avoid dealing with McLean. 'When I felt something wasn't allowed by NFB policy, instead of asking for it on my filmmakers' behalf, and fighting for them, I'd find some memo or rule or regulation to hide behind to avoid raising the issue. Maybe they needed some piece of special equipment. Let's say I knew someone else had a prior right to it, and I felt it wasn't fair to ask for it. I wouldn't even take the chance of asking. Also they felt if I did ask for it, I might ask for it in a "scared" way and might not get it for that reason.

'This kind of limitation is like an invisible wall you can see through, but you can't breathe the air outside it. You don't even realize it's there. Or it always has been there for you, and you assumed it was there for everyone else.'

Daly found this second flaw 'much harder to grasp than the first one. It was harder to watch, harder to put my finger on. And once I was clear there really was something, I still wasn't sure I'd recognize it when it happened. So I asked them if they'd make some kind of signal – since it evidently would be in front of Grant McLean or another similar type – make a gesture, like rubbing the side of their nose, or something of that nature.

'They kind of agreed to try it, but I don't remember it ever coming off quite that way – with some kind of signal – but over a period of time, I began to catch the elusive flavour of this trait of mine. Once the wall had been broken down, somehow I would sense things. For instance, we might be talking about something they said they needed, and one of them would say, "Can we go talk to Grant directly?" I'd know that I was exhibiting that trait again.'

The personality differences between Daly and McLean were underscored by opposing interpretations of Grierson's legacy. Both men admired Grierson and were devoted to what they took to be most valuable in Grierson's documentary idea. For McLean, it was Grierson's emphasis on using film as an instrument of education and social change in the national interest. He accepted without question Grierson's insistence on a close relationship between the government and the Film Board; he agreed with Grierson that the Film Board's move in 1956 to Montreal was a mistake. McLean liked the Grierson who denounced 'art for art's sake,' who proclaimed, 'I look on cinema as a pulpit and use it as a propagandist,' who said film should be 'a hammer, not a mirror,' and who urged the Film Board to 'bang them out and no misses.' But in McLean's opinion, 'Daly had surrounded himself with people who weren't very interested in the Film Act. They wanted to do their own thing rather than follow the Film Act. They didn't give much consideration to distribution, and they hated deadlines.'

McLean was also attracted to Grierson's character. Grierson had political nerve. He respected daring and on-the-spot know-how in others. In his earlier writings, Grierson extolled the virtues of getting around, of achieving intimacy with the subject. To McLean, who had filmed in the midst of shooting wars in foreign lands, Daly really didn't know what documentary was about: 'Daly had never been on location, and filmmakers lack respect for that. Grierson would add "cameraman," for he felt it was effete to be involved in the documentary film medium and not be deeply involved in photography. You can see this in his affection for Rotha, Lorentz, Joe Gibson, Boris Kaufman. He said that while all documentary directors needn't have been cameramen, they must at least have some photographic or painting background. The cutting room is not the world of documentary.'

For Daly, the more compelling side of Grierson's documentary idea was his sense of structure, his interest in 'the whole,' and his insistence that 'a routine average won't do.' Grierson stressed 'actuality' material but also the importance of ordering the material, an insistence embedded in his view of documentary as 'the creative treatment of actuality.' Daly felt a strong affinity for the Grierson who had once said that 'all things are beautiful as long as you have them in the right order,' who peppered his talk with references to the likes of Plato and Tolstoy and Dostoievski, and who, in wartime, had called Norman McLaren the most important filmmaker at the Board.

In 1963, several years after Daly's second confrontation with his filmmakers, the Film Board hosted a conference on films about art. Apparently most of the presentations had emphasized the art of the subject – painting, sculpture – and had ignored consideration of the art of the film treating the subject. In a contribution to a panel discussion, Daly made a case for the importance of the art of film. Now married and a father, he expressed his position in terms of his personal interest in filmmaking:

Many films have the capacity to fill up the mind with new information, but few have the capacity to change the mind itself. Many films have the power to induce emotional reactions or titillate the feelings for an hour, but few have the power to induce new and finer qualities of feeling than we had before. Many films add to our knowledge and information without changing *us*; very few have the quality to open our minds and hearts to a new *growth* of understanding, so that our whole person is changed, and life is never quite the same afterwards.

The moments at which this kind of change can take place are unpredictable. I would like to tell you of one such tiny moment that happened to me only the day before yesterday. My three-year-old son came up to me while I was shaving and said, 'Daddy, will you do me a favour?' Absently wondering what he was cooking up in his mind I said, 'Yes, Tommy.' 'What?' he replied. 'What *kind* of favour?'

It is a very tiny example, but it was one of those moments where awakening takes place and understanding comes. I was 'stumped.' My mind was stopped altogether from running on in its usual pattern. And, in that moment, a great many realizations poured in, about our habitual use of language, how we could use it differently, how we get so used to looking at things in one way that we fail to see them in many possible other ways, and in general that we are almost all the time closed to new perceptions.

Next morning I conducted an experiment. Tommy was back again while I was shaving. I decided to see what he would do when confronted with his own question. So I asked him, 'Tommy, will you do me a favour?' 'Yes,' said Tommy. 'What?' I asked. 'What kind of favour?' Without a moment's hesitation he replied, 'I'll run and get you a book so you can read it to me.'

I must say this produced something of the same effect as the first one ... [Both] were moments of enlightenment.

My personal interest in making films is, through art – and indeed in every other way possible – to try to produce more such moments in the experience of the audience: moments of stopping to question, of being open, so that something new can come in.

... For it is at those moments, and in those states, that not only our understanding but also our actions have a different and more universal quality ...

... There is so much knowledge already available to people that no one has time to encompass it. There are so many films, alone, that unless they have some outstanding quality, *above the ordinary*, they will leave no lasting impression of importance, will change nothing.

But a lot of people at the Film Board – especially managers – did not understand what Daly was trying to articulate. Some who did, did not believe in it. To them, Daly's conception of film seemed ivory-towerish, pretentious, and, as McLean put it, effete. It was a conception of film that, in Daly's case, went with a lack of interest in location work and a dependence on others to bring him material to work on. It seemed to describe a voyeuristic relationship to the world. Some even referred to Daly, among themselves, as 'Peeping Tom.' The feeling was that Daly, as a filmmaker and as a man, was content to remain an observer in life. He seemed innocent – or afraid – of experiences and impulses normal to most people.

Wolf Koenig tells with affection a story that for him sums up Daly's attitude towards detail, towards perfection, but that for others might illustrate a certain incompleteness. 'We were in a theatre, looking at a series of films for a festival or something. Tom, me, a couple of others. One of the films was an air force training film, something about perception under stress. A sequence came up in which an air force instructor in front of a blackboard said something like, "Furthermore, if there are two stimuli, the stronger will override the weaker. For example, in the following sequence count the number of dots." Then the film cut immediately to a close-up of the belly of a belly dancer, undulating very suggestively to some music. Then these little white dots began to appear here and there on the screen, while she kept dancing. I started counting the dots like the instructor asked, but I lost count very quickly. Then the instructor comes back on, and immediately Tom says, "There were sixteen dots." The instructor says, "There were sixteen dots."'

For Koenig, the incident showed how 'once he's locked into something, he's very determined to do it right.' To others, it could suggest Daly's fear of life – a fear that Daly acknowledges he had.

'I was afraid to make mistakes. I'd tend not to take risks. I had to learn how to rely on *them*, on their knowledge and confidence, in order to be an effective producer for them.

'I saw that I was weak, and that I should be strong. First I tried to be like them. But it didn't work. I quickly realized that there are different ways of being strong. If a deer tried to be strong like a lion, it would be sunk. You don't change your nature, but you can be strong in your own way. So I stopped trying to change my nature and tried to discover what was appropriately "strong" for myself.

'I realized that basically I was only afraid of the little mistakes. But in not trying things, I was not trying the things I needed to try for my *life's* sake – and that was a *big* mistake.'

Daly's memory of the confrontation is warmed by gratitude. 'When you're suddenly unsure of yourself, you can be unsure of everything. But they were so supportive. They didn't do to me what I had once done to them – give only the negatives. They got me to see that invisible wall.'

Daly began 'to realize that when I sensed this special flavour of "Gee, we could do that," I should go by it, I should trust it. Going by that feeling has proved very valuable and happy-making in my life.'

His marriage, in December 1958, was in part an early result of his decision to trust. His bride was Ruth Ellen McMullin. She had been married before, to Larry Gosnell, an NFB filmmaker who specialized in agricultural subjects, and had reverted to using her maiden name after their divorce. The marriage would prosper, bring joy, and produce two sons.

At work, Daly became more assertive on behalf of his unit. 'McLean was a bastard to Tom,' Verrall says, 'but Tom would still back us. He'd go down on his knees, so to speak, and humiliate himself to protect his charges.' But now he could act firmly on occasion. Koenig remembers an instance in which 'McLean wanted to fire somebody in the unit, and Tom said no. McLean backed off. Tom didn't realize it was that simple, that if you stand up to a bully, he'll back off.'

McLean says this incident never happened. Koenig insists it did. Daly doesn't remember it. But if it did happen, McLean might have backed off from sheer surprise at Daly's directness. A fairly common complaint about Unit B filmmakers was that they were not always straightforward in their dealings with management. Roger Hart, who recorded sound on *Nobody Waved Good-bye*, believes that 'McLean thought Unit B was kind of sneaky about budgets, that they'd deliberately under-budget a project to get it approved, with no intention of sticking to the budget. *Nobody Waved Good-bye* was budgeted as a half-hour documentary. But everybody knew that Don Owen intended to shoot a feature. Daly knew. McLean knew. What McLean hated was that they tried to deceive him.'

Hans Möller, who as a unit head grew close to McLean, thinks McLean felt that 'as a manager he had a right to oversee what they were doing. Grant felt he wasn't being told the whole story, that they weren't being frank with him.'

McLean's perception of underhandedness on the part of Daly and those around him tainted his interactions with Daly and may have coloured his perception of their philosophical differences about documentary film. An incident that dramatizes their conflicting emphases on photography and editing – and happens, as well, to mark an important moment in French-language filmmaking at the NFB – shows also the distrust. Around the time he was working as a cameraman on *The Days Before Christmas*, Michel Brault and Gilles Groulx were assigned to shoot some newsreel footage of a snowshoe congress in Quebec. Brault admits to having 'cheated. I took more footage than I should have, and I brought sound equipment along. When Grant saw the rushes, he declared that they were no good and should be sent to the stock-shot library. But we kept the material and started editing it at night. We showed a rough-cut to Daly. When he saw it, he declared the film should be made. He helped us change Grant McLean's decision.' (Daly says that Guy Glover was equally supportive of the project.) The result was *Les Raquetteurs* (1958), a short film that got Brault invited to the Robert Flaherty Seminar in 1960, where Jean Rouch discovered French-Canadian filmmaking.

Edouard Davidovici 'was working in a cutting room next to Gilles Groulx at the time of the secret editing' and then was assigned to Unit B for a short stint. For Davidovici, now head of French postproduction, the affair summed up the difference between McLean's and Daly's approaches to film: 'You look at the rushes, it was nothing. It comes out of the editing room, it's a great film. Grant was a cameraman. He was interested in how a shot was done, the physical aspect of the shot. He cared about the the angle of the shot, what lens was used. Tom looked at it from the point of view of what he could do with it in the editing.' But Davidovici's memory of Unit B also could be interpreted to support the impression of sneakiness on the part of Unit B. 'Grant McLean would say, "You can't do that." Tom would say, "Yessir," and then go do it under the table.'

Most of the filmmakers who admired Unit B's creativity also liked

McLean – or grew to like him. At the time of *Les Raquetteurs*, Brault found McLean 'frightening. We'd never see him in the cafeteria, never see him in the corridor. He'd look at rushes alone. He'd declare things from his office. But I met him again much later, and he's wonderful. He is not the guy I used to think he was.' Davidovici remembers that McLean 'was out of the Grierson school, and very authoritarian, but in dealing with him I found him to be fair and a darn good director of production. I really liked him, person to person.'

Hans Möller loved working for McLean: 'He was a born, imaginative manager. When I'd report to him with a problem, I'd leave very quickly, with everything resolved. He'd say, "Do this. I'll take the rap." He was decisive and incredibly loyal.' And, for Möller, anything but a bully: 'I'd tell him about a budget problem. After laying it out, I'd say, "It's even worse, Grant." Grant would just laugh. Even when he disagreed with you, he was very supportive. He was a very fine, warm-hearted person who really cared about people.'

Donald Haldane, whose commercial credits include *The Reincarnate*, the Walt Disney feature *Nikki, Wild Dog of the North*, and numerous CBC programs, directed several NFB documentaries that McLean produced. In 1963, he directed the NFB feature film *Drylanders*, a somewhat stiffly acted but often beautiful and moving film. Although it received less acclaim at the time than its near contemporary *Nobody Waved Good-bye*, it has worn well over the years and now seems the richer film. Haldane says that McLean 'was one of the best producers I ever worked with. His sensitivity to the problems I was having [while shooting] was apparent in the reports [on the rushes] that he sent to me.' When Haldane was about to commence location shooting on *Drylanders*, which had been approved for 35mm photography, 'the equipment arrived, and it was 16mm! I was livid. McLean was out of the country, in Moscow. I sent him a three-page telegram explaining why the film had to be shot on 35mm. We didn't hear back, but the next day the 35mm equipment came out. He had just called up the Film Board from Moscow and said, "Send it."'

But the trust that warmed the dealings between McLean and many filmmakers, and between Daly and many filmmakers (some got along well with both), never favoured the relationship between McLean and Daly. Low laments that 'they found communication almost impossible. There was constant hostility. Tom's films always won the prizes, and management couldn't understand that.' Macartney-Filgate sums up the conflict as one between 'art and industry. McLean was a propagandist, Daly a perfectionist. McLean was out of the rambunctious side of the Film Board, Daly out of the intelligentsia. McLean was incisive, adventurous. Tom was cautious, deliberative. It was like oil and water.'

An irony shadows the running conflict between Daly and McLean. McLean, who seems to have possessed an outlaw's temperament, which can be close to that of the artist (and his camerawork in films like *The People Between* and others suggests he was an artist), would invoke reasonable but conventionally bureaucratic values in his feud with Daly. Daly, in so many ways the consummate civil servant, correct and dutiful, had learned to defy norms and break the rules in pursuit of art. As Grierson had said to Legg, 'Always cast against type.'

But McLean's loyalty to the Film Act was genuine and passionate. Möller recalls that 'McLean had very high standards, high ideals about film. He was deeply influenced by Grierson's ideal of civil service. You are entrusted by the government to do this and that, and you should do it.' Even Koenig agrees: 'McLean was on the side of the Film Board, on doing the right kinds of films for the Film Board. No question about it.'

The friction between Daly and McLean was the visible, dramatic focus for a broader, more diffuse conflict. Resentment of Unit B was spreading through the Board. Much of it seconded McLean's criticisms: Unit B was arrogant and pretentious; it avoided sponsored work; its films went over budget and past schedule; and it lacked devotion to the Film Act.

A suggestion of how other filmmakers regarded Unit B survives in a transcript of a sound skit prepared for Donald Brittain's wedding party in 1963. Brittain had joined the Film Board in 1954 and had worked mostly in sponsored films. He was a friend of McLean's and very popular with other filmmakers. The skit took the form of a BBC radio documentary about the Film Board. 'Lumpkin' is a BBC reporter. 'Lou' is a Film Board guide assigned to him. At one point, a Film Board official asks Lou to take Lumpkin to drop in on 'Unit P' so that he can see 'something highbrow.'

LOU: Yes, Mr. Lumpkin. This is a rare opportunity to see our famous Unit P in action. They're having a script conference. It's really fascinating.

LUMPKIN (*interested*): Ah?

LOU: Yes, come this way, please.

Corridor footsteps
Creaky door opens

LOU (*whisper*): Come in. But we have to be very quiet. Let's listen to their animated conversation.

Five seconds silence

LUMPKIN (*whisper*): I say, this *is* fascinating. Who is that executive chap there?

LOU: That is Tom Yearly, their leader. Ssssh ... Let us listen.

Five seconds silence

LUMPKIN (*whisper*): And who is that, sitting at Tom Yearly's left?

LOU (*whisper*): That is his right-hand man, Human Loiter.

LUMPKIN (*whisper*): And at his right?

LOU (*whisper*): His left-hand man, Wolfgang Kong. But hush, let us listen to their animated conversation.

Five seconds silence

HUMAN *emits a slow groan.*

WOLFGANG: What a mess!

TOM YEARLY: I don't see why you're so discouraged. After all, it's only five years since we started. A film has to mature, find its shape. We've only shot 738,000 feet. But it's all hand-held. So cheer up, boys.

HUMAN (*bitterly*): Sure, sure. Trim a frame here, trim a frame there. But this time it won't work, Tom.

TOM (*cheerfully*): Look, all it needs is a little re-structuring. We can do this right here, before the Centennial, and meanwhile, we can send a crew to Leipzig and see what happens. You re-structure a bit, you re-shoot a bit, and it all falls into place.

The scene concludes with a debate about whether or not to invite Brittain, who had developed a reputation as an effective troubleshooter, to come in and 'save the film.' 'Yearly' is given the last word. He decides

against involving Brittain, who, Yearly says, 'has always been a bit ambivalent on the dichotomy of foreground relevance in documentary weltan-
schauung. Even Stuart Legge [*sic*] said so.'

'We were considered a bunch of fairies,' Koenig says. 'They couldn't
cope with our softer nature.' Colin Low suggests an additional line of
demarcation: 'McLean belonged to the booze culture. About half the Film
Board did. The booze culture and all the macho stuff that went with it. We
were the arty types.'

Drinking was, for many, an emblem of the documentary ethos that
informed and infused the Board. Grierson typically was described as a
'hard-drinking Scot' or a 'gin-drinking terror.' Others followed suit. The
script that lampoons Unit B's pretensions celebrates, without a hint of
embarrassment, Brittain's reputation as a heavy drinker. When Brittain first
appears, he is shuffling down the hall dragging a cart on which his cameraman is sprawled out unconscious. The BBC host reports to his audience
that Brittain stops, goes back to the cameraman, 'and he's digging into the
cameraman's pocket. How deft! He's not even waking him up. Yes ... he's
taking a huge flask from his pocket. He's drinking thirstily from it. What a
charming picture, ladies and gentlemen. I wish you could see it in full
colour. This chap leaning wearily against his *charette*, or cart, slaking his
thirst and gazing into the westering sun.'

The drinking faction was the stronger one, sociologically speaking, in
those days. Non-drinkers were the oddballs. Koenig, however, was the
only teetotalling Unit B principal. Daly had failed his initiation into the
'booze culture' during the war. Others similarly had tried to fit in. Low and
Verrall each say they tried heavy drinking once, got sick, and then drank
only socially and in moderation.

Kroitor, in his early years at the Film Board, had made a more serious
effort: 'I tried to emulate the heavies, but it was fairly pathetic. These guys
were experienced drinkers. I would try to match them quart by quart. I did
some incredibly stupid things in those days.'

Before his marriage and the NFB's move to Montreal, Kroitor shared a
cottage on the Ottawa River with Stanley Jackson. One night, they had
three friends over for dinner. 'One of them was making Singapore Slings,
or something. Very strong. We were all sitting around the table, having a
very merry time. I remember that somebody rose to consciousness and
said, "Gosh, I think there's a fire." The fire was rising from the middle of
the table and just about reaching the ceiling. Finally, it got through to us
that there was a fire about to burn the house down, and we put it out just in
time.

'Then we all got in a little coupe that I drove. We were off to another party. We were going along a road that came to a tee at the Ottawa airport, at the end of some runway. I was supposed to turn, but I was going too fast and drove straight ahead. We went down into this deep ditch and then leapt a Frost fence that lined the airport.

'There we were, sitting on the runway. We thought, if we're caught, that's no good. The only thing to do was to drive out. We hoped no planes were landing. We drove up and down the runway, went past a terminal, and finally found a gate to an access road. We drove right past the guard. He stood there with his mouth open. He was apparently so startled that he didn't even try to stop us.'

But if the Unit B filmmakers were deficient in certain attributes of the macho culture of the time, they weren't necessarily any the nicer for it. 'Our softness,' says Koenig, 'was often a cover for ruthlessness. And we could be terribly, brutally critical of other people's films. I remember Kroitor being stopped in the hall by someone whose film we had just seen. The filmmaker asked Kroitor what he thought of his film. Kroitor told him, "It was shit." Kroitor had the guts to say it outright, but we all probably signalled this kind of arrogance to others.'

Kroitor remembers 'feeling that we had a deeper sense than others that there's more than meets the eye in what you see around you. It seemed to me at the time – quite incorrectly – that this was a privileged view, that others went around with blindfolds on.

'I was insufferably arrogant. I wasn't consciously that way. My view at the time was that I was applying standards that I thought were important. But I didn't distinguish between that, and how to put it so that people wouldn't be hurt. I wasn't aware of how I hurt people's feelings. It was blindness on my part.'

Some filmmakers simply resented Unit B's success. Daly remembers learning that a producer (now dead) he respected was 'bad-mouthing our unit. Of all people, I didn't expect it from him. I went to him and said I had heard he had some objections to our unit, and that I would like to hear them directly. Perhaps we could talk about them. So we went to a beer parlour and had a good clearing session. To my amazement, just as we were leaving to go back to work, he added, "I guess it was jealousy."'

Daly believes the other criticisms were unfair. While Unit B probably did less sponsored work than other units, one reason was, in Daly's view at least, that 'government departments wanted to work with *one* executive producer, not several different ones that had different methods. They wanted to work with the ones whose programs had *their* kind of subject. So

we got the sponsored work that came with our subjects, or occasional odd-
ments that came along. Other units forgot that part of our sponsored work
was animation films, which were going on upstairs. Roman had sponsored
films like *Farm Calendar* and a civil defence film for the army on how to
liberate victims from a bombed, collapsed house.' And *It's a Crime* was a
sponsored film.

'But,' Daly maintains, 'for "sponsored films" you could read "unwanted" films, and it came to about the same thing. Nobody really wanted
the "foreign versions," which we did on the unit's own money but which
offered no creative opportunity for those who did them. We took them on
because I and some of our people believed in the importance of reaching
other countries with our films. Classroom films was another category that
others did not want. They had to fit curricula of all the provinces but be
paid for out of our own money. [*The Romance of Transportation, Roughnecks*, and *Universe* were classroom films.] Then for quite a while people
were complaining about "having to do TV films" – which in the early days
were rushed, and technically and artistically limited – and trying to avoid
doing them. That was when Roman and Wolf developed their *Candid Eye*
program, to take advantage of some of that "unwanted" money to develop
a new method of cinema. Another example was films about Canada as a
whole, sponsored or unsponsored. Nobody really wanted to tackle them,
as they had to have a little of everything in them to satisfy all regions and
provinces. And it turned out that we got all, or almost all, of those to do,
partly because we believed in the purpose behind them, partly because I
knew the stock-shot library so well, and partly to give us our "share" of
sponsored films.'

Daly resents the perception that he was duplicitous in his dealings with
McLean. He denies the stories suggesting he would say one thing to
McLean and then do another. 'It may have been done to me. But I didn't do
that to Grant or anyone else.' For Daly, the perception of underhandedness
is the product of gossip 'escalating into generalities that then become
"accepted."'

Daly acknowledges that Unit B films often went over their original budgets, but he believes the result was usually 'a much more usable film. I
never could – and still can't – see the value of making a not-much-wanted
film within budget, if it could be made useful with more. The first is a total
waste of the money, and the second not necessarily a waste, in the end, at
all.'

But for McLean, Daly's reasons were and remain no more than rational-
izations: 'It is not true that taking longer to make a film makes it better. I

have often seen it made worse. And if, for example, you can spend $100,000 and achieve 85 per cent of a film's potential, should one spend $20,000 more just to achieve 90 per cent of it? One can never reach 100 per cent.

'One must realize,' McLean maintains, 'unless one is completely selfish, that an over-expenditure results in another film not being made. Is it worth it?'

In McLean's view, budget overages and missed deadlines were particularly devastating in the case of sponsored films. To make films for other government agencies was one of the purposes for which the Film Board had been established. Sponsored films also brought income to the Board. They provided training opportunities for young filmmakers. Beginning in the 1960s, the Film Board's always-resented monopoly over sponsored films began gradually to erode. By the 1990s, sponsored films had been given over entirely to the private sector. McLean blames this development on the attitudes exemplified by Unit B and absorbed by others.

Yet even if Unit B got a disproportionate share of the Film Board's discretionary production money, even if there was an element of fiscal irresponsibility in their budgeting, and whether Daly and his protégés were interested in the Film Act or not, the Act's language sanctioned the kinds of films they were making. The original 'Act to Create a National Film Board' of 1939 had directed the Film Board to concern itself with 'films designed to help Canadians in all parts of Canada to understand the ways of living and the problems of Canadians in other parts.' In 1950, a revised Act defined NFB films more broadly as 'films designed to interpret Canada to Canadians and to other nations.' One would be hard put to argue that Unit B films did not interpret Canada favourably, at home or abroad. And Unit B's preference for films that did not address pressing public issues found support in high places. Albert Trueman, who served as the Film Board's commissioner from July 1953 to April 1957 and who had supported Unit B's position on *Universe*, recalled in his memoirs that he found the Film Board at the time

burdened with what seemed to me an excess of social conscience, a do-the-people-good-whether-they-like-it-or-not complex, which led them – from my point of view – into rather too much attention to "educational" films on the drug habit, crime in general, housing, and so on and on. To my mind, one film we made showing a Canadian cowboy roping a young, partially broken horse in the corral, cutting him out from his bucking, plunging fellows, bridling him, saddling him, and dashing off for a glorious hell-for-leather gallop across the prairie was worth any two of the so-called "educational" efforts we made.

It is true that Grierson insisted on the subordination of personal artistic ambitions to the needs of public service. Visiting the Film Board during its twenty-fifth anniversary celebration in 1964, Grierson was appalled by the same apparent lack of discipline and a sense of service that had eaten at McLean. Still later, when he was teaching at McGill University, Grierson (according to the Canadian Radio and Television Commission's 'Grierson Transcripts: Interviews with John Grierson, 1969–1971') criticized Daly for seeming to endorse and favour the production of films that dissented from government policy and priorities. Grierson often complained about the Film Board's pursuit of prizes and awards.

But Grierson's most fundamental rhetorical trait was a penchant for contradiction, and a striking feature of his documentary conception is its resistance to reduction. Although the propagandistic aspect of his documentary idea is widely emphasized – as it was, as well, by him – he valued the aesthetic side just as highly. Propaganda was documentary's bottom line, but documentary aspired to 'the power of poetry and prophecy.' In *John Grierson: Film Master*, James Beveridge appended to his portrait of Grierson the detailed written response Grierson gave to a questionnaire presented to him in the late 1960s by a group of Cambridge University students. When asked about the relative importance of education, art, and philosophy in his conception of documentary in the government service, Grierson said they were 'all part of the same thing as far as I'm concerned.' The documentary idea, he went on, involved not just propaganda but, equally, aesthetics. This latter intention, Grierson implied, more or less has to be kept secret, but the powers that be will sense that it is there.

So you will always be subject to a certain mistrust and even a certain inarticulate opposition, at many points of your bureaucratic journey. After all, you *are*, from many a point of view, taking the wooden horse of aesthetic into Troy. The story of the documentary movement is in part the story of how, not without a scar or two, we got by. Maybe you win more or less for keeps, as in the case of the National Film Board of Canada. Maybe you lose.

In response to another question, Grierson insisted that the documentary filmmaker should seek 'the noumenal,' the truth or reality that underlies whatever phenomena are being filmed. To do this, the filmmaker has to refer – always – to some larger context, social or poetic. If you make a film, 'be sure you are not pursuing the shadow instead of the substance.'

When asked if there was a current filmmaker whose work he particularly admired, Grierson said that the only ones who interested him were those who had 'broken through to economic viability in modern progressive terms' and were sharing the breakthrough with others, initiating or influencing new waves of filmmaking. He named six: Joris Ivens, Arthur Elton, Bert Haanstra, Edgar Anstey, Henri Storck, and Tom Daly.

According to Margaret Ann Elton:

After Grierson's fruitful sessions at McGill, he came back one Christmas a year or so before he died, rang me up (as usual), and said: No One Will Ever Know What the Film Board Owes to the Persistence of Tom Daly.

In hindsight, McLean's and Daly's opposing interpretations of Grierson's legacy, no matter how hard to reconcile in practice, appear to emphasize different sides of the same Griersonian coin. Daly, who found it so hard to break rules, sensed this. 'When there was someone at the NFB big enough to contain us both in full flight, there was an ongoing resolution of the differences that enabled both of us to fully operate in the best way our natures permitted and limited, without getting in each other's way. It is this factor which makes Grierson into a far greater overall figure than either of us. His vision and capacities included the best of both, and he refused to see these differences as divisory, but rather included them all together as grist for the whole mill.'

McLean may have sensed it as well. He seems never to have denied Unit B a budget overage or a deadline extension on an important film. Despite his avowals of disapproval, he tolerated Unit B until the unit system itself was dismantled. However loudly he railed against Unit B's profligacy, he continued to sign off on budget increases and to support new projects. When Daly would present him with an argument that Don Owen's material ought to become a feature or that Michel Brault's footage would make a good film, McLean would relent and give his administrative backing. Roger Hart thinks that the reason McLean didn't stop production on *Nobody Waved Good-bye* even though he suspected it had been deliberately under-budgeted was that 'he didn't want to. He thought it might turn out to be an important film.' Daly agrees with Hart's interpretation: 'When Grant and I discussed it, and I showed him the material, he saw that it was in fact good material, and could make a good film and bring possible new kudos to the NFB. He agreed to support my proposal to be responsible for the result, and provided the necessary funds ... which he didn't in any way have to do.' Stanley Jackson once recalled an incident in which, when a producer crowed about consistently coming in under budget, McLean stepped out into the hall and bellowed, "I don't give a damn. I want good films."'

In an indirect way, Jackson may have been the one point of understanding between Daly and McLean. In Low's words, 'Stanley danced between the two of them with his wit, and with his wisdom.'

Jackson was beloved in Unit B. He was a bachelor and apparently had no close relatives. Unit B was his family. For two years he paid the private-school tuition fee for Roman Kroitor's son. Kroitor remembers that Jackson also 'had a friend we never met, from some African country. He needed help. Stanley gave him something like ten thousand bucks. He was very, very generous.' He was also a gifted raconteur. Low recalls, 'I was often under the table, doubled up with laughter. He was funny largely because he laughed at himself a lot.'

McLean and his circle loved Jackson's stories, too. Jackson was fun. He was always welcome to join them at the Taverne Principale, known informally as the 'T.P. Tavern,' a popular hangout for NFB filmmakers and administrators. 'In a way,' says Wolf Koenig, 'Stanley was the court jester for Grant. He had a way of playing the fool, but he was very smart. It was a wonderful camouflage.'

Skilled as he was in storytelling or film analysis, Jackson had a peculiar habit of standing up in the middle of a discussion, walking away without explanation, and returning minutes, hours, or days later ready to resume the discussion exactly where it had left off. He was similarly eccentric in his work habits, whether writing commentary or recording it.

'Grant and I knew,' sighs Daly, 'that Stanley was irreplaceable in the commentary field. Even if you "fired" him, you couldn't get another to compose anything like the same quality and effectiveness of commentary. And even if you got another narrator to read Stanley's commentary, it never came off with anything like the convincing effect of Stanley's own voice.

'So in our own ways, we each realized we had to suffer whatever was necessary to get the real stuff out of Stanley. Consequently, Grant would be hard put to actually fire any of our people for missing deadlines, since they would all be less guilty than Stanley!'

In budgeting a film, Daly 'would ask Stanley carefully how much time *at the most* he felt he needed for his commentary to work. Then I'd double it without telling him, and keep the contingency on it. It was rarely, if ever, enough. It was all very well to deal with him on a film entirely within our own unit, but when Stanley made us miss scheduled sponsors' screenings, when the sponsors had come all the way from Ottawa to Montreal for it, and without warning us that he wasn't ready, it was just too much.'

Daly once asked Kroitor to use his influence to help get Jackson to adhere to more reasonable scheduling. 'But Roman simply said, "Don't fob off your own problems on me." And I realized he was basically right. In any case, nothing changed.'

One suspects that, deep down, McLean had a grudging respect for Unit B and its films. Perhaps at some level he understood, through his friendship with Jackson, that Unit B's budget overages were not the result of mere wilfulness or intentional deceit. But he was under more, and more varied, pressure than Daly. It was part of McLean's job to demand fiscal responsibility and promote equity among units. And it wasn't just a few disgruntled producers or filmmakers who were complaining. Almost all of them were.

Filmmakers in other units respected Unit B's commitment to quality but resented its apparent dispensation from the restrictions to which others were held. Their goal was not to force Unit B to follow the rules but to enjoy some of Unit B's apparent freedoms for themselves. They craved opportunities to develop projects from their own ideas and free from rigid schedules and efficient budgets. This, in turn, threatened the more traditional producers. 'All the bright people in the place,' Verrall says, 'came to Tom. They didn't go to the other producers. They felt they wouldn't get a hearing. McLean would get an earful of this from other producers, his card-playing buddies.'

Daly looks back with understanding at what took him by surprise at the time: 'I was so busy that I wasn't really aware of how unhappy other people in other units were. I can see how they might complain.'

The filmmaker who perhaps best understood both points of view was none other than Donald Brittain, and he seems to have played a key role in the unit system's demise. Verrall remembers the Brittain of those days as part of 'the T.P. Tavern crowd, who used to enjoy trading stories about "Uncle Tom and his gang of fairies." But one day Roman told Wolf and me we'd better get in the theatre and take a look at this film. We did. It was *Fields of Sacrifice*. We were absolutely blown away. We had thought of Brittain as just a clown, into his booze.'

Brittain directed and produced *Fields of Sacrifice* (1964). Peter Jones was its executive producer. A tribute to Canadian war dead and funded by the Department of Veterans Affairs, the film was engaging and moving despite its solemn subject and sponsored origin. It suggested that Brittain had a special ability. *Bethune*, completed in 1964, confirmed Brittain's talent. It is an engaging, sympathetic biography of the Canadian physician Norman Bethune, who served with the loyalists in the Spanish civil war and with Mao in China. Although it lacks the organic fluidity characteristic of Unit B's best work, it deals with a messier topic. The film presaged Brittain's

genius for weaving stylistically diverse material – still photos, archival footage, candid material, interviews – into rich, sometimes profound essays,
with inspired commentary as the thread.

Brittain respected McLean enormously. Forces in the government were
unhappy about *Bethune*'s favourable depiction of a doctor who served radical causes. When the Film Board, under pressure, agreed to restrict the film's
circulation abroad, McLean responded with the same outrage that the censorship of *The People Between* had provoked in him. He attacked the restrictions passionately and aggressively. On 7 February 1966, McLean wrote to
the commissioner that the reaction within the Film Board to the restriction
'has been one of shock and bewilderment.' Among filmmakers, 'respect for
NFB management has been seriously undermined.' The decision 'has no
basis in common sense.' It is 'shameful and destructive because it does a great
disservice to the principles of truth and courage, principles on which this
organization has been built.' If not reversed, the decision 'could actually
redefine the NFB in terms that few of us could live with.' Some think out-
spokenness of this sort – and style – was a factor in the government's decision not to appoint McLean as commissioner (after a year as acting
commissioner), but it won him a reputation among filmmakers like Brittain
for fearlessness in the defence of the Film Board's journalistic integrity.

When McLean, passed over for the job of commissioner, left the Film
Board in 1967 for private industry, the Film Board staff fêted him with a
gala send-off. Brittain was the main speaker. His remarks survive in an
off-the-books, undistributed, quick-and-dirty black-and-white film record
(titled *The National Film Board Grant McLean Spectacular 1967*) of the
event. The film shows an aspect of McLean that is absent from the stories
depicting his derring-do and rough-edged manner. Here he is soft-spoken,
shy. He seems almost *gentle*. Scores of staffers, including numerous women
and several filmmakers whom no one who knew them would call 'macho,'
look on with respect and affection.

The film also suggests the prominence at the time of what Colin Low had
called a 'booze culture.' After the brief ceremony, the liquor flows liberally.
It attracts an admiring camera. And in his opening remarks, Brittain regales
the audience with stories about McLean's love of gambling, his athletic
skills, and, especially, his drinking prowess:

Another thing one can learn from Grant is how to cope with strong drink, a lesson
we should all keep in mind this evening. I learned to drink at a very early age in a very
hard school, but when I met McLean I realized I was in for a certain amount of
postgraduate work. He is the absolute master of the hangover. How many of us, after

an evening with Grant McLean, have eased ourselves into the office, bleeding heavily from both eyes, at three o'clock in the afternoon, only to discover that McLean has been making crisp – or reasonably crisp – decisions since eight-thirty a.m.

But after a few more stories, Brittain assumes a more serious tone:

There are other stories that I could tell of Grant, and they are serious stories, and they would embarrass him probably. Stories that tell of his strength, his dedication, his dignity, his personal integrity.

In concluding, Brittain turns to address McLean himself:

We, who have fought a hundred battles with you in the kitchens of a hundred house parties – we who have watched the sparks fly and the energies burn, and the integrity hold fast – we who have seen you, on our behalf, fight off the bureaucrats, the technocrats, the politicians and the cowards – we who have seen your fine acts of private kindness – we say this: you may not be the smoothest customer in the world, but we like you, we respect you, and as a man and a colleague, we salute you.

Brittain also had written the text for a framed scroll that the new commissioner, Hugo McPherson, presents to McLean:

Let it be known that Grant McLean, filmmaker and public servant of a high order, loyal friend and courageous colleague, possessor of that fierce thing they call a conscience, who departs after twenty-six years to this day, carries with him in full measure the abiding affection and respect of the men and women of the National Film Board of Canada.

But Brittain also admired Daly and Unit B. It was Daly who had brought him into the Film Board. Brittain later recalled being 'absolutely terrified of his intellectualism. But he was very good at drawing me out. From the first day, I started learning about films from him.' In their 1974 article 'Donald Brittain: Green Stripe and Common Sense' in *Cinema Canada*, Ronald Blumer and Susan Schouten quote Brittain as saying:

Kroitor, Koenig, Daly, these were men I really respected. A film like *Lonely Boy* knocked me out when I first saw it, it showed me what could be done with film. But these guys, they worked! I think they used to sleep in the hallways at night. Maybe I started to feel guilty because in the early sixties I seemed to be spending most of my time playing football during working hours with the guys in distribution. You see a film like *Lonely Boy* and you say to yourself, 'Shit, I wouldn't mind making something half decent.'

In the fall of 1963, rumours were afoot that management was contemplating a change in the structure of the English Production Branch. Filmmakers in the Branch met to discuss how they might have some say in the reorganization. They asked Brittain and John Kemeny (*Bethune*'s producer) to interview confidentially all persons involved in creative work in the Branch. Of seventy such persons, sixty-eight were interviewed. (Two were unavailable.)

The filmmakers' report ('A Summary of Staff Opinion on the Structure and Organization of the English Production Branch,' 16 December 1963) announced that there was 'a widespread lack of esprit de corps in the English-language units,' a deeply felt 'absence of a sense of purpose,' a 'mustiness.' Acknowledging that the NFB filmmaker had 'to perform a very difficult dual role [as] both a craftsman working in the realm of ideas and ... a public servant,' the report claimed that 'the Civil Service mentality has become destructively predominant, with depressing effect.' Filmmakers blamed this imbalance on the unit structure, and urged that it be replaced by a 'pool' system that would give filmmakers 'final creative responsibility.'

The filmmakers took pains to distinguish the position of executive producer from the individuals occupying the position. In the case of two executive producers, however, the filmmakers went further – the only instance in which the report names individuals:

There is grave concern for the future of Executive Producers. It is felt that each of them [has] real and vital contributions to make in the future development of the Board. There is particular anxiety over the the future roles of the two senior Executive Producers, Guy Glover and Tom Daly. Their wealth of experience, their wisdom, dedication, guidance and criticism should be made readily available to all film-makers under any reorganization. Their talents could perhaps be even better utilized under a new structure.

The judgment pronounced upon the the office of executive producer was harsh: it was an obstacle to production. The recommended new structure would eliminate the position. Producers, who would have no ongoing authority over individuals, would perform most of the executive producers' functions. In the fluid, flexible system that was envisioned, filmmakers could choose among projects and producers. The pool system would distribute creative independence equally among all the filmmakers.

Two months later, in a memorandum (28 February 1964) to all producers, directors, editors, and writers in the English Production Branch, McLean announced the establishment of a pool system incorporating most of the filmmakers' recommendations. All creative personnel – those to whom the memo was addressed – would belong to a pool. The position of executive producer was eliminated. Producers would have no authority over other creative personnel. A program committee of senior personnel would guide production. Filmmaking teams would form largely by free association. Although the memo attempted to explain how the new system would work, doubt crept into the text. 'It is exceedingly difficult,' McLean acknowledged, 'to come up with a structural diagram which fully explains the direct and indirect lines of communication' in the new system. He anticipated that 'considerable confusion will mark the [system's] initial months.'

The dismantling of the unit system was a crushing defeat for Daly and his inner circle. But senior managers who took satisfaction in Daly's fall would now have to deal with the apparent triumph of some of the values he represented. In a certain sense, the new system attempted to reproduce for the entire English Production Branch the fluid, flexible, filmmaker-centred dynamic that existed at the core of Unit B. It was an attempt to institutionalize the authority of filmmaking over administration.

For some, it worked as envisioned. Brittain flourished. In 1965, he made (with John Spotton, and with Kemeny as producer) *Memorandum*, still one of the most moving and complex films about the Holocaust. In *Memorandum*, Brittain drew on what he admired both in Grant McLean and in Tom Daly. Like the best of what would become Brittain's large body of documentary work, *Memorandum* addresses political power. It looks into the depths of the abyss that was the Holocaust. And it exhibits political courage in examining relentlessly the shameful recent past of a current ally. But it is also a work of cinematic art. Spotton's brilliant *vérité* footage anchors the film's diverse material. The film has a richly intertwining structure that emerged from nine months of struggle in the editing room. It went about forty per cent over budget. If it had a deadline, it didn't meet it. Over the next two decades Brittain developed into the Film Board's most widely honoured documentary director, with films like *Never a Backward Step* (1966), *Volcano* (1976), and *Henry Ford's America* (1977).

But the pool system evidently released as well the very energies that management was trying to contain. Only seven months after the system's implementation, two senior producers sent a lengthy memorandum (29 September 1964) to the film commissioner, Guy Roberge, laying out their concern that the Board's filmmakers had lost interest in public service and in audiences:

Preferences in subject-matter are being increasingly dictated by the priorities of the film-maker's private aesthetic adventure rather than by the demands of Canadian social reality ...

[There is] an effort to create an environment of total license for the film-maker ...

They conceive of the film-maker as the repository of autonomous TALENT, unique, absolutely unchallengeable, operating within the priorities of its own laws to which all other rules take second place. The truly proper environment for such beings would give them maximum control over artistic expression, size, form, type, and purpose, *and* maximum freedom, *and* maximum government support ...

Only two years later, McLean himself, in a generally upbeat article in *Journal of the University Film Producers Association* about the Film Board's status and plans, lamented that increasingly filmmakers were 'inclined to the view ... that the only restraints which are creatively relevant are those self-imposed by the artist himself – and that all others are intolerable and destructive.'

By 1970, the pool system would be judged a mistake. Its implementation, however, had coincided roughly with a period of administrative turmoil at the Film Board. In 1966, Commissioner Guy Roberge resigned. It was then that McLean was appointed acting commissioner. McPherson was named commissioner in 1967. McPherson, consensus has it, turned out to be a weak administrator easily distressed by conflict and strife. In the late 1960s, labour-management tension spread throughout government service. Separatist impulses quickened in Quebec and found sympathetic spokesmen in the Film Board's French Production Branch. It is hard not to wonder how the new structure might have fared had McLean, a politically fearless man, a straight shooter, and a filmmakers' administrator despite his differences with Unit B, been named commissioner.

The Unit B team enjoyed a last hurrah of sorts the same year that McLean left. In 1964, the Canadian Corporation for the 1967 World Exposition, which the city of Montreal would host, had commissioned the Film Board to create an exhibit. The exposition's theme was to be 'Man and His World.' Most projects proposed and accepted for Expo 67 emphasized the conquest of nature. Under Roman Kroitor's direction, the Film Board developed an idea for an exhibit exploring 'man's conquest of himself.' The exhibit, called *Labyrinthe*, would attempt to retell, in architecture and film, the myth of Theseus and the Minotaur.

In a 30 January 1964 memorandum to Grant McLean – only a month before the demise of Unit B – Kroitor specified three categories of staffing required for the project: full-time, part-time, and occasional. Colin Low, Wolf Koenig, and Hugh O'Connor, who had headed the science film sub-unit within Unit B, were the three full-time personnel mentioned by name. Low would take charge of the project design, Koenig would act as a consultant, and O'Connor would manage it. (Koenig lost interest in the project and dropped out after the initial planning; O'Connor, Low, and Kroitor wound up as the project's directors.) Kroitor named four more people for the part-time category. For the third category, he estimated he would need about four additional directors and editors. And he had one request that didn't fit into a category:

In addition to the above, I should like to have access to the skills and knowledge of Tom Daly, in whatever ways they seem best applicable, and in such a manner that it does not preclude him from fulfilling the other responsibilities he may be called on to carry in the Board

In addition to contributing to the conceptual development of the project, Daly would edit the most complex film and sound effects portions of the presentation.

The project also would be a culmination of Unit B's attempt to integrate the immediate into a vision of something whole. The key developers of the project believed they had selected a universal theme, something that meaningfully embraced all human beings and cultures. Northrop Frye would be a chief consultant during the development of the idea. Film crews would be sent around the world to gather unscripted material with which to express the idea. The footage would be edited into a multiscreen production. But the structure for this direct-cinema material would be more than elaborately cinematic: the film would be exhibited in a building designed specifically for showing it.

The film team was already somewhat familiar with Frye's work. In 1961, Kroitor had produced and Stanley Jackson directed a documentary called *University*. The film included a scene of one of Frye's seminars.

On 12 May 1974, Frye met with the filmmakers at a ski lodge in St-Jovite to discuss the *Labyrinthe* project. As John Ayre reports in his biography of Frye, Daly took fifty-eight pages of notes in the day-long session. Frye's knowledge awed Daly: 'It was like he had an encyclopaedia of all his researches right there in his brain. He was able to document not only the history of the Minotaur legend in Western literature but also a great deal about myths of a different nature in other cultures, which covered all the stages of human psychological development, and what those stages were and are – seven in all, from birth, through childhood, youth, and wilderness, confronting the Minotaur, all the way to death and rebirth. We were very gratified, because we were afraid we might be trying to make too much of the Minotaur myth by generalizing it, that it was too much a personal, wishful choice.'

What impressed Daly the most were remarks of Frye's that personalized the myth. As recorded in the shorthand form of Daly's notes, Frye told the filmmakers (implied words or meanings appear in brackets; abbreviated words are spelled out and periods are added without brackets; all emphases are in the original notes):

There's only one story – the story of your life.
[The] only choice for man is (a) to recognize he is 'in it' [i.e., in the labyrinth] *or* (b) to remain ignorant of it.
[The] walls of [the] labyrinth are [the] walls that wall you off from yourself.
[The] *Tyrant* figure = *ego – tyrant in every* man's soul.
[The] Minotaur *has* to be something you created yourself.
The monster is externalization.

But

Theseus, going into [the labyrinth], knew there *was* a minotaur but he didn't know *what* it was.

Daly remembers being 'struck with wonder' by how Frye's response to a question about the purpose of ritual led back to the challenge the filmmakers had taken on:

To awaken awareness that one is in [the labyrinth, no]? Our aim – something like self-realization or the heightening of consciousness & [this] is what great works of art are supposed to *do*.

Frye understood the difficulties of creating such art. When asked how the myth of the Labyrinth could be communicated to a modern audience, he responded:

[The] public doesn't know [the] stories [in the] Bible [or the] myths – [therefore you] can't allude to them.

Present [it] in terms familiar in present-day terminology.

[The] purpose of discussing [the] central myth is not to dress up this story, but to have it in your mind in presenting the film sequences.

[You're] going to rely on parallels and comparisons.

[The] job now is – select what Eliot calls 'objective correlatives.'

Originally the team envisioned building seven theatres, one for each of seven stages of development, but economic constraints forced a compaction of the idea. Ultimately *Labyrinthe* – the French spelling was in deference to the host city – was housed in a five-storey building divided into three chambers. Each chamber featured images, sounds, music, and a brief commentary in two versions – French, by Claude Jutra, and English, by Donald Brittain – written under the team's general guidance after the picture and sound editing had been completed.

Chamber I was a theatre in which audiences on four levels of narrow balconies on two sides of the chamber watched a twenty-minute film. The film consisted of images of birth, childhood, and youth. It was projected onto two massive screens. One screen lay flat on the chamber's floor. The other rose from the floor thirty-eight feet up a third wall. Together, they created a huge L-shaped projection surface that forced a split in the viewer's attention. The commentary guided the viewers' interpretation of the experience:

This is the Labyrinthe in modern dress. It has been constructed from appropriate bits and pieces of this planet. You in the balconies, each one of you, is the hero of this story.

We begin with the world, waiting for the hero.

The hero: he comes in four colours, two sexes, and thinks in the future tense.

You are no longer just a splendid animal at play. You come from a long line of working men, and if all things are not possible, you are not yet prepared to admit it.

One day you are confronted by your mortality but, peculiar creature that you are, you did not choose to accept it.

Our great adventure appears to have ended rather badly. The surroundings are angry and uncomfortable. But this journey is only half-done and the Labyrinthe has many corridors.

Daly's memory of *Labyrinthe* remains so vivid that he often uses the present tense in recalling it even though it no longer exists: Chamber I 'ends in disillusionment. It seems universal that youth thinks it will go further and do better than its elders. But after a certain point, youth doesn't get any further. Things seem to get in the way. The disillusionment has to do with the feeling that there must be something more to life than just this. It hasn't led to happiness, even if it has led to pleasure – and maybe displeasure as you see your achievements dismantled.

'Now the audience has to make a move that corresponds to the move you have to make to get out of that, to look for a clue to what more there is to life. So the audience has symbolically to make that move into Chamber II, the maze, symbolizing the labyrinthine passages of uncertainty and not-knowing.' The maze was M-shaped, lined with prisms and mirrors. 'It was dark at the beginning, with eerie sounds passing over your head. At a certain point, tiny coloured lights began to respond to the soundtrack. Bird sounds, music – they made a dance to infinity in all directions – up, down, all around you, totally harmoniously, because of the prisms and mirrors. Then it fades. The sound fades. And then the narration says, in effect, that you've had a glimpse of it, but it doesn't belong to you, so now go ahead and search for it yourself':

In legend the hero is told of a monstrous beast that dwells in the dark heart of the Labyrinthe and has cast a spell on the world. And so, there is urgent business: you must go forth and hunt out the beast and break the terrible spell.

Chamber III was a theatre housing five screens arranged in the form of a massive cross. The presentation – which Daly edited – was twenty-one minutes long. Five projectors created the overall image. The images ranged from the ordinary (such as city traffic), to the exotic (such as religious temples), to the haunting (Churchill's funeral barge), the unsettling (an actress removing make-up and confronting her loss of beauty), and the spooky (a night scene of a man paddling a canoe down a river, hunting and killing a crocodile). The intent was to suggest the unity not only of all peoples but also of all experiences, including death. Visitors were told that

The hardest place to look is inside yourself, but that is where you will find the beast, blocking your path to other men. Conquer it and you can truly join in the world.

Just when you think you have it all, it starts to slip away.

Is the last room empty? Or is it filled with all the shapes and sounds on earth?

In its intended effect, Chamber III 'was totally different from Chamber I, where the images were larger and more dramatic but arranged so you could only look at one or another, but not both, at any given moment. In Chamber III, with your need to know what further is possible, you begin to see with a vision which can incorporate various strands of the whole truth at the same time. In Chamber I, it is as if *one* sensation, or *one* feeling, is fully occupying your attention at any one time, and you're unaware of all the other things that could be true at the same time. In Chamber III, you can begin to see simultaneously, with a higher vision, things that you normally can only deal with separately and at different times.'

For Daly, to whom the last decade had brought first triumph and then pain, the intended universality of *Labyrinthe* reflected – as Frye had said it should – an intensely personal meaning: 'The Labyrinth is the psychological struggle of man. The Minotaur is the ego – whatever gets in the way of things. For me, it was anger, either held in or exhibited. But I found out that that in itself was a kind of cover for fear. It had a destructive effect, as the people in my unit taught me.

'You need those confrontations in order to experience what you are unconsciously covering up. These personal characteristics that one doesn't like or is ashamed of or tries to keep locked up, hidden away where they can't do any harm – if they are kept separate like that they continue to act poisonously. When finally they are acknowledged and included in a larger whole, they can be benign, and affirmed in their own right.'

The only experience of *Labyrinthe* now available is a multiple-image film version (*In the Labyrinth* [1979]) of the Chamber III presentation, but by contemporary accounts *Labyrinthe* was among Expo's most popular exhibits. People waited as long as six hours to get in. Many returned for another visit; apparently the exhibit told the stories of their lives, too.

Although Daly says the time he spent editing the Chamber III presentation 'was one of the happiest years of my life,' it didn't start out that way. The project was the most adventurous the Film Board had ever done, involving architectural, technical, and conceptual challenges of a high and varied order. It was budgeted at more than four million dollars. Visually it pushed the tension between unscripted material and formal structure to a new limit. An enormous amount of footage collected in direct-cinema style from around the world had to be edited into a multi-screen format and had to make sense with minimal commentary.

Sound technology had progressed so rapidly that editing the sound would challenge Daly in a very different way from editing sound in the early NFB years of primitive equipment. 'Everything I knew about sound would come into play in cutting the complex tracks for *Labyrinthe*, with its many available channels and excellent quality of tape and recording. Sound and music strongly touch people's senses and emotions. They round out the effect of a film, and they also can add a strong sense of movement, just off-screen, to rather ordinary static shots. *Labyrinthe* needed as complete and rich a blend of sounds, music, and picture as possible, since there could be very little narration, given the international audience. So I would have to make patterns of sound which, to the senses and emotions, would compare and contrast with previous patterns, whether you even "thought" about it or not.'

Despite the project's ambition and complexity, there could be no give in the production schedule. Daly had to meet a precise deadline – the scheduled opening of the exhibit – and he had to carry out his part while the building and the technology were also under development. The only multi-screen project Daly had edited before was 'a two-screen show of still photos of human faces (*Faces* [1963]) done in four days to an existing music track as a promotion piece for the *Labyrinthe* proposal itself. This time it took me two weeks to put together my first attempt at a rough-cut sequence, and the result was a disaster. I had used up one twenty-sixth of the available editing time, with nothing to show for it, and I had some fifty items to rough-cut and integrate into some sort of meaningful progression. I panicked, and considered backing out. But I realized that I had as much knowledge and experience to work from as any other editor, and that any other editor would have exactly the same problems but even less time than I had, since I was at least familiar with the material. I convinced myself to go on.'

Daly had one assistant. He was Yves Dion, who had been hired only a few months earlier. Dion at first felt out of his element: 'I didn't have any artistic training, and I didn't come from the type of milieu which makes filmmakers, you know, like the small bourgeoisie. I came from a working-class background, where you evolve the kind of mentality where work is something to be done to earn a living. You don't usually like it, but you have to do it.'

When Daly first met him, Dion seemed wary and withdrawn. 'He was very young, and he had a kind of hunted look that reminded me of a caged wolf from the wilds. But he was vigorous – he had to be to manipulate our eight-way synchronizer with eight double reels of 35mm film going back and forth during all the sound editing. And he learned quickly – for example, not to snap the film by stopping too suddenly.'

Dion felt very lucky. 'Here I was, doing something I liked very much, and I was being paid for it – not much, but I was being paid for it, I could make a living out of it. That was incredible. And I was slowly learning that all the people around me were the great names in filmmaking – Colin Low, Roman Kroitor, Don Brittain – they were all coming in to our cutting room. I was cooped up with Tom Daly for like twelve, fifteen hours a day, seven days a week. And whenever we had a break, we'd start talking about things that I had never discussed before, only read, things like Kafka and "Kubla Khan" and Plato. That was simply fantastic, especially with the type of mind that Tom has about filmmaking.'

Daly enjoyed the developing relationship as much as Dion did. 'We were much of the time alone, out there at the edge of town in the Canadair hangar buildings, and we used to go often to a pub across the street to lunch on a beer and a sandwich. As he gradually lost his fear of communicating his inner thoughts, the far-away look began to disappear, and a willing assistant was ever present.'

With Dion's help, Daly tackled the challenge of structuring the enormous collection of disparate sounds and images into something that would represent the original vision. 'The problem, from the very beginning, was how to induce in the audience some degree of *inner experience* corresponding to the stage of development in question. And even if they couldn't understand it, the experience would at least be *compatible* with the psychology of the stage concerned. They would not be just spectators, but *participants* too.

'Chamber III gave the greatest difficulty in that respect – all the material was necessarily photographed from the outside, but all the concentration of the story development was now on the inside, the search: the search for the self, the finding and dealing with one's own greatest inner adversary in this development ... the possible stages beyond ... the possibility of sharing a community where the others are all as important to you as you are to yourself ... the reality of mortality and loss.'

Daly began seeking 'ways to relate the simultaneous progression of images till they began to awaken *in myself* the desired feeling, or the recognition and remembrance of the desired feeling. If I had not been disappointed and frustrated by my own limitation, I would not have embarked on a search for more. And the taste and desire for it seemed to sensitize me to even the tiniest elements of evidence of what we were looking for in the material.

'It was during that year of editing that I began to notice *consciously* a very different form of "thinking" from the usual "trying to figure things out." I had to do all that ordinary thinking ... all my "homework" as I call it – know all sides of all the shots, et cetera – then relax and forget about all that detail and ask myself, What is there in this batch of material that can serve the purpose? And every now and then a sort of non-verbal "suggestion" would come from "somewhere" which would activate that sensitivity, and I knew then that I could make *something* relevant out of it.

'The most remarkable part to me was the way the very end of the film came about. It was the last Thursday of the very last week we could consider making changes. So far we had no real end, only a beautiful scene of horses galloping over the Alberta foothills. Colin, Roman, and Yves gathered on Friday to look through the entire collection of footage for any shot or sequence that any one of us thought might conceivably be useful for making an ending. At the end of the day, we were all depressed. We'd found maybe half a dozen possibly useful single shots. I went to bed very disappointed – only to wake up at five in the morning with images of two shots floating together in the quiet of my mind. One was a shot we already had selected, a shot of Buddhist monks in saffron robes walking in the colonnade beside their golden temple, their highlights and shadows intermittently appearing and disappearing behind the pillars. We'd seen this shot many times. The other was a shot we had totally forgotten till the day before, a different one of the crocodile slayer canoeing down the river – this time in daylight, in the late afternoon sun, with the golden light on his face appearing and disappearing into shadow again as the canoe passes trees on the river bank.

'The visual similarities stuck in my mind and began to attract – almost magically – other images from shots we had seen: shots with the same golden afternoon light, shots of objects made of gold, shots of elderly people in their "golden" age. As this process of attraction continued, I saw more and more ramifications of these images, connecting back to contrasting sequences earlier in the film, like the scene of the crocodile's death. I was so excited that I called Roman as early as I decently could, and told him that I thought I had a clue to a possible ending. He said, "Marvellous – we can come and be available all day if you need us." For the first and only time in my editing career, I said, "No! Don't anybody come! I'm afraid of losing the mood in which the sequence is taking form." So everybody, except Yves, stayed away.

'By nine that night, I had developed a three-part sequence which quite excited me. I screened it for the others. Afterwards there was a long silence, which Roman finally broke. He began suggesting all sorts of changes. "I wonder if we switched the Cretan lady on the east screen with the man on the north one," and so on. My heart sank as he went on. My ending hadn't worked.

'On Sunday, we dutifully made all the suggested changes and screened it at six that evening. There was a silence again, and again Roman broke it: "No, it was better the first way." And, with the exception of one change, that was the way it finally went out – only two weeks overdue but in time for the opening of the exhibit.'

As far removed from the wartime documentary as *Labyrinthe* may seem stylistically, Daly sees them as directly linked in craftsmanship. In his contribution to *How to Make or Not to Make a Canadian Film*, he explained the connection:

It is interesting to look back at the contrast between editing in World War II and editing today. In the war years, material was scarce, thin, often inadequate. You had to be inventive, and stretch it to cover many purposes. By contrast, today we often have more good material than we know what to do with. And it is easy for practically any editor to do a "good-enough" job. I am grateful to the war years for teaching me always to try to find the most that I can see in any material, whatever it is, and to be satisfied with nothing less than trying to bring *that* off.

One day, while Daly was editing *Labyrinthe*, John Spotton decided to pay him a visit. Now working under other producers, Spotton had earned acclaim for *Buster Keaton Rides Again* (1965), an entertaining film about the making of another NFB film, Gerald Potterton's *The Railrodder* (1965), in which an aged Buster Keaton crosses Canada on a railway scooter. Spotton directed, shot, and edited *Buster Keaton Rides Again*. It was 'his' film. But it was a minor one compared to *Memorandum*, on which Spotton, although credited as co-director with Donald Brittain, had worked mainly as cameraman.

Memorandum was the most hectic shoot Spotton had ever been on: 'A third of the film was shot in twenty-four hours. We got off the airplane and started shooting. We had to follow this group on their pilgrimage, and I never knew where I was. So the footage tends to get pretty ... *ragged*, you know. We got a telegram from our producer saying the stuff was useless. But I knew that once we got in the cutting room, we could make it work. I knew this because, as a cameraman, I was paying attention to how things might be used. And this was all because of Tom, Tom constantly talking in the cutting room about what to look for in a shot – never about how to expose it or frame it, but what to look for in it.

'It turned out that both of these films were in the same film festival. They were competing. Now I just *know* that *Memorandum* is a helluva lot better film, but *Keaton* won, and I felt pretty good. The next morning, I went looking for Tom. He was working on *Labyrinthe* in an aircraft hangar a couple of miles from here. It was kind of silly, maybe, but I just kind of wandered about over there. I just wanted to say thank you. Whether I did or not, I'm not sure, but I think he got the message, that this award was a kind of pay-off for what he had done for me.'

4

The Thermometer of Truth

When Daly returned from *Labyrinthe*, the Film Board was in creative ferment but administrative anarchy. Filmmakers ruled the roost. To get a project approved, all they had to do was find a willing producer, who in turn would present the project to an unpredictable but increasingly accommodating program committee. To have something to do, producers had to interest filmmakers in working with them. Consequently the dynamics of their negotiations with directors were such that they had very little power over their projects' development.

At least that is how Daly saw the situation: the new system had 'liberated' the directors partly by 'punishing the old executive producers, demoting them to producers and taking away their authority – "imprisoning" them by leaving them officially responsible for projects but without the authority to carry out their responsibilities. We were even physically uprooted from our central locations and moved together to lesser quarters in a side corridor, which somebody dubbed the "Via Dolorosa."'

Among the filmmakers, Daly says, there was 'euphoria for a little while. The strait-jacket was off. They had "freedom." But the problem of making anything out of it was not thought out. How do you pick your team? How do you get anything done? All the elements of a team working well together, learning from film to film, were lost.'

As the former head of what had been the Film Board's most respected and successful unit, Daly might seem to have had the farthest to fall after the unit system's demise. Gone were not just his authority but also the hard-won sense of community that he had derived from Unit B. 'Tom took the abandonment of the unit system very much to heart,' remembers Robert Verrall. 'A lot of people thought it had been done to clip Tom's wings. He was very demoralized about it.' Colin Low says, 'When the unit system disappeared and he lost his authority, which was very important to him – he had a big ego, and probably still does – he was very hurt.'

Quitting the Film Board was not an option for Daly. He had no ambitions in film external to the Film Board. Even if he had, his deliberative style and particular skills, committed as they were to an extreme perfectionism, probably were unmarketable in the commercial filmmaking world. With his rich experience and impressive credit list, he easily could get a teaching job – film education was rapidly gaining a foothold in universities – but an academic career still held no interest for him. However diminished and demeaned his role now was, his future would be at the Film Board. Yet he was only forty-six years old, nearly two decades from retirement.

If his predicament was a bleakly familiar one in the organizational world, his response was not: 'I could have felt annoyed and said, "To hell with this place," but it wasn't what I felt like. There was so much there to do, still plenty to do of just what I really wished to do. But it was in a new arrangement. Now, I was not required of other people. They sought me out if *they* wanted to. This showed me something about paper authority versus real authority. An executive producer has paper authority. Real authority is where you really understand things, and people sense that and want to work with you. All of a sudden, even as a producer, I didn't have authority. So I could be effective only if the other person wanted to work with me.'

Not everybody did or could. His Unit B team had split up. Kroitor left the Film Board for private industry to promote the IMAX projection system that had been invented for *Labyrinthe*. Koenig and Verrall returned to Animation. Low became an avid pioneer in the Film Board's activist 'Challenge for Change' program. The French-language filmmakers now had an entirely separate production branch. Other directors preferred to work for less meticulous producers.

Those who gravitated to Daly were novice filmmakers looking for support and guidance. They had just joined the Film Board or were trying to move into directing from some other department, as John Spotton had done earlier. One attraction Daly had over his producer colleagues was his still-active interest in the details of editing. Even as an executive producer he had enjoyed editing; although he had never done location work, he had not become a mere 'desk' administrator, either.

He also liked to explore ideas. Many of those who were seeking to become Film Board directors in the latter half of the 1960s were themselves exploring fresh cultural values and new political orientations. The more traditional documentary culture held little interest for most of them; Brittain notwithstanding, the booze culture, suddenly, was passé. Classicist though he was, Daly, with his interest in Native cultures, spiritual development, and non-Western religions, shared several points of interest with them. He was, as Colin Low observes, the one producer with whom 'you could discuss, say, *The Tibetan Book of the Dead.*'

These filmmakers would not, however, coalesce into enduring teams along the lines of Unit B. Although they had in common with the Unit B filmmakers an urge to experiment, they were more individualistic in their approach and their goals, and they wanted to introduce a stronger personal element into documentary content and form. They also tended to be more politically minded than Daly. But several of them became distinguished filmmakers who acknowledge an early debt to Daly's tutelage.

In the mid-1960s, Tony Ianzelo 'was breaking out of the Camera Department. There was an experimental film budget. I dipped into it to get one sequence shot.' Out of this one sequence grew Ianzelo's first film, *Antonio* (1966), which Daly produced. The film is a meditative portrait of Ianzelo's father, a widowed immigrant coming to terms with old age. He wavers between self-pity and resigned affirmation. 'Two rooms in a strange house,' he complains in voice-over. 'I am like an old shoe, a rag. It's tragic. It's tragic.' But he resolves 'to carry my own life the way I find it.' He finds solace in Dante and the Bible, pleasure in concocting his one meal a day ('my invention, my creation'), satisfaction from his skill at making wine, and companionship with a hospitalized, dying friend. *Antonio* conveys sympathy without sentimentality; it is wise without pretension.

'When I saw the material Tony had shot about his own father,' Daly recalls, 'and saw how objectively he had been able to look at him while feeling very deeply about him, I just knew it would make a touching and enduring film and that we had a potentially great filmmaker in the making.' Daly ranks *Antonio* with other 'classic first films, such as *Corral, Paul Tomkowicz,* and *Very Nice, Very Nice.*'

Ianzelo marvels at Daly's 'ability to give total attention to one filmmaker and his project in the morning and to someone else in the afternoon.' But Ianzelo's project required patience as well. 'The editing was laborious, because I still had to work as a camera assistant. I had to come in on weekends to screen materials and cut sequences. Tom understood all that. It is so easy to get discouraged, but Tom just talked about the values of the film. He was positive, supportive, encouraging. He would help you bring your best points forward and realize your failings. That's the character of the man. I'll always be indebted to him.'

In the 1970s, Ianzelo emerged as one the Film Board's strongest directors. His many NFB films include *Don't Knock the Ox* (1970), *Goodbye Sousa* (1973), *Cree Hunters of Mistassini* (1974), *Our Land Is Our Life* (1974), *Musicanada* (1975), *High Grass Circus* (1976), *Blackwood* (1976), *North China Commune* (1979), *North China Factory* (1980), and IMAX films *Emergency* (1987) and *The First Emperor of China* (1989). In cinematic style, however, he was arguably the most traditional of the filmmakers whom Daly helped get started during these years.

Michael Rubbo, an Australian who in 1965 was studying film at Stanford University, had got interested in the Film Board and in Daly from watching Unit B films in class. 'They had a sort of openness, they were always unusual in some way, like *Lonely Boy* and *The Back-breaking Leaf*, and all those. I decided I'd try to do an internship at the Film Board, and I sent Daly my thesis film, *The True Source of Knowledge*. I waited and waited, but got no reply. Finally, I decided to hitchhike across the United States. I was in New York. It was winter. I called the Film Board. Tom was about to go on holidays or something, so I was told to hurry up and get there the next day, which I did.

'I didn't know what it was going to be like – was it going to be a high-pressure production house, or what. Anyway, when I got there he was in a screening. They said if I wanted to go into the screening room, that was okay. So I slipped into the back. It was my film they were screening! Daly, Koenig, Kroitor, maybe some others. I could just see the back of their heads, and of course didn't know who they were anyway. When the lights went up, one of them asked, "Who made this?" "Oh, some guy in California." "He really seems to understand what's happening with youth. We should get in touch with him." Then I revealed myself.

'He and some other people took me to lunch. He had a sort of serenity about him that was fascinating. He made me think of the place as a bit like a university, and he was a little like a university professor.

'Out of that lunch came the offer of a job. He must have had something to do with it, but we pretty much lost track of each other, because there were little power centres at the Film Board. I sort of got into John Kemeny's. Kemeny sent me off to make a film on trucks. It didn't turn out too well. Then I got ill for a while, and after that I had nothing to do, and I was quite demoralized. I picked up films that nobody else wanted, some little films on animals. They turned out okay in a corny sort of way. But I knew I was at a turning-point. So I went to see Tom, and told him I'd like to do a film with him, and he, in his roundabout way, said something like, "Well, I think you should think seriously about whether you're a filmmaker or not. And if not, maybe you should try something else."

'I was quite shocked by that. I'd never had any doubts about it, and here was somebody whose judgment I trusted saying in a very polite way that maybe I was in the wrong profession. So we made a sort of deal, where I would try one film with him, and if it didn't work out, then, well, I'd leave. I don't know if it was ever spelled out that way, but I took it that way.'

The film was about a drama teacher who had a reputation for creative approaches to teaching recalcitrant students. During the shooting, Rubbo discovered that the situation wasn't quite what he had expected. 'These were tough kids from downtown Toronto. They didn't seem to like the teacher. They thought the whole thing was sappy and stupid. So the first rushes were ... chaos. I really have to credit just having those rushes to Martin Duckworth. He kept on filming, while I was huddling in a corner, thinking I had really made a disastrous mistake. Somehow I was expecting the class to be magical, that these kids would just flower somehow. But when Tom saw the rushes, he said, "Well, you know, it's not what you thought it would be, but it's very interesting anyway."'

Rubbo went back several more times to film, and the documentary, *Mrs. Ryan's Drama Class* (1969), began to take shape. 'I think he enjoyed the fact that once I'd got over my initial confusion I was able to film in that exploratory spirit. It wasn't earth-shattering, but it looked like a film, it had excitement, there was change going on, something was evolving.'

After two or three other unremarkable projects, Rubbo wanted to make a film about the war in Vietnam. Support for a film condemning the war outright would not be forthcoming, but, with Daly's support, Rubbo got approval for a film about a Canadian-sponsored foster parents plan in Saigon. When Rubbo arrived with his small crew, he found that the foster parents plan wasn't as interesting as he had hoped, and he began exploring the city for himself, using some of the children as a kind of thread. He discovered a trio of idealistic, antiwar young American journalists, whose work and views could serve as an anchor for his filming. Via telex, 'Tom backed me up, saying that that really wasn't the subject, but to go ahead if that's what I really wanted to do. We started shooting, and sent our rushes back, and he'd look at them, and send quite full telex reports on the rushes, right down to shot numbers. He would *interpret*, he'd guess what I was after. He'd say, "Good atmospheric stuff of kids in slum, gives feeling of tension of war on children," or something like that. He'd get at the meaning behind the surface meaning.'

The eventual film, somewhat misleadingly entitled *Sad Song of Yellow Skin* (1970), is an exploration of the war's corrupting effect on the culture of Saigon. Using the three journalists as guides, the film interweaves three main locations: a home for orphaned shoeshine boys (who also pimp, steal, and gamble), a refugee slum built on a cemetery, and an island in the Mekong Delta governed by a Buddhist monk who, every day, walks along a three-dimensional map from Saigon to Hanoi in a symbolic act of peace-making. The more we see, however, the less we understand. In his commentary, Rubbo acknowledges his difficulties in penetrating cultural barriers and personal defences. Halfway into the film he confesses that 'by the end of the fourth day, we knew that our research was not going past the superficial.' His American guides admit to limitations on their own ability to establish intimate contact with the people they are trying to help. But as the difficulties of understanding are made explicit and the levels of mediation are compounded, the film becomes increasingly compelling. The last twenty minutes, in which the film lingers first on a funeral in the refugee compound and then at the Island of Peace, range across a spectrum of images and emotions that are unforgettable. The film undermines simplistic idealism, but not cynically. Rubbo's struggle to make sense out of what he saw in Saigon, to find some moral point of view on the subject, transforms a film that could have been a self-righteous moral travelogue into a profoundly moving, disturbing film that may prove to be the most enduring documentary on the war.

This quality was the result of arduous editing and restructuring. Daly had seen all the material as rushes and in rough assembly and, he says, 'had, as usual, got an unformed general impression of the sort of stature and quality of film that could be made from the material. In this case it was a very strong impression, very exciting. But when Mike invited me finally to his first rough-cut, I had a devastating feeling of disappointment. It was so far from the potential of the material that there was no way I could see of editing and improving this form of it to bring out the quality. But I could not understand the reason, or see what was the centre of the problem. Mike was himself upset with the effect of it, but even more so because I was obviously unhappy with it, too.

'Mike had chosen to use a discussion between the journalists as a framework of linkages, allowing him to go back and forth between them and their meaningful comments, and the images of reality they were talking about. It was a frequently used "essay" form of film, which allowed considerable freedom for the filmmaker to express his own ideas and feelings in logical order. *But I couldn't feel that I cared about it.*

'In the course of pondering over the problem, I realized that before Mike went to Vietnam for the filming, his ideas about the place were rather different, more like mine still were, not having gone there. And all of a sudden it hit me that I couldn't *feel* his film because I couldn't connect with his conclusions. What I needed was to follow him step by step in the process of the changing flow of his own understanding. How did he get "from here to there"? What were the influences along the way that effected the changes?

'I told him of this, and asked him what his *first* impression was on arrival in Saigon. It was of a kaleidoscope of colour and confusion. Then what happened? He looked around for something to hang on to, and met the three American journalists in a little office. They were themselves exploring in their own way the consequences of the war and the American presence, and trying to bring a positive action to it. This had interested Mike, and it was in following what they did in their everyday lives that he came upon and shot all the subjects in the film.

'At this point I suggested that he simply structure the line of development by following the gradual unfolding of his own discoveries and understandings, and it would lead us along an adventurous line where nothing predictable would lie ahead. He decided to try it, and the very next rough-cut showed the promise of what the film could become. But it ended up of even higher quality and mood than I had envisioned at best.'

Daly remembers the experience as one of discovery 'about the forming and shaping of films. The difference between the meaning of an "essay" and a "story" in communicating between people threw much light for me on many other things thereafter.'

A key to the effectiveness of the structure is the personal nature of the commentary. Rubbo speaks it himself and makes no effort to professionalize it, leaving in his hesitations, his 'ers' and 'ahs'. Rubbo credits Daly for the personal commentary. From Vietnam, 'I had written him these long, vivid letters, "word-pictures" really. I think they had stuck in his mind. He thought, "This guy's a storyteller, and it's all personal, so *get that into the movie*." He was the one who encouraged me to use the word "I". He gave me the confidence of my own convictions. I was retreating from that which was okay in a letter, because a letter was just to an audience of one. I was retreating back to something more formal. And he was saying, well, that it was not that sort of material.'

The director's personal commentary, so widely accepted now, was then generally considered intrusive. Daly remembers that a buyer from the CBC 'was very much taken by *Sad Song* and included it in his recommendations for purchase and broadcast. Later he called back very crestfallen, because he had been overruled by his superior, who didn't like films in which the director took part himself. However, the film went over well elsewhere, including the United States. About a year later, the CBC ran it themselves, in spite of their "policy," since it now had status that they recognized as acceptable.'

After *Sad Song*, Rubbo carried his newly discovered first-person approach an important step further. Beginning with *Wet Earth and Warm People* (1971), he stepped in front of the camera when necessary, not to report to the audience as a journalist but to become one of his film's active characters. He employed this method in several subsequent films, most notoriously in *Waiting for Fidel* (1974), where the process of filmmaking itself supplants the film's ostensible subject.

Mort Ransen joined the Film Board in 1961. The films he made in his first few years were unremarkable educational or military training films. The breakup of the unit system freed him to pursue unconventional ideas. Daly produced Ransen's feature film, *Christopher's Movie Matinee* (1968), and two offbeat documentaries on Sweden, *Untouched and Pure* (1970) and *Falling from Ladders* (1969), which were among six films co-produced by the Film Board and the Swedish Institute for Cultural Relations.

Working on these films with Daly gave Ransen a fresh and liberating perspective on editing: 'Tom is the best person I've ever met at judging footage, and figuring out how to manipulate it to work for you. Even the way he starts off is unusual. Most editors begin by looking for something in the material they're watching that might provide a direction. Tom sits and records *everything* on the screen as thoroughly as he can. He writes constantly. I used to think he wasn't seeing what I shot because he was too busy writing, but he has an uncanny ability to write and watch the screen at the same time. His notes were always the best source of what the material consisted of. They were not merely concerned with content, but with potential. Often shots you don't think important Tom would remember weeks or even months later, as a means of, say, making the character more sympathetic, or providing a change of pace, or counterpoint.

'Once past the rough-cut, however, and into the intricacies of the final editing, was when his ability would *really* shine through. It's when he picked up a yellow grease pencil and started to concern himself with the numbers of frames that his editing genius amazed you. "Take two frames out of there," he'd say, and you couldn't see how it possibly could make any difference – and then you'd watch a connection come to life in a way it hadn't before. I tend to play with frames a lot now in editing, and I know it comes totally from Tom.'

Ransen played with a lot more than individual frames. All three of the films challenged filmmaking conventions prevalent at the time. Although a feature film, *Christopher's Movie Matinee* is almost entirely improvised. It is about what happens when a group of alienated teenagers are given a generous film budget, limited control over a professional crew, and access to an experienced director. The result is an alternately tedious and engaging take on the generation gap. The most surprising revelation the film offers is the banality with which the gap typically is expressed. The teenagers are for love, humanity, and peace. The adults sneer at their sappy idealism. The film's aesthetic qualities themselves seem to participate in the debate between the teenagers' anti-authoritarian lack of discipline and the adults' detested values.

Untouched and Pure lampoons what Ransen and his collaborators perceived as Sweden's obsession with planning, control, and measurement. To serve this end, the film juxtaposes unrelated images and sounds for some witty effects. In one recurring scene, a heavy-set woman is delivering a sex-education lecture. Her stern how-to approach presents sexual fulfilment as something achieved by following carefully defined procedures. This scene is intercut with shots of some older women, in a museum, looking askance at the extraordinarily large penises protruding from primitive wooden sculptures. 'I've never seen anything like it' is laid in as voice-over in the museum, and 'At the same time' is cut into the lecture as the educator talks about the man's role in the achievement of simultaneous orgasm. Underlying the humour are glimpses and whispers suggesting anxiety about sex, death, and happiness. A scene that seems to encapsulate the filmmaker's assessment of the Swedish condition occurs after a policeman has interrupted a performance of street music. The film's vivacious female guide protests that 'the people need music.' The stony policeman answers that people must follow regulations.

Falling from Ladders, nine minutes long, isolates the obsession with numbers that Ransen saw in Swedish culture. Every shot is of a Swede reciting, directly to the camera, a statistic about Swedish life: the numbers of reindeer, cows, tandem bikes, persons arrested for drunkenness, women having orgasms, people waiting for flats, policemen, government workers, persons who fall from ladders each year, schoolteachers, old people's homes, lakes, foreign visitors, dental students, and so on. As the film nears its end, just the numbers themselves are recited, without their referents. The statistics are actual; the recitations are contrived, but edited so as to let the audience in on the contrivance.

'With *Untouched and Pure*,' Ransen says, 'I was trying to show the limitations of documentary. It was an "anti-documentary," against documentary's tendency to manipulate. I was doing it right here in the temple of documentary filmmaking, and getting away with it. This was largely Tom's doing. Here's an example of his openness. I was attacking the whole method of editing, the central idea – central to him, too – that you hide your cuts because you don't want the audience to see the cuts, to be distracted by them. What we did was try to find ways of *showing* the cuts, of making the audience aware that they were being manipulated. For example, there were a lot of interviews. We would deliberately repeat lines, or take them obviously out of context, showing the audience that you could manipulate anything, that seeing should not be believing.'

Ransen remembers a similar instance of support during the editing of *Christopher's Movie Matinee*. 'There was a sequence where the kids were talking about education. I had put them in an abandoned classroom, had them sit at their desks, so they could re-experience it as they talked. When I was editing it, I thought the sequence was too long, and boring in parts. The kids were completely happy with it. When I showed it to other people, the reaction was really sympathetic to the agony and tedium the kids were describing, but they thought it was too long, too. Every time I tried to cut out the parts I thought were boring, the sequence didn't work. It was faster, but the sympathy was gone. Tom tried a cut of his own on this sequence. When we looked at it, we both agreed that the kids were essentially right. The audience might be bored in places, but it was worth it, it was needed for the main objective of the sequence.

'I don't know if there's another producer at the Film Board who would have made that decision.'

Daly remembers that John Grierson, who saw *Christopher's Movie Matinee* while teaching at McGill University and praised lavishly its contribution to understanding the complaints of young people, also thought that the film 'shouldn't have been more than an hour long. I agreed with him about the ideal length, but we couldn't see at the time how to suppress one-third of the film without destroying the natural mood, tempo, and development of events.' Of *Untouched and Pure*, Daly says, 'For me, there is a lot of fun in this film. Mort made no attempt to balance matters judiciously but selected certain aspects or characteristics that interested him, then played with them cinematically as well as logically – or anti-logically. But I would have been happier if the film had been tighter and more compact. Repetitions could have been fewer in some cases, with more total effect. Optimum is not maximum. It is often more effective to underplay an effect than to give all of it one has. If a scene lasts a second longer than you want it to, you already begin to be impatient. Much better to be several seconds too soon, leaving people wishing for more. But of course the "right" length of time for different people varies enormously.'

When time came to send a test print of *Untouched and Pure* to the Film Board's Swedish partners, it fell upon Daly to prepare the Institute for a film that could be misinterpreted as mocking. His 29 June 1970 letter to the Institute exemplifies the diplomatic tasks that fell to Film Board producers of innovative co-productions. He began by noting that the film's title was taken

as you will see from a song in the film, and refers to that enduring 'something of value' which is to be found beneath all the shifting and changing, happiness and struggle, seriousness and laughter of life – in countries as in individuals, in Sweden and Swedes as everywhere else.

This ... is a very unusual film, quite original, and breaking new ground in film-making methods as well as in ways of viewing things. In my opinion it is a synthesis of both personal film-making and a challenge-for-change attitude, in which the film-makers have sought new ways of probing into the characterstics of a people. It is about Sweden 'behind the mask.'

No doubt most people will look for their favourite stereotypes and clichés when they hear it is about Sweden. Outdoor enthusiasts will look for landscapes and sports and the body beautiful; welfare enthusiasts will look for the famous examples of their pre-occupations; labour buffs will look for an expression of Sweden's leadership in this field; and so forth. Most of the usual facts and information are not there, and therefore many people may be disappointed at first. But not, I feel, for long.

The fact is that all the usual facts and information have been given a hundred times over, and in better forms than this film can satisfy. There is no point to repeating the same things over again. The film-makers have stuck their necks out and launched into a form of cinematic observation and comment which offers an entirely new experience of things Swedish. Things that are never normally seen together are brought into cross-relations so that one can feel complexities and even paradoxes from more than one point of view at once.

I find that the film grows on people. It is like a ferment which works even after the tasting is over. People go back and back to it in their minds, and it doesn't seem to be so important whether they 'like' or 'dislike' the film. Most people seem to like it very much ... When it was shown to a theater full of our people here, before we finished the cutting copy, it was warmly applauded afterward – a rather rare expression of approbation from notoriously critical and jealous film-makers.

It is definitely a film to be best seen with a good-sized audience. All the fun, recognition of ironies, and changes of mood are best felt in company with others. It is when one is alone that one is inclined to be most critical.

I think perhaps our people are a little afraid that the film will be taken in Sweden as 'Canadians laughing at Sweden.' It is not meant that way, though as Mort says, it couldn't have been made anywhere else than in Sweden. Here, certainly, it is taken as a film in which we laugh at ourselves, at our strengths and weaknesses, character and foibles, mirrored in Swedes. We hope it will be taken in the same way in Sweden.

After several additional paragraphs on the film's intended effect, the letter concludes with some detailed information about the test print.

In *A Film for Max* (1970), Derek May's contempt for narrative convention made Ransen's look tame. The scriptless, plotless, and, some would say, pointless feature film seems to be a meditation not on the meaning of life or on one's place in the world but on the experience of utter uncertainty about either. It may be the most self-referential narrative film to emerge from the Film Board. Director May and his wife are the film's two main characters. They don't so much play themselves as simply be themselves. Max is their son. The cameraman and soundman become characters as well, the former most prominently as a mediator between May and his wife after a spat, the latter as a kind of comic foil. The Film Board itself is given a role as an off-camera Philistine: in one scene, May reads from an internal Film Board document on restrictive budgetary measures.

Almost everything about *A Film for Max* would seem to flout common-sense principles of communication as well as accumulated knowledge of the craft of film. At times, the film seems to have been shot at a 1:1 ratio. In places, the shots seem strung together rather than edited. Some shots stay on the screen long after the typical viewer has become bored with them.

'Usually,' Daly reflects in defence of May, 'shots are held only so long as the usual surface interest in them holds, and the audience's attention is carried along by a controlled momentum, which often prevents it from having to question the meaning of what is in front of it. Derek felt – at least he said so at the time – that if shots were left on the screen longer than usual, people would begin to find and see other meanings than the obvious ones. Even if they became bored with the film, they would have to wake up to their own passivity and learn to take action of some sort, either finding something to interest them, in any situation, or, even, getting up and walking out.

'There may have been not a few who have walked out. But sometimes it is just as important to make films, with all one's heart and belief, entirely appropriate to only a narrow segment of the public as it is to make more broadly popular ones – especially in the experimental field, if the experiment has any depth to it, and is sincere.'

Although it tests the viewer's receptivity, *A Film for Max* has some fine moments. In a breakfast scene, May and his crew stagger around sleepily. Nothing seems to be happening. A crew member off-camera asks May if the cameraman should keep shooting. May answers, 'I don't care if he goes on shooting or not.' The exasperated soundman tells May, 'Do something you enjoy. I enjoy taking sounds, he enjoys shooting.' After a pause, May responds, 'I enjoy directing,' and laughs.

May took full advantage of Daly's support. 'He'd encourage you to experiment, to have a good time, to *play* – which was wonderful! And he'd have as good a time as was being offered. He was interested in the process.

'He may not agree with the tone of the film. He may not agree with the stance I take. But that won't get in the way. He's a conservative soul ... but game enough to allow the other voices to be heard.'

Albert Kish was an editor hoping to become a director. 'I had an idea, which I wrote on a piece of toilet paper, and I stopped Tom Daly in the corridor – I hardly knew him – and I asked him to read it. First he corrected the spelling mistakes in it and then he said it was an interesting idea but had to be developed further. The thing is, he didn't dismiss me. So I wrote it up again, and really embellished it. He fought for the project when I was trying to get it approved.'

The result was *This Is a Photograph* (1971), a short film on the immigrant experience. 'When looking at immigrants' photo albums,' Daly recalls, 'Albert had noticed how frequently the same tendencies turned up in all the different families. On arrival, they took photos of what was different here from their homeland. On getting their first job, they would find a way of showing that. On having their first dwelling-place, they would show what it was like. And their first bathtub, frigidaire, TV, or automobile. Then there were the family memories – culture and costumes and ancestors from the homeland – not to forget. All these were collected in their albums and treasured.'

Using photos from these albums with snippets of voice-over dialogue and a commentary, Kish structured his film like a letter back home. Its theme is the immigrant's gradual assimilation into Canadian society and culture. A visually striking sequence superimposes thick-flaked snow falling across photographs of winter scenes. But it is the 'wry and sly details' (Daly's phrase) that are most intriguing: photos of immigrants posing by cars that relatives back home will assume belong to the prosperous correspondent; a remark that the trusting Canadians 'will believe anything' when a job-seeking immigrant presents his 'qualifications.' The film won several awards and demonstrated Kish's directorial abilities. In between editing assignments, Kish directed numerous films, among them the highly successful *Our Street Was Paved with Gold* (1973), *Los Canadienses* (1975), and *Paper Wheat* (1979).

'What's really interesting about working with Daly,' Kish remembers, 'is that he has a way of telling you that the film is a piece of *shit* without *saying* this, by pointing out the good things in it. He'll look at the whole film and then say,"Oh, this [cut or shot or sequence] is brilliant." So right away you get the idea that the rest is not so brilliant. And where the weaknesses are. And without destroying your ego. You feel that the idea comes from you, not from him. He's helping you find the story, and he's never overbearing. And you must realize that *This Is a Photograph* was severely criticized. It is very harsh on Canada, it gives a very harsh view of the immigrant experience. But the first version I showed him was the very usual view, the "grateful immigrant" view of Canada. Daly looked at it and said, "I don't think you are telling the truth. This is not your feeling." But he didn't tell me what my feeling was. I had to search out my feelings and discover what they really were. He's a great teacher. In all my professional life, and my school years as well, Daly is the greatest teacher I've ever had.

'After *This Is a Photograph*, he rejected many of my ideas. He was right, every time. I remember once I was *furious*. I was *frothing*. But as I was walking out, and reread the idea, I saw that he was right, and I'd have to rewrite it, and find the *concept* in the film – *why* I want to make the film. What is the point I'm trying to make? What is personal in it, what is universal? How will the world be richer by this experience? Or is it just a flicker on the screen? And Daly, once the concept is clarified, is like a compass pointing to the right direction, and so during shooting you take advantage of all the good accidents, because you know where you're going.'

Robin Spry joined the Film Board in 1965. In the late sixties, he made two films exploring the left-leaning counter-culture of the time: *Flowers on a One-way Street* (1967) and *Prologue* (1969), the latter under Daly. *Prologue* is an attempt to weave a fictional story into actual unfolding events. The story follows the faltering relationship between the activist Jesse and the more contemplative Karen. While Karen follows a spacey hippie to an idyllic rural commune, Jesse goes to Chicago to observe the 1968 Democratic party convention. The film cuts back and forth between the two stories to contrast the separate paths chosen. Much of the Chicago footage is observational material of 'name' protesters: Abbie Hoffman, Jean Genet, Dick Gregory, Allen Ginsberg, and William Burroughs. Even the economist John Kenneth Galbraith makes an appearance.

The main editing challenge that Daly remembers was how to achieve a balance between the documentary and the dramatic material. 'The strength of numbers, and the presence of big names among the people in the park, made the documentary footage really important, and Jesse's presence at so many points in the midst of this documentary footage gave an unforeseen fascination to this part of the film story. It was very hard not to give maximum space for this highly topical footage. Now it might seem over-proportioned, but at the time it was still fresh and fascinating. And it remains useful as an important documentary record.'

And the footage was not irrelevant: 'The big names gave the film a certain "cachet" even to our personal story. Allen Ginsberg's scene of Hindu chanting showed the power of Eastern thought and practice alluded to by one of our characters. Jean Genet added an international validity beyond the usual U.S.-Canada connection, and was an extra touch of interest for French Canada. Abbie Hoffman, by coming to Montreal before the Chicago convention, was able to take part briefly in the personal part of the film when he helped to improvise effectively a motivation for Jesse to go to Chicago. John Kenneth Galbraith had the wit and wisdom to provide an emotional switch of mood, for our film as well as for the people in the park, when he said to them over the loudspeaker that they didn't look very dangerous to him, and that when the men in uniform behind them went home at the end of their shift, he wouldn't be surprised if many of them would change their clothes and come back to join their protest.'

Most of the young filmmakers who worked with Daly in the late 1960s were concerned with the political issues of the day, but only Spry overtly explored them in his films. The others were more inclined to challenge the accepted norms of filmmaking – and thus habits of perception – than to confront the political establishment directly. Rubbo was attracted to political themes, but he developed a personal, questioning approach to them. Ransen wanted to expose the constructed character of the supposedly transparent, straightforward documentary. Derek May sought new transparencies.

The politics of the English-language filmmakers were soft perhaps because the filmmakers were in no personal danger from what offended them. In 1968, after the Soviet invasion of Czechoslovakia, Daly and some others at the Film Board got involved in a project which posed real risks for some of the non-NFB participants. The project was the completion of a film made from underground footage of the invasion, and it was carried out so secretly, Daly says, that 'we took no notes, spoke about it to no one else, and even tried to get it out of our heads for fear of blurting something out.'

Daly keeps his secrets. '"Someone" had brought the film material to the Film Board, "someone" edited it and put it together, our lab supplied its services on "somebody's" NFB budget on another film. "Someone" wrote a commentary in Czech. And it fell to me to take the film to New York – also on another budget – to have the commentary read by an émigré Czech there, who was a well-known figure and well-known voice in Czechoslovakia.

'I do not know anything further about the fate of the finished film, but it was in fact taken back for use in the underground. But it can now be said that the name of the Czech émigré in New York was Vladimir Valenta.' Several years later, the Film Board hired Valenta to develop scripts for short dramatic films.

Meanwhile, a political cauldron of another sort was boiling up right at home: Quebec separatism. Ironically, Daly's informed detachment from close-to-home partisan politics and topical issues, which probably contributed to the political softness of the English-language films he produced, won him a degree of trust among radical French-Canadian filmmakers. Just as he had been the anglophone most responsive to the cinematic aspirations of younger French-Canadian filmmakers in the late fifties and early sixties, now the separatist filmmakers looked to him when they needed an anglophone producer for one of their projects.

The film was *Un pays sans bon sens!* (1970). It had been programmed as a documentary presenting French-Canadian attitudes to English audiences. (An English voice-over was added and the film retitled *Wake up, mes bons amis* [1970] for English-language distribution.) Its director, Pierre Perrault, was arguably the Film Board's most celebrated French-language filmmaker. Although Perrault had not worked with Daly, the film's two cameramen, Michel Brault and Bernard Gosselin, had, as had another producer on the film, Guy L. Coté.

Daly believes he was asked to serve as a producer in the administrative sense only, 'more symbolic than active and practical.' And he remembers entering the project with some ambivalence about its aim: 'I have never been very sympathetic with politics in general, and especially with the kind of view that dividing up peoples who differ will somehow thereby bring greater freedom and happiness. At the same time I felt it was very important for other Canadians to know much more clearly what the militant French-Canadian separatists were saying to each other. I was one of the relatively few producers in English production who could read French fairly fluently and write and speak it to some extent quite happily.'

Perrault's film explored the meaning and possibilities of patriotism for French-speaking Canadians. Although the film mixes metaphors, likening French-Canadians sometimes to laboratory mice and other times to hunted caribou, in doing so it offers a rich montage of attitudes, ideas, frustrations, and insights regarding the meaning of 'liberation.' The film's main argument is that French-Canadians are spiritually lost and will stay that way until they have a country of their own. The film attacks the picturesque portrayal of Quebec, exposes 'the trap of assimilation,' extols Quebec's 'inherited eloquence' that embraces more than just language, and concludes that the time has come to make English Canada 'pace up and down.'

The October Crisis of 1970 made English Canada pace up and down, and suddenly the film was controversial. Politicans and commentators wondered why the Film Board, a national organization, supported the work of separatists. In early 1971, the Film Board commissioner, Sydney Newman, asked Daly for an account of the project. Daly easily could have dissociated himself from the film. Instead he defended it. His 5 March 1971 reply to Newman contained a reasoned statement of principle regarding the role of free political expression in a government media production organization. Early in the memo he emphasized that

the whole point was that the film should express the undiluted *French* attitudes of the people in it and of its distinguished director ... For English audiences, the intention was to preface the film with the thought that while the ideas and questions contained in it were not necessarily those of the NFB itself, they were ideas and questions which would have to be understood and met squarely by English-speaking Canadians generally.

Daly reported that Perrault originally had intended that the film be about René Lévesque, but, after agreeing that the focus should be less immediately political,

found a different centre of gravity around which to make the film – namely, the concept of UN PAYS (Homeland) and what it meant to French Canadians. This could provide a positive focus and at the same time [explore] historical and current questions in a more timeless manner. The editing was done with this focus in mind. More shooting was done [in order to gather] more widespread views on the 'Homeland' question, taking the subject abroad to expatriate French Canadians in Paris, and to the independent attitude of citizens of Brittany, whence Jacques Cartier set off for his discoveries of Canada.

I am completely satisfied that the new direction taken in the film editing is better, more meaningful, less 'political', and more enduring than that originally proposed for the film. It is probable that the exact balance achieved among the differing viewpoints in such a film will always be a matter for argument or dispute. But, in my opinion, the present balance was arrived at by the Director sincerely and responsibly.

It should be noted that Perrault has already been criticized in some quarters for including hardly anything of the outspoken extremism of present day youth in Quebec. And some have even urged him to eliminate the Indian question from the film, as embarrassing to the separatists. But he has stuck to his guns that all sides of the question needed to be seen, felt, and aired.

After discussing the language difficulties the film presented to English-speaking audiences and how that limited the film's distribution potential, Daly concluded with tactful but forceful support for the film:

It is important to note that the film was made, completed, and shown months before any of the terrible events of the Laporte case took place. It is clear that these events have created an anxiety and emotionally charged atmosphere in relation to almost everything connected with the French-English question. It is to be hoped that these emotions will not obscure the real values of the film. It is probable that if we had a document in our hands of a similar character taken in the year 1867, we would cherish it as a priceless historical document. At the very least, this film documents some equally important questions and characters of our own days.

Newman adopted Daly's position. He defended Perrault, the film, and the importance of presenting a variety of opinions. He also restricted the film to non-theatrical, non-broadcast distribution. He would impose tougher restrictions on some separatist films in which Daly was not involved: *Cap d'espoir* (1969); *On est au coton* (1970); *24 heures ou plus* (1973).

Two years later, Daly's instinctive aversion to political confrontation and his acquired skills for defusing it helped secure the timely release of Robin Spry's *Action: The October Crisis of 1970*, which Spry completed in 1973 along with a companion film, *Reaction: A Portrait of a Society in Crisis*. On one level, *Action* is a debate about the measures a democracy may take to defend itself and remain a democracy. But it also reveals how news media affect the tenor of a political issue by distorting, merely from commercial imperatives, what people say. The film is compiled mostly from footage taken originally by television, and much of this footage is of political figures delivering opinions on the crisis. This strategy allows the crisis to unfold as most Canadians experienced it, but with an important difference: several sequences are allowed to run far longer here than they had in the news media. In one sequence, a cool, unflappable Prime Minister Pierre

Trudeau responds for almost ten minutes to a reporter's criticism of his security measures; in most news reports, only the reporter's final question and Trudeau's 'Just watch me' had been selected, showing Trudeau as merely testy and arrogant. In another sequence, René Lévesque, upset and irascible, refuses to adapt his statement to fit neatly into a sixty-second slot. After the quiet newsroom anouncement of Pierre Laporte's death, the studio empties in near silence. The film incorporates historical material on Quebec nationalism and separatism and expresses some sympathy for their aims.

Because the crisis itself was still a touchy political issue, Daly remembers having 'a lot of difficulty getting acceptance at all levels. But we got the project programmed by our peers, and then we got it accepted as a project at the internal administrative level.' Then, during production, there 'was a certain trickiness about what could be included and what couldn't be included, not just from us but from the people we got the material from. Anyway, there finally came a point where the final cutting copy was okayed by the director of production. Then it was seen by the commissioner, and he okayed it. But it still had to be shown to the Board of Governors, because it was so hot a political thing that everybody felt, including us, that it would be a good thing to pass it through them, so that we would have their support when the film was released. And we got a very good response back from the Board of Governors, except for one problem. Somebody had more or less figured out that the statements by the various political parties about what the government had done were not of equal "air time," that the New Democratic party's statements were out of proportion, the Conservative party's statements were too small, and so on. We were asked what we could do about it.

'The immediate reaction was that this was political censorship, that the film was very good the way it was. But then Robin and I sat down and thought, okay, this is a problem, an obstacle, but instead of seeing it as something negative, what if we could meet the objection and *improve* the film at the same time? If we could, we would *want* to. So instead of thinking of it as good or bad, we would first see what we could do, what changes could be made without changing the content. And there were nine little changes that could be made, nine little trims. We examined them very carefully in the cutting room to see how we would deal with the sound cut, how we would deal with the picture cut, and so on. Three of them we found could *not* be made without showing an obvious cut, which would give a mistaken impression that something substantive had been cut out, so we didn't do them. Of the remaining six, three were possible to make without anybody noticing, and we *liked* them. They simplified or cleaned up something a little better than it was, and we hadn't thought of that before. And we made them. The other three could be done technically and nobody would notice, but they changed the impression, they changed the meaning a little bit, and we refused to make them.

'We documented these nine things to the commissioner and said this is what we're doing. He was delighted. And we had no problem with the members of the Board of Governors. I think they appreciated it very much. And in *fact* they were behind it from there on. So it was not a question of satisfying *our* sense of responsibility on the issue, or *their* sense of responsibility, but of finding a bigger solution that we could *share*.'

Spry later made an experimental film, *Face* (1975), and another feature, *One Man* (1977), under Daly before leaving the Film Board to direct commercial features (among them *Suzanne* [1980], *Keeping Track* [1986], *Obsessed* [1987]). Spry says that 'even when Tom was not involved in a project, he somehow was always around. He inspired a conviction that making films can be an important activity – depending on what you put into it, why you do it, how you do it. He would always treat what you were doing as if it was potentially something very important. It made you feel that the often dreary activity of sitting in some dungeon trying to make sense of all that footage is somehow worthwhile.

'He also had a fascination for those moments of truth, those moments in a film that truly work. And he had tremendous creative generosity. At the end of a screening, he would give you thirty pages of notes and he'd analyse the film shot by shot.

'Outside, I miss that. Too often, any intense discussion tends to be just about money and schedules. What I miss of the NFB is the qualities that Tom brought to it. True, as long as you're trying to make something good, those qualities are still applicable outside. Whenever there's a possibility of doing something better, I always take the time. I haven't learned yet just to crank them out.'

Although he supported political films, it was on the personal and the experimental film that Daly's influence probably was most significant in this period. No one was more personal and experimental than Martin Duckworth, cameraman for Rubbo and collaborator with Ransen on the Swedish films. His first film of his own, *The Wish* (1970), is about Duckworth's beautiful twin daughters spending seemingly joyous summer days with their grandparents but experiencing some unspoken anxiety. Most of the footage is colour, candid observation of the girls, but each time one of them happens to look towards the camera, the frame freezes, and black-

and-white still photographs are cut in briefly. The photos seem to relate, in every case, to their 'absent' parents. (Their parents, we gather, are separated or divorced. During the girls' visit with their grandparents, the mother is absent physically; the father is present but as a filmmaker.) Although consistent in mood and editorial style, the film nearly succumbs to home-movie hermeticism; an audience not privy to the family relationships entwined in the movie has trouble deciphering them. Nevertheless, the film has persisting charm and marvellous moments. When picnicking beside a graveyard with the grandparents, one of the girls asks a devilishly profound question only a child would think of: 'What if we were having a picnic in a graveyard, and someone suddenly died – say of a heart attack – would you bury the person in the same place you had the picnic?'

In a final two-shot (apparently a continuation of the film's opening shot), the girls are pulling at a wishbone. Someone off-camera asks if the wish ever comes true. The girls answer, simultaneously, 'We don't know yet' and 'So far.'

But for Duckworth, Daly's contribution to *Accident* (1973) best exemplifies his memorable qualities as a producer. The film is a meditation on a light-plane crash suffered and survived by a good friend of Duckworth's, Pat Crawley. The crash itself had been filmed, and after visiting Crawley in the hospital and seeing how the crash had affected him, Duckworth thought that an interesting film could be made about the accident and its effect on Crawley. He scrounged a few rolls of film and phoned Daly. It was a weekend. Daly gave him permission to film what he could and then got the director of production to authorize the project on his 'emergency authority.'

Duckworth had been in a car accident himself, and 'had had a close brush with death. I was unconscious for ten days with a fractured skull. Tom would come visit me in the hospital while I was recovering. I was depressed, and he was a real breath of life for me. I had a hard time with this depression until Pat had *his* crash. I saw making a film about it as a way of getting out of my mental dead end.'

The film communicates the heightened awareness of life's brevity that Duckworth's friend experienced immediately after the accident. As Daly remembers it, however, the sustained emotion was not achieved easily. The original footage of the crash had been in 35mm colour. It had to be mixed with the 16mm black-and-white footage Duckworth had shot on the weekend following the crash. In addition, the action footage was too thin, and some additional shooting was required. But 'the biggest problem was that as Pat's convalescence improved, his experiencing of life became more and more "ordinary" again, so that the film progressed from the most dramatic and engrossing material, at the beginning, towards the least unusual at the end – if we were to follow the usual approach. Martin finally came up with the solution to the dramatic problem by replaying the accident shots in different ways, with different time warps, corresponding to Pat's memories still present in his mending state. This finally maintained the sense of mystery and out-of-the-ordinary feeling, right to the end.'

In Duckworth's view, 'Tom's role as a craft-teacher may be more of a spiritual than a technical one. He taught me the importance and the joy, the spiritual joy, of editing, of finding connections among disparate things, things you never dreamed could be connected. He gives you a sense of what is of lasting value in a frame or cut.'

Daly's role in the development of new filmmakers validated one of the lesser intentions behind the dismantling of the unit system. Whatever its flaws, the pool system did make Daly easily available to any young filmmaker interested in working with him. It accelerated his development into a gifted and generous teacher.

It might seem that Daly gave a lot more than he got back. Filmmakers who in effect apprenticed with him became significantly better filmmakers, and several of them owe their subsequent success largely to what they learned from Daly. But Daly never has looked at it in that way: 'Teaching is not a one-way street, just giving knowledge to others. Any *real* teaching, where something new actually lights up in the other person, is accompanied by an equivalent something received by the so-called teacher. It is not just a kind of personal "satisfaction," though that is inevitable in it. It has to do with a continual learning process *in oneself* which bursts into flower again, as a result of the work together, that arrives at these moments of understanding. There were always completely new and fresh problems to solve, which required not only past knowledge and experience, but quite new solutions, not known and met before. There were many new understandings that came to me in the course of trying to explain something, trying to grapple with something that had to be resolved in a limited time. I can't put quantitative values on it, but I could say that I feel that in those moments of understanding with the one I was working with, I received as much "light" as the other. Although each person feels individually that "I" got something, it seems that in reality there is an *exchange* of energies, that it is *one* experience, with two outlets. I'm sure this has something to do with feeling "less tired" after good work that brings such moments of understanding.'

Even in more conventional teaching contexts, Daly tried to go beyond merely conveying technical skills or conventional solutions to film problems. Since the early 1950s, he occasionally had given editing workshops for younger filmmakers. In the 1970s, when the Film Board's regionalization program brought filmmakers from all across Canada into the Film Board's ambit, Daly was asked to offer workshops through the Film Board's regional offices. Terry Ryan, a marketing officer for the Film Board during those years, recalled later:

[Because] I had organized a lot of seminars and workshops, I had the benefit of watching Tom Daly in action on a number of occasions. When we asked him to do something specific, like a session on editing, he would always prepare something, even if he was very busy, which he almost always was. He was a natural teacher, so it was a pleasure to watch him work in a seminar situation. He was very good at drawing people out, so he always made things relevant to the group he was with, whether they were a school-age audience or adults.

Daly brought the same kind of intensity to this teaching that he did to reviewing a director's freshly printed rushes:

Of course, he was at his best in a discussion following the screening of an earlier assembly of material. The copious notes he took in the dark are legendary. I didn't think he needed them, because his memory was phenomenal. But he had formed the habit in his first days [at the NFB] when he was logging footage and it never left him.

And just as he did with his other work, Daly viewed his teaching in the context of larger structures:

In those discussions around works in progress, Tom's comments were nearly always down to earth and practical but they had a certain special resonance because they all related to a very coherent philosophy of film and the National Film Board, and this ordered conceptual framework was obviously part of an equally coherent but much vaster philosophy, which he never commented on – at least to me.

The combination of practicality and philosophy noted by Ryan can be glimpsed in a transcript from a tape recording of an editing session Daly conducted for beginning filmmakers at the Film Board on 21 February 1973. (Apparently the recording was technically flawed; the transcript is garbled in places, and there are large and frequent gaps in the students' responses.) At one point in his presentation, Daly propounded his view that a person responds to a film or any aspect of it according to which aspect of his psyche is the strongest: the physical, intellectual, or emotional. But he also explained at length, and illustrated with visual examples, several specific, deceptively simple editing principles that he had learned over the years: almost any shot is potentially a long-shot, medium-shot, or close-up, depending on its context; an overlap between two such shots can serve as a 'hinge' between one perspective and another; even a two-frame adjustment (one-twelfth of a second) can alter the effect of a cut; a shot's centre of gravity attracts the viewer's eye, affecting how the shot is interpreted. In one longer passage, Daly elaborated on finding a good cutting point in a shot:

I find it very helpful to occasionally examine the shot for starting points and finishing points all the way through it. For instance, there's a cup of tea on the table. I reach out, take the cup, drink, put it down, and take my hand away. Well, there would be a number of starting points, like just [at] the very first, seeing it there before I reach out, or where this starts, or where I start to lift up the cup, or where I start to tilt it to drink, or where I start to take it away, or where I start to put it down, [or] where I start to put my hand away. Those are all good starting points for a piece of that shot. And again, in the same way, you know I could end it where my hand reaches the cup, where it reaches up here, where I take it away from my mouth, and so on. There are a whole lot of ending points in that shot and they're all interlaced. And there is one other factor which is obvious – but is it all that obvious? – [and that is] there is something going on. You want to connect shots that [show actions of different speeds or direction. For instance, in *Corral*] the horses are still running, you know, they haven't stopped running and they're still running at the same pace. They may stop running and start trotting, or they may stop going left and go right. So there are continuing actions, beginning actions, and ending actions, and a continuing action may be so short that you can't make it a whole shot but you can get into a movement that another shot can pick up, where it's just going on like that. For instance, continuing to move toward the cup or continuing to move up this way, continuing to turn just briefly, and continuing to drink maybe quite a while, and so on. There's a little bit in the middle where the same action is still going on. And that is the third element [of the action in a shot] you can use for connecting to another shot. Now all that is very formal and kind of wordy till you run into a problem of actual cutting where you haven't much to work with ... you may have a little tool at hand. If you know things like that, you can help yourself figure out what is possible to do.

At times, Daly sounded like someone just discovering how editing works:

It's strange – I think the essential editing factor is the interesting relationships. I mean, as long as there's more than one shot, what is the relationship between the two, you know? There is something in each shot and there's something that happens at the join ... It can flow or it can be a shock or it can be something to do with rhythm. It can be anything you're interested ... in relating [for some purpose]. If you take a pan shot, for instance ... [and cut from the middle of it to a static shot] there's an uncomfortable jar, which just doesn't correspond to any actual reality. [If] it's Charlie Chaplin turning a corner, he has to slow down or stick his leg out to kind of compensate for getting round the corner. There's always some factor in momentum [such] that if you're going to stop, it [first] slows down ... There has to be a taper to a stop.

... [But] as always you can use a rule the other way around. You can create a jarred effect on people if you [want to]. And the only thing is, you have to make sure that the jar is dramatically right for what it is and not that they feel jarred about the way you do it to them ... [Recall] *Great Expectations*, where the little boy is running away from those terrible trees and runs bang smack into the man. Do you remember seeing that? It's scary ... [It] happens so fast that there's practically only one or two frames of stop.

When in the mid-1960s there was talk of creating a national film school with extensive Film Board involvement, Daly was asked for his thoughts about such a school. He prepared a brief proposal, 'Some Notes and Observations on the Subject of a National Film School or Film Training Centre for Canada,' but nothing ever came of it. Its chief interest lies in its originality of vision and its suggestion of how Daly's practical and philosophical sides might have been realized in a public institution of his own design.

Daly's school would be selective and rigorous: 'There should be no room for mediocrity.' Twenty students (five from abroad) would be admitted for the first year of a three-year program. Fifteen would be allowed to complete the second year. Ten would complete the third year. Daly's reasoning was that 'competition for the continuing places would tend to ensure harder work and better standards among the students.'

Daly stressed that what was needed 'is a school for *creative* filmmakers – not for technicians' and that the school 'should be essentially *practical*, a school for film-*making*' rather than appreciation, criticism, theory, or history. The practical side of the curriculum would cover film writing, directing, cinematography, editing, sound effects, music – but also budgeting and audiences. Students would acquire skills mostly from working on their own films and on the projects of visiting filmmakers.

In equal measure to its practicality, Daly's ideal school had a flavour of the Greek academy:

Since the film course is meant to develop film-makers who can appeal to the 'whole man' in the audience, it is necessary to awaken certain concerns in the film-maker himself, and to try to make sure that the 'whole man' in him is being touched. Certain academic studies can help this, for example:

(a) *Philosophy* – Raise the question again: why is the student here on earth? Everyone has a point of view whether they know it or not, different values, and so forth. The film-maker has to get messages across to many kinds of people, since he is dealing with a mass medium. The students' own points of view and values would be probed, in relation to one another, so as to awaken them to the need of always considering the point of view of the films they make in relation to their goal.
(b) *Psychology* – The study of the relationship and associations between thought, feeling, sensation, action. By observation of the flow of attention in himself and other people, a film-maker can direct and edit his film in such a way as to have far greater control over an audience. By this means he can also come to understand how one person is convinced by logical continuity, another by emotional progression, and a third by physical demonstration, and how necessary it is to become master of all three if he is to reach everyone.
(c) *Comparison of the Arts* – This is meant not so much from an 'aesthetic' point of view as from the point of view of how to recognize what is suited to each form of art. It would be a study of things that film can do better, as compared with what film-strip, literature, painting, sculpture, the live stage, radio, or TV can do better. The goal is to perceive what is practical, for film purposes (if any), in any given subject that may be suggested.
(d) *The changing world around us* – Some actual study of the fundamental changes that are taking place in the world (in science, education, jobs, etc.) will give the student some idea of what he and his audience will have to cope with in the years to come. This would give a relevant and valid context for dealing with almost any film topic he may come up against.

It will be seen from the kind of 'academic' subjects to be studied that they would be less effective in the form of book-learning than they would be as live seminars, where questions and answers and confrontations can take place at all times. These questions would be related directly to any practical film work being done at the time. The subjects given here are for the sake of example. Perhaps better ones could be chosen. But the aim should remain the same – not to stuff the student's head with undigested information, but to awaken him to his own real questions, so he in turn will know how to awaken his audience. In this case any 'information' learned becomes ten times more valuable and practical.

But the most exciting teaching for Daly remained the one-on-one inter-action that occurred naturally when working with a receptive filmmaker on a real project. In teaching, in which his effectiveness as a producer lay, he seems not to have missed having an external structure for authority. He preferred the 'real authority' that his demotion had revealed to him.

For Daly, real authority is described in Aesop's fable 'The Wind and the Sun.' In the fable, Aesop recounts that the wind and the sun were arguing about which one was the stronger. When they saw a traveller coming down the road, the sun proposed that they resolve the dispute by seeing which one could get the traveller to take his coat off. The sun withdrew behind a cloud while the wind began to blow. But the harder the wind blew, the more tightly the traveller wrapped himself in his coat. When the wind gave up in despair, the sun came out and shone on the traveller. It made him warm, and he removed the coat himself.

'Everyone,' Daly says, 'has, so to speak, a "pilot light" in them. Through their own experience, they can get a jet of fuel that lights it now and then. Or it might come from the outside. A teacher can do that for them. I've had that experience so much in my life that I was aware that the first interest in something can come to them the same way, just enough to feed their pilot light, and they can do the rest themselves.'

But, Daly says, 'I never really thought of myself as a teacher in a formal sense. I've never tried to teach as such. What seems to happen, as far as I can make out, is that the arrival of some kind of understanding in myself is very exciting, but it really feels like something alive and meaningful only if I can *apply* it. Then it's not just an idea in my head. And to see that it works for *other* people is even *more* exciting, because it suddenly means that every-thing is not totally subjective and locked up in one's own imagination, that one person can actually reach and touch another. To have a moment of understanding inside yourself is very lonely, in a way. It's a kind of impris-onment. When a moment of understanding is shared between two people, it's outside your own egoism in some way. It includes it, but is also above it somehow.

'Regardless of the differences between people, it is a kind of binding thing. If I really felt I understood what the person was trying to do, and yet the way they'd cut the shots together was *obscuring* that, or going *aside* from that, or *blocking* that, or simply *distracting* from that, I felt I had a positive basis for making a criticism of what they'd done. If I had learned some techniques for not obscuring it, or for bringing it together, then I had that to respond with. I could *show* how it works. And if they felt, when they saw how it works, that that was what they wanted, then I realized I'd actually communicated some kind of practical dress for their feeling or wish or aim. Somehow, I never really had the feeling that as a producer I was trying to get people to make my film or make films my way or anything like that. I had to feel that it was compatible with my way, but I was really trying to find what their way was, and to make the resulting film as *much* that, and *more so*, than they perhaps could do alone. And when this was reached, I felt in the end it was just as much my film as it was their film, although it *was their* film. And that is a very happy kind of conclusion.'

Daly's teaching emphasized the principle behind the application: 'Principles embody themselves in specific forms of the moment. If you try to copy that form, it is sometimes as satisfactory as the original example. But if the conditions change, copying the old example doesn't work. If, however, the *principle* is understood, and not just the *particular example*, then it can be applied in various conditions, taking up a *new form* in new situations. And this was the thing I was trying to pass on to the other filmmakers. It was so practical a point, saving a lot of bumbling about with just trying "anything."

'Sometimes it would work a little differently. Perhaps I understood the aim, but almost any kind of thing I could suggest was not the kind of thing they wanted to do. Maybe they just didn't want that *style*. So I'm making these suggestions, and in the end they will *never* do any of them. But they often would do *something* which they would never have otherwise bothered to do, but do it in their *own way*. And then when *I* got to see how it worked, I got to understand much more how they looked at things, and then I could get closer to *that*, and I would have learned something from *that*.'

Usually such moments of understanding would occur while Daly was struggling with a specific problem in editing, but Terry Ryan remembers an instance in which Arthur Lipsett expressed with elegant simplicity what was for him the essence of Daly's conception of editing. It was in 1969. Lipsett, who had continued to make films along the lines of *Very Nice, Very Nice*, had decided to leave the Film Board. 'He was leaving on an up-note. He wanted to concentrate on sculpture, and other things. But he was a high-strung individual. People were always concerned for him, in a caring kind of way. Tom was very fond of him.

'There was a gathering in Tom's office. Tom always kept a bottle of sherry on hand. He brought it out and poured a small glass for each of us. Then he gave Arthur a going-away present. It was wrapped up neatly. Arthur opened it up. It was three small Chinese porcelain figures, each about an inch high. I think they had been in Tom's family. Tom probably wanted Arthur to take something away with him that was comforting – a good-luck charm.

'Tom said they had a significance that he would explain if Arthur wanted him to, but Arthur said, "Oh, I think I understand it." Then he arranged the three figures in a certain way, and offered an interpretation of what they meant. Then he switched them around, and said, "Or it could mean this," and offered another interpretation. He rearranged them again. "Or this." And he gave a third interpretation.

'It was a marvellous, playful "editing" job. He was kind of one-upping Tom, all in good fun. Tom was delighted with it. We all were.'

Daly speaks with a sense of wonder and gratitude about such moments of understanding with other filmmakers. 'I still remember the surprise of finding that quite unexpected people wanted to make this connection. It was a miracle that I could have that.'

It was 'a miracle' to one whose devastating discovery that he was *like that* had been foreshadowed in his school years. 'People would call me up and ask me what the answer was to a Latin question, for example. But I realized that they never called me up to talk to me. I had a lot of acquaintances but no friends. And I envied the people around me who had friends, hail-fellow-well-met people, always joking around with each other.

'I tried to imitate them, but it didn't have the same effect. There was a sharp cutting edge to my jokes, as if there was something resented at the same time, and they weren't funny.

'Something even then made me wonder why was it that the people I wanted to be friends with didn't want to be friends with me, and the people who would contact me for this and that, I didn't particularly want to be friends with. I realized there was nobody my age I could share anything important with. The fact is, now, when people actually trust me to hear them, it never ceases to be a miracle – that it is possible to really relate to someone, and that someone can be my friend.'

Colin Low was his closest friend. Low says that the 'suffering and failure' that Daly experienced in developing and losing Unit B had a lot to do with the expansiveness that seemed to develop in Daly in his later years at the Film Board. Daly's friendship with Low had begun in the early days of Unit B and survived the crisis of Daly's administrative style. 'After work,' Low recalls, 'we'd just stay around talking about something, and it would last a long time. Often it was about how one dealt with problems. But I was also interested in his metaphysical ideas. His learning was so broad. My background was just high school and art school. I didn't realize what I had missed.' Working together on films such as *Corral, Universe,* and *Circle of the Sun* strengthened the bond between them. 'In the hard business of making films – and for me it's always been very hard, especially to come back and make another one – it was reassuring to have someone you were absolutely certain would help you.' After Daly's marriage, Low adds, 'our wives became very good friends. They still meet once a week to play music together. Having families and children brought us closer.'

The friendship was reinforced through their participation in 'the Gurdjieff work.' Low thinks that just as Daly's involvement in 'the work' (as it is often referred to) had shown him how to learn to respond more effectively as Unit B's administrator, so it helped him transform the disappointment of losing Unit B into the joy of working with others on the simple basis of mutual desire.

Low had met the de Hartmanns through Daly 'first in Toronto and later in New York. I liked them very much. They were absolutely fascinating people. But I didn't understand Ouspensky. I still don't.'

'The group really started growing here in Montreal, after the Film Board moved here from Ottawa. After Thomas de Hartmann died, Madame de Hartmann would come to Montreal frequently.

'One of the people she brought to Montreal was a man who had been specially trained as a boy by Gurdjieff as a teacher of the exercises. They were fascinating. I was terrible at them. In fact, I was unable to do them. But I experienced enough of the discipline of trying to "remember yourself" in the process of doing the movements – the whole point being to try to get the three aspects of the self into some kind of focus or harmony.

'So while Tom is working on films, he is developing an active Gurdjieff group as well. I can't imagine how he had the energy to do all that ... *and* marry and raise a family. But learning how to "see yourself" while something is going on helped him a lot.'

Daly describes his friendship with Low as a bond between two incomplete people who helped each other become whole. 'Colin's experience in the work filled in a side he was lacking. When we first knew him he was wonderfully clean and subtle emotionally. He was very capable in the physical aspect of life – making things work, fixing things. But he was missing something: he could almost never finish a sentence. It was hard to converse with him. It was as if his thinking mind couldn't keep up with the other two. But he began to have glimpses of what it is like to be able to express complex thoughts verbally, and he became trusting of it, not afraid of it. *Now*, he can talk to a committee in Parliament without a problem.

'Colin had the feelings and the physical ability. I had the mind. We've helped each other extend the other things.'

Daly insists that growth does not require, and cannot accomplish, the complete elimination of undesirable traits. Instead, growth is, as the word itself implies, an increase in capacity, an 'enlarging,' that includes one's traits in new and benign combinations, perhaps even creative ones. 'My clearest example is that of oxygen and hydrogen. Separately, they are, so to speak, "afraid of fire," because they are used up and die in the process of fire. But when they are united in a larger whole, in a molecule of water, they are still there but the force holding them together produces a completely different chemical result. The molecule of water can put out fire, or go up in steam and travel around the world.

'I have more and more experiential proof that this principle operates psychologically as well as physically. But the fact remains that when there is no *attention* holding the parts together, the previous, old habits of the individual parts have exactly the same old tendencies as they ever did. But now they are not as likely to stay in that state too long.'

For a two-year interlude in the early 1970s, Daly once again assumed an executive role in production. This happened when, in early 1971, management declared the pool system a failure and attempted to reinstitute a unit structure for production. The disappointment with the pool system had less to do with the overall quality of the work that was produced under it than with its resistance to managerial control. The system had become, in Daly's words, 'a total hodgepodge and unworkable.' Rather than fully admit to error, however, management attempted to reinstate the old unit system 'without daring to call it by that "dirty" name – inventing "studio" as the euphemism.'

Daly was given a studio to run, but his interest in experimental filmmakers and his increasing reluctance to judge came into conflict with the managerial aims behind the studio system. In 1972, the Film Board attempted to rid itself of younger filmmakers who hadn't achieved what management regarded as significant success or shown sufficient promise. On 10 July, Bernard Devlin, the director of English production at the time, addressed the following memorandum to all executive producers:

Certain amongst you have brought to my attention the existence of people in your units whom, if you had a choice, you might otherwise not consider as members of your unit. In some cases these are people who have displayed lack of talent, or lack of motivation, or who are simply people cast in an area of operations for which they are not suited. Some of them may not even belong at the National Film Board.

I think that the worst possible service we can do to one of our employees is to allow such a condition to endure. We cannot repeat the errors of the past and, through negligence, fail to notify these people that they are not really contributing to the NFB's operation. We must either transfer them or, failing that, face up

to the fact that in both the interest of the employee and the NFB, they should
be let go.

I expect every Executive Producer to face up to this responsibility.

I expect you to bring to my attention the names of all people in your unit whose
terms of employment should be reconsidered and to discuss this with me.

In the meantime, I am asking you for personal reports on some cases which I
have already identified. As you know, union regulations require that we build up a
file on such cases before taking action.

Devlin identified five such cases in Daly's unit. One of them was Donald
Winkler, whose experiments in film resembled contemporary experiments
in light fiction. His *Doodle Film* (1970) had won festival awards; *Bannerfilm* (1972) became an enduring favourite with audiences. He had written
the narration for Albert Kish's *Louisbourg* (1972), a film about the restora-
tion of the old French fort on Cape Breton. Daly's report (7 August 1972)
on Winkler was straightforward and devoid of hyperbole. At the same
time, it was upbeat, lacked any tone of defensiveness, and cleverly alluded
to certain needs that management itself had voiced for writers, filmmakers
with a sense of audience, filmmakers willing to do sponsored films, and
filmmakers interested in drama.

You asked for my personal review and analysis of *Donald Winkler's* production
capabilities. Here they are.

A measure of Winkler's capability is to be seen in the Doodle film. It is a slender
item when read on a page, but it is an enormous success as an audience film. It was
among the most effective films in the whole NFB showing recently in Hawaii from
the point of view of audience response. Winkler's method, manner, and language
can be gentle and disarming, but the impact can be considerable.

There is usually a sense of humor and whimsy about Don's work, no matter how
serious the point may be. And he can structure his writing so that the theme or
story develops as it goes. At present his experience is best fitted for something
under half an hour, but is not limited in principle.

His main work until recently has been as writer, either of commentary or narrative 'voice over', or of dramatic sketches or stories. He has written commentary for
other people's films, not only his own. He has not been a particularly fast worker,
but quality and craftsmanship are definite words I would apply to his work. He
hates to leave loose ends or approximations. When he learns to speed up his pace
and can turn out greater quantity, he could be valuable in a variety of ways.

He is not averse to sponsorship. Already he pleased the Parks Branch with his
narration for 'Louisbourg'. He will probably do their 4 clips also. Right now, the

Environment department is interested in a film suggestion of his on 'Garbage'. It would be great if he could score a first success for a sponsor with his whimsical originality.

His first live action film directed by himself, is 'Bannerfilm' (on the work of the artist Laliberté) which I think is very creditable, and should be very useful in the series on Canadian artists. Albert Kish edited the film. They make a good team together.

Training in film editing would also probably help his work as writer and as director. He has not had that much of it. Perhaps if he has blocks of unallotted time this could be arranged.

I would like to see him complete 'The Cuckold', which would be a useful item in the family life and mental health area, in which Ian MacNeill is also interested. It would also show how well he can *direct* whimsy, as well as write it.

Daly's reports on the other four 'cases' identified by the director of production were similarly positive in tone and almost defiantly sensible. None of the filmmakers was dismissed; one left the Film Board voluntarily. Although 'The Cuckold' never got beyond script stage, Winkler continued to make experimental films. His *Travel Log* (1978) won several awards. In 1989, it was one of thirty-nine films selected by New York's Museum of Modern Art for its fiftieth-anniversary tribute to the National Film Board. He made another film on crafts, *In Praise of Hands* (1974), also an award-winner. And in the 1980s he became one of the Film Board's most prolific directors, making several penetrating documentary portraits of Canadian poets: *Earle Birney: Portrait of a Poet* (1981); *F.R. Scott: Rhyme and Reason* (1982); *Poet: Irving Layton Observed* (1986); *Al Purdy: A Sensitive Man* (1988); and *Winter Prophecies: The Poetry of Ralph Gustafson* (1988). And Daly's observation that Winkler and Kish made 'a good team' proved more than insightful. They would work together often. Kish edited *In Praise of Hands* and the films on Scott and Purdy. In 1994, he and Winkler co-directed *The Summer of '67*, a videotape that mixes clips from *Christopher's Movie Matinee* and *Flowers on a One-way Street* with the present-day reactions of several people who had figured prominently in the films.

Undeniably, however, several of the films made in Daly's studio were inept and inane, and some of Daly's colleagues remembered the failures, such as *Anger after Death* (1971) and *One Hand Clapping* (1972), more readily than the successes. A filmmaker who had been at the Board for a long time and who respected Daly's discipline is still shocked that a man 'schooled by Grierson and Legg could support such atrocious films. It was a very expensive way to get something out of the filmmaker's system.'

Donald Brittain also thought Daly was too indulgent in those years: 'There were many cases where it was clear there was no filmmaking talent there – very bright people, but they should have been running countries or banks, or teaching history, getting the Nobel Prize for something, but they shouldn't have been making films.'

The perception of overindulgence was in stark opposition to the impression of hypercritical prissiness that had so riled others in the early days of Unit B. Wolf Koenig, who knew the earlier Daly, now said of him, 'Tom is so open-hearted. He's a set-up for a con job. He'd say, "Well, maybe they've got something."' Paul Cowan, who joined the Film Board in 1973, agrees: 'You see, it is in Tom's nature always to find goodness in people and also in films. I mean, he can look at *dreck*, and find something good to say about it, and instead of saying, "That's garbage, throw it out, put it on the shelf, let's not finish it," he'd try to find something good in it even when it was worthless.' And for Giles Walker, who joined in 1972, 'the films of the flower era – well, all Tom was doing was helping the filmmakers achieve what they wanted to do. It was happening all over the world. However bad they were, they would have been worse without him.' Mort Ransen notes that 'in the sixties, "experimental" was a good word. In the seventies, you just crossed it out. But Tom always accepted that if you experiment, you might fail.'

Ransen was the central figure in an experiment that was decisive in ending Daly's brief second stint as an executive producer. The project was a feature film, provisionally called 'Conflict Comedy' but retitled *Running Time* by the time it was released in 1974. It was produced jointly by Daly and the head of another studio, George Pearson, himself an accomplished producer. It was to be a story about a teen-age boy and an old lady who fall in love, run off, and then are pursued by the boy's father and the woman's son. Ransen's intent, as Daly recalls it, was 'to express some of the mood of the sixties through an acted drama of humour and spoof, poking fun at some of our hallowed institutions but touching us here and there with the difference between real and artificial relationships, and suggesting how sometimes the accepted social codes of conduct become the tail that wags the dog of real morality.' Ransen wanted to tie his social comment to a demystification of the mechanisms of drama, just as his essays on Sweden also exposed the manipulations of documentary in *Untouched and Pure* and *Falling from Ladders*. For example, he would show the actors having their make-up applied. And he designed a single stylized, blatantly artificial set for the entire film. The design would permit any scene to be shot in any order, and it would allow Ransen to film the progression from one scene to another as the actors moved from one part of the set to another.

Although the project came to be viewed as an example of Film Board profligacy, Ransen had conceived it in response to financial problems that had just begun to plague the Film Board. Ransen remembers 'walking through the halls of the Film Board. Everybody was depressed. We had been hit by the first of what would prove to be a long series of budget cuts. Management was having trouble figuring out how people on staff could make films. It particularly hit people making drama, especially those who, like me, felt they were ready to make a feature.

'I walked onto the shooting stage. Not much was going on. I started looking at all the equipment that was in the place. Everything you needed for a feature was right in the building – equipment, crew, shooting stage, lab ... The only thing lacking was actors. I could write a script in which there would be no outside costs except the actors – and some music.'

Inside costs were essentially costs that the Film Board incurred whether it produced anything or not. Idle or busy, a filmmaker received his salary. The same was true for clerks, administrators, artists, and technicians. Facilities, equipment, and maintenance were inside costs. The main issue regarding inside costs was one of accounting: where to allocate them. Ransen's film would draw primarily upon resources that had been paid for but not allocated.

'This is why management approved the project. But I took this idea one stage further: I would try to find work on the project for any NFB person who wanted work. They could charge their time to the film. So a lot of people worked on it, who normally would not have been brought on. It seemed to make sense not to worry about the inside money.'

But problems plagued the filming from early on. Tension developed between Ransen and his lead actress. The film needed considerable lab work for process shots, some of which had to be completed before certain live-action scenes could be filmed. Some administrators above Daly disliked the film's irreverent counter-cultural values, such as its sympathetic look at marijuana and unusual sexual pairing.

The project needed constant defence. 'As the production continued, time and costs mounted,' Daly recalls, 'and the question of how or whether to continue was raised on a number of occasions, by more than one director of production and by more than one commissioner. But on each occasion, after full discussion at the highest level, the decision was always to continue to completion.'

Bernard Devlin had been the first director of production to approve the project. Robert Verrall, who succeeded Devlin in September 1972, continued approving expenditures on it. But he was very unhappy about doing so. Verrall says bluntly, 'I hated that whole project.'

The project's various problems exacerbated each other. Delays in lab work caused other inside costs to rise as crew members waited. Ransen says that he allowed his disputes with management to distract him from his directorial responsibilities, especially with regard to his lead actress. 'That was the real source of the problem with her. While I was supposed to be rehearsing her, I was busy arguing with Bob Verrall. I was gone all the time. I couldn't tell her why. I didn't want her to know how up in the air it all was.'

In his arguments with management, Ransen maintained that the high costs were largely illusory. He still does: 'The film came in on time and on budget – of *outside* money. It went *enormously* over budget on *inside* money, on *inside* time.' But Verrall rejected Ransen's argument, and still does: 'Mort was never able to understand that inside money was real money. For example, some people were forced to go outside for services that Mort was hogging.'

Early in 1973, long before the film was completed, the one-time member of Unit B's inner circle dismissed his one-time mentor from his executive producership. 'I didn't think,' Verrall recalls, 'that Tom was faring well. There were signs that he was not the old Tom in charge of a strong unit. It was as if he were at the mercy of people he was a little bit out of sync with. Mort was one of them. I couldn't understand why Tom had let himself get caught up in a project that was breaking the bank. I thought that at this stage in Tom's career it was probably the right thing for him to have a program of films within a unit and have the leisure to go with it – and not on the front line. We had a long soul-searching lunch over it. Although I sensed a certain amount of hurt, I think he felt good about it. And I put him under the wing of someone he loved very much – Colin. I didn't put him under someone he didn't respect.'

In Daly's view, a perverse political agenda had intruded subtly into the project and, in a way, possessed it. 'In the end, I felt it had been like a complex chess game, played between forces that were trying to win with a certain vision, and forces that were needing to be efficient and economical, for the sake of the whole program of films. And these forces were not polarized *between* people but in *each* of us – director, producers, directors of production, and commissioners. The outcome was a sort of draw. Neither force really won or lost. But I can't look at the finished film without missing the vision that had been really possible of realization at the outset.'

And for Ransen, working with Daly was not what it had been with *Untouched and Pure*, *Falling from Ladders*, and *Christopher's Movie Matinee*: 'Tom and I and everyone else became involved in a much larger political battle which made that old, unpressured working relationship impossible.'

Nevertheless, Ransen looks back on the ordeal philosophically, without rancour. 'The most important thing I learned from all of this was from Tom. He was suddenly the executive producer of a film the Film Board adamantly did not want. I was absolutely determined to persevere with the film. He was at the centre of this turmoil and trying to be loyal to both sides. *Now*, I look at my own stance as a kind of arrogance.

'At one point, Tom said to me, "It doesn't matter how talented and persistent you are, Mort, you still can't grow a rose in the wintertime." What he was trying to tell me is that it takes a lot of people and a lot of resources to make a movie, and you need to have everybody working in the same direction. If I were in that situation today, I'd recognize that administrators are human beings, that the film matters to them, too. I would have decided not to go ahead with the film even if I was right. It was a battle I should have been willing to lose. But at the time, I was just too bullheaded.'

When *Running Time* was completed in 1974, its cost had exceeded a million dollars. Even if most of this figure represented inside costs, it was exorbitant for an NFB film at the time, especially a film that seemed to offer little more than a painful glimpse at failed zaniness. Its difficulties were immortalized in an article called 'It Didn't Start Out to Be a Disaster Movie ... But *Running Time* Is Canadian Film History's Worst Catastrophe,' by Martin Knelman, published in *Saturday Night*. In addition to recounting the film's troubled production history, Knelman described a preview screening in which those who didn't walk out booed and hissed throughout, cheering only when the projector broke down.

In retrospect, the film seems to have been over-maligned, perhaps uncreatively marketed, and made the scapegoat for a generally disappointing national feature film industry. The final budget figure is misleading if compared to that of a commercial production. Canada has produced many feature films worse and more expensive than *Running Time*. According to Ransen, audiences at some test screenings responded warmly to the film; an imaginative distribution plan might have enabled the film to reach an audience of respectable size.

The film has a cinematically imaginative concept at its core. Devoting only about thirty minutes of screen time to its plot, the film plays on images, makes jokes about filmmaking, toys with film clichés, and fools around with musical asides. A very funny joke – one that might have offended some administrators – involves a rear-screen projectionist who, having been fed brownies laced with marijuana, makes some people in a car seem to be driving across snowfields, down streams, and ultimately deep into space. The film may fail as drama, but it has originality and intelligence. And Ransen, after leaving the Film Board for commercial directing, developed a reputation for speed and economy.

Daly never felt a need to apologize for his support of experimental film-makers or to avoid the topic. To the charge that he supported filmmakers indiscriminately, without regard to their promise or seriousness, Daly relates an incident that predates his discovery of Gurdjieff but is consistent with Gurdjieff's insistence on striving for an unbiased attitude towards oneself and others. Perhaps it also answers, for Daly, those sceptical of Gurdjieff's own seriousness, or even those who suspect Daly of a fundamental gullibility. 'I was still living in our big house in Toronto, so I couldn't have been much older than twenty. There was a moment – my mother was there, and I was looking out the window. It was a summer day. Two Catholic student priests were walking down the street in big, floppy black hats and long soutanes. I became aware of an expression on my face and an inner attitude of superciliousness, looking down my nose on that ... on how anyone could believe in the infallibility of popes or the virgin birth, that kind of thing.

'I was shocked, because we had been brought up thoroughly to be equally respectful of all people's religious beliefs, and I had thought I didn't have this kind of attitude. And something happened just then that gave me a symbol for all time to come. I saw, as it were, a kind of "thermometer of truth," with the greatest and completest truth at the top, and the least at the bottom. Everybody in the world was somewhere on that thermometer, and it was everybody's function in life to try to rise up one degree, and not to fall down one degree. I thought that even if there were charlatans at the bottom trying to make money out of gullible people by using "words of truth" that they'd heard from someone else, it still might operate for the gullible person as the first words of truth they'd come across, and lead them to go further, perhaps discovering how false the charlatan was, and not wishing to stay there.

'And what I saw from all of this was that everyone in the world is in the same boat. Whatever our starting-point, it is as big and unknown a step to move that one degree up as it is for anyone else at their place to move one degree up. Those that have bigger responsibilities need to have more resources to work with. Those that have little, may have less to accomplish. But it is the same relative problem.

'Some people say I saw good where there wasn't any. It is quite true that you wouldn't put an incapable person in a job that needed the capability he lacked, but this is a separate issue from whether someone needs to know something in their position, and wants to know. So caring for them at that point is just as important as caring for a more capable person at their point. Maybe the former needs more.'

Not long after his demotion, Daly, in the September 1973 issue of the NFB newsletter *Pot Pourri*, addressed his encouragement and support of experimental filmmakers. It is not an apology but an apologia. Although never mentioned, Daly's 'thermometer of truth' informs his argument and is applied to filmmakers, audiences, and himself.

When new ideas come up and there seems to be a possibility of originality in them, I am interested wherever possible in taking the chance to find out if there really is something in it. In doing so you're going to have some successes and some abject failures, but in order to have something of a new kind you have to try many things.

There's something to do with perception in it. Very few people can perceive in a new way, and very few of those who can perceive in a new way can bring it into reality, can actualize it. Of those who can, some of them may be great and others probably not. And for me there is a difference in kind, between trying to relate to the real and living thing that one can sense differently perhaps from others, trying to bring it into reality, and doing what is already known, done, safe. The known, done and safe isn't necessarily wrong. Perhaps it is the great centre of gravity, of stability in life. People have carried on the same kind of activities for thousands of years and it doesn't mean they're wrong. But I'm interested in fresh and original perception and the possibility of realising it in action, and communicating that to people in a way they can care about and which, perhaps, makes life more meaningful and more worthwhile.

And I can say that I've learned something for myself in the course of working with these people. For instance, I am by craft a film editor, so I have my own feelings about the correct length of shots and the right order of shots – not *the* right order, there are many right orders, but the kind of organic relationship between things that hold together. And in the case of, say, working with Derek May, we disagreed sometimes very much on the length of shots and each of us had our own reason. But again without saying whether either was right, what I learned was that when he held a shot much longer than what seemed to me to be the filmic, or dramatic, or story-telling value of that shot, he could explain that he wished me to run out of my habitual reaction to that shot and come to the point where I was still left with it and had to begin to have a new relation to it. He wasn't going to give me another shot just at the moment that I would like to have it, so I would have to deal with the fact that the shot was still going on. I could get angry ... or be bored, or I could find a new interest, but I would have to make a decision of my own about it, and for him that was the interesting thing. And I don't personally care whether he thought up this answer in reaction to a question of mine or an attack of mine just on the spur of the moment, or whether he had really thought that way from the beginning. I don't care whether he really meant it or didn't mean it, whether he was conning me or not conning me. The fact is that it made a new interest for me, which I think is a very right kind of interest.

It applies in life. When we run past the end of our habit patterns, we're suddenly on our own and have to have a new, real, relation with life. And, in effect, what's the difference between that and experiencing the same thing with a new moment in film? If a film goes by in every way conforming with what you already like, you may say it's a great film but it may not touch you in any real way ...

It's equally possible when you're disturbed, to simply follow habit, get annoyed, and say it's no good, which is very frequent. But I think it is not the quality of a real man or woman to do that ...

What interests me ... are the elements that can help wake up that perception in us that really wishes to live off the truth, pleasant or unpleasant, and wants to question itself, and is not afraid of that, no matter what it sees. It is not the function of standard films usually to do that. These films give us knowledge, or satisfy an appetite. They may raise mental questions, questions of whether to do this, or do that, and so on. But to wake up the person himself is another function which is very valuable. If the person is awake he will think about social situations in a different way, he will relate to other people in a different way, everything will be done with a different quality. Very few solutions to problems are discovered from the ordinary level. So it matters if there are ways to help out the possibility of loosening us in ourselves and letting ourselves approach new perceptions and new possibilities ...

I call certain films 'difficult' films because so many people say they are difficult for them to care about, to understand, to sit through. I don't deny that they may seem exactly that for a lot of people, but in this case I wish to suggest to them that perhaps they are only trying to understand with one part of themselves. And if they let their attention flow to other parts of themselves rather than trying to grasp it all with their mind they might find they have a different connection with the film in another way. I'm not saying they will, but I find that when some individual presents the material to the audience in that way, others frequently find that they too have several other ways of relating to the film, and they begin to see it in a different light. They discover that they have more resources in themselves than they really knew they had.

Typically for Daly, his interest in experimentation was rooted in a vital, almost immediate, always fresh relationship to the origins of philosophical culture:

There may be a lot of nonsense perpetrated in the realm of the experimental film and the personal, unusual, or difficult film. I'm quite sure there is. But sometimes it's not nonsense. What is there in archetypes, and symbols and myths, that's so deep that it goes on for centuries and centuries, touching people in new ways they cannot define? For instance, the image of the sphinx, or the image described by Socrates, that man is composed of three elements, a multi-headed monster, a lion, and a man, and that they are inextricably connected with each other. There's something fascinating about it. It's a kind of image that is very fertile in meaning if you ponder on it. Where did it come from? Was it out of his own intuition, from something he'd seen? Logic is not enough to deal with it. It's images. It's something you see, something you feel something about.

In any case, for

people [who are willing to look within themselves] I think some of these films are extremely good. I think that in every form of this inner awakening the hope of the world is to be found, and if this is one of the ways to do it, then I'm for it.

I think films of this kind can be accused of conning people ... One can be accused of doing the fashionable thing – giving someone money to do their thing. The films can be accused of double values. They can be accused of many things, and some of that is probably true. But some of it is not, and in what area of life is it not that way? ...

I can only go by my own inner sense of sincerity and validity, such as it is, in receiving a suggestion, or working with a person, or looking at a film. And I believe it's my job as a producer not to have them make their film my way, but for me to try to understand what they're doing and, if I'm backing them in the first place, to try to help them do it their way.

Although the Film Board's institutional memory has filed away the experimental era of the late sixties and early seventies as a failure for which Daly was largely responsible, a dispassionate assessment would have to acknowledge several complicating factors. Poor NFB films are not unique to that era or to Daly. Every NFB producer has had his or her share of failures. Daly also supported some of the best new filmmakers of the era and produced some of the most memorable films, such as *Prologue, Accident, This Is a Photograph, Untouched and Pure*, and *Sad Song of Yellow Skin. A Film for Max* and *Running Time* offer unexpected pleasures. Tony Ianzelo, Michael Rubbo, Albert Kish, and Donald Winkler became four of the NFB's most productive directors of the seventies and eighties. Mort Ransen, Robin Spry, and, later, Michael Rubbo established themselves outside the Film Board as commercial film directors. In 1995, Rubbo was hired by the Australian Broadcasting Corporation to head its documentary division. Martin Duckworth forged a productive career in independent film. And the major experiments of this era – Spry's mingling of documentary with dramatic footage; Rubbo's transformation of the director into a character; Ransen's inversion of editing conventions; May's attempt to eliminate all artifice; Duckworth's introspective lyricism; their common interest in the political dimension of film aesthetics – influenced subsequent documentary both at the Film Board and elsewhere.

The opportunity to experiment with form, content, or voice enriched their work and the Film Board documentary generally, but perhaps the most interesting example is that of Derek May. Daly's encouragement of May's work found some critical justification in Piers Handling's 1980 Canadian Film Institute monograph on May. Acknowledging difficulties and disappointments in May's films, Handling's close analysis also finds 'a consistent aesthetic at work' in a search for personal identity that parallels Canada's larger political problems. And there is no doubt that *A Film for Max* helped puncture the illusory power of the film image.

In 1974, with Daly as his producer, May turned his iconoclastic eye onto a documentary subject, and made an unusual film about art, *Sananguagat: Inuit Masterworks*. The film conveys a sensual, emotional appreciation of Inuit sculpture. Numerous individual pieces are shown, almost always rotating slowly in abstract space. These shots are intercut with images of ordinary, contemporary Inuit life. Sounds from the latter are extended over the shots of the sculptures, and there is a recurring sound of what seems to be a rasp working a stone but also sounds like heavy, anxious breathing. Apparently it is a kind of throat-singing performed by Inuit women. The exhibitionary intent of the shots of carvings constrasts mysteriously with the indirect, allusive, anti-expository character of the location scenes. The two realities are connected literally only once; the effect is startling for both its unexpectedness and its felicity. The film bears the personal imprint of Derek May in nearly every frame, yet its quirky artistry enhances rather than competes with the art that is the film's subject. Its gnomic surface complements a deeper lucidity.

Sananguagat: Inuit Masterworks can be viewed as a companion film – and stylistic response – to John Feeney's equally beautiful but comparatively straightforward *The Living Stone* and *Eskimo Artist: Kenojuak*. Like these earlier, Unit B films, *Sananguagat* attempts to communicate or at least suggest the mythical aspect of some of the Inuit carvings, 'in which,' in Daly's words, 'mankind, animal and god elements are interwoven in the same direct, non-intellectualized art object that corresponds to the direct-ness of their nature as we see it.' Daly also sees a progression from *A Film for Max*. In that film, 'there are some brilliant shots, and many ordinary ones, that do not actually show "ordinariness" brilliantly. There is some feeling that the director does not actually care whether *we* care or not. But in this film, every one of the chosen sculptures is truly a masterwork, and we are permitted to see them all rather fully with appropriate lighting. There is no feeling of too much time or too little. All the works are good to look at for as much time as we are given.

'The shots of Inuit life are chosen to illustrate normal activity, normal time passing, natural character, the people's own language. But this time, they are chosen with clearer purpose – for example, to contrast the empti-ness of the "outside" with peace and simple self-work on the inside. Here again, the shots are long enough – but they could also be longer, or shorter, because inside *us* we are busy experiencing *them*.'

But *Sananguagat* is more than a simple progression from *A Film for Max*, more than a rejection of youthful conceits. It owes something to that earlier film. *Sananguagat*'s peculiarly haunting charm would not likely have evolved from a background in conventional documentary.

May sensed what he owed to Daly. He once said that 'the great thing about Daly is his *unwavering* availability to talk over ideas, projects – not necessarily head on, direct, about the particular project, but more general.

'And he's incredibly *patient*. There was one of the – who was he? – some biblical guy – who had a lot of patience. Well, Daly's got *more*.'

5

The Copper Beech Tree

Daly didn't blame anyone in particular for his demotion. He saw it as a consequence of a new and enervating form of bureaucratic control creeping into the Film Board. It was 'a homogenization of things, making different kinds of people fit the same pattern, doing the same things, instead of the more natural organic groupings, around function and theme. Decisions got more and more remote from the doers. As the government put in computerization, it also adopted the practices of big business – for example, budgeting people's time by hours and days and weeks on specific films long before you could know how much would be needed. Only the programs which were repetitive could be budgeted with reasonable accuracy. The new system was a Procrustean bed, requiring everything to fit the computer printouts. While this may have given the deciders in far places a feeling of satisfaction in that they were getting the information they asked for, we had to go through all the old human, natural methods anyway in order to figure out what had to be rearranged to fit the desired computer language. When secretaries are asked to record their time spent on each separate project, I call that bad administration.'

While its procedures were being newly rationalized, the Film Board's assets were undergoing a kind of privatization. 'Management and commissioners were more and more appointed on politics and attitude. There were efforts to sell the stock-shot library, and turn over other facilities to the private sector. There was little concern for the NFB as a visual arts centrepiece, for its leadership in film technology and artistic standards. The new politics seemed to be turning more and more of the Film Board's resources to serve outside business interests.'

The touch of resentment in Daly's recollection of the Film Board of his later years rises from a feeling that a great institution and cultural treasure was being betrayed. He seems to have avoided or at least defeated personal bitterness. And he found strength in the attitude that had sustained him when he lost Unit B. 'Not being politically minded or inclined to activism, I didn't spend much time and energy on being sorry for myself over what seemed an unavoidable trend. I was glad not to be wanted as an executive producer in later years, since they had less and less time for direct creative work, and more and more meetings and paperwork. Being a "mere" producer turned out to be not "mere" for me. I could spend all my time and energy directly on the films themselves, with whichever filmmakers were interested in working with me.'

Opportunities to ply his craft and share his knowledge were less obvious or abundant than had been after the earlier set-back. The 1960s were a time of optimism, experimentation, and, at the Film Board, generous budgets for new projects and for hiring new people. There was openness to big ideas about both film and life. Daly had *Labyrinthe*, the greatest editing challenge of his career, to occupy much of his time for three years. After that, there were talented new filmmakers to support and teach. The 1970s, by contrast, were turning out to be a time of tightened budgets, cut-backs in hiring, and a turn towards more conventional filmmaking.

Daly's contribution for the rest of the 1970s thus would be more of a hodgepodge than the 'program of films' that Verrall had envisioned for him. He would produce about seven or eight films a year on average. Two new filmmakers would apprentice under him. He would also produce for now-accomplished filmmakers like Ianzelo, Rubbo, and Winkler and take on his share of unexciting projects that no one else wanted. His diplomatic skills would make him a natural choice for co-productions with film units from other countries. And increasingly he would be called upon to help out film projects that had been bogged down in the editing.

Yet underlying this scattered deployment of his abilities was a unifying theme. In his last decade at the Film Board, Daly's attitude towards film production grew even more philosophical than before. Increasingly he was interested more in the existential and ethical implications of a project than in whether or not it was a 'good' or 'successful' film. Just as Grierson had defined art as 'a by-product of a job of work done,' Daly would see value in film as a by-product of the right thing done. Some filmmakers welcomed this reflectiveness; others were impatient with it. But Daly's philosophical approach to the problems of filmmaking would linger in filmmakers' minds even as Daly's direct involvement in production waned. Near the end of his career, whatever influence Daly exerted at the Film Board stemmed largely from his sheer presence.

Giles Walker was one of the last two staff filmmakers to apprentice with Daly. Daly produced three of Walker's early films: *Descent* (1975), *No Way They Want to Slow Down* (1975), and *The Sword of the Lord* (1976). Later, Walker's interests shifted to drama. Under other producers, he directed the half-hour *Bravery in the Field* (1979) and the features *90 Days* (1985) and *Princes in Exile* (1990) before leaving the Film Board for commercial film-making.

Walker says that Daly 'can make the most devastating criticism seem positive. But he doesn't just say that it will turn out all right. He goes through in enormous detail the film's missed potential. It's extraordinary. Usually he starts slowly, first with a long list of the good things. Then he gradually eases into the things that are wrong, and how to fix them. For the filmmaker – even though Tom has completely negated what the filmmaker has done – it is an extremely positive experience.'

Walker's *The Sword of the Lord* records the attempt by Jim Hunter, a deeply religious skier employed as a farm-hand in Saskatchewan, to win the 1974 World Cup competition. Hunter trains rigorously and does well in practice but fails even to come close to winning. When he begins to realize that he will fail, he blames his ski suit, then the waxing on the skis. He becomes defeatist: 'It's like they got the clock set two seconds against you at the start.' A colleague tries to get Hunter to see that his problem lies within himself: he is too serious, he can't relax. Although Hunter acknowledges that he has 'never been able to let go,' he seems confused by his failure and opines that maybe God wants him to learn how to lose graciously. In the end, his religiosity seems to be a substitute for self-knowledge.

In recalling the film, Daly skips over technical or structural matters to ponder the film's failure to achieve the popular success that Daly had expected of it. 'I feel much clearer now about it, looking back on the film with "emotion recollected in tranquillity." The film looks even better than I thought it did when we made it. But I now read the content with more of an inner eye, and not just an outer eye.

'I see that this young skier is a pure product of the mass-belief of our times, that winning is everything, that winning will surely bring you happiness, that if you don't win a medal you are a failure. And spectators have the idea that if the team wins, they win, and if the team loses, they lose.

'Jim Hunter is too much like that. He makes every effort *himself* to bring about his winning, but – as of the time the film was being made – he does not see that it is the very over-intensity of his training and performance that is doing him in. The fact that he does better in practice runs than he does in the actual races is the clue. Always the "waxing," the "skis," or "mistakes" are to blame. But the *big* mistake is not looked at, and when near the end of the film it is suggested to him directly, he walks out, offended.

'Film audiences are no different from sports audiences. They want their heroes (or anti-heroes) to win, and then they can go away feeling that *they* have won something, *they* have understood something. But when they are faced with watching someone, even in high places, who cannot bear, yet, to see the truth of his own nature, it is too much a mirror of their own lack, their own fatal flaw, their own chief fault, and this they can't bear to face.

'It is hard to face the fact that many of us will actually make really great efforts – except the most important one. It is as if we go to all lengths to be busy with great efforts so we won't have "time" to face what we really need to face.

'In my case, my expectations that this film was going to win popularity belong to the same unconscious teaching of our time. But the film can have a long life among those who really want to face their own truth, on the inside as well as on the outside. And I hope Jim Hunter was able to do just that in the years that have passed since the film was made.'

When he directed his first major film, *Coaches* (1976), Paul Cowan became the last new staff filmmaker to apprentice under Daly. The documentary follows four coaches preparing their Canadian teams – men's volleyball and basketball, women's volleyball and equestrian – for pre-Olympics competition. Each coach drives his or her athletes very hard and demands the seemingly unreasonable or impossible from them, but each also shows genuine concern for their personal growth. The film is disarmingly straightforward in style and structure. The four stories are left intact rather than interwoven.

The strongest moment in the equestrian sequence presented Cowan with an ethical issue reminiscent of *Blood and Fire*. 'I had asked the coach a question, which was heard off-camera, about one of the riders who seemed to be losing her nerve trying to get her horse to go over a jump. And I said something to the effect that, "She's losing her nerve, isn't she?" And the coach said, "Yes, she is," or something to that effect. Well, one of the big shots from the equestrian team, a millionaire from Toronto, came and saw that sequence, and he was adamant that we take that interchange out, that it was going to hurt the girl to see herself portrayed as a coward on film. Tom and I argued very strongly that it should be kept in, that it reflected the truth of the situation. This guy made some not-too-veiled threats about what he'd do if we left it in. We debated for a long time about whether I had led the coach into saying what she said, but we decided I had not. And in the end, this girl has a great moral victory. She gets her horse to jump and goes on to win the Gold Medal. So we left it in.'

After making *I'll Go Again* (1977) with Daly, Cowan directed *Going the Distance* (1979), *The Kid Who Couldn't Miss* (1982), *Democracy on Trial: The Morgentaler Affair* (1984), and *Double or Nothing: The Rise and Fall of Robert Campeau* (1992) under other producers. But Daly remained for Cowan an informal consultant on ethical issues. 'On several occasions, I have gone to him for a kind of ethical judgment, cases where I thought I might have a conflict of interest. But Tom was never prissy about it. If he feels you can honestly put something in the film which is hard on a character, okay, but you've got to be honest, and it's got to be very, very fair.'

But filmmakers stimulated by Daly's philosophical approach to even the routine problems of making films could also find it relentless and exhausting. For Giles Walker, 'Tom's greatest strength – a lot of people don't credit him with it – is discussing an idea. He can take any idea and expand on it a hundredfold. Its full potential gets revealed. You might have thought of ten sequences and you come out of the meeting with a hundred possibilities, some of which are really good. But Tom can overwhelm you. With him the process never stops. There's always something you can improve. He's still spewing forth ideas, while you're feeling the film is as good as it's ever going to be.'

Daly's philosophical bent, and his desire to give liberal expression to it, often annoyed his fellow producers and other admininstrators. 'Supposing you sit at lunch with Tom,' explains filmmaker and producer Daisy de Bellefeuille, 'and you say, "Tom, I have an idea of making a film about the life of a lobster." He'll say, "That's interesting," and before you know it, he will connect it to the court of Louis XIV, to the history of the Vatican, to, uh, the present problem of pollution, to possibly the Republican convention – *to every single thing that ever existed*. And by the time you finish *you don't know what film you're going to make any more*.'

George Pearson was a veteran producer with an impressive list of films behind him when he worked with Daly for the first time, as his co-producer, on *Running Time*. That project had reinforced for Pearson the image of Daly that many of Pearson's colleagues in administration had of him. 'He could, on occasion, be arrogant, vain, hard-headed, and patronizing. He drove higher-level managers to distraction with what they considered his unrealistic, even unworldly, approach to matters of administration, organization, financing, and policy. Even now as I look back, I see him in his office or at the conference table laboriously setting forth a set of ideas, clouded in allusion and strung out with analogies, everyone wishing he would just get on with it. Because when Tom would start philosophizing, the analogy that he adduced could seem more complicated than the reality it was supposed to illustrate. He might begin, "It's like in the Ming Dynasty when ..." So you wondered: Where does the man get his reputation? Why do filmmakers hook up with him?

'I later discovered that when you get him down to a concrete editing problem, an awe-inspiring transformation takes place – not in him, but in your perception of him. In this image, I see him perched on a stool in front of the editing machine, meticulously developing an argument for retaining, eliminating, or moving a sequence using the same forms of analogy and the same flights of allusion, but here we listen carefully and nod thoughtfully. With almost any other editor, if you ask, "Why did you cut *there*, and why did you place this sequence *here*?" the answer usually comes back, "Because it *feels* right." Or he quotes some well-known rule of editing that he has learned somewhere. Or he gives you an explanation based on what simply makes sense to him. Tom does all that, and often it's enough. But with an intricate cut or a difficult placement he has a special capacity to go beyond that and explain in clear, logical, and precise terms the "why" of the cut or placement. He can root it in a clear definition of what the film is all about or in the art of documentary itself. He'll go from the cut to a generalization and then back down to the cut. When this happens you not only solve the question at hand, you also learn something that will guide you in similar situations in the future. When I saw that facet, I realized why everyone saw him as a great film teacher. It is easy – so easy – to misjudge him if you haven't experienced that.'

Pearson made this discovery during a re-edit of *Cold Journey* (1972), a dramatic feature about a young Indian's acculturation problems and conflicts. Pearson produced the film. Martin Defalco was its director. His previous films included a pair of enchanting sponsored documentaries, *Northern Fisherman* (1966) and *Trawler Fishermen* (1966), a documentary portrait, *Don Messer: His Land and His Music* (1971), and *The Other Side of the Ledger* (1972), a withering indictment of the Hudson's Bay Company's treatment of Canadian Indians. When a test print of *Cold Journey* was screened at the Film Board, the general reaction was negative. The dialogue and acting were often wooden and the characterizations somehow unsatisfying. No one in management thought the film had any significant theatrical potential. The film's problems arose from the script and were thought to be deeper than anything that could be corrected by minor editing. Robert Verrall, the director of production, says that he was considering cancelling the project when he arranged a private screening of the film for himself and Alanis Obomsawin, a Canadian Indian who had just joined the Film Board. After the screening, 'she said, "This film is too important to kill. There's just too much in it that has to be shown and discussed."' Verrall then decided to bring Daly onto the project to recut the film and Stanley Jackson to write a voice-over narration for the film's main character.

Daly was not initially hopeful about the film's prospects. Its problems were rooted 'in a dramatic error that permeated the material. It seemed as if "real people" – the Indians, the good guys – were pitted dramatically against "cartoon stereotypes" – the white people, the bad guys. The two sides weren't cognate. There was no real struggle between two sets of equally believable characters. For me, the whole tragic purpose of the story was weakened by this. Martin was trying too hard to give the Indians their rightful due.'

Daly tried trimming the film down, but he found that the imbalance between the two sets of characters was too systemic to be eliminated in that way. Then he started looking at the out-takes. 'I began to see a good many bits and passages of the same scenes with different impressions, and this changed my mind about the possibilities of the film.'

'Sequence by sequence,' Daly started 'to join all the usable takes back together as the rushes once were, and then systematically to cut out any lengths of these shots which had that offending flavour. So I was left with a total block of material which I could see as emotionally believable for the purposes of drama, whether it came from the Indian side or the white side. Almost all that was left behind was on the white side, but not totally. And there were a number of gems of really fine material that had never made it into the original cut, possibly from not knowing how to fit it in. Whenever I was in doubt or could see alternatives, I'd find out from Martin what his intention was and work towards realizing his original aim.'

Although Pearson and Defalco welcomed Daly's and Jackson's help, they felt as if, in Pearson's words, they had been 'ordered off the field so the first string could come in and win the game.' They nevertheless assumed that with Daly's re-editing and Jackson's narration, the film would now work better. But at a test screening of the new version, it was Pearson's and Defalco's turn to react negatively. 'They had made this cut,' Defalco remembers, 'and they were ready to mix it. It was a disaster. I think they weren't very happy with it, either. I was shocked that they were proceeding anyway.' 'Martin,' Pearson recalls, 'was upset at the loss of certain sequences. He felt that even if they had problems, they must be retained to keep faith with the validity of the situation being portrayed. I was much more upset by what I felt was an inept and utterly inadequate narration.'

The narration's failure surprised Daly: 'For the first time, we all discovered that while Stanley could write and read a narration as himself, he absolutely could not write a narration "in character," as a dramatic character, from somebody else's real point of view.'

Pearson went to Colin Low, now the project's executive producer, and asked for a go at writing the narration himself. Low, who respected Pearson enormously for his record as a producer, agreed, even though Pearson had never written a narration before. 'It turned out,' Daly acknowledges, 'that he really had the knack, and the narration worked wonderfully well, even to the point of being able to resurrect some of Martin's other scenes or passages.'

Defalco thinks that Daly was pleased at his and Pearson's reaction to the Daly-Jackson cut. 'The powers that be had forced a completion on them. Now, Tom swung right around. He became tremendously helpful.' Pearson agrees: 'I have no doubt in my mind that he saw himself being sent in as a "film doctor," to bring back to health a very sick film. That's probably the way it was presented to him. I think he discovered that we were as dedicated to making it a better film as he was, had a great deal more knowledge about the subject than he had, and had our own strong ideas on how to go about it. He stepped out of his role as film doctor and into one of collaborator.'

While *Cold Journey* enjoyed no conventional theatrical success, it served as a catalyst for public discussion of the issues it treated. 'The film played to packed houses across the North,' Verrall says, 'bringing whites and Indians looking at the same film together.' Pearson and Defalco say that Indians loved some of the sequences that executives at the NFB had found worrisome. The film was screened for government officials and cited by Parliament. And Alanis Obomsawin, who would make several films of her own and eventually receive the Order of Canada for her work on behalf of Native peoples, cut a half-hour version of *Cold Journey* for children's educational television.

Writing the narration brought Pearson into close involvement with Daly's editing, especially during the last days of postproduction, when Daly's cutting consisted mainly in shortening or lengthening shots by one or two frames. 'On many days,' Pearson recalls, 'I worked well into the evening and, after a long day, would hit a point where I needed to get away from the writing at hand and do something else for a while in order to get back to it fresh. One thing I would do would be to take Tom's cuts apart and put them back again to see the difference. I was fascinated that they had been done so quickly and with so little hesitation, and I wanted to see for myself if they were really as expertly done as they seemed. They were.'

Pearson also experienced firsthand a model of producing that is rare in the film world, even in the NFB: 'Daly has an amazing tolerance for other people's creative ideas. He always puts himself in the role of, "How do I get the best of what this guy has to offer? And if I don't understand it, it's my job to do that." So he'll always take the time. I've learned to try to do this myself from Tom.'

'From a guy like Tom,' observes Defalco, 'you learn that you don't have to quit on a film. If you do quit, get off. But if you don't quit, you stick with it all the way. It's not going to be easy, and the solution won't come from some trick or technicality. It has to be integrated as a whole. Tom wants to talk philosophy. I think that's a way of helping the filmmaker – making connections with him – so it's not just an editing problem in the technical sense.'

Defalco's perception was shared by Donald Brittain, one of the many filmmakers who appreciated Daly's editing-room genius for relating the apparent minutiae of fine-cutting to broad but apt ideas. 'He is so meticulous when dealing with the final few frames [to be cut],' reflected Brittain, 'that you tend to think that maybe he's lost sight of the big picture. But he knows what you're trying to do, and he's absolutely brilliant in helping you to achieve it. He can see how two frames here and three frames there can help your overall idea. I always try to bring him in to look at a rough-cut or assembly.'

Although filmmakers again and again refer to Daly's ability to point out where adding or subtracting two or three frames will improve the effect of a shot or a cut or a line of dialogue, specific instances would occur during the hands-on process of editing. They are not easily recalled, by filmmakers or by Daly. Daly can, however, explain some of the governing principles behind such cutting decisions.

One of them has to do with '"apparent" sync, when a musical chord or sound effect is meant to "synchronize" dramatically with the cut to a new shot. The obvious approach is to have the first striations of the chord or sound effect begin exactly at the splice on the synchronizer. I found in practice, though, that the sound then appears to arrive just *before* the shot is seen.

'Why is this? It is because the ear hears the new sound begin exactly at the same time as the striations of the new sound begin, however much the outgoing sound is mingled with it. The eye, however, has a short, variable period of adjustment *before* it fully adapts to the new shot. This is clearly checkable when you look at a bright red object and then look at a white wall: there will be a green after-image of the previous object on the white wall until the eye adjusts.

'So, although the ear hears the sound change exactly in sync with the splice, the sound will appear to have occurred ahead of the point where the eye fully takes in the new shot, which to the eye, will be the "apparent" proper sync point of the picture and sound.

'It is like a very short "lap-dissolve," in the eye, of the old and new images. And just as a musical chord syncs most comfortably to the new shot at the *end* of a lap-dissolve (and not in the middle), so also here the chord will apparently sync best at the point where the eye sees the new shot in the clear.'

To illustrate how this works, Daly describes a cut to a shot of a cannon firing. 'The firing is visible only at the first frame of smoke and flame. But if you cut to that as the first frame of the gun, you won't "see" what is firing, as it is already only smoke and flame. To see it as a gun firing, you need one or more frames of the gun first, for the eye to perceive it as a gun, which fires "immediately."'

Daly adds that the exact point of cutting according to this principle – and to any other principle – varies with factors having different dramatic effects, such as the difference between a close-up and a long-shot, or between light and shadow.

Another principle involves the different speeds with which various functions of the mind and body react. An instinctive reaction, such as recoiling from contact with a hot stove, often occurs before the mind is even aware of a need to react. An emotional reaction is almost as fast as an instinctive one, but it still begins 'only after the realization *hits* you that you've been insulted or received a million dollars.' A deliberate physical reaction 'has some inertia at the start of it that takes a tiny bit more time.' Thinking before speaking takes still longer. And 'a pause between spoken sentences is longer on the average than a pause between clauses in a sentence. A pause between different sections of thought on a subject is longer still, while a pause before starting on a new subject usually takes the mind a bit longer to start again.'

The application of this principle, like the principle of 'apparent sync,' varies with numerous other cinematic factors, including the richness of the material. 'One can make a pause "more emotional" or "more thoughtful" by shortening or lengthening it, but only, of course, if there is some visual emotion or some thought in the first place.'

Reflecting back on his attempts to explain these and other principles to filmmakers and editors, Daly believes that 'those who listened to the *idea*, and saw from practical examples that it was worth the effort, usually put it into good practice when they felt a problem. Those who listened to the *reasons behind* the idea, and saw the difference in practice, usually had as much fun with it as I did, so long as the material warranted the time.'

Some listened to the ideas and to the reasons behind them but felt only a little wiser for it. Eddie Le Lorrain was no novice when he joined the Film Board in 1967. He had trained in Holland under Bert Haanstra and then spent ten years at the BBC. In 1972, he was asked to do some fine-cutting on *Cowboy and Indian*, directed by Don Owen and produced by Daly. The film was about two painters who also play musical instruments. Le Lorrain remembers working on a sequence that began with 'a jam session inside a farmhouse, then cut outside to a 360-degree pan around the farm and back to the house. When it came back to the house, they were playing a new piece of music. I had to find an out-point from the first piece of music and a starting point for the new piece of music so that the film was in sync when it got back to the farmhouse.

'Tom very patiently explained a complicated formula for determining exactly where to make the cut. It was a kind of mathematical-slash-musical way of determining the exact point.

'I got lost during the explanation. I just nodded in agreement even though I didn't understand a thing. Tom left, and then I went at the problem my own way, and made a cut that worked for me. When Tom came back and looked at it, he said the cut worked perfectly.

'I had just approached it intuitively and arrived at the same solution. I didn't have the heart to tell him. Anyway, I was pleased with my cut. And I was pleased that Tom was pleased that his theory had worked.'

In this instance, Le Lorrain had been brought in to work on a film that Daly was producing. More often in these years, as with *Cold Journey*, Daly found himself giving advice on projects other than his own. Filmmaker Robert Fortier believes that sometimes Daly got sent into situations where his presence wasn't wanted. In the early 1970s, 'Verrall imposed Tom on everybody. It was as if Verrall had said, "No film is complete in this organization until Tom Daly has blessed it."' Fortier remembers Daly being sent in to consult on Michael Scott's *Station 10* (1973), which Fortier was editing. 'We resisted him. We weren't saying that his style was bad, but that there were other ways to make films. He had a lot of suggestions, but we said no. It was like a revolt. This wasn't Tom's fault. He didn't like being imposed on people.'

In George Pearson's view, 'Verrall had this hero-worship. He idolized

Tom. Tom could speak no wrong, do no wrong. Everything he said was pure wisdom. Any opposition was the work of the devil. "Why would you refuse to work with a genius? What's wrong with you?" It really only lasted for a while. Tom probably pulled Verrall off.'

Verrall acknowledges having assigned Daly to consult or advise on several productions other than Daly's own. 'There were a number of people in English Production who had never worked with Tom. They hadn't been in Unit B. They had worked in other units. I was convinced there could be some real benefit if they were exposed to Tom.'

Daly was unaware of Verrall's scheme. 'What did happen a lot,' he remembers, 'was that all types of people would, for instance, stop me in the hall and ask me to come to a rough-cut screening or something. And I would. Of course, it is possible that in some cases they had been *told* to ask me! But I don't remember anything like that.'

The 'other ways' to make films usually meant faster, rougher, and more openly didactic. Le Lorrain admits to having learned from Daly: 'Things have rubbed off from just listening to him, being around him, that have helped me in my career. For instance, he would point at the image on the editor and say, "Your eye is focused right here. Your next shot should have its centre of gravity right here, so your eye doesn't have to switch."' Le Lorrain also admires the 'hang-in-there attitude' that Daly brought to even the least promising of projects. 'But,' he adds, 'if you have enough money and enough time, you can go on and on and on, and get a perfect film. *Corral* is perfect. *Universe* is perfect. But who else in the world can do this? It's not fair, in a way.' In 1982 Le Lorrain produced *If You Love This Planet*, which is constructed around a speech by the nuclear arms critic Dr Helen Caldicott. It is a 'rough' film, but direct, unwavering – even crude – in its didactic purpose. It is far from perfect. It won an Oscar and wide distribution.

The two approaches to editing recall Daly's and McLean's conflicting interpretations of Grierson's documentary idea. What came to be thought of as 'the Daly approach' emphasized structure, and it sought to forge structure out of the material presented for editing. The competing approach emphasized function, and was happy to shape the material to the didactic aim motivating the production. The difference is suggested in a taped conversation between another British-trained editor, David Wilson, and Robert Fortier that took place in the early 1980s. By that time, Fortier had invited Daly in on a film of his own and was pleased with his suggestions.

Fortier: I don't start small and expand. I start big and come down. I cut the 'Tom Daly' way.

Wilson: Yeah, part of the strength of this place is that films take a long time to cut. When I started cutting in England, I knew I had, say, six weeks to cut. You have to look at the footage, decide what the film is, and work it out in your mind, and make the cut.

Fortier: When you only have a limited amount of time, then you *have* to cut it that way. But why do you do that *here*? I mean, you have the time, right? You could work that way if you wanted to.

Wilson: I couldn't. It would drive me crazy. I did it once ... [The director] had a hundred thousand feet of film. We cut it to six hours ... four hours ... two hours. I was on it eight months. It's crazy. He had a hundred thousand feet of original footage, and he insisted he was going to stretch the film out with stock footage. The BBC cuts much faster. Six weeks to cut a half-hour is a luxury, in England.

Fortier: But the films there lack the polish ...

Wilson: The kind of films that I like to cut are about issues, films worth doing for their subject matter, like *The Other Side of the Ledger*. I ask, what is this film supposed to do? What can we say, given the footage available? I personally couldn't sit down and start to cut a film unless I knew where I was going. I can't just sort of chip away at it, and cut sequence by sequence.

Fortier: I like to see *everything*. I like to see all the possibilities. If I shoot fifty sequences, I have to *see* them *with* other sequences that *maybe* won't work, but maybe *will* work. I don't know the answer until I see them on the screen, and because I have the *time* here to see them, I do.

Wilson: I won't cut a documentary from beginning to end. I will identify the critical sequences and cut them first. Generally, if I'm going for an hour film, my first cut may be *under* an hour, and then I'll build on that.

Fortier: I'll go the other way around. I'll do all the sequences, stick them all in, and then *lose* them.

Wilson: But if you don't know where a sequence is going, what it is supposed to do, I don't see how you can cut it efficiently.

Until recently, the 'Daly approach' to editing seems to have been the dominant one at the Film Board. Even Eddie Le Lorrain, who managed as well as any to resist it, sighs, 'I don't think I could go back and edit films for the BBC anymore. I'd be afraid. My whole approach is now different. Film Board films have to have a longer life, and they're superbly crafted, but for TV the main use is to be shown once or twice. But I'm not so sure our films are that much better.'

The thoroughness that characterized the 'Daly approach' to editing also described his producing. Dutch filmmaker Nico Crama discovered this when he directed *It Wasn't Easy* ... (1978), a co-production between the

Netherlands and Canada on the history of Dutch immigration to Canada. Crama was forty-two years old and had produced more than fifty films. They included an early short by Paul Verhoeven, *The Wrestler* (1970), an Academy Award nominee, and numerous enduring films on art and artists. As accomplished as he was, Crama was surprised by what Daly could teach him about producing. 'He helped me tremendously with all the bureaucratic problems of making a film here, and his editing knowledge was truly great, but what is really amazing is that he takes his *time* with you. He's very busy, he has a tremendous amount of work to do, but when you talk with him, there doesn't seem to exist any time pressure any more. And I think I learned that from him: that no matter what's happening outside, producing a film *creatively* takes time. And he takes the time.

'As a producer, he doesn't impose his will on you but helps you discover your own abilities – and your weaknesses, also. This is so important, especially in a case like mine, when you've done a lot of films, you have a lot of experience, and you rediscover what you can and what you cannot do. And he does that for you in a very gentle way. He tries to teach you how to find a way to do it yourself.

'Here was a man who put all his energy into creative producing – and this is so rare in the film world.'

Daly's example altered the direction of Crama's career. 'It's intriguing – and this is very personal – that someone else can change your life when you're older, that you suddenly find a teacher after you're established, and already have your own methods. *It Wasn't Easy* ... was the first film I'd directed in years. I wanted to get back into directing. But he made me also want to go back into producing. He made me feel that you're not necessarily more creative as a director than as a producer, that producing is as worthwhile as directing. When I returned to producing, I stopped paying too much attention to the administrative aspect of it, and I tried to put more emphasis on the human side.'

Daly was a producer on two other films Crama later made with the NFB: *Co Hoedeman, Animator* (1980), which Crama directed, and *From the Ashes of War* (1980), which Crama co-produced with Daly. Since then, Crama has produced a documentary for American public television (*The Dutch Connection*, 1982), an award-winning film for Pepsico, *Passage: A Richard Erdman Sculpture* (1985), and numerous animation films. In 1988, he co-produced another NFB-Dutch venture, *The Boulevard of Broken Dreams*, a documentary directed by Derek May, and in 1990 he produced an independent feature film, *Vincent and Me*, directed by Michael Rubbo, who had left the Film Board a few years earlier. Commenting on a recent project beset by unusual problems, Crama remarks, 'On several occasions, when I was in a difficult situation, I thought: "How would Tom have handled this?" It certainly helped me achieve a reasonably good final result.'

The 'emphasis on the human side' that impressed Crama showed itself clearly in another international project that Daly co-produced. The film was *Mr. Symbol Man* (1974), directed by Bruce Moir, a young filmmaker with Film Australia (and later its head). The documentary celebrates the magnificent obsession of septuagenarian Charles Bliss. A survivor of Buchenwald, Bliss fled to England and then migrated to Shanghai, where he worked as a photographer and filmmaker. He finally settled in Australia, where, convinced that the miseries of his time were rooted in misunderstandings among peoples, he doggedly pursued a dream of inventing a universal symbolic language free of cultural bias and baggage. His work had met only indifference and rejection, however, until psychologists at the Ontario Centre for Crippled Children discovered that his language of symbols could enable victims of cerebral palsy to communicate with each other, their teachers, and their families.

The film foregrounds Bliss's exuberance while hinting at an underlying streak of anguish. He lives with his brother Henry, who is taciturn, intellectually ordinary, happy to help around the house. Conventionally but carefully structured, the film is enriched by cinematic embellishments organic to the material: Bliss's own footage of Shanghai, for example, and part of a drawn-on-film animation used for teaching Bliss's symbolic language to the children. At one point, Bliss himself, having once made films, brashly tells the cameraman when to cut.

After taking a test print to Sydney, and screening it for Bliss and the Australian component of the film team, Daly received a letter from Bliss objecting to the shot of Bliss 'directing' the film, the use of only part of the cartoon, and the depiction of Henry. In his reply to Bliss, Daly justified each sequence in question with patience, decisiveness, and a sensitivity to the needs of both a film's subject and its audience:

Many thanks for your kind letter of January 20. I enjoyed all the news and all the comments and suggestions. You ask me what I think of your three requests. I've been thinking about them a good deal and here are my quite clear feelings about them:

(1) The word 'cut' which you say at the end of the mind-words sequence: I wouldn't cut this out for the world. For the audience it is one of the unexpected charms of the film and of yourself. It is a reminder that you were a film-maker as well as an inventor of a symbol system, and furthermore the reminder comes in a

dramatic manner and not by "telling" the audience in commentary; they come upon it by themselves. Audiences simply love it, and it puts them in a good mood for hearing and accepting the sequences and information that follow. When the scene was shot, you may not have intended it to be in, but I'm sure we're right that it is a real advantage to the film and to the audience's enjoyment of you to keep it in.

(2) The cartoon: In itself, what is in the film works charmingly. It is intended to show the *relationship* between the children and the cartoon, to show how it really affects them. Technically we had some difficulties in that the children's reactions were recorded during an actual run of the cartoon, and so the wonderful natural reactions of the children were tied to certain parts of the music, so we couldn't show *both* the children *and* the whole cartoon in the film even if we wanted to. But with all due respect I think we have a *better* solution to the problem than your suggestion: we intend to finish the *complete* cartoon ($3\frac{1}{2}$ minutes) as a separate little film, available independently, as a teaching aid for use in classes in just the same way as it was used by the teacher in the film. This way, we can have our cake and eat it too!

To suggest that there was more to his brother Henry than he thought the film implied, Bliss had sent along a photograph of Henry in a Masonic hat. In reply, Daly first mentions a beloved uncle that had been a thirty-third-degree Mason. But:

I simply don't agree with you about the impression the film gives of Henry. His character is a very necessary complement to your own. In fact, I think it would have been very hard for you to have succeeded without him, had you been so unlucky as not to have him with you. We know from the whole story that the two of you did not have a big source of money to carry out your work, and that you had to do all necessary work yourselves in order to manage it, including work around the house.

For young people today this quality of you both, but of Henry in particular (of being happy and willing to serve a cause with hard and patient work), is a very attractive quality. It is not taken at all as 'menial' work, but as an expression of readiness and ability to work voluntarily. The days of maids and such are over. People in general have to do their own work now, and that is 'normal.' In fact, far from 'humiliating' Henry, these scenes give people the sense that he has a natural humility. And true humility and service to community causes are both qualities which I believe the Masons admire and aspire to.

But it is in recalling the test screening itself that Daly's concern for the people involved in a project shows how far it could reach. During the filming, Bliss had discovered that one of the teachers had adapted his symbols in a way contrary to what Bliss had specified in his writings. 'He became very angry, and he developed an irrational dislike of this thoroughly responsible person. It bordered on real hatred. This was still the situation when I took the film to Australia. The showing went very well, and since Bliss was in such a good humour, I took the opportunity to mention that there was only one thing I was sorry about, and didn't know if I should mention it. He insisted I do so, and I said that the one thing I could not bear was that, after all the good he had brought to the children and to the world, he might die with this hatred of that teacher on his conscience, unresolved.

'Bliss was truly touched, and suggested at once that he make a full apology. In fact, he suggested that we cover it as a film interview in which he could speak directly to her through the camera with all his feeling evident. We all were happy to agree, and a crew was made immediately available. However, Bliss indicated that he was tired just then, and it was lunchtime. After lunch, and after his obligatory nap after lunch, we would do the interview.

'All went as planned, except that he had taken the time of his "nap" to memorize his message and rehearse it to perfection. All the spontaneity and unrehearsed feeling that had welled up in the morning had totally disappeared. The result was worse than not doing it at all. The rest of us were terribly disappointed, but we said nothing. His change of heart, which was permanent, was duly passed on to the lady concerned, to her great relief. But the interview was quietly consigned to oblivion.'

Tony Ianzelo admires this kind sensitivity to the personal and psychological needs of others: 'Besides all the craftsmanship, Tom's also a guy who likes to get people together. He knows how to get people contributing, so that the whole is greater than the sum. I saw that often. And he's an incredible diplomat. He knows how to say no and be firm. I heard him on the phone chew someone out who was quite capable of defending himself. The guy had treated some lab person badly. It went on for twenty minutes. This was not the usual soft, easygoing Tom. There wasn't even time to ask me to leave. The tone was so firm, the words well chosen. But there was no ranting and raving.'

Michael Rubbo gives an example of Daly's ability to soften disputes during a production. In the early 1970s, Rubbo successfully proposed a co-production (*The Man Who Can't Stop* [1973]) between the Film Board and Film Australia on Rubbo's Australian uncle, Francis Sutton, a crusader against pollution. 'Film Australia, fearing that I was doing a number on them and just getting *their* money to make *my* film, which they would never see again, insisted that I use an Australian editor. So they sent one of their editors over here. He was a good editor, but we had problems from the very beginning. I never really felt that he believed in the material, in Francis.

'Tom had this job of mediating between us as our squabbles got more and more intense. They went on for months and months. Both of us were running to Tom with tales about the other person. Tom had to work very, very hard on that, because – complicating matters – the editor had overstayed his stay by months and months. He was staying downtown, in a hotel, at great expense. The people at Film Australia were getting very nervous about that. Tom had to calm all that down, and in a way sort of educate Film Australia about the way the Film Board works, that there was nothing particularly disastrous about what was happening, that it was just par for the course, that that was how interesting and unusual things often got made.'

Daly's acceptance of unexpected problems and reversals helped Rubbo turn his next project, *Waiting for Fidel*, from a potential bust into Rubbo's most influential film. The film's motivation is an invitation received by Joey Smallwood, the Liberal ex-premier of Newfoundland, a self-styled 'socialist,' to film an interview with Fidel Castro. Smallwood, Rubbo, and Geoff Stirling, a media mogul who has put up the film's outside costs, all take on roles as characters in the film. Smallwood hopes the resulting film will contribute to international understanding. Stirling is looking for a nice profit. Rubbo wants to make an insightful documentary on the Cuban experiment. As they wait in Cuba for the promised interview and begin to suspect they will not get it, they turn on each other. They argue about Cuba and bicker about the production.

Midway into the project, Daly made a decision which would have been beyond his capacity in his early days as a producer. When Rubbo realized that the promised interview probably would not be granted, he phoned Daly. As Daly remembers it, Rubbo proposed that 'instead of calling off the film altogether, a film could be made building on the material they had shot already. It was full of character and frank talk, and could equally well be the start of a different subject. Rather than waste all the money already spent, I felt it was a good idea. And knowing Mike's ability, like a cat, to fall on his feet when upset, I didn't feel the project was all that "experimental." Although I personally would be afraid to try such a thing, I knew he could pull it off. So I got official approval for the changed project.'

The result is indeed an insightful documentary, not about Cuba directly, but about the perception of Cuba, and how perception is coloured by expectations. And it is very funny, rich in character, and revelatory about the process of documentary filmmaking.

Daly's responsiveness was a key reason that Tony Ianzelo and Boyce Richardson asked him to produce their two warm but observational documentaries on China, *North China Commune* and *North China Factory*. 'When you're on location,' Ianzelo explained shortly after the films were made, 'he wires reports on rushes. He's almost got the rushes cut in his head. He can tell you that, say, the harvest scene will cut well. You rely on that. It gives tremendous confidence. He also senses when your spirits are low, and he gives extra info on the rushes that makes everyone feel good and want to keep on going. You need that. In China, for example, one guy on the crew got sick. Boyce broke his toe. I was sick. Someone had ulcers.'

Daly's comments on *North China Commune* reveal another kind of responsiveness: to the personality, talent, and goals of the filmmaker. The film's best quality, for Daly, 'is the feeling that we, the audience, are visiting the Wuxing commune ourselves, not just hearing about someone else's visit. It is as if there are no veils between us and the people and life of the commune.' Daly attributes this quality to Ianzelo's 'natural desire to get to know and enjoy people as they are, without any axe to grind or thesis to find support for. He researches with no hurry to come to conclusions, observes with eyes and feelings and thoughtful mind, and shoots what most touches him. And he has a wonderful capacity when shooting to keep both eyes open: one eye sees exactly what he is getting inside the lens, the other sees what is approaching or going on off-screen. This enables him to zoom back or pan around to take in unexpected actions at just the right time, with the smoothest camera movement. This natural and organic sense of timing makes for few empty moments in his shooting, and also lets him know, without having to think about it, whether to cut the camera sooner or later during the rhythm of an action.'

No matter how deeply they respected him, however, filmmakers who had flourished under Daly grew independent of him as the 1970s wore on. They might work with him from time to time, but they also worked with other producers or, as they gained more experience, produced their films themselves. Martin Duckworth believes that the kind of guidance Daly provided 'is needed in the formation of new, young filmmakers. But when you mature, you want to break loose, make your own way.' In Paul Cowan's words, 'Everything becomes a *lesson* with Tom. And at a certain point, you don't want to have a lesson every time you seek an opinion. You just want the opinion. It's not that you don't want him. You want him in a different way.' Giles Walker observes that 'it seems that about two or three years are about all you can last with Tom. Some people grow out of the nest, others have to jump out, because they can't stand it. He can seem like a smothering influence, a consuming presence. He demands a certain intellectual honesty ... When you're young, and eager to learn, you're willing to do that. He's a continuing influence in my life, but I spend less and less time with him. I can't ... do him justice.'

Although he continued to work with Daly more often than most of his contemporaries did, Ianzelo acknowledges that Daly 'can get so involved that you think you might be over-guided.' Despite Daly's helpfulness, with *Waiting for Fidel* Rubbo began 'shutting him out a little bit. But he's not demanding of loyalty. Once you've had enough, he doesn't sort of say, "Hey, you owe me this," and he was never the sort of person who'd remind you that he'd thought of an idea you had used. He doesn't need to take the credit. He's a very self-effacing person. *Too* self-effacing.'

'Overwhelming' and 'self-effacing': these two apparently contradictory qualities recur in descriptions of Daly. Pierre Lasry, whose films often deal with psychology (*Healing* [1977], *Captive Minds: Hypnosis and Beyond* [1983], *The Myths of Mental Illness* [1988]), perceives the two traits as aspects of a single essence: 'Tom is a true artist, which means he is both a megalomaniac and a humble person at the same time. If you get into an argument with him, you realize his perception of reality is a mystical one. He talks in prophetic terms. He relies on either bullshit or prophecy. Like the artist.

'To challenge his perception of reality is not an easy undertaking. Deep down, like all men of Grierson's school, he has the Truth. A faith. An axiom. So while he's a great artist, he can be a pain in the ass, just like me. I wouldn't let him get near my movie. I'm afraid I'd find him too powerful.'

Martin Defalco was first surprised, then impressed by that power. 'He looks like a pushover, but he's *very* deceptive. There's a tremendous tenacity about him. He becomes as demanding of the material as you are. He gets a proprietary interest. This bothers a lot of people, but I think all artists – and he's an artist – claim ownership. The problem is then to re-establish your *own* ownership, so it becomes a true collaboration. It's like the Arab in the tent. Once you invite him in, don't say, "This is my camel, get out." He makes the same demands as the Arab in the tent.'

Robert Fortier remembers how this influence worked on him: 'I was directing a stock-shot film and cutting it myself. I was really defensive about it. I was arguing with him on everything in this ten-minute film. And finally one day, after a really bitter session – we'd sat there all morning, going back and forth – he said to me, "Look, there's about two hundred cuts in this film. I'd like you to change three of them. There's going to be a hundred and ninety-seven that are yours. Three will be mine. It's your film." And you know, this put it into a whole different perspective. I said to myself, "Hey, wait a minute, why am I arguing so strongly here?" I realized that he was right.

'The most important thing I learned that day was that filmmaking is a group process. There are many views and ideas on a film from all the people around you, and they really do have the film in mind when they make suggestions. It is not a personal attack.'

In Giles Walker's view, 'Tom completely subordinates his ego to the film and to the filmmaker. I'm sure he got an enormous amount of Tom Daly into every film he worked on, but the filmmaker probably doesn't realize how it got there. You never have an ego battle with Tom Daly.'

For Daly (as for Lasry), these conflicting perceptions of him – overbearing, at times pretentious; humble, self-effacing – are both true. But it is a conclusion in which, by recognizing and accepting it, he finds liberation and enlightenment, not despair. Shortly after Daly had met him, Thomas de Hartmann 'said something very, very simple and very, very strong. He said, "*Not* this *or* that." And his finger went up to his nose, and he shook his finger and turned his head left with "this" and right with "that". Then he said, with affirmation, "*And* this *and* that!" He said it in English, but it was the Russian way of saying, "*Both* this *and* that." I felt he was absolutely right, and I think I remember nodding my head in agreement, but in fact I didn't yet know what he meant.'

Walker knew only the mature Daly and had been at the Film Board for several years before hearing, to his astonishment, 'that apparently there was a time when Daly was very, very disliked, that he was considered an opinionated, arrogant prick. Some people wanted to get him out of the NFB. Apparently he underwent an enormous personality change. The Tom Daly you see today – according to some people – is totally opposite from the Tom Daly they once knew. But some would say that he hasn't really changed.'

Walker adds that he finds it 'hard to believe that the Tom Daly I know could have been that way. I don't see any evidence of those traits they say he had.'

But Daly sees truth in what Walker finds hard to believe – even the part about not having changed. For him the matter is addressed in a cherished passage from *A New Model of the Universe*, in which Ouspensky retells a Talmudic legend, 'A Portrait of Moses.' The legend recounts that the king of Aribistan, having heard of Moses' great accomplishments, sent his best painter to Israel to paint Moses' portrait. When the painter returned, the king asked his sages to describe Moses' character from the portrait. The sages said that the portrait showed 'a man cruel, haughty, greedy of gain, possessed by desire for power and by all the vices which exist in the world.' The king thought the painter must have misrepresented Moses, but the painter insisted that he had painted Moses accurately. To resolve the dispute, the king went to see Moses for himself. When he saw that the painting was indeed accurate, the king concluded that his sages and their wisdom must be worthless. But Moses told the king that both the painter and the sages were right. Indeed, Moses added, his vices were by nature even worse than was evident to the sages from the portrait. 'But,' Moses explained, 'I struggled with my vices by long and intense efforts of the will and gradually overcame and suppressed them in myself until all opposed to them became my second nature. And in this lies my greatest pride.'

For Daly, the parable is about the nature of truth as well as the self. 'What becomes clear is that there's truth in most seemingly opposite statements. If you choose only one, you leave out the other. This doesn't mean they are both true in equal measure. You have to balance them. Put the fulcrum near the big one, and you can get balance. But you need to include the truth of both sides to have a result which will stick.

'Otherwise you'll have what you have in the world right now – this polarization, where each side is absolutely unwilling to include the other's truth.'

Daly would apply the parable to films as well. To have genuine value, a film has to strive to tell the whole truth, in the sense of including the bad with the good, in appropriate measure. A film that shows only one side of the truth tells a 'dead' truth – no truth at all. It is a position remindful of Grierson, who once said that 'all things are beautiful as long as you've got them in the right order.'

Opportunities to share this perception and others like it with younger filmmakers became rarer as the 1970s wore on. Experienced filmmakers were pulling away, and the Film Board was hiring few new young people to replace them. The lack of young people to teach may have been a harsher deprivation than the second demotion to producer. Martin Duckworth thinks that Daly 'suffered as much as anybody from the budget cuts that started in the seventies. Austerity cut off the influx of new blood. His special talent had been restricted.'

One filmmaker who had an opportunity to learn from him was Irene Angelico, a freelance who asked Daly's help on her first directing job, a short film on Tai Chi (*Meditation in Motion* [1978]). The subject's philosophical aspect attracted Daly. His philosophical bent stimulated Angelico: 'The most important thing I remember about working with him was that he helped me take something that I knew intellectually and make it into a reality, to see filmmaking as part of life, as an extension of life. That it's not something separate. The film kept reminding us of what we were doing, and we kept reminding ourselves to interject that awareness into the film. That is something very special about him, that for him everything has an organic connection, everything is part of a larger philosophy. It was an absolutely wonderful introduction into film – a wonderful and living lesson that film is an expression of life and that you always have to remember that.'

After *Meditation in Motion*, Angelico worked on several commercial projects. Compared to the freelance commercial film world the Film Board seemed like a secure cocoon. But it was there, at the Film Board, that she confronted something extremely difficult for her. Her parents were survivors of the Holocaust. 'It was a subject I had avoided. I never went to see films about it, never read books, and basically put off people who tried to talk to me about it, because it was just too painful. Then Marcel Ophuls came to the Film Board to show films and to talk. Tom, I think without knowing anything about my background, suggested that as a filmmaker and as a person I would find it worthwhile seeing Ophuls's films and coming to his workshop. I explained that I found it too painful to see films about the Holocaust. We talked about it. And as a result of that talk, I decided to go see the film that Ophuls was showing – *Memory of Justice* – and it had an enormous impact.

'I was ready for it, but I had needed a push. I could easily have stayed in my cocoon, but Tom told me that maybe I should really consider taking a look at this subject and be open to exploring it. You know, I'm finding these things are much more painful if you hide them away and pretend that they're not there than if you face them. So in the same way this film I'm now working on – the connection between filmmaking and my life is very real in this film as well.'

The film Angelico was working on was *Dark Lullabies*, which, after years of struggling as a freelance with partial budgets, she completed in 1985. It won first prize at the Mannheim International Festival that year.

As production budgets tightened over the years, the length of time that could be lavished on a project steadily shrank. Robert Fortier, thinking back on his dialogue with David Wilson about editing, says, 'Things have changed ... Now there is a little more pressure to cut films in a shorter time,' and wanting to '"see all the possibilities" is getting to be more and more unrealistic. With fifty sequences there can be many, many possibilities. So today [in the 1990s] we probably shoot less, [and] therefore have fewer possibilities and less time to edit.'

Daly viewed these trends as more than simple economizing. They were part of, or perhaps the effect of, a general drift away from 'the living, organic structure that in 1940 I had *by luck* landed in and marvelled at. It had begun by taking off the excess, but everything began to be tightened for everybody, for all of us. It was less possible to program sudden possibilities. There was less interest in experiment, less money for technical development. There was not only less money for bringing fresh blood into the place, the already-trained people had no new blood to train. *They* began to move out, and so senior positions tended to be filled by people who didn't know much about film. And they did not *want* the continuation of former attitudes. They wanted to get rid of that, to have a go in another direction.'

Even the need for a stock-shot library – Daly's first significant contribution to the Film Board and long an essential source of material for such films as *Guilty Men*, *Memorandum*, and *Bethune* – had been called into question. The argument was that the library was used too little for its costs to be recovered. Management proposed selling it.

In his 1977 response ('Notes on NFB Stock Shot Library'), Daly tried to explain to management how a lack of understanding of Film Board production had led to a wrong judgment about the library's function and value. He first argued that 'the deficit position is not nearly so great as is being made out.' The reason was

that a system that once worked well, when the stock shot library was in the Production Branch, has broken down since the stock shot library was transferred to the Technical Services Branch.

The stock shot library is waiting for film-makers or unit administrators to report on final stock shot use. Film-makers assume all this is handled automatically by the stock shot library. New unit administrators have never heard of the old system. Many editors, younger film-makers, producers, even executive producers do not know of the old system. And many freelancers know nothing of it at all.

Consequently most films that get made using stock shots never report to the library on their final use.

Daly then reported on his research into a few individual cases that he knew of in which stock shots were used but not properly accounted for. He inferred from this that the library's real cost-effectiveness was probably much higher than it appeared. The library 'should be credited for the actual work they have done and which they have done excellently with an ever dwindling staff.' And even if there was still a deficit,

the stock shot library has probably never been a self-paying operation. That was not
its purpose. It was an important resource and a service, both inside and outside the
Board – like the book library, which I am sure does not pay for itself, but it would
be ridiculous to suggest we should therefore dispense with it.

In Daly's attempt to describe and persuade, one can begin to see that an
aspect of what he called 'organic structure' was an intimacy between a
worker and the details of his or her job. This intimacy, as suggested in his
recommendations, is the most practical starting-point for creating an
administrative procedure. For example:

Gilberte [Mayerovitch]'s system of reporting stock shots should be activated everywhere. Most administrators have been keeping the initial minimum stock shot work
orders in their compartment files until the charge goes through the laboratory, then
they file them (and forget). Gilberte, remembering they are for stock shots, keeps
them till the picture cutting copy goes to negative cutting and then pesters the film
editor for a list of footage of all stock shots used (from sources inside or outside the
Board). She then writes a memo to the Stock Shot Library itemizing these various
listings, and asking to be billed. This system works whether the editor is an outside
or inside editor, whether the director is here or away on a new job, whether the
film-maker is freelance or NFB, etc.

There was even a note of nostalgia for an old nemesis:

In Grant McLean's day, the stock shot library was a going concern, active, with
good morale, reporting directly to Grant McLean as Director of Production, and
consulted and involved as a matter of course in stock shot policies.
    Even then, its costs were never fully recovered, but the value of the service was
understood and accepted as a desirable aim of film production.

Daly concluded his report with a list of detailed suggestions, the leading
one of which was to transfer the library 'back to Production where it is
wanted, which it is meant to serve, and which pays for its deficit anyway.'
The library was not sold.
    In his last years at the Film Board, with fewer projects and dwindling
responsibilities, Daly contributed by example as much as by direct inter-
action. And it was the Film Board's most accomplished filmmakers who
recognized this contribution in the clearest, least equivocal terms. Tony
Ianzelo attests that Daly 'brought to the Board an incredible integrity in
filmmaking. The content should be first-class. He's not interested in cheap

shots. I think Tom's standards are the NFB's standards. He is the *one* guy around here who has so much integrity that he's been a guiding light.' For Donald Brittain, Daly represented 'the spirit of the Film Board, sort of ever present: if he's not in the cutting room he's going to see your film on television. So you feel you better meet a standard. I always feel I need something like that to get my juices flowing, someone I respect a great deal that I've got to really impress.'

A few years after Daly's retirement, Wolf Koenig likened this standard to 'a kind of torch – a commitment to some goal that a group would decide on, some goal outside ourselves that we could agree was good.

'Daly got it from Grierson. We got it from Daly. I think it's coming back, emerging again. We're trying to pass it on to the new people.

'He was always quoting Plato. It's amazing that somehow that kind of thing – from Plato – is being passed on, kept alive, twenty-five hundred years later.'

Yet Daly's role in the Film Board's history has not been widely known outside Film Board circles. His name is omitted from or barely mentioned in histories of documentary. In 1980, Concordia University awarded Daly an honorary doctor of laws degree for his contributions to the Film Board as an editor, producer, and teacher, and 'the person who gave final editing advice to a generation of Canada's best N.F.B. filmmakers.' It is the only such academic recognition he has received.

At the Film Board, Daly tried not to be elevated – or reduced – to the status of a symbol. At the same time, he knew his career was nearing an end. For a man who saw film as an extension of life rather than an end in itself, offering his total commitment to a project was getting harder to do. But in 1980, his fortieth year at the Film Board, a project came his way that engaged him completely. It was a documentary called *The Last Days of Living* (1980), directed and edited by Malca Gillson and produced by Daly. The film was about the work of Montreal's Royal Victoria Hospital Palliative Care Unit, an innovative approach to helping terminally ill patients die with dignity. It is a straightforward documentary, filmed over a four-week period, that shows several patients, their families, and medical staff working together to make the patients' last days not merely bearable but rewarding. A line of narration summarizes one reason for Daly's interest in the program and probably reflects it as well: 'The patient becomes part of a team, which is focused on the physical, social, spiritual, and psychological needs of the whole person.'

The film doesn't claim that the program works for every patient all the time. To a suggestion that he get some fresh air on a beautiful day, a patient responds, ' I don't see that that would do me much good.' In commiseration with an old man who can't change his position even half an inch, an attendant acknowledges that it must be discouraging; the patient responds, 'It's more than discouraging. You ask for death.' Another patient says the doctors 'seem to have all the answers ... but ... I have to ask the question ... but I don't know the question.'

The successes are dramatic. Placidly, without resentment, a young mother describes how her husband has taken over her maternal role. A woman who has returned home for her final days sheds tears of gratitude when she recalls how the people involved in the program had helped her overcome her fears.

Michael Charette's story is the film's centrepiece. He is only twenty-two, he has inoperable cancer, his face is cadaverous, yet he seems always to smile. 'When I first found out I was going to die, it was very traumatic,' he confesses, but 'it didn't take long for me to start thinking about dying rather than being afraid of it.' He now regards death as 'the highlight of living, the ultimate gift.' He has decided to forgo further treatment and wants to go home. He plans to use money he had saved for marriage to buy a sound system. When the head of the Palliative Care Unit, Dr Balfour Mount, asks him about his parents, Michael says that while his mother seems strong and accepting, his father is taking it harder, still hoping that 'some supernatural thing' will intervene.

It is the intervention, not the supernatural itself, that rouses Michael's scepticism. He observes that while 'there's so many different religions [and] they're all man-made ... they all seem to [revolve] around the same type of idea: something supernatural created us, and the earth, and the universe. I mean, it's all so gigantic, something had to start it.' When asked how being sick has changed him, Michael says simply, 'It made me more aware of the importance of people and their feelings.'

After Michael has moved back home and shortly before his death, he and his father are together in his room. Michael puts a tape on his new sound system. His father is cradling a guitar. The narrator explains that they had written the song together on a fishing trip. The melody is soft and lilting. The narrator speaks the words:

> When there's nothing left to hide
> And no need to turn away
> You can make a moment last a lifetime
> And a lifetime last a day.

The patients' bravery affected Daly during the production itself. He remembers being 'astonished that there was no problem getting permissions from them. They seemed to be very clear about it, that if it would help anybody, they'd like to do it, they'd be glad to do it. It was the staff who were uneasy about it, even though they're all the time counselling other people in relation to the same subject. That was typical: when you are *really* in a situation, really and truly in a situation, there is a kind of direct understanding that you have access to. And it can make you very peaceful at very difficult times. Whereas if you're not in that situation, you get all anxious about the possibility of being in it.

'There was a case, elsewhere, of a young girl of about thirteen who was dying and her family couldn't bear it. When they visited her, they were full of terrible anxiety, saying to her, "Don't leave us!" "Hang on, we'll find ways!" – things like that. She knew very well there was no hope of recovery, but that didn't bother her. What bothered her was her family's terrible fear and anxiety, which was not helping her. She needed to be helped peacefully to go through what she had to go through. So, one day she asked them to go home and bring her one of her cherished possessions. She felt that she couldn't bear to die in their presence, that it would be too excruciating for them. So, although only thirteen, she wisely had them go off to do something special for her – which was what they *were* doing, without knowing how fully – and then she let herself die in peace. This is a very touching kind of natural wisdom that everybody has some possibility to get to, but which is rarely touched, and usually only in extreme, urgent situations.

'So we found that the work with the unit was not at all tiring, exhausting, saddening, depressing, because the unit itself was full of a buoyant, positive spirit aimed at making the life of these people as comfortable and happy as possible, and as meaningful as possible, for even one more day, and then the next day, and the next day.

'It was a very positive experience for Malca and me, because neither of us was afraid of it. We had both been through the loss of very, very close ones. I had been with my parents when they died, and I had all kinds of fears about it in advance, but when it actually came there was some kind of very intense, positive exhilaration in responding to the needs of my parents at this time. It absolutely astounded me, because I hadn't the slightest expectation of it, and I found myself just helping them to go at their own pace, and not trying to stop it or change it. Except once, when my sister had arrived at the airport and my mother was very nearly gone. The nurse helped by suggesting we call my mother back to explain the situation, and to ask if she wouldn't wait. She could hear us, but she couldn't speak. And she waited. My sister arrived, and was able to say some last things to her. About twenty minutes later my mother died. So you can understand that with so many people having terrible fears about the subject, it felt like a really good thing to do, to try to make a film that would express these positive feelings about the whole subject of death.'

One of the happiest experiences in Daly's career occurred when the Film Board held a private screening of the film for the families of the deceased. 'Here they were, all these different families who practically never knew each other but now were meeting together in this common purpose of looking at the film. Michael's father had been uncertain whether to come or not. Michael's death had been extremely painful for him. He wanted to come. And then he was afraid to come, afraid that it would open up all the old wounds that had just been healing. He was so scared of that, and yet he really wanted to see the film. The day before he had decided he wouldn't come. But on the night of the screening, he came. And when the film was over, he was like a happy young man. It had not opened old wounds. It had reinforced all the positive feelings he had come through with, and he was *so* relieved and *so* happy that in fact it worked out like that.

'The whole evening, for everybody, was a celebration. The families stayed, practically to a person, for three hours, relating to each other and telling their own stories to each other and to us. You could tell that the film was just *exactly* the honest expression of what they had felt when those events had happened. There wasn't a single example of anybody feeling that it wasn't just the way they had known it. And I was very happy about that. It showed that we weren't over-dramatizing the material.'

Shortly after the film was completed, Gillson recalled the ethical issues involved in making the film. 'Tom and I both felt from the outset that we had to be very careful about how things in the film were presented. You could have taken some of that footage and manipulated it to convey meanings that might have been interesting on film but could have hurt the living. Tom and I agreed that unless someone can have a rebuttal, we couldn't use that kind of material – that you can't give just the one person's point of view even if it might be fantastic in the film. Tom seems to have a kind of eighth sense or something. He's the epitome of what a documentary filmmaker should be. That's the only way I can express it. I just wish he'd never leave here.' After making two more films on the Palliative Care Unit (*Time for Caring* and *Reflections on Suffering* [both 1982]) and two films on music (*Singing: A Joy in Any Language* [1983] and *Musical Magic: Gilbert and Sullivan in Stratford* [1984]), Gillson herself left the Film Board in 1987 to start her own film company.

As a producer, Daly still had responsibilities with regard to several other projects. One of them was *The Lost Pharaoh: The Search for Akhenaten*

(1980), directed by Nicholas Kendall, narrated by Donald Brittain, and edited by Judith Merritt. A brief excerpt from a transcript of a random half-hour of Daly working with Kendall and Merritt during the final stages of editing provides a glimpse of Daly's meticulousness and his application of certain of his principles of editing. Daly, Merritt, and Kendall are at the Steenbeck, working on a short narrated sequence, replaying the passage as needed.

Daly: It sounds too ... slow.

Merritt: You mean the way he [Brittain] says it?

Daly: The way he says it. Everytime I hear it I get the same impression. You should take a few frames out between the sentences. I'll tell you why. 'The word has spread ...' It sounds like it should go on with a colon: 'the Canadians are back.' But he reads it as if it were two separate sentences that have nothing to do with each other. I think it should be 'The word has spread: the Canadians are back.' He says, 'The word has spread. The Canadians are back.' Let's listen.

Narrator: 'Along the banks of the Nile, the word has spread –'

Daly: 'The Canadians are back.' You'll find it quite a bit shorter. And then the guy's reaction at the very end of the line [of narration] is going to be in the clear. He does some big gesture at the end of the –

Merritt: Yeah.

Daly: See – quite often he [Brittain] does that. Now he's doing it partly to make sure that the breaths in between can be cut out. But he's expecting us to adjust it accordingly.

Narrator: 'The Canadians are back.'

Daly: It's generally all the same *pace*.

Merritt: Yeah.

Daly: You'll have a variety, things tighter together, some *really* dramatic pauses – because they're the *only* ones. And that will give more space at the end. *(Merritt tightens the space between the two clauses and then replays the passage.)*

Narrator: 'Along the banks of the Nile, the word has spread: the Canadians are back.'

Daly: Still more. *(Merritt cuts out another frame.)* It's sort of like running over logs in a log boom: if you don't do it fast enough, each one sinks. It's *exactly* like that.

Narrator: 'Along the banks of the Nile, the word has spread: the Canadians are back.'

Daly: You see, the *different pace* means that there's excitement among them [the people in the picture]. The faster it goes together, the more they're emotional about [the Canadians' return], and the slower it goes, the more lethargic they are about it. It's got to do with the *meaning* of it.

Kendall: So what we have to – what you're taking out –
Daly: Goes back at the end. That's right.
Narrator: '... the word has spread: the Canadians are back. They pay sixty-five piastres a day – with an hour for lunch.'
Daly: Stop there. Uh ... if there's time to do this, I would be inclined to take about ... five or six frames out earlier, and then after something about banks of the Nile.
Narrator: '... the word has spread ...'
Daly: '... along the banks of the Nile, the word has spread: the Canadians are back.'

From this her only experience of working with Daly, Merritt says, 'I learned basic principles of editing that I still refer to today, such as: use a problem to solve a problem; find your opening and ending and the rest will somehow find its form; present your characters sympathetically at the beginning in order to engage the audience no matter what you do with them later.' She remembers that Daly also 'took the time to write a very long and detailed evaluation report on my work, listing pros and cons, which I found invaluable. It gave me a direction for my professional development. He was a great teacher.'

Daly's evaluation report (31 October 1980) was a piece of paperwork required by policy at the time. In the bureaucratic scheme of things, Merritt was in a probationary period as an editor. She had freelanced at the Film Board for many years, but now she was on staff, and this was her first experience editing a major film with an extensive narration. The report was addressed to the film's executive producer, Roman Kroitor, who had returned to the Film Board briefly, primarily but not exclusively to develop a program of dramatic films. Yet this unassuming, potentially perfunctory report crystallizes much of what had characterized Daly's career and made it distinctive. He tactfully addresses the needs of both Merritt's supervisors and Merritt herself. He first devotes three paragraphs to describing the background of the production. Shooting problems and legal issues had caused delays in the editing; Daly takes pains to ensure that Merritt cannot be blamed for them. The rest of the report reflects Daly's concern with the person, his notion of commitment to craft, his sense of what collaborative filmmaking should entail, his overriding concern for structure, his educational impulses, and his sense of passing something on or giving back (his suggestions regarding Merritt's further training echo the memo Stuart Legg wrote about Daly's Toronto script forty years earlier):

Judith is a most pleasant person to work with, always trying to please her colleagues and serve the needs of the film. She willingly manages to be available whenever there is a need, evenings and weekends if necessary. And she seems to really enjoy her work.

She is very open to trying things that the director & producer may want, even though she may feel differently herself. But I am glad to say that she feels increasingly free to express her own opinions and wishes and desires, even where they go counter to the other team members. I think this is a very important development as she has very good ideas and responses, and the film would be less effective if they were not expressed. I think in this respect that Judith is gaining more self-confidence all the time in her work, and that helps her to be more decisive. If there was any weak spot it tended to be a sort of uncertainty or indecision sometimes before a set of conflicting alternatives or pieces of advice, or responsibilities competing for the same time frame.

For that reason she sometimes wanted or needed strong guidance in structuring the material, which in this case was particularly difficult to structure, being composed as it was of 4 simultaneous elements or strands of story. The Akhenaten mystery story itself, the arts and writings of Akhenaten's time, the explanation of the archaeological dig, and the present day life of Egyptians in the neighborhood of the dig. There was no easy sure-fire line through this complex material. And Nick Kendall, Judith & I all needed Don Brittain finally to put into words that story-telling structural certainty that he has so well.

Judith seems very at home with scripted material & readily sees the choices available in the material to follow that line. One way to extend her capabilities into new fields would be to give her small-scale blocks of film to edit, where there is no script and the structure must be developed in the cutting room by the editor. In this way a facility for feeling out structures could be exercised where the variables are few, and then extended into larger scale films as the confidence grows.

I would gladly work with Judith again any time.

Daly was still asked, occasionally, to help improve a troubled film. Around 1980, Rosemarie Shapley (later the associate producer of Paul Cowan's *Double or Nothing: The Rise and Fall of Robert Campeau*) worked as Daly's editing assistant on one such film. Her memory of the experience sounds a bit like Daly's recollection of working at the side of Stuart Legg: Daly would 'kind of talk as he was cutting. He'd find philosophical justifications for things that at first seemed insignificant – for example, about whether something needed a pause at a certain point. Then, almost as an aside, he'd draw a connection on some different plane that would show how the pause might contribute to the film's overall emotional impact.' What impressed Shapley even more was Daly's '*enthusiasm* for the project, even if it wasn't all that good and he couldn't have that much control over it. A boyish enthusiasm. He was never jaded about it. His attitude was always, "Oh, let's give it a try," or "Oh, this is going to be fun." The project was always far more important than his ego.'

Barbara Greene, who joined the Film Board in 1972 after a career in broadcasting with the BBC and CBC, found Daly's love of discourse as stimulating as his editing insights were helpful. 'Sometimes,' she writes,

when I needed a break from the cutting room, I would wander along to his office on the chance that Tom might be free. He seldom was, but he'd suggest we make a date for lunch, flipping through his crowded desk calendar and plunk me down, leaving an open space after my name. I imagined we'd be going out to some restaurant nearby and needed more time than the usual cafeteria lunch hour. Usually, our dates ended upstairs in that noisy crowded centre of indifferent food.

Tom had a voracious appetite. It was amazing to watch him as he appraised the mundane offerings of the cafeteria menu. With the enthusiasm of a hungry school-boy, he'd choose at least six different dishes – soup, salad, bread, dessert, juice and possibly a piece of cake. 'Come on, come on,' he'd say, 'Get what you want,' as if we'd come to dine at an exclusive French restaurant. No matter how ordinary, these things were cause for celebration. Like thoughts, words, imaginings – the more the merrier. Then, with a full tray he'd scan the crowded cafeteria and lead me over to a far table near a window.

We'd eat, talking all the while, and long after the food was gone and the cafeteria was closing down at 4, I'd realize that Tom had left his calendar open, just in case we might need the time. It wasn't that we'd discovered anything unusual nor that our thoughts were particularly lofty, but there was no doubt, we'd both travelled somewhere new and enjoyed the trip ... We had darted from one thought to another, never knowing where we might end up, sharing a sense of elation and liberation.

In 1980, Daly wanted to recognize the contributions of a retiring NFB employee. The man's name was Russ True, a general maintenance man. Perhaps he reminded Daly of what his own career had been largely about. Daly 'never knew Russ's official title' and the Film Board has no record of one. 'He was a troubleshooter, a guy who would arrange, or get, or fix any-thing whenever you needed it. He brought you editing supplies or carted away your editing machine when it had to be serviced. You knew when he was coming, because he would toot a little horn he'd rigged up to his cart – one of those bulblike things that you squeeze.

'He was open to everybody. His function seemed to be to interconnect with all types of people at the Board, not just certain types. He was an example of that lingering wartime spirit where roles, titles, rules, and so forth, were not important – one of those many people at the Film Board whose particular job wasn't as important as the way they affected people. So I just wanted to recognize that.'

Daly carefully printed his tribute to Russ True in a style of script resembling the individualized printing that appears on diplomas and citations. It read:

> To Russ True
> December 22, 1980
>
> Dear kindly, considerate generous Russ
> You'll never know all that you mean to us.
> Helpful, resourceful, dependable, true,
> These are integral parts of you.
>
> Others write memos and argue and fuss,
> But when we want something, we go round to Russ.
> And the cheery 'toot! toot!' of your musical bus
> Is a heart-warming sound to the coldest of us.
>
> There's one other point we don't need to discuss:
> There's no one around here we'll miss more than Russ.
> And no one lives up to your name more than you.
>
> – And that's True. –

One of the last producing assignments to come Daly's way was Donald Winkler's *F.R. Scott: Rhyme and Reason* (1982), a lucid career biography of a complex man, a poet who fought for social justice and a lawyer who defended the arts. The film shifts deftly back and forth between Scott's poetry and his activism without confusing the audience or letting it forget Scott's other dimension. Scott reads from a number of his poems, but the most compelling sequence is one in which Scott explains, with straightforward, logically consistent eloquence, his approval of Trudeau's invocation of the War Measures Act during the 1970 FLQ crisis, while others decry it.

Daly thinks the film will become 'one of the important historical documents of our century. It grows larger, broader, and deeper' as it unfolds, offering 'a profound glimpse of the forces of Canada's "two solitudes," French and English, that dominate our politics. We see Scott as one of the most able of Anglo-Canadians to consort happily with his French-Canadian counterparts. He brings the two forces ever so close together by the force of his character and his caring, but we still see at the end how history pulled away from him again, without in any way lessening his historic presence, and without reducing him to disappointment.'

Daly's interested objectivity with respect to the conflict between French and English Canada inspired Richard Millette, who joined the Film Board in 1977 as a projectionist, to initiate a film project about Daly tentatively called 'The Mentor and the Two Solitudes.' Daly's influence on Millette, however, had begun before Millette knew Daly or even knew of him. As a teenager, he had been given a one-day pass for Expo 67 before the official opening. 'I went and visited *Labyrinthe* four times that day, it touched me so much. It seemed to capture all the fears I had then, but also the joy of life.' At the time, Millette paid no attention to who created *Labyrinthe*, and he met Daly and learned of Daly's role in *Labyrinthe* only after joining the Film Board. 'I screen everything that's shown at the Film Board. Sometimes he'd come into the projection booth while I was screening. I'd ask him a question about the film, and he'd take the time to explain it to me.'

For Millette, Daly is the one person he knows who is capable of bridging the gap between French and English Canada described by Hugh MacLennan in his novel *Two Solitudes*, the inspiration for Millette's working title. 'He's something we don't have in this country. He's the only anglophone around here who would try to ask and learn about Quebec nationalism. He doesn't react to things the way most of us do. Tom is balanced. He has self-control. He takes the time to see every aspect to a problem.

'We French-Canadians see things in an emotional way. The anglophones are more rational in their way of thinking. But *both* production branches say Tom is extremely objective. He's *never* said he liked or disliked a film. He doesn't judge people but tries to see them as they are. He's always tried to see the qualities in everybody and everything, and make those qualities grow. This is very unusual here. He has this objectivity that is incredible.'

Millette would learn something even more important to him about Daly after Daly had retired. 'Just before I joined the Film Board, I had got interested in Gurdjieff, and the interest grew. For years, I looked around for a group led by someone who knew about him. I went to Florida, New York, Boston, but I couldn't find someone close to Gurdjieff's teaching, just people who had learned third-hand or through some splinter group. It wasn't what I was looking for. One day Tom came in to screen some film having to do with Gurdjieff. When he came back into the booth, I asked him if he knew about Gurdjieff. It was a wonderful discovery for me. He'd never mentioned it – and I'd known him for seven years, I'd seen him almost every day.'

Daly's last major project at the Film Board would remind him of some of his best experiences there and become one in its own right. The film's director was his best friend. Its subject recalled one of Unit B's great films. And although Daly began the project as the film's producer, eventually he had to draw on that 'rock-firm thing' he had acquired in the war years: his knowledge of editing.

The film was *Standing Alone* (1982), a one-hour documentary portrait of Pete Standing Alone, who had been the subject of Unit B's *Circle of the Sun*, which Colin Low had directed more than twenty years earlier. The film had originated in a suggestion from Standing Alone in 1976. Low was interested largely because 'Pete's life was at a high point. His marriage was going well, and he was a member of the tribal council. So we started gathering material about him.'

The demands of other projects delayed the editing of the material until several years later. By the time a first cut was completed, Low recalls, 'Pete's situation had changed. His marriage had dissolved, and he was in some political trouble on the reserve, partly because he had a very individualistic point of view. I asked to do some new shooting, to suggest the dark side of the situation.'

There was also a problem with the look of the film. Low remembers Daly telling him that it was 'too "televisiony."' But the editor who had made the first cut was now busy with another project. Low himself was now engaged in administering Film Board regional production as well as finishing up the first IMAX film, *Atmos* (1980), about weather. He could find time to shoot some additional footage, but not to re-edit the film. So Low answered Daly, 'Then you'll have to edit it yourself.'

The Film Board was now a more bureaucratic place than it had been in the days of Unit B, when even an executive producer, if so inclined, could commit a significant portion of his time to editing a project. Daly needed official permission to edit *Standing Alone*. It was an unusual request for a producer of his stature and on the edge of retirement. 'But knowing Colin, knowing Pete Standing Alone, knowing and caring a good deal about the lore of the Plains Indians, having been on the Blood reserve, having cut *Circle of the Sun*, I realized that there wasn't another editor in the place that would know how to relate and balance the many and subtle strands of meaning that criss-crossed through the material.'

Daly had another reason to want the job: 'From time to time one needs to test the apparently broader vision and comprehension by putting it to practical work. Editing *Standing Alone* needed everything I had accumulated and still something more. Colin generally gathered film material around a subject on the basis that it felt intimately connected to the central person or theme – in this case, Pete. With his painter's rich visual sense, Colin had shot scenes and sequences that would be strong visually and engage the main character centrally – sometimes present-day activities, sometimes evoking moments of the past that had impressed Colin vividly at one time or other. The problem for the editor was that while the various sequences were closely related to Pete, they often had little relation to each other. It was like having a wheel hub, with a number of spokes sticking out of it, but no rim around the *outside* connecting them. In a still photo or a painting, you could see them all at once as a pattern, but in film they would have to appear one after another, without an apparent sequential reason or connection.'

The many 'spokes' that wound up in the film included Standing Alone's family life, his work, his relation to the Blood reserve, Indian crafts, religion, ritual, and folklore, historical information, the encroachment of modern ways of life, political concerns, and the Indian relationship to nature. There were scenes of a contemporary sun dance, a ceremony in which a design on Standing Alone's tepee is made his own and he is taught about the old religion, his horses in a corral, horses on the range, a discussion with an anthropologist, a meeting of the tribal council, Indians carrying briefcases below Calgary's modernistic glass skyscrapers, the making of a saddle, and a re-enacted buffalo hunt. There were also scenes depicting various tribal business ventures, including a potato processing plant and a jewellery project.

Daly invokes more than one metaphor to describe his strategy for organizing this material. He strove 'to interweave strands of many "colours," appearing and disappearing as if by chance, as they seem to do in life, but nevertheless having a perceptible pattern of recurring themes, like a woven rug or a finely beaded article of clothing.' He sought to achieve a 'kaleidoscope of near and distant objects, subjects, meanings, feelings, and aspects of life through a perceptible continuity of thousands of years, permeating the film in recurring movement, some things appearing only once, and others returning in choral fashion.'

The viewer can find in *Standing Alone* numerous examples of what Daly sought to accomplish. Colour – especially the combination of yellow and black – is used in a way that could be called kaleidoscopic. The film's first image is of a dark fence-post in magic-hour light. Yellow and black animal designs painted on a tepee reappear as paper cut-outs of horses during a family activity. Black horses gallop over golden prairie grass. Yellow sunlight is refracted off a child's raven hair. The film's last images, over its credits, are silhouettes of Indians on horseback against a deep yellow sky.

A transition that may be the cinematic equivalent of a weaver's stroke starts at the end of the re-enacted buffalo hunt. From the front of Standing Alone's speeding Chevrolet truck, which serves as the buffalo, a tracking point-of-view shot skims along just above the grass. Then come several shots of Charles Russell paintings of a buffalo hunt. Then there is a close-up of a buffalo head. A wider shot reveals it to be a head mounted on a wall. The camera tilts down to a tribal council meeting taking place in a panelled room.

Things near and distant, in both space and time, are linked frequently and subtly. Most of the connections are easily overlooked. Usually Standing Alone's voice-over narration is involved in them. Some are made with the help of clips from *Circle of the Sun* and one with still black-and-white photos of a political demonstration. But one is an astonishing tour de force. It occurs before the buffalo hunt or any hint of it. Standing Alone is in his home, leafing through a book of Charles Russell paintings. After a shot of a painting, there is a close-up of Standing Alone looking contemplative. This is followed by three slow-motion tracking shots of young Indians, wearing buckskin and wielding bows and arrows, on galloping horses. The film cuts back to Standing Alone, now in an extreme close-up. Earlier in the film he had remarked, in voice-over, that he sometimes thinks he would like to have lived in the old days of Indian horse culture; we assume now that he is merely indulging in nostalgic fantasy. Then the film cuts to a scene in his corral, where one of his sons is roping a young horse, and the fantasy is quickly forgotten. Only later does Standing Alone reveal his idea of re-staging a buffalo hunt with his three sons as hunters. He wants them to learn something of their cultural history. The corral scene was part of the preparation. And still later comes the real scene of the re-enacted hunt from which the 'fantasy' images had been taken. Considered as a whole, the sequence accomplishes something rare in documentary film, showing both interiority and action, thinking and doing, entirely with conventional documentary material. The buffalo hunt is not the dramatized re-enactment so rife in contemporary documentary. It is a real re-enactment, asking for no suspension of disbelief, and it has been willed by the film's subject.

An image that recurs in 'choral fashion' is that of a soaring hawk. It appears early in the film, several times in the main body, and again at the end. It seems to signify a spiritual presence, a supernal witness. It not only helps connect the film's disparate scenes; it links the film to other films dear to its editor, such as *Guilty Men* and *Labyrinthe*.

The film's overall achievement, however, is larger than any of Daly's various metaphors can suggest on its own. On the one hand, the film lacks the visual flair and dramatic soundtrack of *Circle of the Sun*. Filmed in the late 1970s after the influence of direct cinema had permeated the Film Board, much of the material – by no means all – has, initially, the prosaic, inconsequential look so hard to avoid in sync-sound, unrehearsed filming. The film relies on the now-standard device of a subject's voice-over narration. The theme of the sun as a unifying being is present here, but more as context, not with the sometimes overbearing emphasis given it in the earlier film. On the other hand, the philosophical attitudes behind the film's structure, or embedded in it, mesh naturally, unobtrusively, with the film's material and seem to give it a glow of meaning. The musical score – again by Eldon Rathburn – is subdued and self-effacing. In a relaxed, matter-of-fact tone, Standing Alone explains to the anthropologist that an Indian 'offering tobacco to the creator ... [goes] through the Elder because it will get there faster ... the same principle as the White Man uses the priest.' When Standing Alone says – although not all in one passage – that everything changes, that nothing stays the same except for the sun dance, he seems to be expressing the essence of the spiritual impulse, the sun dance being but one embodiment of it. It is compelling largely because the tone of the film itself seems to accept change and embrace the everyday. Ultimately the film locates spirituality in a sense of presentness, a heightened awareness of the here and now. The film is unpretentious, joyful, and serene.

The film pleases Daly. 'The comings and goings of these parts, so often even far removed from one another in time and space, nevertheless, for me, have a common centre of gravity, like a solar system, which holds them all together through time and space, and in all moods of nature and of man. Only one section seems to me not on a par with the rest – the section on business projects, which is descriptive of facts, rather than both factual *and* symbolic like the rest of the material.

'The hardest sequence to create was the final one, in which so many of the strands come together – Pete's son, the reverting to ritual drumming, chanting and prayer, in that high place, at sundown, in the presence of a teacher we've come to know, and of the birds in the air and the grasses blowing in the wind, with a small child – so naturally there – who, before our eyes, begins to try to dance to the rhythm of the chanting, in his grandfather's lap.

'Only this time, having discovered the possibility earlier than I had while doing *Labyrinthe*, I built the sequence up quite early in the editing, so I *knew* what I was heading for. And then some of the other material fell into place [as I was] preparing for this sequence by setting up images all along the way.'

Low and Daly drafted a suggested commentary consisting of things that Standing Alone might say to link together the parts of the film that needed narration. For Daly, this was 'the final hurdle. We went over each passage with Pete to see if its point was valid. If so, we would ask him how he would naturally speak about it. I took down what he said, and we evolved a written narration of the right length to fit the necessary places. Then, in the recording, he would sometimes say he didn't feel like saying some word, and we'd find another one together.

'Once he stopped, and said that the sequence on breaking in the horse didn't feel right. So we asked him what should it be, and he said such wonderful fresh things that we knew *that* was what we wanted. But it wasn't on tape. The recordist had stopped when we got into this long discussion. So we asked Pete to tell it to us again. But he couldn't remember what he had said. No matter! My old habit of writing down impressions as I received them had come to my aid, right to the end. I had written down verbatim what he had said, and we soon had a live version of it on tape before he lost the mood of it.'

Standing Alone, now an Elder of the Horn Society of the Blood Indian tribe, attests to the authenticity of the thoughts voiced in the film. 'Where I live, on the reservation, if you say something that isn't true – about yourself, but especially about the people – you can be criticized. Right off the bat, I thought about that. That's why I tried to be honest about myself, and about the reserve. What I said – my thoughts – were true at the time. I still believe that. Things are still changing, still happening.

'Most of the developments failed. The potato project failed. The gemstone jewellery project went down the tubes. At the time they were great, I thought, but a few years later they folded up.'

Standing Alone recalls that in *Circle of the Sun* he had 'predicted there might not be any more sun dance before long. That was my view ... because I was not involved in my religion. I didn't care whether it survived or not. It's strange, but that last scene of *Standing Alone* – that guy holding that little child – for some reason I connect that scene to where our religion is today. It's good the way the film ended, with all that singing. The religion has not died, and the way things are going it is not going to die.

'The Blood Indians liked the film.'

One would not infer from Standing Alone's comments or from Daly's account, which characteristically describes the editing of *Standing Alone* in terms of a search for structure, that a strong political theme quietly under-lies the film. 'Viewed ten years later,' Low explains, 'the film seems pro-phetic, in terms of where the Indian movement is now – holding off the Canadian army at Oka, fighting the second James Bay hydroelectric project, undermining the Meech Lake accord. The film touches on all of these issues. It has been shown in different community halls all across the reserve, by a wide range of people among whom Pete is not very popular. The film has been received very positively ... but they're not so crazy about it as they are about *Circle of the Sun*. They still love that one.'

Daly acknowledges that the film 'will probably never be as popular as *Circle of the Sun*. It is longer, about just one person, more allusive and less explanatory. People without some knowledge or experience of Indian ways may not notice so many of the references and allusions. But that is not important. I cared about all those elements in such a way that I wanted to do my best with the material even if it were to feel right only to Pete, or to Colin, or to anyone looking for the relation of beings in our part of the uni-verse. I would have been happy to do it as a kind of affirmation of thankful-ness for what meaning and vision life has brought to me, even if it would never see the light of day. Work can be a kind of prayer. The juggler of Notre Dame [here Daly is referring to the main character of Anatole France's short story 'Our Lady's Juggler'] comes to mind: he had no other way to express his private feelings than to juggle before the Virgin in the empty cathedral at night.'

Daly had worked for more than forty years for his one and only employer. Even more remarkable, to many, was that he seemed to have changed very little over the years. Neither bureaucratic obtuseness nor intraorganizational meanness had jaded, embittered, or exhausted him. Now in his sixties, he still could bring to a film project an expectant open-ness to possibility rarely associated with civil servants or filmmakers of any age or situation. To have asked to edit a long documentary at his stage of life and career was itself an indication of a resistance to cynicism, compla-cency, or defeat.

One of the Film Board's hardest cases, Donald Brittain, noted this unusual quality in Daly when, in 1980, he said, 'Daly's the one man who over the course of my twenty-six years here has never ceased to surprise me and impress me. Usually people get burned out. We all get burned out. But Tom still manages to generate that enthusiasm which is the essence of what's good about the Film Board.'

Even Stuart Legg, in his letter about Daly's apprentice years, noted this characteristic:

A former guru may perhaps, in conclusion, be allowed a personal comment. Among his other achievements Tom seems to have discovered the secret of eternal youth. To me, his appearance at retiring age is almost exactly the same as it was when he first walked into my office in 1940. He is still tall and lean. His nose is the same breath-taking length. His eyes can still stare you into the ground. His face is remarkably unlined. He is still as well-washed, shaved, dressed, as ever. Only in two respects, as far as I can see, has he changed. Inside, he has acquired a philosophy to me incomprehensible; and outside, a moustache which causes him to resemble a brigand. I do not know the psychological purpose of these accoutrements. Perhaps they are defence-mechanisms; or perhaps intended to endow him with ferocity he does not otherwise possess. In any case, I am sure that he does not need the trappings of either Ouspensky or Stalin. He is, after all, a figure of exceptional stature, as well as a very loveable man, in his own right.

One thing that had helped Daly maintain his enthusiasm for so long was his sense that his experience and abilities were needed and valued. But after *Standing Alone* he began 'to feel there just wasn't much interest, at least from the administration, in what I could bring to the work of the Board. For instance, the commissioner would say we should really have a chat, but we'd never have it. There was really no desire for the chat. Just before my retirement – Jacques Bobet was also retiring – the commissioner saw me in the hall, and the only thing he said to me about it was, "Wouldn't it be a good idea to join the two parties together?" Apparently he was thinking of saving some money. I was looking forward to my own party after forty-three years! But it didn't seem to be much of a concern to him. That tells you a lot. So I happily completed whatever loose ends there were, because I felt it was time to get out.'

Leaving the Film Board was not the wrenching thing that Daly's investment in the organization might portend. Film had never been an end in itself but a means to serve and to search. Retirement would free him to devote all his creative energies to projects related to his philosophical work. One was a definitive edition of Thomas and Olga de Hartmann's *Our Life with Mr. Gurdjieff*, enlarged from earlier editions by the discovery of unpublished texts by both of them. Working with his son, Daly would write a new foreword, offer new biographical data on Gurdjieff and the original authors, and prepare new maps, a new chronology, editors' notes, and an index. His edition was published by Penguin Books in 1992. He would also supply the archives and direct the research for a series of volumes of printed sheet music composed by Gurdjieff and Thomas de Hartmann, the first of which was scheduled to be published in 1995 or 1996.

Daly's particular philosophical interests also fortified him against some-thing else that people naturally dread as they leave middle age: the approach of death. 'At a certain level of awareness,' Daly explains, 'the contradictions of life are simultaneously perceived and felt – my loss and someone else's gain, sadness and happiness together, and the inextricability of life and death together.

'For example, most of the cells of the body die every week. If they didn't die, and stayed the same, your growth could never take place. Everything would stop like a still photograph – neither dead nor alive. Your chance to grow and develop and learn and understand things *depends* on the death of various elements in you at different levels and stages of your life.

'It seems to me that there are three levels of matter in us having to do with three levels of attention and consciousness that can be aware on suc-cessively higher levels ... so that when we are born, for example, the protec-tive cover that protected us in the uterus is thrown off, and it would seem to be a further stage when the physical body is thrown off at the departure of the consciousness. But we can't measure what happens to consciousness without a conscious instrument. We can only surmise.

'In my own experience, the awareness I have had from time to time of being a living part of a very living universe is so convincing that perhaps I've been over-zealous at times in wishing to share that with others. There's a Dervish sect in which no matter how much they know of their truth, the devotees are forbidden to tell it to others unless asked, unless it's wanted.

'All these various wholes in the universe are hierarchically but discontin-uously arranged, not gradually. For example, ice has *one* changing-point to water, water *one* changing-point to steam. There is nothing in between the wholeness of a galaxy and the condensed wholeness of a certain star system in it. But *something* holds it together. It is like those Chinese ivory balls, carved so that one is inside another. The whole system is very simple when you see it, and very ancient.'

And, for Daly, vividly present, immanent: 'My own learning has gone on in the sense of realizing, more and more, the inclusion of the opposites and the contradictions, of life and death, in the larger wholeness. The unity of outer and inner. The sense that the harmony of the universe, or of the ecol-ogy of the planet, is the same as a harmonious relationship among people in a film unit. And that you can't really be happy unless others are happy, too.'

One autumn Daly had a vision that remains for him the most powerful image he has had of this view of life and the universe: 'It was during a coffee break at a Gurdjieff meeting near New York. I went out in a courtyard, and

there was a copper beech tree there with nothing around it. It was a tremendous tree with all these long branches going out in all directions. It was full,
beautiful with colour. The sun was glistening off of it. I burst into tears,
because I immediately saw it as like the world: all our differences stretched
out from a common trunk, a common root, and no branch was more
important than any other. It was a vision of overflowing perfection.

'It was so beautiful that I went over to pick a leaf as a memento of the
moment. The first leaf I pulled had a wormhole in it. Another had another
leaf stuck to it. The third had caterpillar damage. I could not find a perfect
leaf. And then I had a still deeper moment of vision: this perfect thing was
made up of all these imperfections!'

Despite what he felt as indifference to him on the part of the administration, the Film Board did give Daly a party of his own. On 18 May 1984,
nearly a thousand friends and colleagues gathered in the Film Board's
shooting stage to bid him farewell. It was a party with content. It was at
one and the same time a recapitulation of a career and an expression of
gratitude.

When Daly entered the stage, he immediately perceived 'the enormous
amount of work people had done just to *prepare* for it.' Hundreds of com-
memorative posters, featuring a portrait of Daly along with a list of his film
titles, were being given out. In various corners of the stage, video machines
played excerpts of favourite moments from films Daly had produced or
edited. Along the walls were six snapshots that had been greatly enlarged.
Each depicted a different era in Daly's life.

The first of the enlarged photographs was a shot of Daly, his brother,
and two cousins taken during a summer at a lake. The second was a formal
portrait of Daly taken by Malak Karsh (brother of Yousuf), who roomed
with Daly when Daly first went to Ottawa to work at the Film Board. The
third showed Daly editing, surrounded by shelves of film tins. The fourth
was a shot of him as an executive producer. The fifth was a picture of Daly
and Ruth on their wedding day. The sixth was a snapshot that Wolf Koenig
had taken at Concordia University when Daly received his honorary
degree. Daly, in full academic regalia, is holding out a glass of champagne
towards Koenig. This photo had been blown up to a gigantic eleven by fifteen feet and placed on the wall behind the platform where Daly was to sit.
'It had the effect of myself toasting the gathered throng throughout the
evening. They never knew how I secretly blessed them for it, since it went
so well with what I wanted to say to all those friends.'

Malca Gillson ushered Daly to a yellow canvas director's chair on the
dais. Whatever he wanted to say would have to wait until nineteen of his

colleagues had made brief speeches about how he had professionally helped or personally touched them and excerpts were read from a selection of scores of congratulatory telegrams that had been received by the party's organizers.

Most of the telegrams were from people that many in the gathered assembly had only heard about or vaguely known. Stanley Hawes, Daly's first boss at the Film Board, the man who gave him the job of organizing what would become the stock-shot library, wired from Australia. After the war, he had become the first commissioner of Australia's national film unit and had settled there. Basil Wright, director of *Song of Ceylon* and co-conspirator in Daly's only hangover, had sent a wire. Margaret Ann Elton, whom, as Margaret Ann Adamson, Daly had trained to succeed him as Legg's special assistant, collecting newsreel footage 'and acting as hostess where I could only be butler,' joined her husband Arthur Elton and Daphne Anstey in a telegram. The latter had been in charge of negative cutting during the war before being 'snatched from us by marriage to Edgar Anstey,' who, like Elton, was a major figure in British documentary during the 1930s and 1940s.

Wires were read or announced from former NFB commissioners Guy Roberge, Sydney Newman (who, having started out at the Film Board during the war, signed himself as 'Splicer Boy and Commissioner'), and James Domville (an avid sailor communicating 'from somewhere at sea'). Among the many others who had sent wires were representatives from most areas of the Film Board's operation: Nick Balla, a former executive producer with nearly three hundred films to his name; Raymond Garceau, an early French-language filmmaker (*La Drave*, 1957); William Greaves, an editor and filmmaker (*Emergency Ward*) from the *Candid Eye* era; Wally Hewitson, an experienced producer and director now heading the Film Board's sponsored-film program in the NFB's Ottawa office; Gerald Graham, for a long time the Film Board's director of planning; Louis Applebaum, the Film Board's chief composer during the early years; Anthony Kent, a distribution executive; and an NFB film crew shooting in Beijing. Henk Suèr, Daly's Dutch counterpart in Nico Crama's co-productions *It Wasn't Easy* and *From the Ashes of War*, sent a wire. Author and filmmaker Douglas Tunstell sent a wire praising 'the Daly touch' that so many NFB films bear.

Several of the speakers were people who had not been particularly close to Daly or who had known him only briefly, in connection with a specific project or event. Donald Brittain talked about what it meant to filmmakers like himself that there were producers 'who *were* craftsmen, who understood *our* problems. To see that man over the years, going back and forth [between management and the editing machine] was an enormous presence.' Tom Bindon of the Distribution Branch described a two-day editing seminar he conducted with Daly at Queen's University: 'Three people showed up ... [but] I learned more in those two days, I think, than I learned in the twenty years that I've associated with production people in the Film Board.' Robert Duncan, a director of several NFB co-productions about Canadian writers, said, 'We were discussing him last night in a tavern, and I guess the best compliment that I can give Tom is what one of the people in the tavern said. He said' – here Duncan assumed a complaining, dismissive tone – '"Arghh, the trouble with Tom Daly: he sees good in everything."' Tom Radford from the West Region presented Daly with the promise from Pete Standing Alone of a leather belt with a silver buckle that Standing Alone was crafting. (When it arrived, Daly found etched into the leather the titles *Circle of the Sun*, *Standing Alone*, and *Corral*.)

To the surprise of many in the predominantly English-Canadian audience, French-language filmmakers were significantly represented among the speakers. Identifying himself as 'from that other "solitude,"' Marcel Carrière recalled his early involvement with the *Candid Eye* filmmakers. 'I worked in those days mostly with Wolf Koenig and Roman Kroitor. But I could always see that big shadow in the back which was Tom Daly. We seldom met him – or I didn't, because I was in those days a technician – but I could feel his presence everywhere. And many times I ... wondered why we didn't have many more of these people in both English and French production. So, Tom, if I'm still here, it's mainly because you were the big shadow.'

Jacques Godbout, who in his early days at the Film Board often worked on French-language versions of English-language films, bragged, 'I was the only one who was permitted to make his films better: I made them *en français!*' He then attested to the value, for him and other French-language filmmakers, of learning about the craft through working on those versions. Godbout, who had been one of the most outspoken proponents of separate French-language production, confessed to 'wondering, after all these political years,' if having to learn from 'an Englishman' was perhaps not such a bad thing after all, 'even though we wanted to get rid of him [i.e., of anglophone supervision] after that!'

Guy Coté told the gathering that in 1954 he had 'been working at the Film Board for three years, and my job was on the line. The director of production had decided that the time had come to tell me that I wouldn't be a filmmaker. I'd made three films, but they weren't really very good.' Daly, 'with whom I'd worked a little before ... said, "Well, give me a chance, and give Guy a chance, and we'll work together for a couple of years. And I made my first real film with him, and the next one, and the next one ... '

Yves Dion said that when he worked as Daly's assistant on *Labyrinthe*, 'I didn't know how lucky I was, because I was starting in this trade. It was, I think, nearly the last time ... I had a boss who knew what the hell he was talking about.' Daly taught him 'respect for film, respect for the people who make film, and respect for the trade.'

In French, Bernard Gosselin recalled that it was Daly who had encouraged him and Jean Dansereau to make the film that became *Le Jeu de l'hiver*. Gosselin then said that the festive occasion was making him sad. He saw the Film Board as a huge table with only one leg left, and that leg was going away.

Three filmmakers who had apprenticed under Daly during the sixties or seventies shared remembered moments from their experiences. Giles Walker related a version of the log-rolling metaphor for editing that Daly had used when advising on *The Lost Pharaoh*. 'He said it's like creating the illusion of running on water without getting your feet wet. You have to choose the right stream, find your spot, then run quickly, be very nimble, and land on the dry spots of the rocks sticking out of the water – and to the audience, from a distance, it creates the illusion of running on water.'

Alluding to Daly's training in wartime newsreels, Michael Rubbo suggested that one key to Daly's ability to help was that 'he never looked at your footage as if you could have done better with it, but rather looked at it as if it were captured footage. That's what you had to work with, and within that footage there was some truth to be found. The quest for truth has always been what was so exciting with Tom.'

Paul Cowan told how, through several films that Daly had produced for him when Cowan was still a novice, 'he never once told me to do something or that I was doing something wrong. He wants you to find your way through to a discovery ... I remember sitting with Tom through a lot of bad rushes, when stuff I'd shot was out of focus and two stops over, and Tom would always find the one shot that was in focus and was well exposed, and he would say, "Well, we'll build it on that." And Tom would look at a rough-cut that was just pure garbage and find the one sequence in all of that rough-cut that would make eventually a film. And he just said, "You'll find a way." I think that in the end what was much more important to Tom than good films was the process, because he knew that if the process was right, the good films would eventually come anyway.'

Cowan told a story about driving with Daly to Ottawa to show a film to

Prime Minister Trudeau, who had requested a special screening. Cowan had directed the film; Daly produced it. On the way to Ottawa, the car broke down. Cowan thought his car was out of gas. He walked to a gas station and came back with a can of gas. The car wouldn't start. He went for another can of gas, but the car still wouldn't start. 'I had my sponsor suit on, and Tom had his sponsor suit on ... It started to rain. My sponsor suit was getting all wrinkled and I was getting apoplectic. We were by that time within about an hour of the screening and the car still wouldn't start, so we started hitchhiking ... We got picked up by a car full of Jamaicans ... They asked us where we were going, and Tom said we were going to see the prime minister. And they said, "No problem. We'll take you there." They took us to the West Block of the Parliament Buildings. We got there just in time and had the screening. But I remember all the way up there Tom was just making it into a lesson. Something about patience – some Greek myth that had to do with patience was what he was talking about all the way up there, while I was sweating buckets about whether or not we were going to get there in time. And in the end what I remember about that screening is not Trudeau or the other members of government. I can't remember whether they liked the film or not. But I remember the experience with Tom.'

One speaker was not a filmmaker but a film subject. Dr Balfour Mount, director of the Palliative Care Unit at Montreal's Royal Victoria Hospital, recalled his experience in the *Last Days of Living*. When the Film Board approached him about making a film on the unit, he was wary. An earlier film, meant to 'assuage the anxieties of viewers,' had started out with the strong sound of a beating heart. But 'Tom and Malca said, "You can look at the footage, and anything you don't want in, we'll take out. The only problem is, you'll have to watch all the footage."' Dr Mount agreed to that, but after 'eighteen and a half hours [viewing the rushes] I was absolutely blind ... I had a colleague with me furiously scratching notes about things that looked sensitive or might be misinterpreted. We had six or seven points, and I turned around at the end of it, waiting for the gracious time to make these astute comments. And I said, "Well, there were just three or four things." Tom said, "Why don't you tell me about them?" Well, it won't come as a surprise to anyone here that the ones that I had picked up, Tom had already picked up, and pointed out two or three other reasons why they should be deleted, and then mentioned three or four others of his own. That was when I started to learn from Tom ... I'd like to say that ... one of the great privileges of the last few years for me has been to learn something about *my* craft from Tom.'

Of all the speakers, the closest to Daly were the members of the group that had made the best of the Unit B films. Eldon Rathburn declared that as of Daly's retirement 'every film is officially now out of sync' and recalled how in Unit B 'no slipshod work was tolerated.' And he added, echoing Dr Mount, that he believed his experience with Unit B films had helped him in his other musical work.

Stanley Jackson had died in 1981, but Roman Kroitor brought back his memory by relating a story that Jackson told to him not long after Kroitor had joined the Film Board: 'Tom had just taken a trip out west for a holiday, and Stanley came by [to Daly's apartment] – he thought for perhaps five or ten minutes, because he had a question he wanted to ask Tom. Tom said, "Please sit down, and have a drink," and then started to tell him about his trip out west. He took the CN Railway, and to Stanley's growing distress Tom thought that he would be extremely interested in absolutely every single stop that was made, which he described in quite a lot of detail. And about four hours later they were pulling into Vancouver. Stanley said to himself, "Well, it's nearly over." Finally they got there, and Stanley said, "That's really been very very interesting, Tom, thank you very much," [and started to leave], but Tom said, "Oh, I went *out* CN, but I came *back* by CP."'

Kroitor attributed Daly's eminence at the Board and in documentary film to three qualities: 'his terrifically high ideals and his absolutely uncompromising attitude about living up to them both personally and professionally'; his ability 'to listen to new ideas and to be willing to try things that nobody else has tried before'; and his 'incredible capacity for work. I don't know if one could add up all the millions of hours that he has spent making films and helping others to make films, but they would be astronomical.'

Addressing Daly, Robert Verrall recalled that after a month at the Film Board he 'was amazed to find that you'd made it seem perfectly natural that in a converted sawmill, in Ottawa, discussions about that poetic philosopher Plato and that nifty progressive educator Socrates would be very important to the development of Canadian cinema. I think your work, and the best of those ... you've influenced – and that's quite a crowd – prove that you were right.'

Colin Low was the last of Daly's colleagues to speak. He first told about his first impression of Daly: 'Tall, no fat, and straight. No slouch. Tom never slouched ... He called me "Low."' Next Low related an anecdote about a scrape-off job that had failed to meet Daly's expectations of perfection.

Low then asked the audience to skip ahead a few years to 'a cutting room late at night [with] Tom Daly and two budding filmmakers who will be nameless.' Low's audience knew that the film was *Circle of the Sun* and the filmmakers were Low and John Spotton. '"Isn't that a fantastic shot, Tom? Really fantastic – incredible – beautiful, too, eh? What does it *mean*? Well, it's an oil derrick ... in front of the rising sun ... six hundred millimetres. What an effect! Look at the way the heat shimmers! What did we want it to say when we were shooting it? You don't know how hard it was to *get* that shot! We had to get up every morning at four a.m. and drive twenty miles, for a *week*, to get that shot. You don't know what John Spotton was *like* at four o'clock in the morning! Maybe we were wasting our time? You can't be serious, Tom ... Well, I don't know what the shot means, Tom. But it is sort of, well, *cosmic*, wouldn't you say? Yes, definitely *cosmic*" ... In the end the shot got in the film, not in the beginning where I thought it should be, but at the very end – and I still like it there.

'The questions were a joyful game for Tom. He edited a film like playing a game of chess ... In time I got to enjoy the questions as much as the answers ... And so did a lot of other people who found formulating questions difficult, or thinking logically painful. So we learned about Socrates, in the cutting room. We learned that shadows on the wall of the cave are not the real world outside.

'I like to think we taught *him* something, too – sometimes deliberately, and sometimes inadvertently. We brought into the cutting room such inordinate expectations, such a passionate desire to make fine films, such ego, and such frequent despair. Tom had to deal with these human emotions – at first logically, perhaps mystified initially by their intensity. But eventually in his maturing he responded with a marvellous subtlety of feeling and intuition. That's why so many people sought him out. That's why so many people are here tonight. It was as if all the questions had returned to flower in a special faith in people, in the validity of their ideas, the value of their separate searches for meaning in their work and in their lives. And in this faith he contributed a valuable defence of this creative community. It is a paradox that tolerance must be defended – in Tom's case not by battling intolerance, or fighting narrowness of vision, or attacking political expediency, but by affirming the joy of creativity with the generosity of spirit that has so marked his long and luminous career.'

It was now Daly's turn. 'You can't pack forty-three years' worth of memories, feelings, and so on into five minutes ... but it's what I'd like to try to do. I think the reason why I was *most* happy to come here today was not just to enjoy being with you all again at this fantastic event, but because it would give me a chance to tell *you* what *you* have meant to *me* over the years. I don't know if you really know that in a relation between any two people, if one receives some kind of understanding at one end, the other receives an equal something at the other end, but I believe it more and more and more, and it certainly has had a lot to do with the way I've looked at the world, the way I've tried to work with people. And though the process is important, the people are even more important, for me. In fact, I've lived a kind of symbiotic life here at the Board, depending absolutely on the people at the other end of all these relationships. And that's what's meant really so much to me. There's *no question* about the fact that if you felt *you* got something, I got exactly as much. It's full of certain opennesses, and trusts ... It's done a lot for *my life*, and when I hear people sometimes saying very kindly, "You haven't changed a bit," you have to just look around you to see that it's really not true. But more than that, I really hope they're *wrong* ... because *inside*, I feel that something really has come that wasn't there to begin with.

'And I'd like to tell you a little bit of history that I didn't know until the other day myself. You all know the story, probably, of how I got to the Film Board quite by mistake. My old Upper Canada College high school principal gave me a letter to take to a person who was head of the government film organization, John Grierson – it didn't mean a thing to me, but I was interested in getting into some kind of counter-propaganda in 1940 ... It was a sealed letter ... I never saw what was in the letter, but the other day it occurred for the first time that I should look at my file in the Personnel Office at the National Film Board ...'

The letter commending Daly ('virginal of mind, naive to his fingertips ... dog-like devotion') to Grierson was in the file. So was Grierson's reply ('a slight impression of conservativeness of mind'). Legg's critique of Daly's script ('damnably dull') on Toronto was there, too. Daly now read them aloud to the assembly.

'So there you are. That was my beginning. I didn't know anything about these things, [but] Grierson and Legg and Hawes began to be my main teachers. And I went through all this kind of thing that you are telling me back, in a way.

'But some of the people who spoke just now didn't tell you the *other* side of things.' Daly then recalled the time when four of his 'most trusted friends and colleagues, the people who did the best work,' came to tell him that they couldn't go on working with him if he 'stayed *like that*.'

'I didn't know what they meant by *like that*, and the rest of my time at the Film Board has been *finding out* what they meant by *like that*, and trying to come to terms with it. And somehow or other we never lost a smidgeon of our friendship. It just grew and grew, because it was based on that kind of honesty. And so, you see, if the sort of thing you've been telling me is true ... then I have no fears about leaving the Film Board at this point, because there are so many of you who have learned *all that stuff* from me, and can carry it on all over the world wherever you are, inside the Film Board or outside the Film Board. So here I am, thanking you for so multiply carrying out everything that I ever hoped. And I hope you all have as happy a life as I have had inside filmmaking and outside as well.

'And I just want to let *you* know how much you've really meant to me, and still mean to me. And you can't take that away from me, even if you wanted to.

'Thank you.'

Works Cited

Published Materials

An Act Respecting the National Film Board. Statutes of Canada, 14 George VI, Ch. 44. Ottawa: Edmond Cloutier, 1950.

An Act to Create a National Film Board. Statutes of Canada, 3 George VI, Ch. 2. Ottawa: Joseph Oscar Patenaude, 1939.

Ayre, John. *Northrop Frye: A Biography*. Toronto: Random House, 1989. *Labyrinthe* is discussed on pp. 300–2.

Barnouw, Erik. *Documentary: A History of the Non-fiction Film*. 2nd rev. ed. Oxford University Press, 1993.

Beveridge, James. *John Grierson: Film Master*. New York: Macmillan, 1978. The Cambridge questionnaire with Grierson's responses begins on p. 341.

Blumer, Ronald, and Susan Schouten. 'Donald Brittain: Green Stripe and Common Sense.' *Cinema Canada*, August–September 1974. Repr. in Feldman and Nelson, eds, *The Canadian Film Reader*, pp. 103–11.

Cartier-Bresson, Henri. *The Decisive Moment*. New York: Simon and Schuster, 1952.

Daly, Tom. 'The Audience Is Part of the Film.' *Canadian Newsreel*, August 1954.

– 'The Growth of a Craft: My Debt to Legg and Grierson.' In *John Grierson and the NFB*. The John Grierson Project, McGill University. Toronto: ECW Press, 1984.

– Interview. *Pot Pourri*, September 1973.

– 'It's the Mind That Moves.' Interview. *Pot Pourri*, Summer 1977.

de Hartmann, Thomas. *Our Life with Mr. Gurdjieff*. Penguin, 1972.

de Hartmann, Thomas and Olga. *Our Life with Mr. Gurdjieff*. Definitive ed. Ed. by T.C. Daly and T.A.G. Daly. Penguin, 1992.

Edwards, Natalie. 'Who's Don Owen?' *Cinema Canada*, June–July 1973. Repr. in Feldman and Nelson, eds, *The Canadian Film Reader*, pp. 160–78.

Elder, Bruce. 'On the Candid-Eye Movement.' In Feldman and Nelson, eds, *The Canadian Film Reader*, pp. 86–93.

Evans, Gary. *In the National Interest: A Chronicle of the National Film Board of Canada from 1949 to 1989*. University of Toronto Press, 1991.

– *John Grierson and the National Film Board: The Politics of Wartime Propaganda*. University of Toronto Press, 1984.

Feldman, Seth, ed. *Take Two*. Toronto: Irwin, 1984.

Feldman, Seth, and Joyce Nelson, eds. *The Canadian Film Reader*. Toronto: Peter Martin, 1977.

Freund, Gisèle. *Mexique précolombien*. Neuchatel: Editions Ides et Calendes, 1954. The model for the mask is depicted in plate no. 1.

Grierson, John. *Grierson on Documentary*. Ed. by Forsyth Hardy. London: Faber and Faber, 1966.

Gurdjieff, G.I., and Thomas de Hartmann. *Music for the Piano*. Ed. by Linda Daniel-Spitz, Charles Ketcham, and Laurence Rosenthal. Research and Archives by Thomas C. Daly. Vols I and II. Mainz: Schott, forthcoming 1995 or 1996.

Handling, Piers. *Derek May*. Ottawa: Canadian Film Institute, 1980.

– , ed. *Self-Portraits: Essays on the Canadian and Quebec Cinemas* (English edition). Ottawa: Canadian Film Institute, 1980.

Harcourt, Peter. 'The Innocent Eye.' *Sight and Sound* 34, no. 1 (Winter 1964–5). Repr. in Feldman and Nelson, eds, *The Canadian Film Reader*, pp. 67–76.

– *Movies & Mythologies: Towards a National Cinema*. Toronto: CBC Publications, 1977.

Hardy, Forsyth. *John Grierson: A Documentary Biography*. London: Faber and Faber, 1979.

John Grierson and the NFB. The John Grierson Project, McGill University. Toronto: ECW Press, 1984.

Jones, D.B. *Movies and Memoranda: An Interpretative History of the National Film Board of Canada*. Ottawa: Deneau, 1981.

Knelman, Martin. 'It Didn't Start Out to Be a Disaster Movie ... But *Running Time* Is Canadian Film History's Worst Catastrophe.' *Saturday Night*, May 1978.

Mackinder, Halford J. *Democratic Ideals and Reality*. New York: Holt, Rinehart and Winston, 1942.

MacLennan, Hugh. *Two Solitudes*. New York: Duell, Sloan and Pearce, 1945.

McLean, Grant. 'The National Film Board of Canada – Present Status and Future Plans.' *Journal of the University Film Producers Association* 18, no. 1 (1966): 16–20. The quotation about filmmakers is from p. 18.

Mitgang, Herbert. 'Imprint.' *New Yorker*, 2 August 1982. Profile of Helen Wolff.

Morris, Peter. 'Re-thinking Grierson: The Ideology of John Grierson.' *Dialogue 3*. Ed. by Pierre Véronneau, et al. Montreal: Mediatexte, 1987.

Nelson, Joyce. *The Colonized Eye: Rethinking the Grierson Legend*. Toronto: Between the Lines, 1988.

The NFB Film Guide: The Productions of the National Film Board of Canada from 1939 to 1989. Ed. by Donald Bidd. Montreal: National Film Board of Canada, 1991. Two volumes: English-language productions; French-language productions.

Nichols, Bill. *Representing Reality: Issues and Concepts in Documentary*. Indiana University Press, 1991.

Ouspensky, P.D. *In Search of the Miraculous*. New York: Harcourt Brace Jovanovich, 1977. The 'ray of creation' is discussed at the beginning of chapter 5.

– *A New Model of the Universe*. New York: Alfred A. Knopf, 1948. The paragraph remembered as two pages is on p. 154 and begins 'The "grain" played ...' 'A Portrait of Moses' is on p. 130.

Pâquet, André, ed. *How to Make or Not to Make a Canadian Film*. Montreal: La Cinémathèque canadienne, 1967.

Reeve, John. 'Grant McLean.' *Quest*, November 1974.

Report of the Royal Commission on National Development in the Arts, Letters and Sciences, 1949–1951. Ottawa: Edmond Cloutier, 1951 (the 'Massey Report').

Taylor, Fraser. *Standing Alone: A Contemporary Blackfoot Indian*. Halfmoon Bay, B.C: Arbitus Bay, 1989.

Trueman, Albert W. *A Second View of Things: A Memoir*. Toronto: McClelland and Stewart, 1982. The quotation is from p. 120.

Varley, Peter. *Varley*. Toronto: Key Porter, 1983. *Portrait Group: Mrs. R.A. Daly and Her Sons Dick and Tom* appears on p. 104. Tom Daly is the son in the foreground.

Winston, Brian. *Claiming the Real: The Documentary Film Revisited*. London: British Film Institute, 1995.

National Film Board Internal Documents

Badgley, Frank. Memo to Ross McLean responding to Grierson's and McLean's request for the return of Tom Daly. 13 March 1941.

Daly, Tom. Letter to Colin Low about *Circle of the Sun* footage. 23 July 1957.

– Letter to Colin Low about *Circle of the Sun* footage. 25 July 1957.

– 'Discussions on the Future of the Labyrinthe Project: St. Jovite, May 12, 1964.'

- 'Some Notes and Observations on the Subject of a National Film School or Film Training Centre for Canada.' 10 March 1965.
- Letter to Lars Björkbom about *Untouched and Pure*. 29 June 1970.
- Memo to Sydney Newman about *Un pays sans bon sens!* 5 March 1971.
- Memo to Bernard Devlin replying to Devlin's request of 10 July 1972. 7 August 1972.
- Letter to Charles Bliss about certain scenes in *Mr. Symbol Man*. 29 January 1975.
- 'Notes on NFB Stock Shot Library.' 14 March 1977.
- Memo to Roman Kroitor on Judith Merritt. 31 October 1980.

Devlin, Bernard. Memo to Executive Producers about underperforming filmmakers. 10 July 1972.

Grierson, John. Letter to T.W.[L.] MacDermot about Grierson's meeting with Daly. 23 September 1940.
- Letter to the Chairman of the NFB about the creative needs of a film organization. 27 November 1940.
- Memo to Frank Badgley requesting the return of Tom Daly. 7 March 1941.

Johnston, Tom. Memo to Des Dew containing some anecdotes about Tom Daly. The memo begins with a reference to the *Winnipeg Free Press*. 20 May 1966.

Koenig, Wolf. Memo about adding technical staff to *Candid Eye* crews. 21 April 1958.

Kroitor, Roman. Memo to Grant McLean about the *Labyrinthe* project. 30 January 1964.

Legg, Stuart. Memo to John Grierson about Tom Daly's script on Toronto. 28 September 1940.
- 'Talk on Cutting.' Transcript or notes. 17 January 1946.

Letter to Guy Roberge, Government Film Commissioner, about the loss of a sense of duty among filmmakers. The document is undated and unsigned. Attached to it was an unaddressed note from Nick Balla and Don Fraser saying the letter was sent on 29 September 1964.

MacDermot, [T.W.L.]. Letter to John Grierson. 14 August 1940.

McLean, Grant. Memo to English production personnel. 28 February 1964.
- Memo to Guy Roberge, NFB Commissioner. 7 February 1966.

McLean, Ross. Memo to Frank Badgley requesting the return of Tom Daly. 12 March 1941.

The National Film Board Grant McLean Spectacular 1967. Film. No credits other than 'From all of us.'

'A Summary of Staff Opinion on the Structure and Organization of the English Production Branch.' No author given. 16 December, 1963.

Woods, J.D., and Gordon Ltd. 'The National Film Board: A Survey of Organization and Business Administration.' March 1950.

Miscellaneous

Daly, Tom. 'Response to John Read's Presentation.' Notes from panel discussion at NFB on films about art. No date. Circa 1963.

– 'Editors' Workshop.' Transcript of tape recording. 21 February 1973.

Daly, Tom, Nicholas Kendall, and Judith Merritt. Editing session on *The Last Pharaoh*. Audiotape. Circa 1980.

Donald Brittain's wedding party. Script for a sound introduction. No title, no author. 2 July 1963.

Elton, Margaret Ann. Letter to the author. 10 October 1980.

Fortier, Robert, and David Wilson. Discussion about editing. Audiotape. Early 1980s.

Greene, Barbara. Letter to the author. 6 October 1994.

'Grierson Transcripts: Interviews with John Grierson, 1969–1971.' Canadian Radio and Television Commission, 1973. Grierson's account of his disagreement with Daly at McGill is found in vol. 4, pp. 435–40.

Hawes, Stanley. Letter to the author. 26 September 1980.

Koenig, Wolf. Memo to Tom Daly about Unit B. 22 October 1976.

Legg, Stuart. Letter to the author. 25 July 1983.

Ryan, Terry. Letter to the author. 21 October 1987.

Tom Daly's retirement party. Audiotape. 18 May 1984.

A Tom Daly Filmography

The credit information in this filmography was compiled with considerable help from the National Film Board's archival services, *The NFB Film Guide*, and Tom Daly. Wartime films typically did not list credits, and records are scanty for some of these films. An asterisk (*) marks those films on which Daly's role (given here as he remembers it) is not given in the *Film Guide*. A section mark (§) indicates films in which Daly's role (given here) differs from that given in the *Guide*. A dagger (†) denotes films in which credits other than Daly's differ from what is given in the *Guide*. A number sign (#) marks films that do not appear in the *Guide*. According to Daly, the *Guide* erroneously includes him among the credits for one film, *The Homeless Ones*.

In keeping with the collaborative character of Daly's film career, other major credits are listed for each film for which the information is available. This filmography does not, however, include the countless films on which Daly was consulted but not officially credited. *The NFB Film Guide* contains a brief synopsis of each film and mention of major awards.

A Is for Architecture
Direction: Gerald Budner, Robert Verrall. Camera: Douglas Poulter. Script, editing: James Beveridge. Narration: William Needles. Music: Eldon Rathburn. Production: Colin Low, Tom Daly. Colour. 14 mins. 1960.

Above the Horizon
Direction: Roman Kroitor, Hugh O'Connor. Camera: Jean Roy. Animation: Sidney Goldsmith. Commentary: Stanley Jackson. Music: Eldon Rathburn. Production: Roman Kroitor, Hugh O'Connor, Tom Daly. Colour. 21 mins. 1964. Produced for the American Meteorological Society through the Canadian Commercial Corporation.

Accident
Direction: Martin Duckworth, Pat Crawley. Camera, editing: Martin Duckworth. Narrator: Sandy Crawley. Music: Larry Crosley. Production: Tom Daly. Colour. 16 mins. 1973.

Across Arctic Ungava
Editing, script: Doug Wilkinson. Camera: Jean P. Micheau. Production: Tom Daly. B&W. 20 mins. 1949. Produced in cooperation with the National Museum of Canada.

Action: The October Crisis of 1970
Direction, script: Robin Spry. Editing: Shelagh Mackenzie, Joan Henson. Production: Normand Cloutier, Robin Spry, Tom Daly. Colour. 87 mins. 1973.

Age of the Beaver
Direction: Colin Low. Camera: Gordon Petty, Lyle Enright. Animation: Sidney Goldsmith, Robert Verrall. Editing: Roman Kroitor. Production: Tom Daly. B&W. 17 mins. 1952.

Alberta Girls
Direction: Malca Gillson, Tony Ianzelo. Camera: Tony Ianzelo, Savas Kalogeras. Editing: Malca Gillson. Producer: Tom Daly. Executive producer: Colin Low. Colour. 8 mins. 1975.

Anger after Death
Direction: Rick Raxlen. Script: Donald Winkler. Camera: Douglas Kiefer, Barry Perles. Editing: Margaret Wescott. Music: Alain Clavier.

Producer: Tom Daly. Colour. 29 mins. 1971.

Antigonish
Direction: Stanley Jackson. Camera: Mogens Gander. Editing: David Mayerovitch. Production: Tom Daly. B&W. 21 mins. 1964.

Antonio
Direction, camera: Tony Ianzelo. Editing: Martin Defalco, Tony Ianzelo. Commentary: Antonio Ianuziello, Harold Arthur, Elspeth Chisholm. Narrator: Alfonso Cisterna. Music: Robert Fleming. Production: Tom Daly. B&W. 28 mins. 1966.

Arctic Outpost (Pangnirtung, N.W.T.)
Direction, script, editing: John Feeney. Camera: Patrick Carey. Production: Tom Daly. Colour. 20 mins. 1960.

Atlantic Crossroads
Direction, editing: Tom Daly. Photography: John Norwood. Production: Grant McLean, Tom Daly. B&W. 10 mins. 1945.

The Atlantic Region
Direction, script, camera: Donald Fraser. Editing: Betty Brunke. Production: Tom Daly. B&W. 23 mins. 1957.

Atomic Juggernaut
Direction, camera: Eugene Boyko. Editing: Albert Kish. Narrator: Donald Brittain. Production: Walford Hewitson, Tom Daly. Colour. 17 mins. 1971.

Produced in cooperation with the Department of Atomic Energy of the Government of India.

Back Alley Blue
Direction: Bill Reid. Camera: Savas Kalogeras, Julian White. Additional photography: Lois Segal. Script: Peter Madden, Bill Reid. Editing: David Wilson, Tom Daly. Music: Bruce Mackay. Production: Vladimir Valenta. Executive producer: Roman Kroitor. Colour. 25 mins. 1977.

The Back-breaking Leaf
Direction: Terence Macartney-Filgate. Camera: Terence Macartney-Filgate, Gilles Gascon. Editing: John Spotton. Commentary: Stanley Jackson. Music: Eldon Rathburn. Production: Wolf Koenig, Roman Kroitor. Executive producer: Tom Daly. B&W. 29 mins. 1959.

Balkan Powder Keg*
Direction, script, editing, production: Stuart Legg. Assistant: Tom Daly. B&W. 19 mins. 1944.

Bannerfilm
Direction: Donald Winkler. Photography: Roger Rochat. Editing: Albert Kish. Music: Alain Clavier. Production: Tom Daly. Colour. 10 mins. 1972.

Battle for Oil*
Direction, editing: Stuart Legg. Camera: Radford Crawley, Donald Fraser. Narrator: Lorne Greene. Stock shot research: Tom Daly. Production: Raymond Spottiswoode. B&W. 19 mins. 1942.

Battle Is Their Birthright*
Direction, editing, commentary, production: Stuart Legg. Music: Lucio Agostini. Narrator: Lorne Greene. Research, sound editing: Tom Daly. B&W. 18 mins. 1943.

Battle of Brains*
Direction, production: Stanley Hawes. Camera: J.B. Scott. Sound: W.H. Lane, C.J. Quick. Editing: Milton Shifman. Music: Godfrey Ridout. Research: Tom Daly. B&W. 11 mins. 1941.

Battle of Europe§
Production, script, editing: Stuart Legg. Research, picture editing: Tom Daly. B&W. 15 mins. 1944.

Beware, Beware, My Beauty Fair
Direction, script, editing: Jean Lafleur, Peter Svatek. Camera: Douglas Kiefer, Ernest McNabb. Music: Jeff Crelinsten. Production: Michael Rubbo. Executive producer: Tom Daly. Colour. 29 mins. 1972.

Blackwood
Direction: Tony Ianzelo, Andy Thomson. Camera: Tony Ianzelo. Editing: Les Halman. Commentary: Barry Cowling. Narrator: Gordon Pinsent. Music: Ben Low. Production: Tom Daly. Executive producer: Colin Low. Colour. 28 mins. 1976.

Blood and Fire
Direction: Terence Macartney-Filgate.
Camera: Wolf Koenig. Editing:
William Greaves. Production: Wolf
Koenig, Roman Kroitor. Executive
producer: Tom Daly. B&W. 29 mins.
1958.

Blue Vanguard (Revised)
Direction: Ian MacNeill. Camera:
Denis Gillson. Editing: Marion
Meadows. Music: Colin McPhee. Pro-
duction: Tom Daly. B&W. 60 mins.
1957. Produced for the United
Nations.

Breakdown
Direction, script, production: Robert
Anderson. Camera: Osmond H. Borra-
daile. Editing: Victor Jobin. Music:
Maurice Blackburn. Executive pro-
ducer: Tom Daly. B&W. 40 mins. 1951.
Produced for the Mental Health
Authorities of the Provinces of Canada
in cooperation with the Department of
National Health and Welfare, Mental
Health Division.

The Burden They Carry
Direction: Mort Ransen. Camera:
Martin Duckworth. Editing: Donald
Rennick. Commentary: Jim Carney.
Production: Tom Daly, John Kemeny.
B&W. 28 mins. 1970. A co-production
with the Swedish Institute for Cultural
Relations.

Canada: World Trader
Direction, editing, production: Tom
Daly. B&W. 11 mins. 1946.

Canada's Awakening North
Direction, script: Ronald Dick. Cam-
era: Osmond H. Borradaile. Music:
Robert Fleming. Production: Tom
Daly. B&W. 32 mins. 1951. Produced
by the NFB for the Department of
Resources and Development.

Canadian International Trade Fair
Direction: Ronald Dick. Camera: Robert Humble, Norman Quick. Production: Tom Daly. Colour. 17 mins. 1948.
Produced for the Canadian Government Exhibition Commission.

Canadian Notebook
Direction, script: David Bennett. Cam-
era: Donald Wilder. Editing: Douglas
Tunstell. Music: Maurice Blackburn.
Production: Tom Daly. B&W. 32 mins.
1953. Produced for the Department of
Citizenship and Immigration.

Canadian Profile
Direction, script, editing: Allan War-
gon. Camera: John Spotton. Music:
Louis Applebaum. Production: Tom
Daly. B&W. 53 mins. 1957.

Canadian Venture
Direction, script: Caryl Doncaster.
Camera: Donald Wilder. Editing:
William Greaves. Narrator: Richard
Campbell. Music: Robert Fleming.
Production: Tom Daly. B&W. 23 mins.
1956. Produced for the Department of
Citizenship and Immigration.

The Canadians
Direction, editing, production: Tom

Daly. Executive producer: Roman
Kroitor. B&W. 21 mins. 1961.

Caribou Hunters
Direction: Stephen Greenlees. Camera:
Julien St-Georges. Editing: Victor
Jobin. Narration: John Drainie. Music:
Maurice Blackburn. Production: Tom
Daly. Colour. 18 mins. 1951.

The Cars in Your Life
Direction: Terence Macartney-Filgate.
Camera: Wolf Koenig. Editing: Bruce
Parsons. Commentary: Stanley Jack-
son. Production: Wolf Koenig, Roman
Kroitor. Executive producer: Tom
Daly. B&W. 29 mins. 1960.

Cattle Ranch
Direction, script, editing: Guy L. Coté.
Camera: Robert Humble. Commentary: Guy Glover. Narrator: Frances
Hyland. Music: Pete Seeger. Executive
producer: Tom Daly. Colour. 20 mins.
1961.

Centaur
Direction, editing: Susan Gibbard.
Camera: Eugene Boyko. Music: Paul
Horn. Production: Tom Daly. Colour.
10 mins. 1972.

The Challenge of Housing
Editing, production: Tom Daly. B&W.
10 mins. 1946.

The Changing Forest
Direction: Maurice Constant. Camera:
Grant Crabtree. Editing: Hubert
Schuurman. Commentary: Hubert

Schuurman, J.V. Durden. Production:
J.V. Durden. Executive producer: Tom
Daly. Colour. 18 mins. 1958.

Chantons Noël
Direction, production: Jim MacKay.
Executive Producer: Tom Daly.
Colour. 9 mins. 1948.

*Child, Part 1: Jamie, Ethan and
Marlon: The First Two Months*
Direction, camera: Robert Humble.
Editing: Margaret Wescott. Com-
mentary, narrator: Stanley Jackson.
Production: Tom Daly. Executive pro-
ducer: Colin Low. Colour. 29 mins.
1973.

*Child, Part 2: Jamie, Ethan and
Keir: 2–14 Months*
Direction, camera: Robert Humble.
Editing: Margaret Wescott. Com-
mentary, narrator: Stanley Jackson.
Production: Tom Daly. Executive pro-
ducer: Colin Low. Colour. 29 mins.
1973.

*Child, Part 3: Debbie and Robert:
12-24 Months*
Direction, camera: Robert Humble.
Editing: Margaret Wescott. Commentary, narrator: Stanley Jackson.
Production: Tom Daly. Executive
producer: Colin Low. Colour. 29 mins.
1974.

*Child, Part 4: Kathy and Ian:
Three-Year-Olds*
Direction, camera: Robert Humble.
Editing: Margaret Wescott. Commen-

tary, narrator: Stanley Jackson. Production: Tom Daly. Executive producer: Colin Low. Colour. 29 mins. 1977.

Child, Part 5: 4 years – 6 years
Direction, camera: Robert Humble. Editing: Richard Todd. Commentary, narrator: Stanley Jackson. Production: Tom Daly, Dorothy Courtois. Executive producer: Peter Katadotis. Colour. 27 mins. 1978.

Children's Concert
Direction, production: Gudrun Parker. Camera: Denis Gillson. Sound: Joseph Champagne. Music: Eldon Rathburn. Sound editing: Peter Jones. Editing: Tom Daly. B&W. 41 mins. 1949.

China: A Land Transformed
Direction: Tony Ianzelo, Boyce Richardson. Camera: Tony Ianzelo. Editing: Margaret Wong. Production: Tom Daly. Executive producer: Barrie Howells. Colour. 25 mins. 1980.

Christmas Cracker
Direction: Norman McLaren, Jeff Hale, Gerald Potterton, Grant Munro. Music: Maurice Blackburn, Eldon Rathburn. Executive producer: Tom Daly. Colour. 9 mins. 1963.

A Christmas Fantasy
Direction, camera, editing: John Feeney. Animation: Wally Gentleman.

Music: Eldon Rathburn. Production: Tom Daly. Colour. 8 mins. 1963.

Christopher's Movie Matinee
Direction, editing: Mort Ransen. Camera: Martin Duckworth. Production: Joseph Koenig, Tom Daly. Colour. 87 mins. 1968.

Churchill's Island*
Direction, production, editing, commentary: Stuart Legg. Narrator: Lorne Greene. Research assistant: Tom Daly. B&W. 21 mins. 1941.

Circle of the Sun
Direction: Colin Low. Camera, John Spotton, Dalton Muir. Commentary: Stanley Jackson. Narration: Pete Standing Alone. Music: Eldon Rathburn. Editing, production: Tom Daly. Colour. 29 mins. 1961.

City of Gold
Direction, location camera: Wolf Koenig, Colin Low. Animation camera: Douglas Roberts. Commentary, narrator: Pierre Berton. Music: Eldon Rathburn. Editing, executive producer: Tom Daly. B&W. 22 mins. 1957.

City Out of Time
Direction: Colin Low. Camera: Georges Dufaux. Commentary: James Beveridge. Narrator: William Shatner. Music: Robert Fleming. Production: Tom Daly. Colour. 16 mins. 1959.

The Climates of North America
Direction, script: Joseph Koenig. Exec-

utive producer: Tom Daly. Colour. 16 mins. 1962.

Co Hoedeman, Animator
Direction: Nico Crama. Camera: Andreas Poulsson. Editing: Stephan Steinhouse. Commentary: Strowan Robertson. Music: Normand Roger. Production: Tom Daly. Executive producers: Barrie Howells, Henk Suèr. Colour. 28 mins. 1980. Co-produced with Nederlandse Omroep Stichting.

Coaches
Direction, commentary: Paul Cowan. Camera: Bill Casey. Editing: Ian Rankin, Paul Cowan. Production: Tom Daly. Executive producer: Colin Low. Colour. 57 mins. 1976. Co-produced with Fitness and Amateur Sport.

Cold Journey
Direction: Martin Defalco. Screenplay: David Jones. Camera: Tony Ianzelo. Editing: Tom Daly, Torben Schioler. Narration: George Pearson. Music: Eldon Rathburn, Willie Dunn. Production: George Pearson. Executive producer: Colin Low. Colour. 75 mins. 1972.

Cold Pizza
Direction: Larry Kent. Camera: Savas Kalogeras. Editing: Werner Nold. Production: Michael Rubbo. Executive producer: Tom Daly. Colour. 19 mins. 1972.

Come to the Fair
Direction: Jim MacKay. Production:

Tom Daly, Jim MacKay. Colour. 6 mins. 1949.

Coming Home
Direction: Bill Reid. Camera: Barry Perles. Editing: David Wilson. Production: Tom Daly, Colin Low. Colour. 84 mins. 1973.

Corral
Direction: Colin Low. Camera: Wolf Koenig. Music: Eldon Rathburn. Editing, production: Tom Daly. B&W. 11 mins. 1954.

Country Auction
Direction, editing: Roy Nolan, Ron Tunis. Camera: Bernard Longpré. Production: Roy Nolan, Ron Tunis, Tom Daly. B&W. 11 mins. 1964.

Country Threshing
Direction: Wolf Koenig. Camera: Georges Dufaux, Terence Macartney-Filgate, Jean Roy. Editing: James Beveridge. Music: The George Little Singers. Production: Roman Kroitor, Wolf Koenig. Executive producer: Tom Daly. B&W. 30 mins. 1958.

Cowboy and Indian
Direction, editing: Don Owen. Camera: Douglas Kiefer. Production: Tom Daly. Colour. 45 mins. 1972.

Dance Class
Direction: Joan Henson. Camera: Douglas Kiefer. Editing: John Kramer. Executive producer: Tom Daly. Colour. 9 mins. 1971.

Danny and Nicky
Direction, production, editing:
Douglas Jackson. Camera: Douglas
Kiefer. Narrator: Patrick Watson.
Music: Eldon Rathburn. Executive
producer: Tom Daly. Colour. 56 mins.
1969.

The Days Before Christmas
Direction: Terence Macartney-Filgate,
Stanley Jackson, Wolf Koenig. Camera:
Michel Brault, Georges Dufaux. Edit-
ing: Roman Kroitor, René Laporte,
Wolf Koenig. Production: Roman
Kroitor, Wolf Koenig. Executive pro-
ducer: Tom Daly. B&W. 30 mins. 1958.

The Days of Whiskey Gap
Director: Colin Low. Camera: John
Spotton, Jim Wilson, Roy Nolan. Edit-
ing: Kathleen Shannon, John Spotton.
Commentary: Stanley Jackson. Pro-
ducer: Roman Kroitor, Wolf Koenig.
Executive producer: Tom Daly. B&W.
28 mins. 1961.

Descent
Direction: Giles Walker, Paul Cowan.
Camera: Paul Cowan, John Dyer. Editing: John Laing. Production: Tom
Daly, Desmond Dew. Executive producer: Colin Low. Colour. 11 mins.
1975. Co-produced with the Department of External Affairs.

Dick Hickey – Blacksmith
Direction, editing, production: David
Bennett. Camera: Lorne C. Batchelor.
Executive producer: Tom Daly. B&W.
8 mins. 1953.

Do You Know the Milky Way?
Direction: Colin Low. Editing: Les
Halman. Executive producer: Tom
Daly. B&W. 8 mins. 1961. Produced by
the NFB for the Vancouver Interna-
tional Festival.

Downhill
Direction: Robin Spry. Script: Ian
MacNeill. Camera: Douglas Kiefer.
Editing: Edward Le Lorrain, Claude
Letournay. Music: Karl Duplessis. Pro-
duction: Robin Spry, Tom Daly.
Colour. 36 mins. 1973.

Earle Birney: Portrait of a Poet
Direction: Donald Winkler. Camera:
Barry Perles. Editing: Susan Shanks.
Reading: Earl Pennington. Narrator:
Mavor Moore. Music: Alain Clavier.
Production: Tom Daly. Executive pro-
ducer: Barrie Howells. Colour. 53
mins. 1981.

Earthware
Direction: Rick Raxlen, Donald
Winkler. Camera: Michel Thomas-
d'Hoste. Editing: Rick Raxlen, Bill
Graziadei. Production: Rick Raxlen,
Colin Low, Tom Daly. Colour. 10
mins. 1975.

An Easy Pill to Swallow
Direction, script: Robert Lang.
Camera: Andreas Poulsson. Editing:
Gerald Vansier. Commentary: Ian
MacNeill. Music: Charlie Frederick.
Production: Tom Daly. Executive pro-
ducer: Arthur Hammond. Colour.
29 mins. 1978.

The Edge of the Barrens
Direction, camera: Dalton Muir. Editing: John Spotton. Commentary, production: Hugh O'Connor. Music: Robert Fleming. Executive producer: Tom Daly. Colour. 14 mins. 1964.

Emergency Ward
Direction, editing: William Greaves. Camera: Wolf Koenig. Commentary: Stanley Jackson. Production: Roman Kroitor, Wolf Koenig. Executive producer: Tom Daly. B&W. 30 mins. 1959.

End of the Line
Direction: Terence Macartney-Filgate. Camera: Georges Dufaux, Terence Macartney-Filgate. Music: Pete Seeger, Sonny Terry. Production: Roman Kroitor, Wolf Koenig. Executive producer: Tom Daly. Colour. 30 mins. 1959.

Eskimo Artist: Kenojuak
Direction, script, editing: John Feeney. Camera: Francois Séguillon. Animation: Pierre L'Amare. Music: Eldon Rathbun. Production: Tom Daly. Colour. 20 mins. 1964.

Espolio
Direction: Sidney Goldsmith. Camera: Kjeld Nielson. Editing: Lucien Marleau. Narrator: Walter Massey. Production: Tom Daly. Colour. 6 mins. 1970.

An Essay on Science
Direction: Guy L. Coté. Camera: Reginald Morris. Animation: Colin Low,

Pierre L'Amare. Music: Maurice Blackburn, Raymond Daveluy. Production: Tom Daly. Colour. 20 mins. 1964. Produced for the National Research Council of Canada.

Experienced Hands
Direction: Theodore Conant. Script: Elspeth Chisholm. Camera: John Foster, Mike Lente, Laval Fortier. Producer: Elspeth Chisholm. Executive producer: Tom Daly. B&W. 24 mins. 1965.

Experimental Film
Direction, editing: Arthur Lipsett. Camera: Wolf Koenig. Production: Tom Daly. B&W. 28 mins. 1963.

Eyes on Canada
Production: Tom Daly. B&W. 11 mins. 1947.

F.R. Scott: Rhyme and Reason
Direction: Donald Winkler. Camera: Barry Perles. Editing: Albert Kish. Production: Tom Daly. Executive producer: Barrie Howells. Colour. 58 mins. 1982.

Face
Direction, editing: Robin Spry. Camera: Robin Spry, Kjeld Nielsen. Music: Karl Duplessis. Production: Robin Spry, Tom Daly. Colour. 17 mins. 1975.

The Face of the High Arctic
Direction, camera: Dalton Muir. Commentary: Strowan Robertson.

Narrator: Michael Kane. Editing:
William Greaves. Music: Robert
Fleming. Production: Hugh
O'Connor. Executive producer:
Tom Daly. Colour. 13 mins.1958.

Faces#
Editing: Tom Daly. 1963. (Test film for
Labyrinthe.)

Falling from Ladders
Direction, editing: Mort Ransen. Camera: Martin Duckworth. Production:
John Kemeny, Joseph Koenig,
Tom Daly. B&W. 9 mins. 1969. Co-
produced with the Swedish Institute
for Cultural Relations.

Family Circles
Direction: Morten Parker. Script:
Morten Parker, Gudrun Parker. Cam-
era: Grant McLean. Editing: Horace
Clarke. Music: Eldon Rathburn. Pro-
duction: Tom Daly, Gudrun Parker.
B&W. 28 mins. 1949.

Family Tree
Direction, animation: George Dun-
ning, Evelyn Lambart. Music: Eldon
Rathburn. Production: Tom Daly.
Colour. 15 mins. 1950.

Farm Calendar
Direction, script: Roman Kroitor.
Camera: Jean Roy, Walter A.
Sutton, Donald Wilder, Wolf Koenig,
Grant Crabtree. Narrator: Harry
Boyle. Music: Maurice Blackburn.
Production: Tom Daly. B&W.
44 mins. 1955. Produced for the

Department of Citizenship and Immigration.

Feelings of Depression
Direction, script: Stanley Jackson.
Camera: Denis Gillson. Editing: Vic-
tor Jobin. Production: Tom Daly.
B&W. 30 mins. 1950. Produced for the
Department of National Health and
Welfare.

Festival in Puerto Rico
Direction, editing: Wolf Koenig,
Roman Kroitor. Script: Strowan Robertson. Camera: Michel Brault. Production: Roman Kroitor. Executive
producer: Tom Daly. B&W. 27 mins.
1961.

Fifty Miles from Poona
Direction, camera: Fali Bilimoria.
Commentary, editing: John Feeney.
Production: Tom Daly. B&W. 19 mins.
1959.

*Fighting Forest Fires with Hand
Tools*
Direction: Lawrence Cherry. Camera:
Lawrence Cherry, John Spotton. Production: Tom Daly. Colour. 20 mins.
1951. Produced for the Canadian Forestry Service.

*Fighting Forest Fires with Power
Pumps*
Direction: Lawrence Cherry.
Camera: Lawrence Cherry, Charles
Beddoe. Editing: Betty Brunke.
Production: Tom Daly. Colour.
22 mins. 1953. Produced by the NFB

for the Canadian Forestry
Service.

A Film for Max
Direction, editing: Derek May.
Camera: Martin Duckworth, Claude
Beaugrand. Production: Tom Daly.
Colour. 74 mins. 1970.

Five Men of Australia#
Picture editing: Tom Daly. 1941.
(20-minute version of an Australian
film, *A Hundred Thousand
Cobbers.*)

Fishermen
Direction, script, editing: Guy L. Coté.
Camera: John Spotton. Animation:
Neil Shakery. Narrator: William Needles. Music: Robert Fleming. Executive
producer: Tom Daly. B&W. 22 mins.
1959.

Fluxes
Direction, editing: Arthur Lipsett.
Animatin: Kaj Pindal. Production: Guy
Glover, Tom Daly. B&W. 24 mins.
1967.

Folksong Fantasy
Direction, camera: Lyle Enright.
Animation: Alma Duncan. Production: Tom Daly. Colour. 7 mins.
1951.

Food: Secret of the Peace
Direction, script, editing, producing:
Stuart Legg. Assistant: Tom Daly.
B&W. 11 mins. 1945.

*Food, Weapon of Conquest**
Direction, editing, production: Stuart
Legg. Research: Margaret Ann Adamson. Sound editing: Tom Daly. B&W.
22 mins. 1941.

A Foreign Language
Direction: Stanley Jackson. Camera:
Reginald Morris. Production: Roman
Kroitor, Wolf Koenig. Executive pro-
ducer: Tom Daly. B&W. 29 mins. 1958.

The Forest
Direction, camera, editing: John Spot-
ton. Commentary: Stanley Jackson.
Music: Louis Applebaum. Production:
Tom Daly. B&W. 21 mins. 1965.

Forest Fire Suppression
Direction, commentary: Lawrence
Cherry. Camera: Geoffrey Taylor.
Editing: William Greaves. Animation:
Wolf Koenig. Narrator: Fred Davis.
Production: Tom Daly. B&W. 22 mins.
1956. Produced for the Department of
Northern Affairs and National
Resources.

The Forest Watchers
Direction, script: Peter Raymont.
Camera: Andreas Poulsson. Anima-
tion camera: Raymond Dumas. Edit-
ing: Laurie Wright. Music: Larry
Crosley. Production: Tom Daly. Exec-
utive producer: Colin Low. Colour. 25
mins. 1975. Produced for the Canadian
Forestry Service of Environment
Canada.

*Fortress Japan**
Direction, production, script, editing:

Stuart Legg. Assistant: Tom Daly. B&W. 17 mins. 1944.

4 Songs by 4 Gentlemen
Direction, production: Michael Spencer. Animation: Jean-Paul Ladouceur, Ray Roy. Sound: Clarke Daprato. Executive producer: Tom Daly. B&W. 8 mins. 1950.

Fraternité
Script: Jacques Brunet, Paul Thériault. Editing, production: Tom Daly. B&W. 10 mins. 1947.

Free Fall
Direction, camera, editing: Arthur Lipsett. Production: Tom Daly, Colin Low. B&W. 9 mins. 1964.

Freighters under Fire*
Direction, production, commentary: Stuart Legg. Research, sound editing: Tom Daly. B&W. 26 mins. 1942.

A Friend at the Door
Direction, script: Leslie McFarlane. Camera: Wallace Hamilton, John Foster. Editing: David Mayerovitch. Music: Louis Applebaum. Producers: James Beveridge, Tom Daly. B&W. 28 mins. 1950.

From the Ashes of War
Direction, editing: Michael McKennirey. Camera: Savas Kalogeras, Kent Nason, Barry Perles, Don Virgo. Commentary: Barry Cowling. Narrator: Alex Colville. Music: Allan Rae. Production: Tom Daly, Nico Crama.

Executive producers: Barrie Howells, Henk Suèr. Colour. 30 mins. 1980. Co-produced with Nederlandse Omroep Stichting.

Garden
Direction, camera: Christopher Nutter. Music: Bruce Mackay. Production: Tom Daly. Colour. 5 mins. 1971.

Gateway to Asia§
Direction, production, commentary, editing: Tom Daly. Narrator: Lorne Greene. B&W. 10 mins. 1945.

Geopolitik – Hitler's Plan for Empire*
Direction, commentary, editing: Stuart Legg. Narrator: Lorne Greene. Research, sound editing: Tom Daly. B&W. 20 mins. 1942.

Girls of Mountain Street
Direction, editing: Susan Gibbard. Camera: Michel Thomas-d'Hoste. Production: Tom Daly. Colour. 10 mins. 1970.

Glenn Gould – Off the Record
Direction, production: Roman Kroitor, Wolf Koenig. Camera: Wolf Koenig. Editing: James Beveridge. Commentary: Stanley Jackson. Executive producer: Tom Daly. B&W. 29 mins. 1959.

Glenn Gould – On the Record
Direction, production: Roman Kroitor, Wolf Koenig. Camera: Wolf Koenig. Editing: James Beveridge. Commen-

tary: Stanley Jackson. Executive producer: Tom Daly. B&W. 29 mins. 1959.

Global Air Routes*†
Direction, production, script: Stuart Legg. Animation: Eve Lambart. Editing assistant: Tom Daly. B&W. 14 mins. 1944.

God Help the Man Who Would Part with His Land
Direction: George C. Stoney. Camera: Tony Ianzelo, David de Volpi. Editing: Bill Reid. Music: Shannon Two Feathers. Production: Colin Low, Tom Daly. B&W. 47 mins. 1971.

Gold
Direction: Colin Low. Camera, editing: Wolf Koenig. Music: Eldon Rathburn. Production: Tom Daly. B&W. 11 mins. 1955.

Grain Handling in Canada
Direction: Guy L. Coté. Camera: John Spotton. Editing: Douglas Tunstell. Commentary: Norman Klenman. Narrator: James B. McGeachy. Music: Robert Fleming. Production: Tom Daly. Colour. 24 mins. 1955. Produced for the Department of Trade and Commerce.

The Great Clean-up
Direction: James Carney. Camera: Laval Fortier, Savas Kalogeras, Robert Humble. Editing: Ivan Horsky. Commentary, narrator: Stanley Jackson. Music: Karl Duplessis, Malca Gillson. Production: Tom Daly.

Executive producer: Colin Low. Colour. 52 mins. 1976. Presented jointly with the United States Environmental Protection Agency and Environment Canada.

The Great Lakes – St. Lawrence Lowlands
Direction, script, editing: Betty Brunke. Camera: Felix Lazarus. Production: Tom Daly. B&W. 22 mins. 1956.

The Great Plains
Direction, editing: Roman Kroitor. Camera: Donald Wilder. Animation: Allan Mardon. Production: Tom Daly. Colour. 23 mins. 1957.

The Great Toy Robbery
Direction: Jeffrey Hale. Camera: James Wilson, Murray Fallen. Storyboard, design: Derek Lamb. Animation: Jeffrey Hale, Cameron Guess. Music: Donald Douglas. Production: Wolf Koenig, Robert Verrall. Executive producer: Tom Daly. Colour. 7 mins. 1964.

Guilty Men
Direction, writing, editing, production: Tom Daly. Music: Lucio Agostini. B&W. 11 mins. 1945.

Half-Half-Three-quarters-Full
Camera: Martin Duckworth. Editing: Christopher Cordeaux. Music: Bruce Mackay. Production: Barrie Howells, Tom Daly. Colour. 8 mins. 1970.

Helicopter Canada
Direction, camera: Eugene Boyko.
Commentary: Donald Brittain, Derek
May. Editing: Rex Tasker. Narrator:
Stanley Jackson. Production: Peter
Jones, Tom Daly. Colour. 50 mins.
1966. Produced for the Centennial
Commission.

Here's to Harry's Grandfather
Direction, editing: Michael Rubbo.
Camera: Tony Ianzelo. Music: Eldon
Rathburn. Production: Tom Daly.
Colour. 58 mins. 1970.

*Heroes of the Atlantic**
Direction, camera: J.D. Davidson,
Donald Fraser. Production: Stanley
Hawes. Research assistance: Tom Daly.
B&W. 15 mins. 1941.

High Arctic: Life on the Land
Direction, camera: Dalton Muir. Editing: William Greaves. Commentary:
Strowan Robertson. Narrator: Michael
Kane. Music: Maurice Blackburn. Production: Hugh O'Connor. Executive
producer: Tom Daly. Colour. 21 mins.
1958.

Hinchinbrook Diary
Direction: Rick Raxlen. Camera: Savas
Kalogeras. Editing: Rick Raxlen,
Donald Rennick. Music: Daisy
Debolt, Celia Brickman. Production:
Tom Daly. Executive producer: Colin
Low. Colour. 14 mins. 1975.

House of History
Direction, script: Gordon Burwash.

Camera: Eugene Boyko. Editing:
Ronald Dick. Executive producer: Tom
Daly. B&W. 19 mins. 1954.

Hungry Minds†
Direction, research, writing, editing,
production: Tom Daly. Assistance:
Ronald Dick, George Brandt. B&W. 11
mins. 1948. Produced for the Canadian
Council for Reconstruction through
UNESCO.

The Huntsman
Direction, production, screenplay:
Douglas Jackson. Camera: Denis
Gillson. Editing: Edward Le Lorrain,
Douglas Jackson. Music: Eldon
Rathburn. Executive producer: Tom
Daly. Colour. 16 mins. 1972.

The Hutterites
Direction: Colin Low. Camera, editing:
John Spotton. Commentary: Stanley
Jackson. Production: Roman Kroitor,
Tom Daly. B&W. 28 mins. 1964.

I Am an Old Tree
Director, editing, narration: Michael
Rubbo. Camera: Andreas Poulsson.
Production: Tom Daly, Michael
Rubbo. Executive producer: Colin
Low. Colour. 57 mins. 1975.

I Hate to Lose
Direction, editing, narration:
Michael Rubbo. Camera: Andreas
Poulsson. Music: Angèle Arsenault.
Production: Tom Daly. Executive
producer: Arthur Hammond. Colour.
57 mins. 1977.

*I Know an Old Lady Who
Swallowed a Fly*
Direction: Derek Lamb. Camera: Jim
Wilson, Murray Fallen. Animation: Kaj
Pindal. Music: Burl Ives. Production:
Colin Low. Executive producer: Tom
Daly. Colour. 6 mins. 1964.

I Was a Ninety-pound Weakling
Direction: Wolf Koenig, Georges Dufaux. Camera: Georges Dufaux. Editing: John Spotton. Production: Roman
Kroitor, Wolf Koenig. Executive producer: Tom Daly. B&W. 24 mins. 1960.

'If He Is Devoured, I Win'
Direction, editing: Rick Raxlen. Cam-
era: Jacques Fogel, Andreas Poulsson.
Music: Bruce Mackay. Production:
Stanley Jackson, Tom Daly. Colour. 5
mins. 1969.

I'll Go Again
Direction, camera, editing: Paul
Cowan. Music: Ben Low. Production:
Tom Daly. Executive producer:
Michael McKennirey. Colour. 41 mins.
1977. Co-produced with Fitness and
Amateur Sports.

Improv
Direction: Joan Henson. Camera:
Douglas Kiefer. Editing: John Kramer.
Production: Tom Daly. Colour. 19
mins. 1971.

In Praise of Hands
Direction: Donald Winkler. Camera:
Michel Thomas-d'Hoste. Editing:
Albert Kish. Music: Alain Clavier.

Production: Tom Daly. Executive producer: Colin Low. Colour. 28 mins.
1974. Produced in cooperation with the
World Crafts Council and the Sports
and Recreation Bureau of the Province
of Ontario.

In the Labyrinth
Direction: Roman Kroitor, Colin Low,
Hugh O'Connor. Camera: Michel
Thomas-d'Hoste, Walter Lassally,
Gilles Gascon, Georges Dufaux,
V.V. Dombrovsky, Alex O. Krasnov.
Editing: Tom Daly. Music: Eldon
Rathburn, performed by Louis Apple-
baum. Production: Tom Daly, Roman
Kroitor. Executive producer: Desmond
Dew. Colour. 21 mins. 1979.

Inside France§
Direction, production: Stuart Legg.
Research, editing: Tom Daly. B&W. 21
mins. 1944.

Interview with Linus Pauling
Direction: Joseph Koenig. Camera:
Wolf Koenig. Production: Hugh
O'Connor. Executive producer: Tom
Daly. B&W. 56 mins. 1960.

Introducing Canada
Editing: Roman Kroitor, Tom Daly.
Script: Stanley Jackson. Narrator: Rob-
ert Beatty. Music: Eldon Rathburn.
Production: Tom Daly. B&W. 24 mins.
1956. Produced for the North Atlantic
Treaty Organization.

Iron from the North
Direction: Walford Hewitson. Camera:

Felix Lazarus, Jean-Marie Couture, Julien St-Georges. Script: Len Peterson. Editing: Betty Brunke. Production: Tom Daly. B&W. 20 mins. 1955.

Island Observed
Direction, camera: Hector Lemieux. Editing: David Mayerovitch. Commentary: Stanley Jackson. Narrator: Henry Ramer. Music: Norman Bigras. Production: Tom Daly. Colour. 28 mins. 1966.

It Wasn't Easy ...
Direction: Nico Crama. Camera: Andreas Poulsson. Editing: Steven Kellar, Malca Gillson. Production: Tom Daly, Henk Suèr. Executive producer: Arthur Hammond. Colour. 46 mins. 1978. Co-produced with Nederlandse Omroep Stichting.

It's a Crime
Direction: Wolf Koenig. Story: Roman Kroitor. Layout, design: Colin Low. Camera: Douglas Poulter, James Wilson. Animation: Gerald Potterton. Narrator: Guy Glover. Music: Eldon Rathburn, Ernst Maser. Executive producer: Tom Daly. B&W. 13 mins. 1957. Produced for the Department of Labour.

Jalan, Jalan: A Journey in Sundanese Java
Direction, editing: Michael Rubbo. Camera: Paul Leach. Production: Tom Daly. Colour. 20 mins. 1973.

Jet Pilot
Direction: Joseph Koenig. Camera: Eugene Boyko, Jean Roy. Commentary: Stanley Jackson. Production: Tom Daly. Colour. 17 mins. 1964.

Le Jeu de l'hiver
Direction: Jean Dansereau, Bernard Gosselin. Camera: Michel Brault, Jean Dansereau, Bernard Gosselin. Editing: Victor Jobin. Music: Tony Romandini, Yvan Landry, Donald Habib, Maurice Blackburn. Executive producer: Tom Daly. B&W. 15 mins. 1962.

The Jolifou Inn
Direction, editing, production: Colin Low. Camera: Lyle Enright, Douglas Roberts. Music: Louis Applebaum. Executive producer: Tom Daly. Colour. 10 minutes. 1955.

Kindergarten
Direction, editing: Guy L. Coté. Camera: Georges Dufaux. Production: Tom Daly. B&W. 21 mins. 1962.

Kurelek
Direction, editing: William Pettigrew. Animation camera: Wayne Trickett, Kjeld Nielsen. Commentary: John Sims, William Kurelek. Narrator: Richard Gilbert. Music: Robert Fleming. Production: Robert Verrall, Tom Daly. Colour. 10 mins. 1966.

Labyrinthe#
Editing of Chambers I and III: Tom Daly. Assistant: Yves Dion. 1967. (Part of Expo 67 exhibit.)

The Last Days of Living
Direction, editing: Malca Gillson.
Camera: Robert Humble, Barry
Perles. Production: Tom Daly. Execu-
tive producers: Arthur Hammond,
Barrie Howells. Colour. 58 mins. 1980.

Legault's Place
Direction, editing: Suzanne Angel.
Camera: John Spotton. Commentary:
Stanley Jackson. Production: Roman
Kroitor, Tom Daly. B&W. 10 mins.
1964.

Legend
Direction: Rick Raxlen. Camera: David
de Volpi. Editing: Margaret Wescott.
Music: Bruce Mackay. Production:
Tom Daly. Colour. 15 mins. 1970.

Life in the Woodlot
Direction, camera: Dalton Muir. Production: Hugh O'Connor. Executive
producer: Tom Daly. Colour. 16 mins.
1960.

Light to Starboard
Direction, script, editing: Jerry Krepa-
kevich. Camera: Savas Kalogeras. Ani-
mation: Gerry Roach, Judith Mancini.
Executive producer: Tom Daly.
Colour. 48 mins. 1972. Produced for
Transport Canada.

Lismer
Direction, script: Allan Wargon.
Camera: Robert Humble. Editing:
Victor Jobin. Music: Maurice
Blackburn. Production: Tom Daly.
Colour. 19 minutes. 1952.

The Living Machine
Direction: Roman Kroitor. Camera:
Wolf Koenig. Editing: Guy L. Coté.
Animation: Pierre L'Amare. Produc-
tion: Roman Kroitor, Tom Daly.
B&W. 56 mins. 1962.

The Living Stone
Direction, script, editing: John Feeney.
Camera: Patrick Carey. Narrator:
George Whalley. Music: Maurice
Blackburn. Production: Tom Daly.
Colour. 30 mins. 1958.

Lonely Boy
Direction: Wolf Koenig, Roman
Kroitor. Camera: Wolf Koenig. Editing: John Spotton, Guy L. Coté. Production: Roman Kroitor. Executive
producer: Tom Daly. B&W. 27 mins.
1961.

The Longhouse People
Direction, script, editing: Allan War-
gon. Camera: Hector Lemieux, Denis
Gillson. Production: Tom Daly.
Colour. 23 mins. 1951. Produced in
cooperation with Canadian Six Nations
Iroquois and the National Museum of
Canada.

Look Alert, Stay Unhurt
Direction: Gordon Burwash. Camera:
Eugene Boyko. Commentary: Max
Braithwaite. Editing, production: Tom
Daly. B&W. 14 mins. 1955.

Look Before You Leap
Direction, script, animation: Laurence
Hyde. Camera: Lyle Enright. Execu-

tive producer: Tom Daly. Colour. 2
mins. 1954.

*Looking Beyond ... Story of a Film
Council*
Direction, script: Stanley Jackson.
Camera: Robert Humble. Editing: Wil-
liam Greaves. Production: Tom Daly.
B&W. 19 mins. 1957.

Los Canadienses
Direction, editing: Albert Kish. Cam-
era: Barry Perles. Commentary: Albert
Kish, Làszlò Gefin. Narrator: Donald
Brittain. Music: Ben Low. Production:
Colin Low, Tom Daly. Colour. 57
mins. 1975.

*The Lost Pharaoh: The Search for
Akhenaten*
Direction, camera: Nicholas Kendall.
Commentary: Donald Brittain. Editing: Judith Merritt. Production: Nicholas Kendall, Tom Daly. Executive
producer: Don Hopkins. Colour. 57
mins. 1980. Produced in collaboration
with the CBC.

Louisbourg
Direction: Albert Kish. Camera:
Eugene Boyko. Editing: Albert Kish,
John Kramer. Commentary: Donald
Winkler. Music: Alain Clavier. Produc-
tion: Tom Daly. Colour. 20 mins. 1972.
Produced for Parks Canada.

Lumsden
Direction: Peter Raymont. Camera:
Tony Westman, Barry Perles. Editing:
Janice Brown. Producer: Tom Daly.

Executive producer: Colin Low.
Colour. 20 mins. 1975.

The Magnificent
Direction: Julian Biggs. Camera:
Eugene Boyko. Script: Norman Clen-
man. Editing: Tom Daly. Production:
Robert Anderson. B&W. 30 mins. 1954.

Making Primitive Stone Tools
Direction, script, camera: Douglas
Leechman. Production: Tom Daly.
Colour. 11 mins. 1950. Produced by
the NFB in cooperation with the
National Museum of Canada.

The Man Who Can't Stop
Director, commentary: Michael
Rubbo. Camera: Don McAlpine. Edit-
ing: Graham Chase, Michael Rubbo.
Production: Tom Daly, Richard
Mason. Executive producer: Colin
Low. Colour. 58 mins. 1973. Co-
produced with Film Australia.

The Mask of Nippon†
Direction, script, production: Stuart
Legg. Narrator: Lorne Greene.
Research, sound editing: Tom Daly.
B&W. 21 mins. 1942.

McBus
Direction: Derek May. Camera: Thomas Vamos. Editing Donald Rennick.
Production: Tom Daly. Colour. 15
mins. 1969.

The Mechanical Knee
Direction: Claudia Overing. Camera:
Jean Roy, Eric Chamberlain, Jacques

Tougas, Claudia Overing. Editing:
Lucien Marleau. Music: Norman Big-
ras. Production: Jean Roy, Tom Daly.
Colour. 22 mins. 1971.

Meditation in Motion
Direction, editing: Irene Angelico.
Camera: Douglas Kiefer, Barry Perles.
Music: Eldon Rathburn. Production:
Tom Daly. Executive producers:
Arthur Hammond, Michael McKen-
nirey. Colour. 10 mins. 1978.

Memory of Summer
Direction: Stanley Jackson. Camera:
Wolf Koenig, Terence Macartney-
Filgate, Georges Dufaux. Editing:
Edouard Davidovici. Production:
Roman Kroitor, Wolf Koenig. Execu-
tive producer: Tom Daly. B&W. 30
mins. 1958.

Metal Workers
Direction: Robert Fortier, Donald
Winkler. Camera: Michel Thomas-
d'Hoste. Editing: Robert Fortier. Pro-
duction: Tom Daly, Rick Raxlen, Colin
Low. Colour. 10 mins. 1975.

Microscopic Fungi
Direction, script, editing: J.V. Durden.
Camera: J.V. Durden, Patrick Carey,
Robert Humble. Production: Hugh
O'Connor. Executive producer: Tom
Daly. Colour. 17 mins. 1960.

Mirage
Direction, editing: Rick Raxlen. Production: Tom Daly. Colour. 6 mins.
1972.

Mountains of the West
Direction, script, camera, production:
Donald Fraser. Executive producer:
Tom Daly. B&W. 20 mins. 1954.

Mr. Symbol Man
Direction: Bruce Moir, Bob Kings-
bury. Camera: Mike Edols, Barry
Perles. Editing: Bruce Moir. Anima-
tion: Les Drew. Commentary: Stanley
Jackson. Production: Tom Daly,
Frank Bagnall, Richard Mason.
Colour. 49 mins. 1974. Co-produced
with Film Australia.

Mrs. Ryan's Drama Class
Direction: Michael Rubbo. Camera:
Tony Ianzelo, Paul Leach, Martin
Duckworth, Robert Humble. Editing:
Edward Le Lorrain. Production:
Cecily Burwash, Tom Daly. B&W.
35 mins. 1969.

*Musical Magic: Gilbert and
Sullivan in Stratford*
Direction, editing: Malca Gillson.
Camera: Andreas Poulsson, Andy
Kitzanuk, Tony Ianzelo. Commen-
tary: Barry Cowling. Production:
Tom Daly. Executive producer:
Barrie Howells. Colour. 57 mins.
1984.

Musicanada
Direction: Malca Gillson, Tony Ian-
zelo. Camera: Tony Ianzelo, Douglas
Kiefer, Robert Humble, David de
Volpi. Editing: Malca Gillson. Produc-
tion: Tom Daly. Executive producer:
Colin Low. Colour. 58 mins. 1975.

My Financial Career
Direction, animation: Grant Munro,
Gerald Potterton. Narrator: Stanley
Jackson. Production: Colin Low, Tom
Daly. Colour. 7 mins. 1962.

N-Zone
Direction, editing: Arthur Lipsett. Production: Tom Daly. B&W. 45 mins.
1970.

New York Lightboard
Direction: Norman McLaren. Animation: Norman McLaren and others.
Production: Tom Daly. B&W. 9 mins.
1961. Produced for the Canadian Government Travel Bureau.

The Newcomers
Direction, script: David Bennett.
Camera: Donald Wilder. Editing:
Douglas Tunstell, Fergus McDonell.
Music: Lucio Agostini. Production:
Tom Daly. B&W. 27 mins. 1953.
Produced by the NFB for the Depart-
ment of Citizenship and Immigration.

Niagara Falls
Direction, script: Derek May. Camera:
Martin Duckworth. Editing: Donald
Rennick. Music: Robert Fleming.
Production: Tom Daly. Colour. 28
mins. 1967.

No Longer Vanishing
Direction, script, camera: Grant
McLean. Editing: Ronald Dick.
Commentary: Leslie McFarlane.
Production: Tom Daly. Colour. 28
mins. 1955. Produced for the

Department of Citizenship and Immigration.

No Way They Want to Slow Down
Direction: Giles Walker. Camera: Paul
Cowan. Commentary, editing: John
Laing. Music: Alain Clavier. Produc-
tion: Desmond Dew, Tom Daly. Exec-
utive producer: Colin Low. Colour. 29
mins. 1975. Co-produced with the
Department of External Affairs.

Nobody Waved Good-bye
Direction, script: Don Owen. Camera:
John Spotton. Editing: John Spotton,
Donald Ginsberg. Music: Eldon Rath-
burn. Production: Roman Kroitor,
Don Owen. Executive producer: Tom
Daly. B&W. 80 mins. 1964.

Norman Jewison, Filmmaker
Direction, production: Douglas Jack-
son. Camera: Eugene Boyko. Editing:
Malca Gillson, Edward Le Lorrain, Les
Halman. Executive producer: Tom
Daly. Colour. 49 mins. 1971.

North China Commune
Direction: Boyce Richardson, Tony
Ianzelo. Camera: Tony Ianzelo. Edit-
ing: Ginny Stikeman. Narrator:
Donald Sutherland. Production: Tom
Daly. Executive producers: Arthur
Hammond, Barrie Howells. Colour. 80
mins. 1979.

North China Factory
Direction: Tony Ianzelo, Boyce Richardson. Camera: Tony Ianzelo. Editing: Ginny Stikeman. Narrator:

Donald Sutherland. Production:
Tom Daly. Executive producer:
Barrie Howells. Colour. 57 mins.
1980.

November
Direction, camera: Robert Nichol.
Editing: Donna Nichol. Music: Harry
Freedman. Production: Tom Daly.
Colour. 9 mins. 1970.

*Now – The Peace**
Direction, writing, editing, production:
Stuart Legg. Assistant: Tom Daly.
B&W. 20 mins. 1945.

O Canada (Coat of Arms)
Executive producer: Tom Daly. B&W.
1 min. 1961.

Off the Wall
Direction, script, editing, narrator:
Derek May. Camera: Barry Perles.
Production: Tom Daly. Executive pro-
ducer: Barrie Howells. Colour. 56
mins. 1981.

On Stage
Direction: Ronald Dick. Camera: Rob-
ert Humble. Script: George Brandt,
David Bennett. Editing: Victor Jobin.
Production: Tom Daly. B&W. 30 mins.
1950.

Once ... Agadir
Direction, editing: Jacques
Bensimon. Camera: John Diebold.
Music: Art Phillips. Executive pro-
ducer: Tom Daly. Colour. 27 mins.
1971.

One Hand Clapping
Direction, editing: Joan Henson.
Camera: Eugene Boyko. Executive
producer: Tom Daly. Colour. 10 mins.
1972.

One Little Indian
Direction: Grant Munro. Camera:
Herbert Taylor. Editing: Douglas Tun-
stell. Music: Eldon Rathburn. Com-
mentary: Stanley Jackson. Production:
Colin Low. Executive producer: Tom
Daly. Colour. 16 mins. 1954.

One Man
Direction: Robin Spry. Screenplay:
Robin Spry, Peter Pearson, Peter Mad-
den. Camera: Douglas Kiefer. Editing:
John Kramer. Music: Ben Low. Pro-
duction: Michael Scott, James de B.
Domville, Tom Daly, Vladimir
Valenta, Roman Kroitor. Colour. 87
mins. 1977.

Ordeal by Ice§†
Photography: Hamilton Wright. Editing: David Mayerovitch, Tom Daly.
Production: Tom Daly. B&W. 11 mins.
1945.

The Origins of Weather
Direction, script: Joseph Koenig. Ani-
mation: Kenneth Horn. Commentary:
Stanley Jackson. Executive producer:
Tom Daly. Colour. 12 mins. 1963.

Our Northern Neighbour§
Direction, production: Stuart Legg.
Research, editing: Tom Daly.
Animation: Norman McLaren.

Narrator: Lorne Greene. B&W. 21 mins. 1944.

Out of the Ruins
Direction: Nicholas Read. Script: Rita Greer. Production: Tom Daly. B&W. 32 mins. 1946. Produced in association with the United Nations Relief and Rehabilitation Administration.

Over-Dependency
Direction, script, production: Robert Anderson. Camera: Jean-Marie Couture. Editing: Victor Jobin. Animation: Norman McLaren. Music: Robert Fleming. Executive producer: Tom Daly. B&W. 31 mins. 1949. Produced for the Mental Health Division of the Department of National Health and Welfare.

Overspill
Director: Mort Ransen. Script, editing: Roger Hart. Camera: Martin Duckworth. Production: Tom Daly, John Kemeny. B&W. 28 mins. 1970. Co-produced with the Swedish Institute for Cultural Relations.

Pandora
Direction: Derek May. Camera: Martin Duckworth. Production: Tom Daly. Colour. 5 mins. 1971.

Pangnirtung
Direction, script, editing: John Feeney. Camera: Patrick Carey. Music: Eldon Rathburn. Production: Tom Daly. Colour. 30 mins. 1959.

Paper Boy
Direction, script: Clay Borris. Camera: John F. Phillips. Music: Willie Dunn, Jesse Winchester, Dutch Mills. Production: Tom Daly. B&W. 14 mins. 1971.

Paul Tomkowicz: Street-railway Switchman
Direction, editing: Roman Kroitor. Camera: Lorne C. Batchelor. Narrator: Tommy Tweed. Production: Tom Daly. B&W. 9 mins. 1954.

Pearly Yeats
Direction: Bruce Mackay. Producer: Tom Daly. Colour. 10 mins. 1971.

The Peep Show
Director, script, animation: Kaj Pindal. Narrator: Stanley Jackson. Production: Colin Low. Executive producer: Tom Daly. B&W. 9 mins. 1962.

Pen Point Percussion
Direction: Norman McLaren. Camera: Lorne C. Batchelor. Music: Louis Applebaum. Production: Norman McLaren, Tom Daly. B&W. 6 mins. 1951.

The People Between
Direction, camera: Grant McLean. Music: Louis Applebaum. Editing, production: Tom Daly. Narration: Budd Knapp. B&W. 22 mins. 1947.

Persistent and Finagling
Direction, script, editing: Michael Rubbo. Camera: Jean-Pierre

Lachapelle. Production: Tom Daly. B&W. 56 mins. 1971.

The Persistent Seed
Direction, camera: Christopher Chapman. Editing: Guy L. Coté, Christopher Chapman. Production: Hugh O'Connor. Executive producer: Tom Daly. Colour. 14 mins. 1964.

Physical Regions of Canada
Direction, editing: Betty Brunke. Production: Tom Daly. B&W. 23 mins. 1954.

Pilgrimage
Direction: Terence Macartney-Filgate. Camera: Wolf Koenig. Editing: Tom Daly, Lucien Marleau. Production: Roman Kroitor, Wolf Koenig. Executive producer: Tom Daly. B&W. 30 mins. 1958.

Pillar of Wisdom
Direction: Josef Reeve. Camera: Paul Leach, Martin Duckworth, Wolf Koenig, John Spotton. Editing: Michael McKennirey. Production: Tom Daly. Colour. 9 mins. 1970.

*Pincers on Axis Europe**
Direction, editing: Stuart Legg. Research, sound editing: Tom Daly. B&W. 20 mins. 1943.

A Pinto for the Prince
Direction: Colin Low, John Spotton. Camera: Douglas Kiefer, Eugene Boyko, Robert Reece. Editing: John Laing. Commentary: Stanley Jackson.

Production: Tom Daly. Executive producer: Michael Scott. Colour. 17 mins. 1979.

Pipers and A'
Direction, script, editing: Austin Campbell. Camera: Guy Borremans, Wolf Koenig, Roger Moride, Edward McConnell, James Wilson, Roy Nolan, Michael McKennirey. Narrator: Douglas Rain. Music: Donald Douglas. Producer: Tom Daly. Colour. 9 mins. 1963.

A Place for Everything
Direction, script, editing: Eric M. Nilsson. Camera: Ake Astrand. Narrator: Joan Henson. Production: Joseph Koenig, John Kemeny, Tom Daly. B&W. 29 mins. 1970. Co-produced with the Swedish Institute for Cultural Relations.

The Players
Direction, script: Donald Brittain. Camera: Ron Lowe, Douglas Kiefer. Editing: John Kramer. Production: Tom Daly, Gil Brealey. Executive producer: James de B. Domville. Colour. 58 mins. 1974. Co-produced with the South Australian Film Corporation.

Poen
Direction: Josef Reeve. Production: Tom Daly. B&W. 5 mins. 1967.

Poison Ivy Picnic
Script, animation: Laurence Hyde. Camera: Lyle Enright. Production: Tom Daly. Colour. 2 mins. 1953.

Police
Direction: Terence Macartney-Filgate.
Camera: Georges Dufaux, Terence
Macartney-Filgate, Michel Brault.
Editing: James Beveridge, Bruce
Parsons. Production: Roman
Kroitor, Wolf Koenig. Executive
producer: Tom Daly. B&W. 29 mins.
1958.

Pot-pourri
Direction, animation: Jeff Hale, Austin
Campbell. Production: Tom Daly.
B&W. 7 mins. 1962.

The Precambrian Shield
Direction, script, editing: David Bennett. Camera: Reginald Morris. Production: Tom Daly. B&W. 25 mins.
1957.

The Price of Fire
Direction, camera, editing: Bruce Parsons. Commentary: Strowan Robertson. Narrator: Don Francks. Executive
producer: Tom Daly. B&W. 22 mins.
1961.

Profile of a Problem Drinker
Direction, script: Stanley Jackson.
Camera: Reginald Morris. Editing:
William Greaves. Production: Tom
Daly. B&W. 29 mins. 1957. Produced
in cooperation with the Mental Health
Divisions of the Department of
National Health and Welfare and the
Ontario Department of Health.

Prologue
Direction: Robin Spry. Script: Sher-
wood Forest. Camera: Douglas Kiefer.

Editing: Christopher Cordeaux. Production: Robin Spry, Tom Daly. B&W.
88 mins. 1969.

Putting It Straight
Direction, editing: William Greaves.
Script: Donald Fraser. Camera: Robert
Humble, Reginald Morris. Animation:
Sidney Goldsmith, Evelyn Lambart.
Production: Tom Daly. Colour. 14
mins. 1957. Produced for the
Department of National Health and
Welfare.

Radiation
Direction, production: Hugh O'Con-
nor. Script: Joseph Koenig. Camera:
Robert Humble, Reginald Morris, A.L.
Coquillon. Editing: Lucien Marleau.
Animation: Pierre L'Amare. Executive
producer: Tom Daly. Colour. 26 mins.
1959.

Railroaders
Direction, script, editing: Guy L. Coté.
Camera: John Spotton. Animation:
Sidney Goldsmith. Music: Robert
Fleming. Executive producer: Tom
Daly. B&W. 21 mins. 1958.

*Reaction: A Portrait of a Society in
Crisis*
Direction: Robin Spry. Camera: Doug-
las Kiefer. Animation camera: Simon
Leblanc. Editing: Shelagh Mackenzie.
Production: Normand Cloutier, Robin
Spry, Tom Daly. Colour. 58 mins.
1973.

Reflections on Suffering
Direction, editing: Malca Gillson.

Camera: Susan Trow. Production: Tom Daly. Executive producer: Barrie Howells. Colour. 21 mins. 1982.

Rescue Party

Direction: Roman Kroitor. Camera: Lorne C. Batchelor. Production: Tom Daly. B&W. 29 mins. 1953. Produced for the Department of National Health and Welfare.

Riches of the Earth

Direction: Colin Low. Script, animation: Sidney Goldsmith, Barrie Helmer. Camera: Lyle Enright. Editing: Douglas Tunstell. Narrator: Lister Sinclair. Music: Louis Applebaum. Production: Tom Daly. Colour. 16 mins. 1954.

The Ride

Direction: Gerald Potterton. Camera: Reginald Morris. Music: Eldon Rathburn. Production: Colin Low. Executive producer: Tom Daly. Colour. 7 mins. 1963.

River (Planet Earth)

Direction: Peter Raymont. Script: Michael Rubbo. Camera: Robert Humble. Editing: Michael Rubbo, Ian Rankin, Peter Raymont. Music: Ben Low. Production: Tom Daly. Executive producer: Colin Low. Colour. 28 mins. 1977. Co-produced with Environment Canada.

Road to the Reich§†

Direction, script, editing, production: Tom Daly. B&W. 10 mins. 1944.

The Romance of Transportation in Canada†

Direction: Colin Low. Animation: Wolf Koenig, Robert Verrall, Colin Low. Camera: Lyle Enright. Script, narration: Guy Glover. Music: Eldon Rathburn. Production: Tom Daly. Colour. 11 mins. 1953.

A Rosewood Daydream

Direction, producer: Ian MacNeill. Camera: Eugene Boyko. Editing: Kathleen Shannon. Executive producer: Tom Daly. Colour. 14 mins. 1970.

Roughnecks: The Story of Oil Drillers

Direction, script, editing: Guy L. Coté. Camera: Eugene Boyko. Commentary: Stanley Jackson. Music: Robert Fleming. Production: Tom Daly. B&W. 21 mins. 1960.

'round and 'round

Direction: Barbara Greene. Camera: Douglas Kiefer. Editing: Ginny Stikeman. Production: Tom Daly. Executive producer: Peter Katadotis. Colour. 57 mins. 1978.

Royal Journey

Direction: David Bairstow, Gudrun Parker, Roger Blais. Camera: Osmond H. Borradaile, Grant McLean. Script: Leslie McFarlane. Editing: Ronald Dick, Victor Jobin, Betty Brunke. Music: Louis Applebaum. Production: Tom Daly. Colour. 54 mins. 1951.

Runner

Direction, script: Don Owen. Camera:

John Spotton, Guy Borremans. Commentary: W.H. Auden. Editing: Guy L. Coté, Donald Owen. Music: Don Douglas. Producer: Tom Daly. B&W. 11 mins. 1962.

Running Time
Direction, script, editing: Mort Ransen. Camera: Jean-Pierre Lachapelle, Douglas Kiefer. Music: Bill Brooks. Production: George Pearson, Tom Daly. Executive producer: Colin Low. Colour. 80 mins. 1974.

Sad Song of Yellow Skin
Direction, script, narrator: Michael Rubbo. Camera: Martin Duckworth, Pierre Letarte. Editing: Torben Schioler, Michael Rubbo. Production: Tom Daly. Colour. 58 mins. 1970.

Salt Cod
Direction, script, editing: Allan Wargon. Camera: John Spotton. Narrator: Lamont Tilden. Production: Tom Daly. B&W. 14 mins. 1954. Produced in cooperation with the Canadian Education Association.

Sananguagat: Inuit Masterworks
Direction, editing: Derek May. Camera: David de Volpi. Commentary: Maudie Qitsualik. Production: Tom Daly. Executive producer: Colin Low. Colour. 25 mins. 1974. Co-produced with the Department of Indian and Northern Affairs.

Saskatchewan – 45 Below
Direction: Larry Kent. Camera: David

de Volpi. Editing: Margaret Wescott. Production: Joseph Koenig, Tom Daly. Colour. 14 mins. 1971.

Satan's Choice
Direction, script, editing: Donald Shebib. Camera: Donald Shebib, Martin Duckworth. Music: The Sparrow. Production: Tom Daly. B&W. 28 mins. 1965.

Science at Your Service
Direction, script: Ronald Dick. Camera: Robert Humble. Narration: John Drainie. Music: Maurice Blackburn, Eldon Rathburn. Production, editing: Tom Daly. B&W. 36 mins. 1949. Produced for the Canadian Bureau of Mines.

The Sea
Direction: Bane Jovanovic. Script: Stanley Jackson, Joseph MacInnis. Camera: Gilles Gascon, Denis Gillson, Nels Squires, Al Giddings, Robert Humble, Joseph MacInnis, Jean Chouinard, Eric Chamberlain, Claudia Overing. Editing: Edward Le Lorrain. Music: Eldon Rathburn. Production: William Brind, Colin Low, Tom Daly. Colour. 29 mins. 1971. Co-produced with the Marine Sciences Branch of Environment Canada and the Department of Energy, Mines, and Resources.

The Sea Got in Your Blood
Direction: David Millar. Camera: Michel Thomas-d'Hoste. Editing: Barrie Howells. Narrator: Max Ferguson.

Production: Tom Daly. B&W. 28 mins. 1965.

A Shocking Affair
Direction, script, animation: Laurence Hyde. Camera: Lyle Enright. Executive producer: Tom Daly. Colour. 2 mins. 1953.

Shyness
Direction, script: Stanley Jackson. Camera: Hector J. Lemieux. Editing: Douglas Tunstell. Production: Tom Daly. B&W. 22 mins. 1953. Produced for the Department of National Health and Welfare.

Sing a Little
Animation: Jean-Paul Ladouceur, Evelyn Lambart. Production: Tom Daly. B&W. 9 mins. 1951.

Singing: A Joy in Any Language
Direction, editing: Malca Gillson, Tony Ianzelo. Camera: Tony Ianzelo. Commentary: Robert Duncan. Production: Tom Daly. Executive producer: Barrie Howells. Colour. 57 mins. 1983. Produced in association with the CBC and the Department of External Affairs.

Sir! Sir!
Direction: Michael Rubbo. Camera: Tony Ianzelo, David de Volpi. Editing: Alan Davis. Production: Cecily Burwash, Tom Daly. B&W. 20 mins. 1968.

Sky
Direction, script, editing: John Feeney.

Camera: Patrick Carey. Music: Eldon Rathburn. Production: Tom Daly. Colour. 10 mins. 1963.

The Sloane Affair
Direction, script, production: Douglas Jackson. Camera: Douglas Kiefer. Editing: Edward Le Lorrain, Les Halman, Ginny Stikeman. Production: Tom Daly. Colour. 53 mins. 1972. Produced with the cooperation of Revenue Canada, Taxation.

Smoke and Weather
Direction, script, editing: William Greaves. Camera: Ray Jones. Narrator: Frank Edwards. Executive producer: Tom Daly. Colour. 22 mins. 1958. Produced for the Department of Northern Affairs and National Resources.

Snow
Direction, script, editing: Barrie McLean. Camera: J.V. Durden, Bruno Engler, Barrie McLean. Animation: René Jodoin. Narrator: Strowan Robertson. Music: Eldon Rathburn. Production: Hugh O'Connor. Executive producer: Tom Daly. B&W. 12 mins. 1961.

Stages
Direction, camera: Paul Cowan. Editing: Sidonie Kerr, Paul Cowan. Narrator: Alan Maitland. Production: Tom Daly. Executive producer: Barrie Howells. Colour. 57 mins. 1980. Produced in cooperation with the Department of External Affairs.

Standing Alone
Direction: Colin Low. Camera: Douglas Kiefer, Ernest McNabb. Music: Eldon Rathburn. Editing, production: Tom Daly. Executive producers: Barrie Howells, Michael Scott. Colour. 58 mins. 1982.

Stigma
Direction, script: Stanley Jackson. Camera: Robert Humble. Editing: William Greaves. Production: Tom Daly. B&W. 20 mins. 1958. Produced for the Department of National Health and Welfare.

Stravinsky
Direction: Roman Kroitor, Wolf Koenig. Camera, editing: Wolf Koenig. Commentary: Donald Brittain. Production: Roman Kroitor. Executive producer: Tom Daly. B&W. 49 mins. 1965. Produced in cooperation with the Canadian Broadcasting Corporation.

The Streets of Saigon
Direction, script, editing: Michael Rubbo. Camera: Martin Duckworth. Production: Tom Daly. Colour. 28 mins. 1973.

The Structure of Unions
Direction: Morten Parker. Camera: Lyle Enright. Script, drawings: Wolf Koenig, Robert Verrall. Narrator: John Drainie. Music: Eldon Rathburn. Executive producer: Tom Daly. Colour. 11 mins. 1955. Produced in cooperation with the Canadian and Catholic Confederation of Labour, the Canadian Congress of Labour, the Trades and Labor Congress of Canada, and the Department of Labour.

Summer's Nearly Over
Direction: Michael Rubbo. Camera: Tony Ianzelo. Editing: Edward Le Lorrain, Michael Rubbo. Music: Eldon Rathburn. Production: Tom Daly. Colour. 29 mins. 1971.

Sur le pont d'Avignon
Direction, camera: Wolf Koenig, Jean-Paul Ladouceur. Animation: Gerald Budner, Blackie Morrison. Production: Tom Daly. Colour. 5 mins. 1951.

The Sword of the Lord
Direction: Giles Walker. Camera: Paul Cowan. Editing: John Laing. Music: Ben Low. Production: Desmond Dew, Tom Daly. Executive producer: Colin Low. Colour. 58 mins. 1976.

Symbol Boy
Direction: Bruce Moir. Animation: Les Drew. Music: Karl Duplessis. Production: Tom Daly. Colour. 4 mins. 1975. Co-produced with Film Australia.

Take It from the Top
Direction, camera: Eugene Boyko. Commentary: Donald Brittain, Derek May. Editing: Rex Tasker. Production: Peter Jones, Tom Daly. Colour. 23 mins. 1966.

Teeth Are to Keep
Direction: Jim MacKay, Dino Rigolo.

Script: P.K. Page. Camera: Lyle Enright. Animation: Jim Mackay, Raymond Roy, Dino Rigolo. Narration: Alan Mills. Music: Eldon Rathburn. Production: Tom Daly. Colour. 11 mins. 1949. Produced for the Department of National Health and Welfare.

Têtes blanches
Direction, script, editing: Guy L. Coté. Camera: Robert Humble. Commentary: Jacques Godbout. Narration: Thérèse Arbic. Music: Pete Seeger. Executive Producer: Tom Daly. Colour. 2 mins. 1961.

This Is a Photograph
Direction, still photography, editing: Albert Kish. Animation: Pierre L'Amare. Production: Tom Daly. Colour. 10 mins. 1971.

*This Is Blitz**
Direction: Stuart Legg. Camera: Julian Roffman. Narrator: Lorne Greene. Music: Lucio Agostini. Research, sound editing: Tom Daly. B&W. 22 mins. 1942.

A Thousand Million Years
Script, animation: Sidney Goldsmith; Barry Helmer. Camera: Lyle Enright. Editing: Douglas Tunstell. Commentary: Lister Sinclair. Narration: Budd Knapp. Production: Tom Daly. Colour. 10 mins. 1954.

Threads
Direction, editing: Anne Henderson, Donald Winkler. Camera: Michel Thomas-d'Hoste. Production: Diane Beaudry, Colin Low, Tom Daly. Colour. 10 mins. 1976.

Three Guesses
Direction, editing: Joan Henson. Camera: Douglas Kiefer. Executive producer: Tom Daly. Colour. 29 mins. 1971.

*Three 'I's**
Direction: Mort Ransen, Martin Duckworth, Eric M. Nilsson. Co-production: Tom Daly. B&W. 58 mins. 1970.

Thunderbirds in China
Direction: Les Rose. Camera: Richard Leiterman. Editing: Laurie Wright. Production: Donald Brittain, Tom Daly. Executive producer: James de B. Domville. Colour. 58 mins. 1974.

Tickets s.v.p.
Direction: Pierre Perrault. Camera: Michel Brault, Bernard Gosselin. Animation camera: Pierre Provost. Animation: Don Arioli. Editing: John Kramer, David Mayerovitch. Music: Karl Duplessis. Production: Wolf Koenig, Tom Daly. Executive producer: Robert Verrall. Colour. 9 mins. 1973.

Tigers and Teddy Bears
Direction, script: Michael Rubbo. Camera: Robert Humble, Andreas Poulsson. Editing: Torben Schioler. Production: Tom Daly. Executive producer: Arthur Hammond. Colour. 32 mins. 1978.

Time and Terrain
Direction, animation: Colin Low.
Script: Neil Harris. Camera: Lyle
Enright. Editing: Colin Low, Robert
Verrall. Music: Robert Fleming. Pro-
duction: Jim McKay, Tom Daly.
Colour. 10 mins. 1948.

Time for Caring
Direction, editing: Malca Gillson.
Camera: Susan Trow. Commentary:
Barry Cowling. Production: Tom
Daly. Colour. 40 mins. 1982. Produced
with the financial assistance of the
Richard and Jean Ivey Fund.

To Serve the Mind
Director: Stanley Jackson. Script:
Stanley Jackson, Roman Kroitor.
Camera: Robert Humble. Editing:
Douglas Tunstell. Narrator: Stanley
Jackson, Tom McBride. Music: Eldon
Rathburn. Production: Tom Daly.
B&W. 25 mins. 1955. Produced for the
Department of National Health and
Welfare.

Toronto Jazz
Direction: Don Owen. Camera: Guy
Borremans. Production: Roman
Kroitor. Executive producer: Tom
Daly. B&W. 27 mins. 1964.

Trade Fair
Direction, script: Robert Anderson.
Camera: John Spotton. Production:
Tom Daly. Colour. 17 mins. 1952. Pro-
duced for the Department of Trade and
Commerce and the Canadian Govern-
ment Exhibition Commission.

*Train Busters**
Direction: Sydney Newman. Narrator:
Lorne Greene. Music: Lucio Agostini.
Sound editing: Tom Daly. Production:
Raymond Spottiswoode. B&W. 19
mins. 1943.

Trans Canada Summer
Direction, script: Ronald Dick. Cam-
era: Robert Humble, Reginald Morris,
Jean Roy. Editing: William Greaves.
Commentary: Stanley Jackson. Narra-
tor: Pierre Berton. Music: Eldon Rath-
burn, Malca Gillson. Production: Tom
Daly. Colour. 58 mins. 1958.

Travel Log
Direction, script, still photography:
Donald Winkler. Animation camera:
Raymond Dumas, Richard Moras,
Jacques Avoine. Editing: Torben Schi-
oler. Production: Tom Daly. Executive
producer: Arthur Hammond. Colour.
10 mins. 1978.

Trout Stream
Direction, production: Hugh O'Connor. Camera: William Carrick, J.V.
Durden. Commentary: Strowan Robertson, Barrie McLean. Music: Maurice Blackburn. Executive producer:
Tom Daly. Colour. 9 mins. 1961.

21–87
Direction: Arthur Lipsett. Production:
Colin Low, Tom Daly. B&W. 10 mins.
1964.

Two-and-a-Half
Direction, script: Brian Pearce. Music:

Eldon Rathburn. Production: Tom
Daly. B&W. 8 mins. 1964.

The Unadulterated Truth
Direction, script: Ronald Weyman.
Camera: Lorne C. Batchelor.
Editing: Victor Jobin. Music: Maurice
Blackburn. Production: Tom Daly.
B&W. 21 mins. 1950. Produced
for the Department of National
Health and Welfare, Food and Drug
Divisions.

Universe†
Direction: Roman Kroitor, Colin Low.
Camera: Denis Gillson, Wolf Koenig.
Story-line: Roman Kroitor. Production
design: Colin Low. Special effects:
Wally Gentleman, Herbert Taylor,
James Wilson. Commentary: Stanley
Jackson. Narrator: Douglas Rain.
Music: Eldon Rathburn. Production,
editing: Tom Daly. B&W. 26 mins.
1960.

University
Direction, script: Stanley Jackson.
Camera: Tom Bird. Production:
Roman Kroitor, Wolf Koenig. Execu-
tive producer: Tom Daly. B&W. 58
mins. 1961.

Untouched and Pure
Direction: Mort Ransen,
Christopher Cordeaux, Martin
Duckworth. Production: Martin
Duckworth, Tom Daly. B&W.
46 mins. 1970. Co-produced with
the Swedish Institute for Cultural
Relations.

V for Volunteers
Direction, script: Leslie McFarlane.
Camera: Walter A. Sutton. Editing:
Victor Jobin. Music: Robert Fleming.
Production: Tom Daly. B&W. 21 mins.
1951. Produced for the Association of
Junior Leagues of America in coopera-
tion with the Canadian Welfare Coun-
cil and the Department of National
Health and Welfare.

Varley
Direction: Allan Wargon. Camera:
Denis Gillson. Music: Louis Applebaum. Production: Tom Daly. Colour.
16 mins. 1953.

Very Nice, Very Nice
Direction: Arthur Lipsett. Production:
Colin Low, Tom Daly. B&W. 7 mins.
1961.

Waiting for Fidel
Direction, editing: Michael Rubbo.
Camera: Douglas Kiefer. Production:
Michael Rubbo, Tom Daly. Executive
producer: Colin Low. Colour. 58 mins.
1974.

Wake up, mes bons amis
Direction: Pierre Perrault. Camera:
Bernard Gosselin, Michel Brault. Edit-
ing: Yves Leduc. Production: Paul
Larose, Guy L. Coté, Tom Daly.
B&W. 117 mins. 1970.

*The War for Men's Minds**
Direction, production, script: Stuart
Legg. Assistants: Tom Daly, Gordon
Weisenborn. B&W. 21 mins. 1943.

*Warclouds in the Pacific**
Direction, commentary, production:
Stuart Legg. Research: Margaret Ann
Adamson. Stock-shot research: Tom
Daly. B&W. 22 mins. 1941.

Warp and Weft
Direction, script: Betty Brunke. Camera: Walter A. Sutton. Production:
Tom Daly. Colour. 11 mins. 1952. Produced for the National Council on
Physical Fitness and the Department of
National Health and Welfare.

Water for the Prairies
Direction, camera: Lawrence Cherry.
Script: Jack Ammon, Evelyn Cherry.
Editing: Victor Jobin. Music: Eldon
Rathburn. Production: Evelyn Cherry,
Lawrence Cherry. Executive producer:
Tom Daly. Colour. 19 mins. 1951. Produced in cooperation with the Eastern
Rockies Forest Conservation Board
and the Alberta Forest Service.

Wax and Wool
Direction: Rick Raxlen, Donald Winkler. Camera: Michel Thomas-d'Hoste.
Editing: Rick Raxlen. Production: Tom
Daly. Colour. 10 mins. 1976.

Wet Earth and Warm People
Direction, editing, narrator: Michael
Rubbo. Camera: Paul Leach. Production: Tom Daly. Colour. 59 mins.
1971.

Wheat Rust
Direction, script: Maurice Constant.
Camera: Grant Crabtree, J.V. Durden,

Maurice Constant. Editing: Hubert
Schuurman. Animation: Barry
Helmer. Music: Louis Applebaum.
Production: J.V. Durden. Executive
producer: Tom Daly. Colour. 17 mins.
1958. Produced in cooperation with the
Department of Agriculture.

Where Have All the Farms Gone?
Direction: Michael Brun. Camera:
David de Volpi. Production: Tom
Daly. Colour. 16 mins. 1969.

Who Will Teach Your Child?
Direction, script: Stanley Jackson.
Camera: Grant McLean. Editing: Stanley Jackson, Gudrun Parker, George
Brandt. Narration: Percy Rodriguez.
Music: Eldon Rathburn. Production:
Gudrun Parker, Tom Daly. B&W. 30
mins. 1948. Produced in cooperation
with the Canadian Teachers' Federation.

The Winds of Fogo
Direction: Colin Low. Camera:
Robert Humble. Editing: Edward
Le Lorrain. Production: Tom Daly.
Colour. 20 mins. 1969.

Winter in Canada
Direction, script: Guy L. Coté. Camera: John Foster. Production: Tom
Daly. B&W. 18 mins. 1953.

The Wish
Direction, camera: Martin Duckworth.
Editing: Margaret Wescott. Production: Tom Daly. Colour. 28 mins.
1970.

The World of David Milne
Direction: Gerald Budner. Camera:
James Wilson, Roy Nolan. Music:
Eldon Rathburn. Production: Colin
Low, Tom Daly. Colour. 12 mins.
1963.

Wuxing People's Commune
Direction: Boyce Richardson, Tony
Ianzelo. Camera: Tony Ianzelo.
Production: Tom Daly. Executive
producer: Barrie Howells. Colour.
57 mins. 1980.

Yellowknife, Canada
Direction, script, editing:
Allan Wargon. Camera: Alvin
Armstrong. Production: Tom Daly.
Colour. 11 mins. 1948. Produced with
the financial participation of the
Department of Mines and Resources
and the Northwest Territories Admin-
istration.

You're Eating for Two
Direction, editing: Malca Gillson.
Script: Ian MacNeill. Camera:
Douglas Kiefer. Animation: Paul
Bochner. Music:Ben Low. Production:
Tom Daly. Executive producer: Colin
Low. Colour. 19 mins. 1977.

A Tom Daly Film Chronology

1941
Battle of Brains
Churchill's Island
Five Men of Australia
Food, Weapon of Conquest
Heroes of the Atlantic
Warclouds in the Pacific

1942
Battle for Oil
Freighters under Fire
Geopolitik – Hitler's Plan for Empire
The Mask of Nippon
This Is Blitz

1943
Battle Is Their Birthright
Pincers on Axis Europe
Train Busters
The War for Men's Minds

1944
Balkan Powder Keg
Battle of Europe
Fortress Japan
Global Air Routes

Inside France
Our Northern Neighbour
Road to the Reich

1945
Atlantic Crossroads
Food: Secret of the Peace
Gateway to Asia
Guilty Men
Now – The Peace
Ordeal by Ice

1946
Canada, World Trader
The Challenge of Housing
Out of the Ruins

1947
Eyes on Canada
Fraternité
The People Between

1948
Canadian International Trade Fair
Chantons Noël
Hungry Minds
Time and Terrain

Who Will Teach Your Child?
Yellowknife, Canada

1949
Across Arctic Ungava
Children's Concert
Come to the Fair
Family Circles
Over-Dependency
Science at Your Service
Teeth Are to Keep

1950
Family Tree
Feelings of Depression
4 Songs by 4 Gentlemen
A Friend at the Door
*Making Primitive Stone
    Tools*
On Stage
The Unadulterated Truth

1951
Breakdown
Canada's Awakening North
Caribou Hunters
*Fighting Forest Fires with Hand
    Tools*
Folksong Fantasy
The Longhouse People
Pen Point Percussion
Royal Journey
Sing a Little
Sur le pont d'Avignon
V for Volunteers
Water for the Prairies

1952
Age of the Beaver
Lismer

Trade Fair
Warp and Weft

1953
Canadian Notebook
Dick Hickey – Blacksmith
*Fighting Forest Fires with Power
    Pumps*
The Newcomers
Poison Ivy Picnic
Rescue Party
*The Romance of Transportation
    in Canada*
A Shocking Affair
Shyness
Varley
Winter in Canada

1954
Corral
House of History
Look Before You Leap
*The Magnificent
    Mountains of the West*
One Little Indian
*Paul Tomkowicz: Street-railway
    Switchman*
Physical Regions of Canada
Riches of the Earth
Salt Cod
A Thousand Million Years

1955
Farm Calendar
Gold
Grain Handling in Canada
Iron from the North
The Jolifou Inn
Look Alert, Stay Unhurt
No Longer Vanishing

The Structure of Unions
To Serve the Mind

1956
Canadian Venture
Forest Fire Suppression
The Great Lakes – St. Lawrence
   Lowlands
Introducing Canada

1957
The Atlantic Region
Blue Vanguard (Revised)
Canadian Profile
City of Gold
The Great Plains
It's a Crime
Looking Beyond ... Story of a Film
   Council
The Precambrian Shield
Profile of a Problem Drinker
Putting It Straight

1958
Blood and Fire
The Changing Forest
Country Threshing
The Days Before Christmas
The Face of the High Arctic
A Foreign Language
High Arctic: Life on the Land
The Living Stone
Memory of Summer
Pilgrimage
Police
Railroaders
Smoke and Weather
Stigma
Trans Canada Summer
Wheat Rust

1959
The Back-breaking Leaf
City Out of Time
Emergency Ward
End of the Line
Fifty Miles from Poona
Fishermen
Glenn Gould – Off the Record
Glenn Gould – On the Record
Pangnirtung
Radiation

1960
A Is for Architecture
Arctic Outpost (Pangnirtung, N.W.T.)
The Cars in Your Life
I Was a Ninety-pound Weakling
Interview with Linus Pauling
Life in the Woodlot
Microscopic Fungi
Roughnecks: The Story of Oil
   Drillers
Universe

1961
The Canadians
Cattle Ranch
Circle of the Sun
The Days of Whiskey Gap
Do You Know the Milky Way?
Festival in Puerto Rico
Lonely Boy
New York Lightboard
O Canada (Coat of Arms)
The Price of Fire
Snow
Têtes blanches
Trout Stream
University
Very Nice, Very Nice

1962
The Climates of North America
Le Jeu de l'hiver
Kindergarten
The Living Machine
My Financial Career
The Peep Show
Pot-pourri
Runner

1963
Christmas Cracker
A Christmas Fantasy
Experimental Film
Faces
The Origins of Weather
Pipers and A'
The Ride
Sky
The World of David Milne

1964
Above the Horizon
Antigonish
Country Auction
The Edge of the Barrens
Eskimo Artist: Kenojuak
An Essay on Science
Free Fall
The Great Toy Robbery
The Hutterites
*I Know an Old Lady Who Swallowed
 a Fly*
Jet Pilot
Legault's Place
Nobody Waved Good-bye
The Persistent Seed
Toronto Jazz
21-87
Two-and-a-Half

1965
Experienced Hands
The Forest
Satan's Choice
The Sea Got in Your Blood
Stravinsky

1966
Antonio
Helicopter Canada
Island Observed
Kurelek
Take It from the Top

1967
Fluxes
Labyrinthe
Niagara Falls
Poen

1968
Christopher's Movie Matinee
Sir! Sir!

1969
Danny and Nicky
Falling from Ladders
'If He Is Devoured, I Win'
McBus
Mrs. Ryan's Drama Class
Prologue
Where Have All the Farms Gone?
The Winds of Fogo

1970
The Burden They Carry
Espolio
A Film for Max
Girls of Mountain Street
Half-Half-Three-quarters-Full

Here's to Harry's Grandfather
Legend
N-Zone
November
Overspill
Pillar of Wisdom
A Place for Everything
A Rosewood Daydream
Sad Song of Yellow Skin
Three 'I's
Untouched and Pure
Wake up, mes bons amis
The Wish

1971
Anger after Death
Atomic Juggernaut
Dance Class
Garden
*God Help the Man Who Would Part
   with His Land*
Improv
The Mechanical Knee
Norman Jewison, Filmmaker
Once ... Agadir
Pandora
Paper Boy
Pearly Yeats
Persistent and Finagling
Saskatchewan – 45 Below
The Sea
Summer's Nearly Over
This Is a Photograph
Three Guesses
Wet Earth and Warm People

1972
Bannerfilm
Beware, Beware, My Beauty Fair
Centaur

Cold Journey
Cold Pizza
Cowboy and Indian
The Huntsman
Light to Starboard
Louisbourg
Mirage
One Hand Clapping
The Sloane Affair

1973
Accident
Action: The October Crisis of 1970
Child, Part 1
Child, Part 2
Coming Home
Downhill
*Jalan, Jalan: A Journey in Sundanese
   Java*
The Man Who Can't Stop
*Reaction: A Portrait of a Society in
   Crisis*
The Streets of Saigon
Tickets s.v.p.

1974
Child: Part 3
In Praise of Hands
Mr. Symbol Man
The Players
Running Time
Sananguagat: Inuit Masterworks
Thunderbirds in China
Waiting for Fidel

1975
Alberta Girls
Descent
Earthware
Face

The Forest Watchers
Hinchinbrook Diary
I Am an Old Tree
Los Canadienses
Lumsden
Metal Workers
Musicanada
No Way They Want to Slow
    Down
Symbol Boy

1976
Blackwood
Coaches
The Great Clean-up
The Sword of the Lord
Threads
Wax and Wool

1977
Back Alley Blue
Child: Part 4
I Hate to Lose
I'll Go Again
One Man
River (Planet Earth)
You're Eating for Two

1978
Child: Part 5
An Easy Pill to Swallow
It Wasn't Easy ...
Meditation in Motion
'round and 'round

Tigers and Teddy Bears
Travel Log

1979
In the Labyrinth
North China Commune
A Pinto for the Prince

1980
China: A Land Transformed
Co Hoedeman, Animator
From the Ashes of War
The Last Days of Living
The Lost Pharaoh: The Search for
    Akhenaten
North China Factory
Stages
Wuxing People's Commune

1981
Earle Birney: Portrait of a Poet
Off the Wall

1982
F.R. Scott: Rhyme and Reason
Reflections on Suffering
Standing Alone
Time for Caring

1983
Singing: A Joy in Any Language

1984
Musical Magic: Gilbert and Sullivan in
    Stratford

Index